THE HOSPITALITY CASE MANUAL

DEVELOPING COMPETENCIES IN CRITICAL

THINKING AND PRACTICAL ACTION

Craig C. Lundberg

Cornell University (retired)

Cheri A. Young

University of Nevada, Las Vegas

Prentice Hall
Upper Saddle River, New Jersey

Library of Congress Cataloging-in-Publication Data

Lundberg, Craig C.
The hospitality case manual: developing competencies in critical thinking and practical action /
Craig C. Lundberg, Cheri A. Young.—1st ed.
    p. cm.
Includes index.
ISBN-13: 978-0-13-112089-1
ISBN-10: 0-13-112089-1
1. Hospitality industry—Management—Case studies. I. Young, Cheri Ann. II. Title.

TX911.3.M27L86 2009
647.94′068—dc22   2008027323

Editor in Chief: Vernon Anthony
Acquisitions Editor: William Lawrensen
Development Editor: Dan Trudden
Editorial Assistant: Lara Dimmick
Director of Marketing: David Gesell
Marketing Manager: Leigh Ann Sims
Marketing Assistant: Les Roberts
Production Manager: Kathy Sleys
Creative Director: Jayne Conte
Cover Designer: Bruce Kenselaar
Cover art/image/photo[s]: Mcduff Everton/Getty Images
Manager, Cover Visual Research and Permissions: Karen Sanatar
Full Service/Project Management: Saraswathi Muralidhar/GGS Book Services PMG

Pearson Education Ltd., London   Pearson Education Australia Pty. Limited
Pearson Education Singapore Pte. Ltd.   Pearson Education North Asia Ltd., Hong Kong
Pearson Education Canada, Inc.   Pearson Educación de Mexico, S.A. de C.V.
Pearson Education—Japan   Pearson Education Malaysia Pte. Ltd.

Prentice Hall
is an imprint of

www.pearsonhighered.com

ISBN-13: 978-0-13-112089-1
ISBN-10:   0-13-112089-1

CONTENTS

Part III Cases for Discussion   109

PREFACE

*Knowledge is not practice and practice is not knowledge. The improvement of one
does not lead automatically to an improvement of the other. Each can work fruitfully
for the advancement of the other, but also, unfortunately, each can develop
separately from the other and hence stuntedly in relation to the other.*

—F. J. ROETHLISBERGER

HOW DID THIS BOOK COME TO BE?

Most teaching materials probably originate in the classroom. Faculty members are sometimes
somewhat uncomfortable with the materials currently available and more or less consciously
want something different, better, more useful. There is usually the thought that with some added
ideas and topics, or a different treatment of some topics, or different questions, different examples, or different problems, and so forth, that their students' learning would be enhanced. The origins of this book clearly had these sorts of beginnings. While there are numerous texts that provide much appropriate subject matter coverage and several that are rich in the number of ideas
and several that have good illustrative materials, few contain very many rich descriptions of the
actual sorts of situations that face hospitality managers—situations in which students may realistically apply their knowledge and thus become more skilled practitioners. We wanted such course
materials and began to collect, create, and teach with them. The more we did this, the more we
(and our students) wanted these materials conveniently together. Hence, we wrote this book.

Quite frankly, the phenomena at the heart of the cases collected in this book have always held an intensely felt intrinsic fascination for us: where managers work, what they do,
and the real differences they can and sometimes do make. In addition, the competencies that
can be developed through the careful, repeated discussion of cases seem to us to be vital ones
for both personal and professional development, well-being, and success. Thus this book represents first what we believe to have been our own useful learning experiences, and second,
our wish to provide such experiences for others.

While each of us has fortunately had several great teachers and many fruitful opportunities
to learn, most of our behavioral and managerial competencies have been largely of our own
making. The wisdom of the epigram by Roethlisberger has often been brought home to us—
especially that part that implies knowledge does not neatly or easily lead to skillful practice. While
valid knowledge is potentially powerful for enhancing practice, we believe that the educational
challenge is to find a way for people to experience for themselves the competency-increasing activity of relating knowledge to practice, practice to knowledge, of ideas to facts, and facts to ideas.

WHAT DOES THIS BOOK CONTAIN?

The title, *The Hospitality Case Manual: Developing Competencies in Critical Thinking and
Practical Action,* only generally indicates what this book is about. A glance at the table of contents will show that the book is organized into three main parts. Part I (four short chapters) is

about cases, the case method, and thinking and learning from case work. Part II (six short case-exampled chapters) provides a class-tested, semi-structured guide for preparing cases for class discussion. Part III is a large collection of hospitality management cases to study and learn from.

You will notice that this book is unlike most management books that assert what you should know, leave the application of their prescribed knowledge up to you, and, essentially ask you to believe what they say because the authors or others say it. In contrast, this book provides a general process within which personally useful professional knowledge, skills, and attitudes may be acquired—without specifying precisely what knowledge or which skills or what attitudes. We have assumed that your instructor and other course materials will provide you with such content guidance (we, of course, do provide some). The approach to studying cases and the many cases to study which comprise the bulk of this book are intended to enhance your ability to learn from experience—from the experience of others described in the cases, from the experience of discovering how and what you think and feel about the complex reality that is a case, and from the experience of repeatedly discussing cases with your classmates. Cases, as you will soon discover, are essentially descriptions of actual situations in which one or more people are faced with understanding and possibly taking some action to improve the situations. Since these cases are about situations in hospitality organizations, you will also be able to learn quite a bit about hospitality businesses and practices. Since these cases almost always have one or more persons in them who are managerially responsible, they also provide the opportunity to observe managers behaving both effectively and ineffectively, and the opportunity for you to put yourself in their place. Being able to repeatedly observe, think, and talk about real hospitality situations and real hospitality managers doing what they do will provide you with the vicarious experiences from which to learn how all of us can enhance our own managerial competence.

WHO WILL BENEFIT FROM THIS BOOK?

This book is intended to be used in hospitality courses that focus on the management of persons, places, and things. While it may stand alone, in most courses it will be used in conjunction with readings and/or a text which will provide the ideas, models, theories, and topics of the subject matter that constitute the knowledge of the field. This casebook provides opportunities to use and refine that knowledge. The students who will benefit from using this book are students of professional schools—especially students who aspire to managerial careers in the hospitality industry. The intended audience, therefore, is those persons who aspire to be more competent hospitality managers.

This case manual is not for everyone. *If you merely want to be told what to do, or you believe judgment and wisdom cannot be acquired, do not bother with this book.* The approach advocated in this book requires you to search, reason, and synthesize on your own and with others, over and over. This takes energy and intelligence of course, but it also requires faith in you as a creative learner and a commitment to the process of learning by analyzing cases.

HOW DOES LEARNING OCCUR WITH THE CASE METHOD?

Part of the process of becoming more competent with managerial phenomena in hospitality settings is unlearning. This means discarding some ideas, some habits of mind, and some customary ways of doing things. Like a teacup that is half full with old ideas, if we want to pour in some new ideas, we had better pour out the old ones or the cup will overflow. Another very important part of the process of becoming more competent is to improve our ability to learn from our own experiences. Further, perhaps ideally, it involves enhancing our capabilities of *learning how to learn*. Initially this mode of unlearning/learning means getting focused—focused on the particulars of situations and their circumstances, on relevant ideas, and on our learning goals. With increasing familiarization about and focus upon hospitality realities and the nature of the mental tools (ideas and conceptual models) we use to make sense out of those realities, we enter a period of practice where we attempt to carefully understand what is going on in a situation and what might be done to improve it. Refining, through repeated practice, the ideas and skills and attitudes found to be truly useful, we will eventually, (a) have a tested, personally useful tool kit of ideas and conceptual models, (b) become skilled in using our ideas to understand and think through a variety of situations, and (c) have practiced the process of learning in this way to where we may go on improving our managerial competencies in the future. Chapters 2 and 4 elaborate how such learning occurs.

WHY BOTHER ENHANCING ONE'S MANAGERIAL COMPETENCY?

Let us first acknowledge that we live in an organizational society. The fabric of our culture is woven around many types of organizations and compared to other societies, we simply have more and more kinds of organizations. Each of us contributes to and is dependent upon many organizations, and the effectiveness of these will reflect on our society's productiveness, its potential for adaptive change, and the creation of healthy and satisfying circumstances of work as well as leisure. Therefore, our increased understanding and personal competencies with regard to organizations and their management will very likely enhance the society in which we live and work.

Another reason to enhance our managerial competencies is that our personal lives may be significantly enhanced. While more skill and knowledge may contribute directly to our personal satisfaction, they may also increase the likelihood of our becoming more influential and more contributory on and off the job, as well as increase these opportunities for others, both key factors in personal growth and continuing maturation. By reducing our uncertainties about the world of work and how we can more appropriately behave, we tend to reduce our apprehensions and anxieties. Increased understanding and more effective, responsible performance often leads to feelings of efficacy and reinforces the belief that we can continually improve, grow, and so on.

The marriage of knowledge and practice referred to in the epigram requires considerable effort and skill, and should not be left to chance. It can and should be helped to develop in the classroom. The repetitive, thoughtful study and discussion of cases is one way skillful managerial competencies may be developed. The study of cases not only provides the needed realism—over and over—but also vicariously provides the spectrum of experience that one would get only after a long and varied career. Learning through cases, however, like learning through life experiences, is seldom quick and easy. Rather, learning to be a skillful manager requires persistence and dedication, the repetition of trying one's best and learning from successes and mistakes alike. If we allow ourselves to be excited by such realistic learning, the potential in all of us to be more skillful managers will surely be tapped.

WHAT IS THE BEST WAY TO USE THIS BOOK?

While tempted to respond to this question with exhortations such as thinking, experimenting, asking, and the like, these and similar words, while meaningful at the end of your experience in working with cases, very likely will have little meaning now. Therefore, let us indicate generally first, the nature of the work involved and second, a plan to follow.

This book asks you to initially work and get comfortable on two different fronts. One is with concrete information in all of its situation-specific complexity (the cases)—noticing facts, seeing their similarities and differences, clarifying their meanings, and ordering them in different ways. The other front to work on has to do with ideas, singularly and in combination, getting clear about them and understanding what facts they reveal. With increasing comfortableness and agility with these two fronts, we then encourage combining them—using some facts to trigger appropriate ideas, and using ideas to find appropriate facts. Through practice in working back and forth between facts and ideas, we can make better and better sense out of the situations we examine and how to improve them.

In accordance with the general strategy just sketched, we suggest you begin by reading the four chapters of Part I fairly swiftly. Then, with guidance from your instructor, read, think about, and discuss in class one or two of the shorter cases. Don't be discouraged if the discussion seems messy or inconclusive. It's bound to be! You are just beginning. Next, reread Chapter 3 and use it to think about the knowledge you've acquired from lectures and reading. It is helpful to do this with your colleagues—you'll be pleasantly surprised at how you will be able to sharpen each other's thinking. Now it is time to tackle a series of cases, but in your preparation and discussion, carefully and repeatedly use the steps outlined in Part II, Chapters 5 through 8. With several such careful discussions under your belt, you'll find it useful to reread all of Part I again—you'll not only understand more but also will begin to better appreciate what it says. Then, in class, go forward to some longer and more complicated cases, referring often to Chapters 6, 7, and 8 on analysis, diagnosis, and action planning. Interspersed with your case discussions you will, of course, continue to add ideas to your kit bag through assigned readings and lectures. With knowledge additions and repeated case work, the time will come when understanding work situations and organizations in deep and meaningful ways and how to improve them becomes almost intuitive and natural.

ACKNOWLEDGMENTS

Everyone is substantially indebted to many others, especially those others he or she learns with and from. As authors this is true of us. We have been fortunate in this regard. Our learnings—about higher education, professional schools, management and organizational behavior, case writing and case teaching, and much else—reach out and back to so many others for so much.

A major debt is to our students over the years from coast to coast, for by wrestling with ideas, with cases, with us, and with their own learning and growth, they have helped us see a little more clearly, understand a little better, and strive a little higher.

Another debt we wish to gratefully acknowledge are the authors of some of the included cases and the field researchers (often students like you) whose notes enabled us to write cases.

We are also appreciative to a number of case method models and mentors. William Foote Whyte and Fritz Jules Roethlisberger inspired as well as demonstrated how to observe and describe closely and to ground one's conceptualization carefully. Paul Lawrence, C. Roland Christensen, and many others of several generations at the Harvard Business School, by example and as exemplar, have led the development of teaching through cases. Similarly we are grateful to contemporary case writing guides, especially to Michael Leenders and his associates at the University of Western Ontario, to William and Margaret Naumes at the University of New Hampshire, and to the dedicated champions of the North American Case Research Association, and the Western and the Eastern Casewriters groups.

Our indebtedness as authors also goes to many of our colleagues and to our editors at Prentice Hall. Thanks also to Linda Carlisle and Nadia Khanam for their secretarial and technical support. We also acknowledge the caring and support of our significant others and family who continue to provide a life of punctuated challenges and satisfactions that enable us to be academics. Lastly, we acknowledge each other for the press of intellectual stimulation and the richness of living that makes us more real and more human than we might otherwise be.

For his example of skillfully facilitating case discussions in the classroom as well as his continuing demonstration of education as a calling, we gratefully dedicate this book to John W. Hennessey, Jr.

Craig C. Lundberg
Ithaca, NY

Cheri A. Young
Las Vegas, NV

PART

I

Learning from Cases

All there is to thinking, is seeing something noticeable which makes you see something you weren't noticing which makes you see something that isn't even visible.

—Norman Maclean

Art is the attempt to wrest coherence and meaning out of more reality than we ordinarily deal with.

—Peter Vaill

How can I know what I think until I see what I say?

—Karl Weick

Learning from case discussions is likely to be a quite different experience for you than you have in most of your courses. Because the case method is such a different way of learning, the four chapters of Part I are offered to help you get oriented to and begin to understand case work. This part of the book will assist you in getting an initial feel for cases and what you do with them, and to appreciate what careful, clear thinking can do for you as a student and as a manager.

1

An Introduction to the Case Method

The only real voyage of discovery consists not in seeking new landscapes but in having new eyes . . .

—MARCEL PROUST

Chapter Objectives

▪ Provide a "hands-on" sense of what a case looks like.

▪ Note some of the typical sorts of initial reactions people have to a case.

▪ Begin to indicate what more careful thinking can reveal about a case.

WHAT TO DO WITH THE FOLLOWING CASE

Believe it or not, we strongly recommend that you read the "Boyd's Catering" Case *three* times. Here is how to read it each time and why.

The first time, read the case the way you would read a nonfiction short story—not too fast, not too slow. Get familiar with the case characters, the things they do, where they do what they do, with whom they relate and how, and what happens over time.

For the second reading, read the case *very slowly*. Your task now is to see all of the information in the case, and to really know the facts. This isn't easy, because most of us have been conditioned to read for the main points. So now read very, very slowly—read, pause, read, pause, read, pause. This way you will notice all the details and specifics. Your second reading is to master the many "whats" of the case.

Finally, reread the case for a third time with "how" and "why" in your mind. Try to understand, for example, *why* the events described occurred over time as they did, *why* the case characters acted as they did, and what might happen next. You might even try to see things through the eyes of each of the major case characters—*how* they perceive things, *how* they feel, what they think, etc.

3

THE BOYD'S CATERING CASE

Kirsten stopped cleaning the bakery case and looked to make sure that Emily wasn't watching her.

"Did you hear that Tracy quit yesterday?" she asked.

"Yeah, I couldn't believe it. Everyone thought she would be manager this summer. Tracy has worked here almost three years longer than any of us. She'll be a senior this year, so this will be her last summer working here. It was really a shock to her when Mrs. Boyd put Emily in charge."

"She always seemed to enjoy work until Emily came."

"Didn't we all?" I asked.

We both glanced at Emily. She was sitting up front, flipping through a magazine. Margot, Kirsten, and I were all getting ready to close the store. Closing was the worst part of the day, especially now that we had Emily as manager. She had never picked up a broom or washed a dish since she began working in May. I looked at my watch for what must have been the 100th time. Only 10 minutes left. I decided not to sweep the bakery. Emily probably wouldn't check. As I put the broom away, I realized that two months ago I never would have considered leaving without everything looking perfect for the next day.

While driving home, I tried to figure out why I hated work so much now. I had worked at Boyd's Catering for two years. Mrs. Boyd always had about five high school and college girls working over the summer. She was very selective about hiring people. She looked for those who would present a good image for the store. We were always very conscientious and took pride in the store and our work.

Mrs. Boyd and her partner, Mrs. Thompson, had opened Boyd's Catering four years ago. Mrs. Thompson had moved to Canada shortly after the opening and only visited a few times a year. The shop specialized in gourmet salads, sandwiches, and desserts. About 75 percent of the store's revenue came from catering. The rest was sales in the store. Business had been growing steadily and the shop had recently been reviewed by the *New York Times*. Everyone connected with Boyd's took pride in the high quality of its products and service. Mrs. Boyd managed the store full time during the winter. She was mainly responsible for the store's success. She had established a name for herself by catering out of her home for eight years. She now did little of the store's cooking, working instead as a general overseer. We all respected Mrs. Boyd's knowledge of food and ability to deal with even the most trying customers in a pleasant way. She was interested in every aspect of the business, including the help. She knew where each of us went to school and our special interests. Her concern for us was genuine, and we became equally interested in seeing her succeed in the catering business.

I considered myself lucky to have such a good job. There was always a lot of work to do, but most of the time no one complained. We all liked each other, and being busy helped the time go by quickly.

The problems began when Mrs. Boyd showed up one morning with her daughter Emily, who was home for the summer. Most of us had met Emily before. She was going to be a senior at Smith College and majored in archeology. Emily usually spent her vacations on archeology field trips. Mrs. Boyd loved to talk about Emily and always kept us up on where she was traveling and what she was studying. Emily had visited the store when she was home for breaks. Mrs. Boyd spent about an hour showing Emily how to work the cash register, close the store, and where everything was. She introduced Emily to the kitchen staff and everyone who worked on the floor. Mrs. Boyd informed us that Emily was going to be in charge.

She told Emily to ask Tracy or me what to do if she had any questions. Emily was very pleasant and seemed enthused about the job. Mrs. Boyd then rushed off for an appointment.

We were all stunned. Emily went downstairs to look for something. Margot, Kirsten, and I all looked at Tracy; we had been sure she would be made manager. Tracy looked as shocked as the rest of us.

"Well," she finally said, "we had better get back to those sandwiches, 'cause the lunch crowd will be here soon."

About 10 minutes later, Emily returned with a dusty old stool. She cleaned it up and sat down. Tracy and I looked at each other; no one ever sat down when they were working on the floor. There was always too much work to do: stock the bakery, make sandwiches, or put together special orders. How dare she sit down while we were working?

Emily tried to make conversation, but she only made things worse.

"I'm starving. What would you recommend for lunch?" Emily asked pleasantly. She was looking at Kirsten. Kirsten told Emily what her favorites were. Emily then went around the store and put together a lunch for herself. She sat down again and began to eat. Again we were shocked, but said nothing. No one ever ate in front of customers. We all took our lunches downstairs.

Emily tried again to make conversation. But we all began talking to each other in a conversation that excluded her. Why did she think she deserved so many special privileges? Did she expect us to be her friends when she wouldn't help with the work?

That evening Emily didn't help us close at all. She spent half an hour at the store next door talking with a friend of hers. She came back five minutes before we closed and asked if we were done. Tracy told her that the cases needed to be covered and the garbage taken out. Tracy thought Emily would volunteer to do it.

"Great," said Emily, "you should be out right on time." She then went downstairs to get her purse and punch out. No one could believe that she hadn't helped at all.

Things went downhill in the weeks to come. Emily did help wait on customers some, but we resented her more every day. She came to work wearing whatever she wanted instead of the white shirts the rest of us had to wear. Emily sat around most of the time and ate whenever she wanted. Mrs. Boyd only stopped in a few times a week and she seemed to enjoy having some time off. This created more work for us and killed morale.

Once when Mrs. Boyd came in, Emily was next door visiting with her friend. Mrs. Boyd was mad at her but thought this was an isolated incident. No one wanted to be the one to tell her that it happened all the time.

To make things worse, there was a rumor that Emily was getting paid eight or nine dollars an hour. The rest of us made about half that and worked twice as hard. Gradually we began to slack off. We started to try to aggravate Emily. We moved slowly and stopped wearing the white shirts. There was no point to working hard, because no one seemed to notice when something was done especially well or not at all. We sat down all the time, and began to eat whatever we wanted. We were allowed a half hour for lunch. Since lunch is the busiest time of the day, we had always just taken 10 or 15 minutes to sit downstairs. Now we took exactly half an hour. No one respected Emily at all because she knew so little about the store and had just gotten the job because of her mother. When she asked us to do things, we always took our time. The jobs we used to do without being told, we now had to be nagged to do. The store was not kept as clean as usual. There had been some mix-ups with special orders being sent off incomplete or with the wrong people. Worst of all, none of us cared. The days seemed to drag by. A number of customers had complained, but I doubt these complaints were making their way to Mrs. Boyd.

After about a month, friction began to build up between Tracy and Emily. We all did whatever Tracy asked and went to her when we had a question. Emily really resented this. When Tracy asked one of us to do something, Emily would give her a different job to do. Emily often went out of her way to be very polite when asking us to do things. Did she really think that a few *pleases* and *thank-yous* would make us move any faster? Why should we work when she wouldn't?

Yesterday, Tracy finally quit. She told Mrs. Boyd that she had been offered a job that paid more. Mrs. Boyd was very sorry to see Tracy leave. She had always been hard working and good natured. Mrs. Boyd seemed to have no idea of the problems in the store.

Margot, Kirsten, and I have all talked about quitting, especially now that Tracy is gone. But it's the middle of July, and we would have a hard time getting other jobs. At the same time, I don't know if I can take another month of this. No one is willing to confront Emily because she can tell her mother whatever she pleases about us. And I have to admit we have been slacking off. I would hate to lose Mrs. Boyd's respect. Mrs. Boyd comes in only once or twice a week and is always in a hurry. I would like to tell her about the problems we are having, but I don't know how she would react to criticism of her daughter. Maybe I should start to look for another job.

COMMON REACTIONS

If you actually read the Boyd's Catering Case more than once, you may have just been reminded of something very important that you already knew. The more thoroughly you know the specifics—that is, the detailed facts about a situation—the more there is to think about, the more there is to understand, and the more there is to consider regarding what might be done, and so on.

When people encounter a written case for the first time and are encouraged to understand it, they very often fall back on one or more common and/or habitual ways of responding to it. Some people

- sidestep thinking about the case at all because in their opinion the events described are "unrealistic" or simply "couldn't have happened." "Nobody would leave her daughter in charge like Mrs. Boyd did." "A Smith College senior would never act as insensitively as Emily did." These people are saying in effect that it is silly to expend intellectual energy on fictional or very rare circumstances. We call this avoidance through denial.
- quickly seek someone to blame—which avoids thinking about the complexity of what is going on or the reality of what can be done. "Mrs. Boyd was a fool to put Emily in charge without more adequate training." "Emily is just a spoiled, self-centered brat." "The girls acted pettily. They were mean to Emily." Blaming does little to help one understand the complexities of a case.
- immediately start by interjecting their opinions into the discussion. "Mrs. Boyd should not have hired a relative." "None of this would have happened if there were written job descriptions." "What would anyone expect since Emily wasn't monitored?" Such comments, of course, are just ways to avoid grappling with the actual facts of the case.
- "read into" case information. That is, they interpret and then treat their interpretations as case facts. "Emily is snobby because she attends Smith College." "The narrator won't quit because she needs money to keep her car going" (referring to "driving home"). Comments like these are not facts since they cannot be verified.

- jump to action and give general advice to help fix the situation—before they understand how things got to be as they are. "Communication has to be improved." "Someone should blow the lid off this situation." "The girls should go on strike or quit." Such advice in the form of quick solutions presumes that initial impressions are good enough upon which to base advice, and that "everyone knows" such general advice will be feasible. Jumping to action or advice is another way of avoiding thinking the situation through.
- attempt to explain case events by means of common sense, believing the situations in the case are rather simple to solve. "If the girls were paid more or Emily was paid less, the girls wouldn't resent Emily so much." "The girls were just following Emily's example." "There is obviously a personality conflict between Emily and the girls." Reliance on common sense keeps us thinking only about easily noticed things and often is about things that we have to guess at—which, once again, keeps us from thinking carefully about the actual facts of the situation.

All of the above common reactions boil down to *talking before carefully thinking*. All interrupt or stop our thinking. Most of these common reactions stem from:

focusing on only the case information a person can readily relate to;

using one's own personal experiences as guidelines for examining the case; or

letting unacknowledged feelings from the past influence that to which one pays attention.

It is easier to deny, to blame, to sidestep or read into the facts, to jump to advice, or to stay attuned to surface information than it is to know the facts inside out and to think about the facts impartially, carefully, and systematically. While easier, such mindless, common reactions usually do not lead to increased understanding or to effective actions for any particular case or situation and they seldom contribute to the learning from experience that we call wisdom. You should attempt to develop an ability to hold yourself back from expressing these reactions and/or jumping to conclusions.

While looking closely will reveal more information, be forewarned that you will never know the whole situation. You will never have all the information you would like to have to completely understand the case. Cases, thus, are like your own experiences. Some information is always missing, unknown, or unattainable. In the Boyd's case, for example, what did Mrs. Boyd say to Emily about how to relate to the girls or customers, or, what were Emily's feelings when she was excluded from the girls' conversations? Although there may be information missing, there usually is, nevertheless, a great deal of information when we are able to notice it. For cases, as in everyday life, we have to use the information on hand. We have to create meanings from, and for, the available information.

PEELING THE ONION—LOOKING CLOSER, SEEING AND UNDERSTANDING MORE

These common, but not very useful, reactions are more likely to occur after an initial, casual reading of the case. During subsequent readings of the case, if we focus on the story line, we tend to notice the unfamiliar, the unusual, the dramatic, the big things. When we read a case for a second and third time, we begin to notice quite a lot more. This is what we mean by peeling the onion: noticing some information as factual, some as not; seeing more facts; beginning

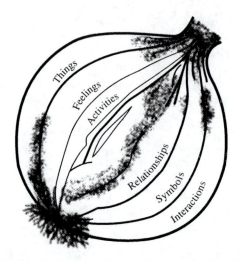

FIGURE 1.1 "Peeling" Layers of Information in a Case.

to see facts that seem to go together; and beginning to make some comparisons across time and between facts (see Figure 1.1). This increased noticing is aided when we have a way of systematically thinking. That is, we have something in mind that helps us notice, classify, and compare.

At the end of the Boyd's Catering Case, you may recall that there are a number of indicators (in Chapter 5 these are termed *symptoms*) that the situation could be better than it is. Emily has to nag the girls to get work done, work is left undone, the girls now resent Emily, their morale is down, customer complaints have increased, Tracy has quit, and the remaining girls are thinking of leaving. We can begin to wonder how and why the situation has changed (see Figure 1.2).

With just a little thought, we may appreciate that some case information has multiple meanings. It acquires significance by the persons involved. Some of this information consists of *things*, such as the stool Emily brings up from the basement and Emily's clothing (that she wears whatever she wishes). Some of this information consists of *activities*, involving what people in the case do (Emily eats her lunch in front of customers), or what they do not do (Emily does not help with closing the store). Regular activities are especially meaningful in this case and are quite noticeable when they *change*. It is as though there is a set of unwritten rules that people follow (called *norms*) regarding how to do the work and relate to one another that are noticeable later because they change. We notice the girls stop wearing white shirts; lunch expands from ten minutes to half an hour; they used to be on their feet and work all the

FIGURE 1.2 Symptoms in the Boyd's Catering Case.

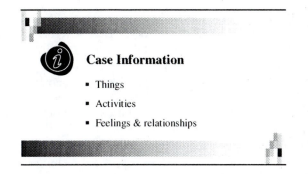

Case Information

- Things
- Activities
- Feelings & relationships

time but later they sit down all the time as well as eat whenever they want; and they used to keep busy and do whatever was needed but later moved slowly and had to be nagged by Emily. Some information is noticeable because it is *new*. Now things occur that didn't before, such as customer complaints and the store being left less clean. Also noticeable is information about people's *feelings and relationships* and how they change during the case. The girls respected and were loyal to Mrs. Boyd, liked one another and relied on Tracy, but by the end of the case they tried to aggravate Emily, were reluctant to tell Mrs. Boyd about what was going on in the store, and were considering leaving the business.

The kinds of noticeable information just listed come from looking at activities, things, relationships, and feelings, before and after Emily was placed in charge. We look *comparatively*. Peeling the onion thus involves using some ideas comparatively and beginning to make sense out of them from the point of view of the case characters. As we will see in later chapters, understanding what goes on in situations is aided by the careful, systematic seeing of information using ideas, and the comparison of the ideas to ideas and facts to facts. Ideas direct our attention. Sets of ideas assist us in making sense of things. Only by carefully making sense of things will we be able to clearly identify problems and predicaments. Without thorough problem and predicament identification, we should not spend time on action planning (finding "solutions").

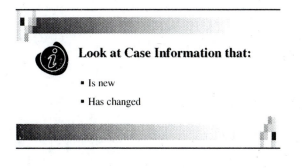

Look at Case Information that:

- Is new
- Has changed

Summary

In this chapter, the case method has been introduced. You have read and studied your first case, noticing it is a lot of information

that describes a real situation and what happened in it. The case has provided us with the opportunity to see several people relate to one another in order to more or less accomplish the tasks by means of which a small business will or won't succeed. The case characters and events, no doubt, prompted your own thoughts and feelings. The chapter also noted a number of common reactions that people have to a case—you may have had one or more of these yourself. It is not important whether your reactions are "good" or "bad" per se, but rather it is important that you do not make quick decisions based on your initial reactions to the case. Our initial reactions are our first reactions, before we have taken the time to fully analyze and diagnose the situation in the case.

In the chapters that follow, you will begin to see how such relatively quick, mindless reactions really don't promote much serious thinking. You will also begin to appreciate what more careful, thoughtful thinking can reveal about a case, and the insights that even a handful of ideas, carefully used, can provide.

While this chapter has provided an initial sense of a case as well as what can be done with its information, in Chapter 2 we turn to a much more careful description of what constitutes teaching cases and what happens in a case discussion.

2

On Cases and the Case Method

The essential fact which makes the case system . . . an educational method of the greatest power is that it arouses the interest of the student by making him an active rather than a passive participant.

—WALLACE B. DONHAM

I define learning as . . . changes a person makes in himself or herself that increase the know-why and/or the know-what and/or the know-how the person possesses with respect to a given subject.

—PETER B. VAIL

Chapter Objectives

- Describe the case method and teaching cases, as well as depict how cases may differ.
- Increase your appreciation for what occurs in case discussions and how participating in discussions contributes to managerial learning.

JUST WHAT IS A TEACHING CASE?

Teaching with cases is an old and widespread form of education. Learning on the job is usually a large part of professional, craft, and other occupational learning and may occur through internships, apprenticeships, and mentoring. All hands-on training is essentially case focused, that is, we attend to one task/activity at a time and try to do it correctly. Cases, in fact, are the mainstay of medical education (the patient as a case) and legal education (the law as a set of precedent-setting cases). Common to these case-based approaches is their prescriptiveness. The cases are used as examples of how a person should behave or as places to practice proper behavior.

11

In the social and behavioral sciences and in business education, cases are usually descriptive of something in its real-life context using multiple sources of evidence. There are two kinds of descriptive cases: research and teaching. *Research cases* are careful, rich descriptions of one or more contemporary events, situations, and/or behaviors where the investigator wishes to learn the answers to questions previously unasked about who, what, where, why, or how (Yin 1984, 23). *Teaching cases* are also for learning, but by students. In the beginning, the intended role of business-related case studies was as follows, as captured in the early classic statement of Harvard Professor Charles Gragg (1954):

> A case typically is a record of a business issue which actually has been faced by business executives, together with surrounding facts, opinions, and prejudices upon which executive decisions have to depend. These real and particularized cases are presented to students for considered analyses, open discussion and final discussion as to the type of action which should be taken. (p. 6)

By the 1950s, Professor Paul Lawrence (1953) more operationally remarked that:

> A good case is the vehicle by which a chunk of reality is brought into the classroom to be worked over by the class and instructor. A good case keeps the class discussion grounded upon some of the stubborn facts that must be faced in real life situations. It is the anchor on academic flights of speculation. It is the record of complex situations that must be literally pulled apart and put together again for the expression of attitudes or ways of thinking brought into the classroom. (p. 215)

More recently, cases have been described simply by Erskine, Leenders, and Mauffett-Leenders (1981) as ". . . a description of an actual administrative situation, commonly involving a decision or problem. It is normally written from the viewpoint of the decision makers involved and allows the student to step figuratively into the shoes of the decision maker or problem solver" (p. 10). Also, recently, Christensen and Hansen (1989), somewhat more eloquently, defined a case as:

> . . . a partial, historical, clinical study of a situation which has confronted a practicing administrator or managerial group. Presented in narrative form to encourage student involvement, it provides data—substantive and process—essential to an analysis of a specific situation, for the framing of alternative action programs, and for their implementation recognizing the complexity and ambiguity of the practical world. (p. 27)

A typical teaching case is, therefore, a record of some situation actually faced by one or more persons (often a manager) with the facts, opinions, and prejudices upon which decisions have to depend. Teaching cases are utilized today in most business fields, such as finance, marketing, operations, etc., as well as courses about the human side of enterprise, those fields which the cases later in this book relate to.

Management cases, it should be emphasized, are not like law cases that summarize important points of law and precedence. Management cases are much more like those dealt with by advanced medical students when treating real patients. A medical student's task is to listen to a patient's complaints, discover other symptoms, and compile a general history and other information about the patient's life circumstances and current state during the examination (e.g., vital signs). From all of this information then, the medical student attempts to reach a diagnosis or a statement of the patient's illness and what might have caused it. Furthermore, treatment is specified, which is some course of action that will remove or ameliorate the diagnosed illness. Of course, the medical student does all of this work under the supervision of an experienced physician.

Management cases are remarkably similar to a medical case history—a more or less complete set of facts, some of them relevant, some less so. A hospitality management student, like a medical student, must utilize the available facts to decide whether there are any difficulties or issues that require one or more actions and, if so, what actions. The situations faced will vary as much as the variety of patients examined by a medical student—from patients in excellent health to those with relatively minor sickness/discomforts to those with multiple, major fractures/illness to life threatening disease or trauma. The major tasks, however, are always the same: to understand and analyze fully, to diagnose accurately, and to take appropriate corrective and/or preventative action.

A management case is a vicarious experience, a situation to learn in and to learn from, without the direct personal involvement and the time investment required to actually live through it. By working with a set of cases, therefore, one can usually acquire, vicariously, both a lot of experience in a relatively short period of time, and perhaps, just as importantly, can confront a wider variety of experiences than can be done in any one or a few actual work assignments.

Just as it is important to say what a case is, it is also important to say what a case is *not*. Teaching cases are not: (1) fictional accounts of situations; (2) just sets of actual organizational data, for example, balance sheets or other records; or (3) articles from business journals or newspapers about a particular company or industry. While each of these "non-cases" may create a great class discussion, they are not true teaching cases. Neither are research cases, those real situations carefully documented by social scientists to explore or elucidate some phenomena of theoretic or pragmatic significance.

As you may have begun to anticipate, teaching cases may be short or long, may be broad in scope or focused, and may have an almost limitless topic range. Some have called cases a snapshot of reality, a slice of life, a story presented as study material, a puzzle, episodes of practice, or other colorful but misleading names (McNair 1971). Distinguishing cases from other teaching materials, however, are several crucial features:

1. A teaching case describes a real situation, based on fieldwork, which brings reality into the classroom.
2. Because it describes reality, a teaching case is information rich and tends not to gloss over specifics.
3. The information in a teaching case is sufficient enough to allow students to identify with the people, situations, and organization described.
4. A teaching case always provides one or more opportunities for analysis, situational understanding, and usually the identification and creation of one or more possible actions.

WHERE DID THE CASE METHOD BEGIN? HOW HAS IT EVOLVED?

When the Harvard Business School was founded in 1908, Dean Gay and his maverick, almost antiacademic, small faculty of seven quickly agreed that business education was not the study of applied economics, and that their purpose was "to give each individual student a practical and professional training suitable to the particular business he plans to enter" (Christensen and Hansen 1989, 22). The key words are *practical* and *professional*. This meant utilizing a pedagogy that linked the classroom to the realities of business and engaged the student in a practice-oriented, problem-solving instructional mode. From the beginning, faculty were advised to use student discussion in addition to lectures. Executives soon were invited to come to classes with a write-up of their own company problems and then lead class discussions of their situations. By 1921, with prodding from the new dean, Wallace B. Donham, the first book of written cases was published. By 1924, the School's Bureau of Business Research had 20 MBA graduates at work preparing cases.

Behind the evolution of the case method is a philosophy of professional education that mates knowledge and action. This philosophy, in the words of Alfred North Whitehead (1947, 218), "rejects the doctrine that students should first learn passively, and then, having learned, should apply knowledge." The case method is based on a philosophy of professional education that mates knowledge and action, not by first passively learning knowledge and then applying it, but in accordance with the principles elucidated by John Dewey, that is, education consists of the cumulative and unending acquisition, combination, and reordering of learning experiences. In Dewey's own words (Soltes 1971, 83),

> Only by wrestling with the conditions of the problem at hand, seeking and finding his own way out, does he think . . . If he cannot devise his own solution (not, of course, in isolation, but in correspondence with the teacher and other pupils) and find his own way out he will not learn, not even if he can recite some correct answer with one hundred percent accuracy.

One of the Harvard Business School's early professors, Arthur Stone Dewing (1931, 49), reflecting on the essence of the case method, stated that since business people must be able to meet in action the problems arising out of new situations in an ever-changing environment, a proper business education, ". . . would consist of acquiring facility to act in the presence of new experience. It asks not how a man be trained to know, but how a man be trained to act."

The original and continuing intent of teaching with cases is to *enhance discussion*—for appreciation, for understanding, for analysis, for action—*in the service of thinking*. And, thinking about the concrete, complex, changeable situations faced by managers means *there is no one way or no one best way to think*.

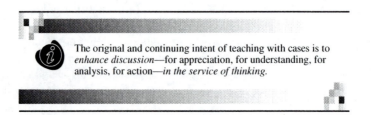

The original and continuing intent of teaching with cases is to *enhance discussion*—for appreciation, for understanding, for analysis, for action—*in the service of thinking*.

Written cases about managerial situations are, as we have noted, descriptions of actual situations. Such cases, however, may vary in several ways.

1. **Length:** Cases vary from short ones of just one or a few paragraphs to quite lengthy ones running upwards of 20 or 30 pages.

2. *Scope:* The situation described can vary from very narrow, for example, just two people talking together in one setting at one time about just one topic, to very wide, for example, a whole company and everything going on in it and outside of it over many years.

3. *Amount of Information:* Regardless of their length or scope, cases can also vary in terms of the level of detail of the description. Some case situations thus are written about in great detail, while others are described somewhat more generally.

In addition to written cases we now sometimes see video and film cases and multimedia cases. Cases have also been linked to other pedagogies such as role plays or structuring the classroom in parallel to the case situation (Lundberg 1994).

WHAT TYPES OF TEACHING CASES ARE THERE?

At present, the form (i.e., the amount and type of information provided, the degree of order and structure given to the information) and learning outcomes of teaching cases continue to evolve. Recently, for example, Lundberg et al. (2001) described 10 different case formats and 14 types of case objectives. This variety, however, can be distilled down into three general types:

- *Iceberg Cases:* These are relatively short cases that describe one or, at most, a few incidents or events or perceptions and opinions. Other, relevant information remains "below the surface"—that is, historical, contextual, and other related information is only hinted at, if at all, and not described in any great detail. Iceberg cases are utilized to practice seeing ideas in information, and to use ideas or sets of ideas to determine what, where, and how additional information might be useful, if acquired. Iceberg cases remind us that having something in mind to prompt seeing and thinking is always desirable. Chapter 9 provides examples and discusses iceberg cases.

- *Analysis Cases:* This type of case can be of any length or scope or detail. They often, but not always, hold someone's opinion that the situation can be improved somehow. Doing a careful analysis is the major opportunity in this case type. The task is to carefully and fully understand some situation, what happens there, and the relationship and behavior of the people involved. A thorough analysis permits us not to get trapped in the sorts of common reactions noted in the Section "Common Reactions" in Chapter 1 or the Section "Action Traps" in Chapter 8.

- *Action-Focused Cases:* These usually longer cases are in a sense an extended form of analysis cases in that they require both an analysis and several types of decisions. These decisions may include determining what issues are salient, whether to take some action and why it is necessary/desirable/warranted, and who, what, where, when, and how to take action, and so on. Action-focused cases thus provide experience in issue identification, information search and assessment, application of conceptual frameworks, contextual understanding, decision making/justification, issue amelioration, and so on.

No matter their purpose or complexity, all three types of cases just described reflect a couple of common themes. One theme, elaborated in Chapter 3, is that to understand something, *ideas* are required. Information alone has no meaning.

An idea is a mental category of thoughts about things, processes, places, people, and so on, that we observe and experience. Most ideas have words (more specifically, a noun) that name, symbolize, or signify them. Some ideas, however, we have no words for them yet. All nouns are ideas in that all nouns refer to a mental category of thought. For example, the idea of "yellow" reflects a mental category of color; the idea of "morale" reflects the mental category of group-level satisfaction; and the idea of "task purpose" reflects the mental category of the work that a unit or department in an organization does—that is, what its purpose is.

Consider the following example of information without an idea to frame it or give it meaning (Bransford and Johnson 1972, 722):

> First you arrange items into different groups. Of course one pile might be sufficient depending on how much there is to do. If you have to go somewhere else due to lack of facilities, then that is the next step; otherwise you are pretty well set. It is important not to overdo things.
>
> That is, it is better to do too few things at once than too many. In the short run this may not seem important but complications can easily arise. A mistake can be expensive as well. At first the whole procedure seems complicated.
>
> Soon however, it will become just another facet of life. It is difficult to see any end to the necessity for this task in the immediate future but then one can never tell. After the procedure is completed, one arranges the material into different groups again. Then they can be put into their appropriate places. Eventually they will be used once more and the whole cycle will have to be repeated. However, that is part of life.

Do you know what this information is about? Without an idea to frame it, to give it meaning, it is difficult to understand. Now read the information again using the idea of "washing clothes." See how ideas work now? This is how ideas work: They help us make sense by giving meaning to information or data.

Information bracketed or framed by an idea is a fact. How facts relate to one another through a set of ideas provides meaning. Another theme reflected in all three types of cases is that understanding is helpful in taking action. Therefore, the fuller and more complete our understanding of a situation, the more likely our behavior in or toward it will be appropriate. Cases have information. Ideas let us notice factual information, make sense of it, and assess

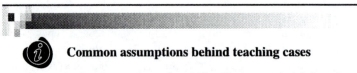

Common assumptions behind teaching cases

1. In order to understand something, ideas are required. Information alone has no meaning. Information that is bracketed, framed, or comprehended by an idea is a fact.

2. Understanding assists in taking action: the fuller and more complete our understanding of a situation, the more likely our behavior in or toward it will be appropriate.

the quality of case information. Ideas also let us order and compare case information. A set of ideas allows us to make sense of particular facts, and, sometimes, even lets us predict what may occur in the future.

WHAT HAPPENS IN A CASE DISCUSSION?

While some general patterns may be discerned for what happens in a case discussion, day-by-day variations will certainly occur. Why? Because there are many factors that mesh together and most of these factors are themselves variable. A couple of important factors are the length of the class period and the classroom setting. Case discussions take time so it is common to schedule classes somewhat longer than for straight lectures, that is, from 60 to 90 minutes instead of 50. Case discussions are also enhanced when they take place in a room where everyone can easily see and hear one another (not just the instructor) and there is a lot of white/black board upon which to capture key points of the discussion.

Other factors influencing a case discussion include the type and complexity of the case being discussed, the classes' experience with case discussions, and the amount and quality of student preparation (both individually and in student groups). At minimum, student preparation is generally acknowledged to require a mastery of the case information and some independent thinking about what the relevant facts are and what they mean. Instructors vary in their beliefs about how much preparation structure they should provide to their students, ranging from providing just a few general questions to insisting upon using a detailed formula. The approach outlined in Part II of this book falls in the middle. Often too, instructors sometimes create a discussion plan for each case, again varying in detail.

The above factors in combination will influence the pattern of a case discussion. Assuming an action-focused case and a class with some case discussion experience, one group of experienced case instructors outline what they call a "normal" case discussion as follows (Mauffette-Leenders, Erskine, and Leenders 1997, 79–82):

> Some instructors start the class discussion by asking someone (or several participants) for his or her solution to the case and then work backwards to derive the analysis. Other instructors start by asking for a definition of the issue(s) at stake and proceed in a logical manner towards the solution and implementation.

Normally, at some stage of the class discussion (although not necessarily at the beginning), considerable deliberation takes place to identify the exact nature of the issue(s) in the case. In some cases this task is trivial because the answer is obvious; in other cases it may constitute the central educational challenge of the discussion.

With a focus on the above issue(s), case class discussions turn to an analysis of the evidence or causal sequence of events. This stage of the discussion is where the tools, techniques, concepts, and theories are used to help make sense of both quantitative and qualitative information available.

A significant part of most case classes deals with the discussion of alternatives. You will be asked to generate alternatives, discuss their respective merits in depth, identify your decision criteria, present your arguments, and justify your decision(s) or recommendation(s).

Discussion of action and implementation strategies and tactics sometimes receives scant attention in case classes because some instructors believe that proper identification and analysis of the problem and discussion of theory are more important. Also, since implementation is logically discussed at the end of class, it often gets lost in the race with the clock. How decisions are executed can be as significant as what decisions are made to solve a problem or address an issue.

The class conclusion is a transition phase. It can be used to close the current discussion, link it to subsequent classes or to the ones so far completed. A student may be asked to summarize the case and its key points, although many instructors do it themselves. Sometimes instructors' summaries will take the form of questions left for students to ponder after class. Other times, the instructor will summarize a set of transparencies and provide his or her own framework and analytical insights that may cover some of the key points discussed in class and attempt to pull the discussion together.

If the case has been very well discussed, several options for further contributions exist. One may be to move to a basic issue discussion: "In this example, the choice of the latest and best technology appeared relatively easy. Surely, there are other situations where this decision might not be so clear cut." For example, another could be to enhance an earlier contribution: "I believe that in this case discussion the comments from Helen really moved us a long way into the right direction. Once we could see how the information in Exhibit 1 could be combined with Exhibit 4, the analysis and need for action became crystal clear."

Regardless of how the discussion closes, students should not expect the instructor to provide his or her solution. Most instructors resist offering students a personal solution so as not to demotivate them from searching for their own answers.

While a general pattern as just outlined can occur, there is no one ideal way to approach a case discussion. In fact, many instructors will intentionally vary what they ask their classes to do. The case method is based upon the belief that *management is a general competency more than it is a collection of techniques or ideas*. The best way to acquire a skill is to practice in an experience-rich, simulation-type process. Thus, the swimmer swims, the pianist plays the piano, and so on. Because it is impractical to have a student manage an organization, much less several, a case provides a vehicle for simulation. Just as every organization is somewhat unique, cases also vary. Just as every case is different from others, case discussions also vary.

What happens in a case discussion?
Expect to learn by being involved in discussions where you are encouraged to:

1. Repeatedly have to confront the intractability of reality (i.e., the absence of needed information, the ever present conflict of objectives, the imbalance of needs/wants and resources).

2. Relate analysis and action (i.e., the application of knowledge, always partial, to the complexities of reality, which requires doable, concrete action) rather than wait for complete or idealized solutions.

3. Practice managerial skills (e.g., observation, listening, analyzing, decoding, persuading, and intervening) as you talk about them.

4. Accept responsibility for your behavior (with an increasing sense of what's critical and possible, and the connectiveness of all organizational resources).

HOW DO CASE DISCUSSIONS ENHANCE LEARNING?

For many students, their initial experiences in discussing cases often do not feel like learning situations at all. Case discussions expect such very different behavior from students:

- Students are expected to speak up and frequently participate in the discussion instead of sitting quietly and taking notes;
- Students are expected to listen attentively even critically to other students instead of just listening to the instructor;
- Students are expected to use case facts to justify their thinking instead of simply expressing opinions or parroting what the instructor says;
- Students are expected to come to class having carefully thought about a case instead of simply coming to listen to the instructor; and
- Instructors mostly ask questions instead of simply providing predigested information.

Early case discussions thus break with the expectations that most students have about what classroom learning is supposed to be like. And, not surprisingly, these early discussions hold dissatisfactions because:

- Cases have no unique, simple answers;
- Case information often seems ambiguous and sometimes even contradictory;
- The issue to work on is not stated or if stated may not be trustworthy;
- Some case information is often redundant or may be irrelevant;
- Note-taking is difficult;
- The instructor is not very authoritative and does not solve the case; and
- Case discussions seem like an inefficient use of class time.

At the outset of your case discussion experience, you need to do several things. One is simply to "hang in" for a while until the unfamiliar becomes more familiar. The other thing to do is suspend any expectations of what a "proper" class or a "good" instructor is. This is why we have written Part I of this book and have suggested you read it early and more than once. It also helps to be tolerant of your classmates, remembering that they may be dealing with unfamiliarity and associated feelings just like you. Preparing each case discussion carefully (Part II elaborates what this means) can be reassuring and will speed up learning.

At this point, you may say, "Okay. I need to expect that for awhile case discussions may feel slow, awkward, unsatisfying, etc. What will happen then?" To respond, we need to be reminded of just how each of us really learns. Take a look at Figure 2.1 before reading further.

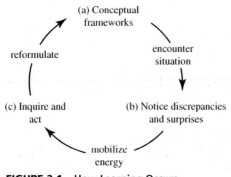

FIGURE 2.1   How Learning Occurs.

We go through life with something in our minds. What we have in mind is, generally speaking, of two kinds. One kind is information about many situations (i.e., situation-specific information) and the other kind is ideas and knowledge for understanding such information (knowledge is defined and examples provided in Chapter 3). With something in mind, we encounter situations one after another (e.g., one teaching case after another). What we have in mind is used to notice the concrete specific facts of the situation and compare what we have noticed to what we expected to notice and what we believe should have occurred. We sometimes notice discrepancies and get surprised. Our conceptual knowledge then lets us make sense out of the situations we encounter. We order information, compare it, analyze it, and so on (more on this in Chapters 4 and 6). If we are sufficiently bothered by whatever discrepancies between desired and actual performances are noticed or we become curious why we are surprised by what is actually going on in the situation, we may feel energized to learn about how the discrepancies occurred and/or why our current understanding prompted our surprise. Basically then we first search for new or more relevant information or for new ideas, and, second, use these ideas and information to make more sense of the situation, and, sometimes, with a deeper understanding, we take action to test our new understanding. If our understandings satisfy and/or our actions seem to work, we have "learned" and we modify what we had in our mind at the outset. Learning thus is an active, cyclical, intellectual–emotional process.

Case discussions enhance learning by providing for repetitive cycling, by consciously noticing, by searching, by making sense, and by acting. We test what we have in mind (our conceptual frameworks) by subjecting them to the concrete realities of a range of situations. Over time we get more adept at thinking and doing (Chapters 3 and 4 will expand on this point).

Discussing a series of cases provides exposure to a lot of first- and second-hand learning experiences. Since every case is about a unique, real situation, you can vicariously acquire a lot of experience in a relatively short time. You can enter and observe many hospitality situations without the time and expense of actually visiting them. And, since they are described in written form you can revisit them again (and again) which, of course, cannot happen in real life. Multiple case discussions also enable you to have multiple first-hand experiences in class where you can practice and perfect several skills that successful managers have, such as active listening, persuasively communicating, thinking-on-the-spot, and learning from experience. In case discussions, since multiple points of view, informational preferences, and communication tactics are exhibited, you can also learn about the effectiveness of your colleagues' skills.

Summary

In this chapter we have endeavored to provide some background on teaching cases, why they were invented, some sense of their variety, and how they may be used. You now have some intellectual insights about cases in general to add to your initial experience with the Boyd's Catering Case in Chapter 1. Let us repeat the essential purposes of teaching and learning from the discussion of cases, namely, that *cases enhance discussion in the service of thinking, and, becoming more thoughtful about real situations leads to more skilled practice.* There are no real shortcuts to repeatedly learning from experience. Knowledge simply does not directly translate into skilled behavior. If it did, all we would have to do is read!

Throughout this chapter we have noted that learning for managers and everyone comes from thinking about their experiences in specific situations. It follows that the clearer and the better we can think about our experiences, the more we will learn from them. And, the more we have learned the more often our behavior will be appropriate.[1]

References for Further Reading

In the list below, sources referenced in the text of this chapter are identified with the superscript.[*] For readers who wish to learn more about the origins and philosophical-educational basis of the case method, types and variety of cases, and, the case teaching process, see superscript.[†] Sources of criticism and debatable issues carry superscript.[‡]

Andrew, K. R. 1953. *The case method of teaching human relations and administration.* Cambridge, MA: Harvard University Press.[†]

Argyris, C. 1980. Some limitations of the case method: Experience in a management development program. *Academy of Management Review* 5: 291–98.[‡]

Barnes, L. B., C. R. Christensen, and A. T. Hansen 1994. *Teaching and the case method.* 3rd ed. Boston: Harvard Business School Press.[†]

Bransford, J. D., and M. K. Johnson. 1972. Contextual prerequisites for understanding: Some investigations of comprehension and recall. *Journal of Verbal Learning and Verbal Behavior* 11: 717–26.[*]

Christensen, C. R., and A. T. Hansen. 1989. *Teaching and the case method.* Boston: Harvard Business School Press.[*,†]

Christensen, C. R., D. A. Garrin, and A. Sweet, eds. 1991. *Education for judgment.* Boston: Harvard Business School Press.[†]

Dewing, A. S. 1931. An introduction to the use of cases. In C. E. Fraser, ed. *A case method of instruction.* New York: McGraw-Hill.[*]

Erskine, J. A., M. R. Leenders, and L. A. Mauffette-Leeders. 1981. *Teaching with cases.* London, Canada: School of Business, University of Western Ontario.[*,†]

Gragg, C. I. 1954. Because wisdom can't be told. In M. P. McNair, ed., *The case method at the Harvard Business School.* New York: McGraw-Hill.[*,†]

Lawrence P. 1953. The preparation of case material. In R. K. Andrews, ed. *The case method of teaching human relations and administration.* Cambridge, MA: Harvard University Press.[*]

Lombard, G. F., ed. 1977. *The elusive phenomena.* Boston: Harvard University Graduate School of Business Administration.[†]

Lundberg, C. C. 1994. Techniques for teaching OB in the college classroom. In J. Greenberg, ed. *Organizational behavior: The state of the science.* Hillsdale, NJ: Lawrence Erlbaum Associates.[†]

Lundberg, C. C., P. Rainsford, J. P. Shay, and C. A. Young. 2001. Case writing reconsidered. *Journal of Management Education* 25: 450–63.[†,‡]

Lundberg, C. and J. Winn. The great casenotes debate.[‡]

Mauffette-Leenders, L. A., J. A. Erskine, and M. R. Leenders. 1997. *Learning with cases.* London, Canada: Richard Ivey School of Business.[*,†]

McNair, M. P. 1971, July–August. McNair on cases. Harvard Business School Bulletin, 10–13.[*,†]

Soltes, J. 1971. J. Dewey. In *Encyclopedia of education* (p. 81). New York: MacMillan.[*]

Vance, C. M., ed. 1993. *Mastering management education: Innovations in teaching effectiveness.* Newbury Park, CA: Sage.[†,‡]

Whitehead, A. N. 1947. *Essays in science and philosophy.* New York: Philosophical Library.[*]

Yin, R. K. 1984. *Case study research: Design and methods.* Beverly Hills, CA: Sage.[*]

---

[1] There is a very, very old joke in business that makes this point. A worker asks his manager why he didn't get a promotion because, "I've got years of experience." The manager replies, "Really, I think you have a small amount of experience that you've had over and over and over again."

3

Toward Clearer Thinking

It is more necessary to think than to know, especially since it is obvious that we never know without thinking.

—Prescott Lecky

Nothing is more common than for men to think that because they are familiar with words, they understand the ideas they stand for.

—J. H. Newman

Essentially (being tough-minded) is the attitude and the qualities and the training that enable one to seize on facts and make these facts a basis for intelligent, courageous action. The tough-minded have a zest for tackling hard problems. They dare to grapple with the unfamiliar and wrest useful truth from stubborn new facts. They are not dismayed by change, for they know that change at an accelerated tempo is the pattern of living, the only pattern on which successful action can be based. Above all, the tough-minded do not wall themselves in with comfortable illusions. They do not rely on the easy precepts of tradition or on mere conformity to regulations. They know the answers are not in the book.

—Malcolm P. McNair

Chapter Objectives

※ Increase your appreciation for clear thinking and why it is desirable.

※ Provide some basic ideas that assist us in thinking more clearly.

※ Sketch the process by which we can continue to develop our thinking competencies.

If being "smart" means being able to think both carefully and clearly so that our behavior is more appropriate and more effective, then most of us would probably wish we were smarter than we are now. What is the antithesis of being smart? The people we say aren't so smart are those who:

- are gullible or easily persuaded;
- treat information as accurate or true regardless of its source or factual basis;
- are slaves to prejudice, bias, doctrine, or emotional reaction;
- are captives of either simplistic or automatic thinking; and
- are locked into one point of view regardless of the situation.

How might we become smarter, more mindful, and think more carefully and more clearly? Part of the answer is to devote ourselves to the preparation and discussion of a lot of good cases. Another part of the answer will come from an awareness and use of some basic ideas about language, ideas, and situational information, as well as understanding the qualitative differences among available information, ways of knowing, and the conceptual tools we use in thinking.

This chapter will provide a rationale for the following assertions:

- Depending upon the loose or inappropriate thoughts or words of others is seldom very useful;
- Good ideas clearly held and carefully applied will result in both greater and better understanding of actual situations;
- A set of related ideas will provide more understanding than single ideas;
- The better we understand a situation we face, the more skillful we are likely to be in respect to it; and
- The more clearly we think, the more, and more easily, we can learn from our experience.

In this chapter we will elaborate on each of these points with the ultimate aim of enabling you to perceive, think, communicate, and act more effectively—in your case work, in your career, and in your life.

WHAT BLOCKS CLEAR THINKING?

In general, clear thinking is thwarted when a person relies primarily or solely on commonsense beliefs, unfounded universal principles, fuzzy ideas, and intuition. This is especially so for thinking about human behavior.

We learn about and communicate *commonsense beliefs* through sayings and maxims such as, "You can't teach an old dog new tricks," "Charity begins at home," "Absence makes the heart grow fonder," "Many hands make light work," "Nothing ventured, nothing gained." We connect with such commonsensical sayings because they seem to hold a grain of truth and because other people seem to firmly believe them. Unfortunately, the same people often simultaneously believe in commonsensical sayings that are contrary or opposite. For example, compare the following maxims to those just listed: "You're never too late to learn," "Love thy neighbor," "Out of sight, out of mind," "Too many cooks spoil the broth," "Look before you leap." These also seem to be heard a lot, to hold a grain of truth, and to reflect some of our experience. The trouble with commonsense beliefs is that they are just partial truths that have no guidance for when to use them. Commonsense sayings would have us believe quite different things, for example, that a risk-taker is reckless or courageous or that a conservative decision-maker is timid or prudent. Was Socrates morally courageous or stubbornly obstinate? Is a business leader pragmatic or principled? *Reliance on commonsense sayings replaces one's own thinking with the partial and usually contradictory truths of others.*

An alternative to commonsense sayings are *universal principles*, those distillations of experience by people who we accept as knowing what they are talking about. A few historical examples will indicate why reliance on them impedes thinking.

Not so long ago everyone believed that the earth was flat and the sun rotated around the earth. While today some people still accept these statements, mounting scientific evidence has replaced them for the majority of educated people. Even today many people are prone to believe in some principle rather than to think in specifics or with evidence. How often have you heard that human behavior is due to our genetic inheritance, the cultures we are born and grow up in, our diets, alien programming, conditioning by television, sunspots, etc.?

Universal principles abound in business as well, as the popularity of one management fad after another demonstrates. Ask your instructor about MBWA, TQM, and MBO. Furthermore, ask whether he or she agrees that they are no longer very popular because they were simple, general principles that did not provide specific, situationally sensitive application guidance.

Universal principles are typically so broad (and their evidential basis so incomplete) that reliance on them instead of careful thinking, just like reliance on common sense, is foolish for a number of reasons. Change makes the advice garnered from universal principles outdated. These universal principles blur the very real variety of circumstances that we face, and selecting one to use is always a very personal and idiosyncratic choice at best. As a hospitality student you will hear many general statements that you are to believe unthinkingly, like "hospitality organizations are unique, not like other kinds of businesses," and "to succeed as a hospitality manager it is smart to adopt the best practices of other successful hospitality managers."

Fuzzy ideas block clear thinking simply because we can never be sure just what we are trying to think about when the ideas used to refer to things are unclear. When we refer to someone as *cool*, for example, do we mean unemotional or that we approve of his or her behavior? Or is it a positive general judgment? Or is a cool person one who conforms to popular culture? Fuzzy ideas have multiple meanings, or a meaning that varies depending on the situation (like "man"), or little meaning at all. Imagine getting a course paper back on which the only comment the instructor writes is, "Hey man, this is cool." The Section "What Are Key Lessons from Semantics for Case Work?" expands on clear ideas.

Intuition, by definition, refers to an unconscious mental process—a person comes to some conclusion but doesn't know how he or she did. Intuition is thus subject to influence by personal mood states, such as depression, anxiety, ecstasy, as well as by nonrelevant biases and attitudes.

Clear thinking is typically blocked when the thinker relies primarily/solely on:
- Common-sense beliefs
- Unfounded universal principles
- Fuzzy ideas
- Intuition

WHAT IS TOUGH-MINDEDNESS?

Before we begin to respond to this question, let us review the quote by McNair at the beginning of this chapter.

> Essentially (being tough-minded) is the attitude and the qualities and the training that enable one to seize on facts and make these facts a basis for intelligent, courageous action. The tough-minded have a zest for tackling hard problems. They dare to grapple with the unfamiliar and wrest useful truth from stubborn new facts. They are not dismayed by change, for they know that change at an accelerated tempo is the pattern of living, the only pattern on which successful action can be based. Above all, the tough-minded do not wall themselves in with comfortable illusions. They do not rely on the easy precepts of tradition or on mere conformity to regulations. They know the answers are not in the book.

William James, a great teacher of philosophy at Harvard University, coined the phrase *tough-minded* early in the twentieth century. James distinguished between people who are tough-minded and people who are tender-minded. *Toughness*, for James, referred to our intellectual capabilities and how we use them. To be tough-minded is to be (1) fact-focused, (2) skeptical of quick or easy answers, and (3) dependent more upon one's own thinking than the thinking of others. To be tough-minded does not mean being either hard-headed (stubborn and closed-minded) or hard-hearted (insensitive to others or unfeeling).

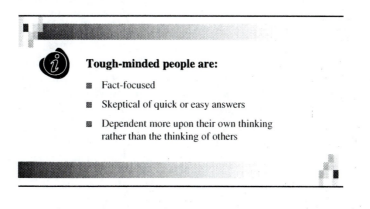

Tough-minded people are:

- Fact-focused
- Skeptical of quick or easy answers
- Dependent more upon their own thinking rather than the thinking of others

We believe that tough-minded managers will be better managers because they are more pragmatic, they see each situation for what it really is, and they make decisions and take action after thinking things through systematically, carefully, and thoroughly. Tough-mindedness is a quality of mind that is useful for doing case work. It is developed through ongoing case preparation and case discussions. It's a lot of what this book is about.

If you were to be tough-minded when thinking about the Boyd's Catering Case, you would not be influenced if one of your classmates said, "I think that Emily should be fired and Tracy should be asked to come back. That would solve everything." Nor would you be influenced by the unfounded yet commonsense belief that one should never hire family members. Instead, you would think carefully about the information in the case using some ideas such as organizational communication, motivation, performance appraisal, and perhaps others, to sift through the information, make sense of the information, and gain a more systematic and sophisticated understanding of the situation before suggesting any kind of action.

WHAT ARE KEY LESSONS FROM SEMANTICS FOR CASE WORK?

So how does one go about becoming more tough-minded? One way is through understanding semantics, which is about words and meanings. Let us begin by considering something you are familiar with as analog-language. All languages have just three elements: words, a dictionary, and a grammar. There is a set of symbols (words), each with one or more meanings (the dictionary), and some rules for arraying the symbols (the grammar). The reason we refer to language is straightforward. Language is the medium for communication, for thinking, for knowing, and hence, for sensemaking. Systematic and sophisticated understanding thus depends upon clear thinking that in turn depends upon the careful use of language.

At the outset we need to remember as best we can to distinguish between the words we use to communicate ideas and that to which the ideas refer. This is sometimes stated in shorthand through the reminder that "the word is not the thing." While obvious, all too often people forget the word is not the thing and use key words as if they were the things to which they refer. Names make the point. Take the name "David," for example. If we have a friend named "David," the name implies a continuity over time. The name continues to refer to our friend today, tomorrow, and years from now. However, "David" the actual person last year was a bundle of cells, thoughts, emotions, attitudes, and so on, which may not have much to do with "David" today or "David" next year. David the organism changes, David the name does not. The word is not the thing! An important and related distinction to remember is captured in the phrase, "The map is not the territory." A map about something does not comprehend all features or facets of that thing. Maps, of course, are symbolic representations of some real phenomenological territory. As is well known, there can be several maps that refer to the same territory, each map focusing our attention on some aspects of the territory but ignoring others. Try driving across country with topographic, soil, population, or political districting maps instead of a road map. This elemental distinction between a map and a territory reminds us that maps are just tools for making our way about in some territory, or for thinking about some territorial features. If we substitute "conceptual frameworks" or "models" or "theories" for map, and "facts," "phenomena" or "reality" for territory, the reminder comes home.

How we use dictionaries may easily confuse the relationship between words and meanings. When we open a dictionary, we find words followed by a definition and that is how we use dictionaries—we look up a word to find its meaning. How misleading. What actually occurred is that people create and agree about a meaning and then further agree that a particular word will stand for (symbolize) the meaning. Dictionaries provide other semantic reminders:

- One word can have more than one definition;
- The same symbol can refer to different phenomena; and,
- One meaning can be symbolized by several different words.

More to the point, meanings are not in the words but in our minds and also very much context dependent. Consider the meaning of the word *fish* in these sentences:

I like fish.

He caught a fish.

You poor fish.

He fished for compliments.

Most of us unconsciously change the meaning of the word fish from a cooked, edible fish to a live fish, to not a fish but a person, to seeking.

Something else to remember as best we can is the common, indispensable convenience of referring to observable things in terms that leave out some of their characteristics. Take our friend David mentioned above. Is he a specific person, or a male, or a human being, or a mammal, or an animal, or a living creature? David is, of course, all of these. The words we used to refer to him became more and more abstract, each progressively both omitting characteristics and including other classes of things as Figure 3.1 shows. This ladder of abstraction is important both for communicating clearly about something (the more concrete, the clearer the referent is known) and for finding verifiable evidence about it (the more abstract, the more likely we are to understand a word by extraneous facts or by more words).

The words we use to think and communicate with also vary in other important ways for managers and everyone. In life, as in cases, we use words to convey information, some of which is factual (and thus independently verifiable by more than one person) and some of which is opinion (what one person thinks or believes, whether it is factual or not). Consider this sentence from the Boyd's Catering Case, "It was really a shock to her (referring to Tracy) when Mrs. Boyd put Emily in charge." That Emily was put in charge is a fact. That Tracy was shocked is the narrator's opinion. We have to be alert to the common practice of stating opinions as if they were facts or of mixing facts and opinions together, as another statement from the Boyd's Catering Case shows: "This created more work for us and killed morale."

Opinions vary as to their certainty and it is useful to be able to discern the degree of certainty being expressed. Figure 3.2 shows a continuum of certainty, anchored at one end by facts. Facts are verifiable information framed by an idea. The point here is that *facts* are preferable to *inferences*. Inferences are judgments based on some facts. Inferences are preferable to

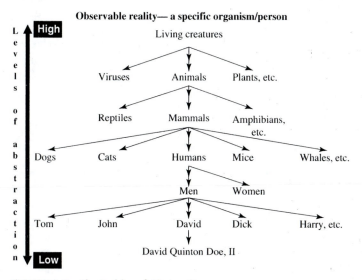

FIGURE 3.1   The Ladder of Abstraction.

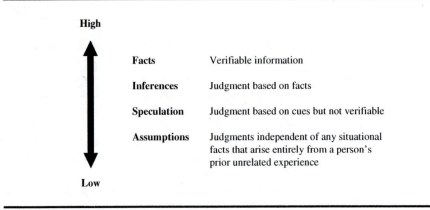

High

Facts	Verifiable information
Inferences	Judgment based on facts
Speculation	Judgment based on cues but not verifiable
Assumptions	Judgments independent of any situational facts that arise entirely from a person's prior unrelated experience

Low

FIGURE 3.2   Certainty of Judgment.

speculations. Speculations are judgments based on information, but are not verifiable. Speculations are preferable to *assumptions*. Assumptions are judgments based on a person's experience, not facts. The more verifiable the information we use in our thinking and communicating, the clearer we will be to ourselves and to others.

Words stand for/symbolize ideas. Ideas are mental categories or any conceptions we have in our minds as a result of mental comprehension, consciousness, or action. So, for example, the word *map* represents the idea of symbolic representations of some real territory. In hospitality management, we could list thousands of ideas most easily, like "front desk," "performance," "attendance," "job title," "leverage," "stockholder equity," etc. The list could go on and on. What you probably noticed is that all these ideas are nouns. Basically, any noun you can think of is an idea. Nouns are ideas. Take the noun "attitude." It is an idea because the eight letters comprising the word "attitude" have come to represent a psychoemotional state of being that influences perception and behavior.

Ideas are important for case work because we use ideas to frame and make sense of information, and this "framed" information we then call facts. Finding facts of a case is very important for making sense of what is going on in a case. Sometimes we notice facts (F) by unconsciously using ideas (I)—we aren't really aware of the ideas we are using. However, once we notice some facts using unconscious ideas, the facts can help us become conscious of the ideas that were previously unconscious (F $\rightarrow$ I) (see Figure 3.3). An example from the Boyd's Catering Case is, "No one ever ate in front of the customers. We all took our lunches downstairs." These two facts about eating lunches downstairs help us become conscious of the idea called a norm (an unwritten rule).

Similarly, we can use ideas to help us notice more facts (I $\rightarrow$ F$_1$, F$_2$, etc.). For example, using the idea of "norms" can let us see more facts in a case, like "No one ever sat down when we were working on the floor," and "We sat down all the time and began to eat whatever we wanted." These are clearly examples of more norms that existed at Boyd's Catering. In addition, ideas are sometimes linked to other ideas (e.g., I$_1$ – I$_2$), in that one idea that we have helps us think of other ideas, which can lead to seeing still other facts. For example, the idea of norms can trigger us to think of the idea of organizational culture (which includes the idea of symbols), which then leads us to see the facts of "[Emily] came to work wearing whatever

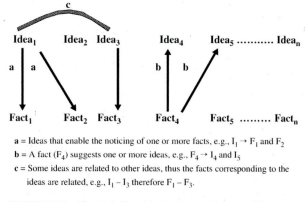

a = Ideas that enable the noticing of one or more facts, e.g., $I_1 \rightarrow F_1$ and F_2
b = A fact (F_4) suggests one or more ideas, e.g., $F_4 \rightarrow I_4$ and I_5
c = Some ideas are related to other ideas, thus the facts corresponding to the
ideas are related, e.g., $I_1 - I_3$ therefore $F_1 - F_3$.

FIGURE 3.3   The Relationship Between Ideas and Facts.

she wanted instead of the white shirts the rest of us had to wear." Her not wearing a white shirt may be symbolic of her different status in the organization. Figure 3.4 presents more interplay of ideas and facts from the Boyd's Catering Case.

This process of ideas triggering our thinking of other ideas (more about this in the Section "What Are Science's Lessons for Case Work?") and our ideas triggering our noticing of facts allow us to be more thorough in case work. Additionally, if we work with facts at the verifiable end of the continuum of certainty—which are concrete rather than abstract—we will be clearer.

Idea leading to one or more facts	$I \longrightarrow F_1, F_2$	
Idea	*Fact 1*	*Fact 2*
Norms	"No one ever sat down when we were working on the floor."	"No one ever ate in front of the customers. We all took our lunches downstairs."

Fact suggesting one or more ideas	$F \longrightarrow I_1, I_2$	
Fact	*Idea 1*	*Idea 2*
"She came to work wearing whatever she wanted instead of the white shirts the rest of us had to wear."	Rule violation	Lack of negative consequences

Idea 1 is related to Idea 2	$I_1 \longleftrightarrow I_2$	
	Idea 1	*Idea 2*
	Norms	Organizational culture

Fact 1 is related to Fact 2	$F_1 \longleftrightarrow F_2$	
	Fact 1	*Fact 2*
	"No one ever sat down when we were working on the floor."	"No one ever ate in front of the customers. We all took our lunches downstairs."

FIGURE 3.4   The Interplay of Ideas and Facts: Examples from Boyd's Catering Case.

HOW DO WE KNOW?

As previously noted, all of us go through life with something in mind, where the "something" is some mixture of bits of more or less factual information, and ideas, more or less abstract, more or less linked to information. An idea that isn't clear and isn't clearly linked to information may enable us to see something, but not accurately. We have also noted that ideas can be related to one another. It may be surprising to learn that a piece of information or a single idea *does not* constitute knowledge. *Knowledge is a statement composed of two or more ideas and how they are related.*

Interestingly, there are just two types of relationships between any two ideas. One is in effect that if one idea is observed, there is some probability that another idea will be observed at the same time. This relationship is called "association" and is described statistically as a correlation. The second form of relating ideas is in effect that if one idea is observed at one point in time, there is some probability that the second idea will be observed at a later time. This relationship is called "causation."

Both types of relating ideas are rigorously expressed in either of two ways: (a) if idea one, then idea two; or (b) the more/less idea one, then the more/less idea two. Most statements relating ideas, however, are more complex. Most statements contain more than two ideas. Thus, the relationships among the ideas are expressed as "if idea one and idea two, then idea three and idea four." The most useable statements also specify under what circumstances we can expect to observe them. For example, given situation X, if idea one, then idea two.

Real knowledge consists of two or more ideas:

- That are low in abstraction;
- That are clearly linked to highly factual information in a particular situation; and
- Where the type and strength of relationship between or among the ideas (association or causation) is known.

Knowledge that does not meet these requirements will be less useful. As you might surmise, a lot of what people have in their minds is a mixture of real knowledge, less-than-real knowledge, bits of information, and ideas of varying quality.

Components of knowledge

Ideas	Mental categories for framing information
Facts	Information framed by an idea
Knowledge	A statement composed of two or more ideas and how they are related
Association	A type of relationship between ideas where if one idea is observed, there is some probability that another idea will be observed at the same time
Causation	A type of relationship between ideas where if one idea is observed, there is some probability that the second idea will be observed at a later time

So, the question, "How do we go about knowing?" really becomes the question: "Where do we acquire more or less real, more or less trustworthy knowledge?" There are several sources and ways of knowing. The major ones are listed here.

- ***Have faith in an "authority."*** Believe without questioning what someone in a high position or who claims expertise states in print or verbally. The risk here, of course, is choosing which authority to believe and whether that person knows what he or she proclaims.
- ***Go with the majority.*** Assume that the more people who state something, the more likely it is to be accurate or true. The risk here is whether the majority actually represents a sample of those persons who are thoughtfully informed on whatever they are agreeing about.
- ***Use a formula.*** Accept as knowledge the answer or solution that some codified practice produces, like from a debate, accounting rules, a jury, a computer program, or a legislative procedure. The risk here is whether you have selected an appropriate formula and applied it properly.
- ***Depend on factual evidence.*** Believe conclusions based upon lots and lots of verifiable facts. This is what scientists do. The risk here is whether you've gathered enough of the right facts and processed them as objectively as possible.

As you can note, all of these ways of knowing have some risk. They vary primarily in how dependent you are on others (from very dependent to not at all dependent) and whether you have to be tough-minded or not (see Figure 3.5).

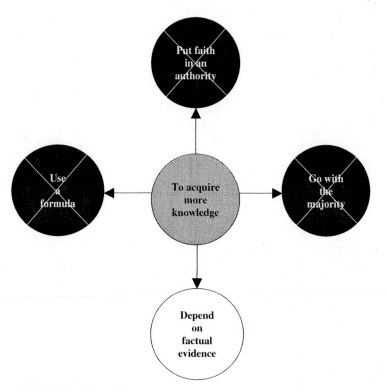

FIGURE 3.5   Ways of Knowing.

WHAT ARE SCIENCE'S LESSONS FOR CASE WORK?

Science provides three main lessons for managers and students discussing cases. They are:

- how ideas differ and relate together;
- how we improve knowledge; and
- how to think about knowing and learning.

As we have seen, words symbolize ideas. Ideas vary in terms of their level of abstraction *and* how easily they can be verified. In serious thinking, we distinguish, as science does, among three types of ideas: constructs, concepts, and variables.

Constructs are ideas without an observable referent. Instead, they are inferred from what can be observed. For example, one cannot observe the idea of "attitude" directly. We see someone exhibiting a behavioral pattern, say avoiding others with a different skin color, and attribute to him or her an attitude of racial bias. Constructs, unfortunately, abound in the vocabularies of managers and everyone else. They blur our thinking simply because two or more persons cannot be very precise in verifying the constructs' existence. What exactly do we mean, for example, when we use such common ideas as responsibility, need, power, norm, authority, organization, or system? And, how do we know of their existence and begin to observe or measure them? Let's emphasize that constructs are ideas inferred from other observables but which are not directly observable. We cannot point to them directly.

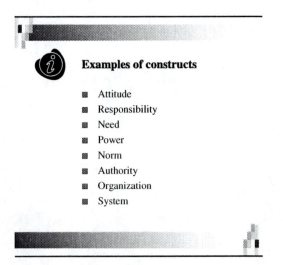

Examples of constructs

- Attitude
- Responsibility
- Need
- Power
- Norm
- Authority
- Organization
- System

In contrast, *concepts* are ideas that *do* have their referent in observable reality. Two or more persons can independently confirm the factualness of a concept. Two or more persons, for example, can each point to a "river" or to a business' "product." Other examples, which we will encounter many times in our cases, are "work group," "interaction," and "performance." The key to identifying a concept is that it permits observation by persons with their sense organs. Concepts assist in clear thinking as well as clear communication because there is little doubt about the meaning of a concept because we have a way of pointing to it.

The best type of idea is a *variable*. A variable is a concept that varies in some observable or measurable way, typically on a continuum, for example, from "low" to "high," or from "hot" to "cold" or from "0" to "100." Variables are the best types of ideas because they provide

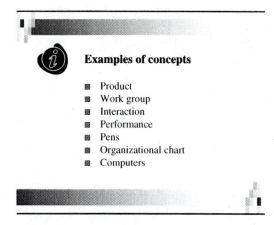

Examples of concepts

- Product
- Work group
- Interaction
- Performance
- Pens
- Organizational chart
- Computers

greater precision and less chance for differing interpretations. They are lower down the ladder of abstraction and thus are more concrete. The more concrete an idea is, the more specific the phenomena to which it refers. Also, the more concrete an idea is, the easier it is to find verifiable evidence about it, since the more abstract an idea is, the more likely we are to understand it by extraneous facts or by more words.

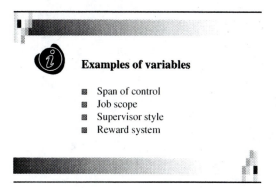

Examples of variables

- Span of control
- Job scope
- Supervisor style
- Reward system

Familiar examples of variables include "temperature," "annual snowfall," and "eggs produced." A managerial example of a variable is "span of control," defined in words (nominally) as the number of subordinates who report to a common superior (supervisor, manager, etc.). Other managerial examples of variables, which we will encounter often in our cases, are "job scope" (the number of tasks included in a job), "supervisor style" (amount and type of communication from a supervisor to a subordinate), and "reward system" (the wages, benefits, and recognition that a person can receive for doing work) (see Figure 3.6).

There are three widely accepted criteria for assessing the adequacy of ideas: scope, clarity, and systematic import. *Scope* simply refers to the number of situations to which the idea applies (this relates to its level of abstraction). Thus, the greater the scope, the greater the number of situations to which the idea applies, and the farther up the ladder of abstraction. *Clarity* refers to the potential an idea has for moving down the ladder of abstraction toward more precision of measurement or accuracy of observation. *Systematic import* refers to whether the idea is or can be linked to other ideas (i.e., can be formulated as knowledge).

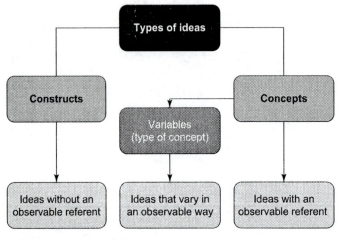

FIGURE 3.6   Types of Ideas.

Ideally we want ideas that have a lot of clarity and systematic import and still retain some reasonable scope. As defined above, variables—and to a lesser extent, concepts—will tend to meet these criteria whereas constructs less often do. Consider the constructs "good" and "beautiful," for example. They are high in scope and abstraction, very low in clarity, and low in systematic import, and as such, cannot contribute to useful knowledge very well. They, of course, fuel debates just because of these features. For clear thinking, we always prefer to use ideas that accurately reflect some phenomena (i.e., are facts per the continuum of certainty). When ideas are neatly and unambiguously linked to facts, we say they are *valid*. We also always prefer ideas whose facts are observed in a consistent way (i.e., when we use an idea to observe with, we always see the same things). If this occurs, we call the ideas *reliable*.

Criteria for assessing ideas

Scope
The number of situations to which an idea applies (this relates to its level of abstraction)

Clarity
The potential an idea has for moving down the ladder of abstraction toward more precision of measurement or accuracy of observation

Systematic import
Whether an idea is or can be linked to other ideas (i.e., can be formulated as knowledge)

Validity
When ideas are neatly and unambiguously linked to facts

Reliability
Ideas whose facts are observed in a consistent way (i.e., when we use an idea to observe with, we always see the same things)

Recall that statements composed of two or more ideas and how the ideas are related we define as knowledge, not ideas alone or facts alone. The clearer the ideas, the clearer their relationship, the clearer are the circumstances to which they relate, and the more verified the statement, the better the knowledge. Verification is critical! A yet-to-be verified statement is merely someone's hunch and we term it a *hypothesis* (or an open question). An example of a hypothesis would be: is or isn't it so that happy workers are productive workers? With reasoning or experience (or better, careful research) that provides a lot of verification we call the statement a *proposition*. Eventually when verification is so great that no one bothers to investigate it anymore we call it a *law*. An example of a law is the psychological "law of effect," that states that "behavior that is rewarded tends to be repeated."

While it is common to hear that a lot of verification of a rigorous statement "proves" it is true, this is misleading. For example, if we come across one million sheep and every one is white, that still does not prove the statement "All sheep are white." Because the first time that we come across a black sheep, we show that the statement is not proven. Proof exists in only logic and mathematics, not in life. A lot of verification means just that, for statements are never absolutely verified. Lapses in verification require reformulating the statement (its ideas and/or relationship) and new verification begins (see Figure 3.7).

Everyone has sets of ideas in their minds. For most people, their ideas are a mixture of fuzzy notions and many constructs with relatively few concepts and variables sprinkled about. All of these ideas vary in terms of their level of abstraction, validity, and reliability. Sometimes the relationships among these ideas are understood, but often they are not.

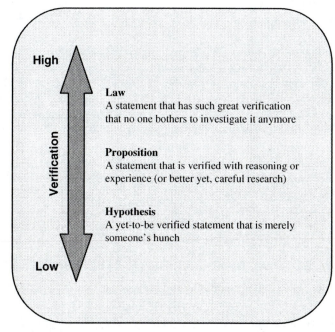

FIGURE 3.7   Levels of Knowledge.

Intuition, personal experiences, and what other people say tend to dominate how ideas are related and verified. Think back to your understanding of why some students were popular in high school. Your specific set of ideas (regarding what makes particular students popular) is termed a *frame of reference*. Everyone has one, and it tends to help us make sense of and understand familiar and relatively unchanging situations. We all have our own unique frame of reference, which is mostly unconscious and, internally, mostly unsystematic. Frames of reference do, however, let us notice features of, and generally comprehend, the familiar situations we find ourselves in.

When we have a known set of ideas, and most of the relationships among the ideas are spelled out, we have a *conceptual framework or model* (for examples of conceptual frameworks or models, take a look at Figures 3.8 and 3.9). These may or may not be linked to facts, and/or, may or may not yet be verified. Of course a conceptual framework not linked to facts is really fiction and, if not at all verified, merely a fantasy. Conceptual frameworks typically center around some identifiable phenomena or set of problems. Examples of these types of sets of problems in management include small-group structure, executive compensation, trust, leadership, and organizational culture.

Such frameworks, at least the more useful ones, will have fewer constructs than concepts. Their ideas will be mostly at the same level of abstraction and possess reasonable clarity. Conceptual frameworks/models, in addition to helping us notice and comprehend as a frame of reference does, also enable us to anticipate and discover as well as better understand how things really work. Over time, with continuing experiences and/or confirmation from research, models/frameworks are fine-tuned to better and better account for the phenomena of interest, or they are discarded and replaced.

When a conceptual framework's statements receive continuing verification they eventually achieve the status of propositions. When there is a set of interrelated, well-verified propositions we call it a *theory*. You will now see that the word *theory* is thus mostly used inaccurately in everyday speech, for example, "my mom's theory about her golf swing." Theories are, in fact, quite rare in business and management. Theories do everything that frames of reference and conceptual frameworks/models do for us, plus they enable us to explain and predict. Thus theories, besides answering the questions regarding the how, what, where, and when of a phenomenon, answer the question of "why" things are occurring the way they are. For example, a conceptual framework might indicate that higher levels of stress can reduce productivity, but a theory regarding this same phenomenon would explain *why* higher levels of stress among workers reduce their productivity. The theory might indicate that workers' cognitive resources are directed away from their jobs and instead redirected at managing their stress, thus reducing their productivity. Such a theory would be very helpful indeed when examining a situation in which workers' productivity appeared to be decreasing (see Figure 3.8).

HOW CAN WE BECOME MORE SOPHISTICATED THINKERS?

Becoming a sophisticated thinker means thinking more clearly, more systematically, and more thoroughly. As we have seen, what we have in mind is crucial for understanding the situations we encounter and acting appropriately in them. When we replace bits of information, common sense, universal principles, and intuitive frames of reference with real knowledge,

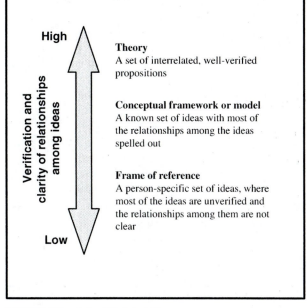

High

Verification and clarity of relationships among ideas

Theory
A set of interrelated, well-verified propositions

Conceptual framework or model
A known set of ideas with most of the relationships among the ideas spelled out

Frame of reference
A person-specific set of ideas, where most of the ideas are unverified and the relationships among them are not clear

Low

FIGURE 3.8   Sets of Related Ideas.

useful conceptual frameworks, and theories, and then use them carefully, we will see more and more realistically and be able to act accordingly.

Let's review for a moment how people behave and learn. In outline it is surprisingly simple. What we have in mind (a frame of reference or a conceptual framework) allows us to notice things. We are not video cameras recording every piece of information. We are more selective, in that what we have in mind not only allows us to notice things, but it also makes it so we do *not* notice other things. That which we notice is either what we expected to observe or not. If we notice what we expected, we tend to either leave the situation alone or continue our normal practices. Either way, we keep in mind what we started with. Sometimes, however, we notice some differences. What we expected to observe is missing or changed or not understood. If differences are noticed, and we believe our understanding of the situation is okay, we take some kind of action to alter the situation so as to make it conform to what we expected. If differences are noticed and we do not think we understand why things have changed, we inquire further about them, gathering more facts about the situation and/or using some different ideas with which we try to understand. By inquiring, whether we act on our enhanced understanding or not, we alter what we had in mind at the outset. We have learned. Figure 3.9 depicts the cycles just described: one that leads to action and leaves our conceptual framework intact, and one that leads to inquiry and modifies our conceptual framework.

At the heart of the processes just described is whether the situation encountered is assessed as being adequately understood. Sometimes it surely is, but often it is not. Most situations in which managers find themselves are changing all the time. In small and larger ways, people, settings, processes, performances, resources, etc., change and hence the situation is seldom what is expected. Managers may take action believing they understand the situation

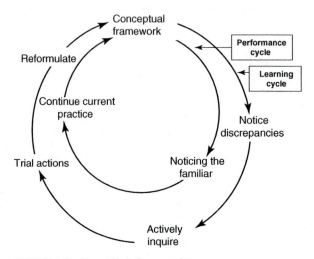

FIGURE 3.9   How We Behave and Learn.

when they do not, and their actions will not be as successful as hoped. In the cases in Part III, you will see this many times.

Becoming a more sophisticated thinker requires us to learn from our experiences—to continue to improve the conceptual frameworks that guide our noticing and the action/inquiry that follows. Figure 3.10 shows how this happens.

In new and unfamiliar situations most of us are relatively naïve in that we have to rely on our general frames of reference that let us notice obvious differences, seek familiar facts, and adopt actions previously learned. If unsuccessful we may then seek or borrow the ways of thinking of more knowledgeable others.

If we use these "new-to-us" conceptual frameworks carefully, we are more able to see both the easily noticeable differences (symptoms) in the situation as well as see more readily what in the situation is producing them. The better the conceptual framework (typically a model) the better the analysis of the situation and the more likely that our actions will effectively deal with the situation's underlying difficulties. We will have moved from naïve practice to systematic practice.

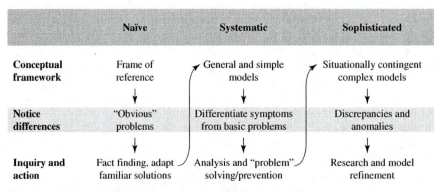

	Naïve	Systematic	Sophisticated
Conceptual framework	Frame of reference	General and simple models	Situationally contingent complex models
Notice differences	"Obvious" problems	Differentiate symptoms from basic problems	Discrepancies and anomalies
Inquiry and action	Fact finding, adapt familiar solutions	Analysis and "problem" solving/prevention	Research and model refinement

FIGURE 3.10   How Thinking Becomes More Sophisticated.

With time and further experience as we recognize the real complexity and changeability of the situations we deal with, we may continue to acquire even better models that permit us to appreciate and behave evermore appropriately. Thus, our practice becomes truly sophisticated.

This process of moving from naïve to more systematic practice and on to becoming a more sophisticated thinker, however, is neither quick nor easy. The repeated application of the approach, suggested in Part II of this book, on case after case after case, however, will enable you to move toward sophistication.

Summary

We believe that the importance of clearer thinking in organizational situations by managers is irrefutable. It just does not happen easily or naturally, and that's why this longer chapter and its many lessons are needed. To think more clearly means several things. It means using language carefully, remembering that words are not things, maps are not territories. It means remembering that the words symbolizing ideas vary in their level of abstraction and in their verifiability, and that there are three types of ideas (constructs, concepts, and variables). It means remembering that we can relate ideas in two ways (association and causation) and that real knowledge is two or more related ideas clearly linked to facts in a specified context. We have also seen that sets of ideas vary qualitatively, from frames of reference to conceptual models to theories. In Chapter 4 we will see that these sets of ideas guide our noticing and then action taking and learning. What we have in mind and how we use it is crucial! Clearer thinking, when used to learn from experience, can eventually replace naivety with sophistication.

References for Further Reading

While there is a very large, often quite specialized, and sometimes very technical literature about the subject matter of this chapter, the following sources are all nicely readable "classics" well worth your attention.

Brown, R. 1956. *Words and things*. New York: The Free Press. (The social psychology of language; humans as categorizers.)

Bruner, J., J. Goodnow, and G. Austin. 1956. *A study of thinking*. New York: Wiley. (Mental labels, thinking and learning, and the benefits of mindfulness.)

Hayakawa, S. I. 1949. *Language in thought and action*. New York: Harcourt, Brace & Co. (Words and meanings—their development and change. Many examples.)

Langer, E. J. 1989. *Mindfulness*. Reading, MA: Addison-Wesley. (How to get out of automatic living and how to acquire a mindset of being more clear, sensitive, and learningful.)

McCaskey, M. B. 1982. *The executive challenge*. Marshfield, MA; Pitman. (A business professor shows how conceptual frameworks guide behavior and innovation.)

Mitroff, I. I., and H. A. Lindstone. 1993. *The unbounded mind*. New York: Oxford University Press. (Lays out and assesses alternative ways of knowing.)

Roethlisberger, F. J. 1968. *Man-in-organization*. Cambridge, MA: Harvard University Press. (Harvard human relations guru on the basics of communications among business members.)

4

Learning from Case Work

First, intimate, habitual, intuitive familiarity with things; secondly, systematic knowledge of things; and thirdly, an effective way of thinking about things.

—L. J. HENDERSON

The teaching business has generated dozens of superstitions. Among the more intriguing of these are the belief that people learn most efficiently when they are taught in an orderly, sequential, and systematic manner; that one's knowledge of anything can be "objectively" measured; and even that the act of "teaching" significantly facilitates what is known as "learning."

—N. POSTMAN AND C. WEINGARTNER

Our life is what our thoughts make it.

—MARCUS AURELIUS

It isn't what you don't know that will hurt you; it's what you do know that isn't true.

—WILL ROGERS

Chapter Objective

▪ Demonstrate how we make sense of and learn from the situations we encounter in life and in cases.

Instructors tend to hold three beliefs about how students learn. These beliefs are usually unconscious and seldom openly stated or discussed. They are usually acted upon habitually. They are quite different from one another. The first, probably most prevalent, belief is that students need to have knowledge before they can apply it. The second belief is that with appropriate experiences, particularized knowledge is easier for students to acquire and use. The third belief is that real competencies (combinations of skills and practical knowledge) are best acquired through repetitive, conceptually informed experiences. The case method and the approach of this book clearly are in agreement with the third belief.

HOW DO WE MAKE SENSE OF AND LEARN FROM EXPERIENCE?

As we go through life, at any moment we are faced with a seemingly enormous array of bits of information. The overwhelming size and nature of this pool of potential stimuli is more than our limited cognitive processing capabilities can possibly deal with. Yet, moment by moment each of us needs to make sense of what's going on so that we can think and act appropriately. Each of us is, fundamentally, a perpetual sensemaker. *Sensemaking* is the process when a person, with something in mind (an idea or conceptual framework) that permits him or her to see *some* things but not all things, notices a particular thing or piece of information (a cue) in the ongoing flow of his or her experience and then uses what he or she has in mind to create a more or less coherent interpretation of the noticed cue.

Sensemaking has, therefore, just three elements: something in mind (a conceptual framework), a cue, and the relationship between framework and cue. Conceptual frameworks (as defined in Chapter 3) are previously learned from sociocultural experiences. Who the sensemaker thinks he or she is at the moment (his or her situational identity) determines which conceptual framework is salient and operative. For example, when in a work environment and in the position of manager, a person may be more likely to use conceptual frameworks regarding the work environment, leadership, etc. If, however, this same person is at home dealing with his or her children, the conceptual frameworks most likely to be salient are those regarding parent—child relationships, rule enforcement, moral upbringing, etc.

Cues are from present moments of perceived experience or occurrences. That is, we experience something and we extract out some stimuli (pieces of information) from the experience or occurrence based on our conceptual frameworks (which are salient based on our situational identity). Thus, cues exist within and are noticeable in terms of a person's current conceptual frame. We then use these cues for sensemaking purposes. Sensemaking, thus, is more about sociocultural plausibility than factual reality. The sensemaking process is the generation of meaning by relating a cue to a conceptual frame. The cue within a conceptual framework is what makes sense, not a cue by itself or a conceptual framework by itself.

Recall the description of washing clothes you read in Chapter 2. Without the conceptual framework of "washing clothes," the description did not make much sense. You likely had no idea what the paragraph was describing. If you are a culinary major, conceptual frameworks regarding various cooking techniques were probably salient and you may have attempted to use them to make sense of the information in the paragraph. Thus, your sensemaking involved noticing and extracting cues from the information provided and then interpreting them (i.e., making sense of them) according to your culinary conceptual framework. You may have interpreted the information as referring to the seemingly endless task of having to make the daily bread needed in a restaurant, or some other culinary process.

This depiction of the sensemaking process once again alerts us to the importance of our conceptual frameworks. Without situationally appropriate (and hopefully reality based, not overly simple) conceptual frameworks we would not be able to create the meaningfulness that leads to clear thinking and wise behavior. When we are able to notice cues that indicate things are as our conceptual framework leads us to expect, we both retain the framework and continue our behavior. When we notice cues that indicate that things are not as we expect and we think our frame is right, we usually act to change things to bring them into accord with our framework. When, however, we notice cues that are surprising or puzzling in terms of our conceptual framework, we have the opportunity to reformulate it or adopt another one.

Let us elaborate on this last possibility, for it is how we learn from our experience. The process of learning is as follows:

1. We encounter a situation, and if curious enough, notice cues that indicate things aren't as expected; that is, there are things that don't make sense;
2. These noticed discrepancies and surprises, if they bother us enough, will energize us to actively inquire and seek new information and/or ideas to create new knowledge; and
3. If this new knowledge seems to provide a better understanding of the situation, we reformulate our initial conceptual framework via substitution or incorporation.

A reformulated conceptual framework constitutes learning. Figure 4.1 visually summarizes this learning process.

However, there are several impediments to learning from our situational experience (both first-hand as well as second-hand like through teaching cases). Referring to Figure 4.1, you'll note that learning may not occur for many reasons, most of which concern not paying attention or being bothered by what we see. Learning from experience can be interrupted in so many ways it is no wonder that it isn't automatic or easy.

The focus of this section was commented on over 50 years ago by Harvard Business School Professor Fritz Roethlisberger and his words are a fitting conclusion.

Let us explore more carefully this idea of learning from experience. One of the interesting things about experience is how personalized it becomes, how important to each of us our

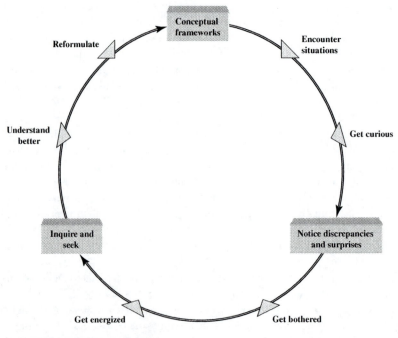

FIGURE 4.1 How Learning Occurs.

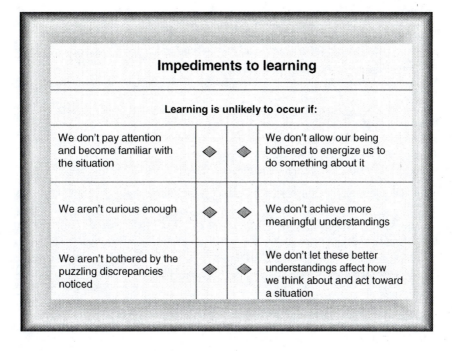

Impediments to learning

Learning is unlikely to occur if:

We don't pay attention and become familiar with the situation	◈	◈	We don't allow our being bothered to energize us to do something about it
We aren't curious enough	◈	◈	We don't achieve more meaningful understandings
We aren't bothered by the puzzling discrepancies noticed	◈	◈	We don't let these better understandings affect how we think about and act toward a situation

own experience is, and how difficult it is to communicate this importance to others. What does personal experience teach us? Astonishingly enough, personal experience seems to teach different lessons. It often teaches the "wrong" as well as the "right" lessons. The "School of hard knocks" makes criminals as well as businessmen.

WHY IS COMPARISON SO BASIC?

The general answer is simply because comparison is what we mostly do. As described earlier, as we move through life we notice and make sense of each situation in terms of some conceptual framework at a point in time. Noticing is comparative work: one or more ideas permit us to see whether there are associated facts or if expected facts are missing or whether the facts are different than expected. Similarly, we are able to compare types of facts across *time*. For example, in the Boyd's Catering Case, when we use the idea of norms to make sense of the situation, we see worker norms that exist before and after Emily enters the situation. In addition to time, one can compare facts across *space*. For example, within a department one may find a work group that has high morale while another work group does not. Also, commonly, we compare what actually happens with what is supposed to happen, and we make comparisons between the same kind of facts and notice similarities and differences.

Another way we make comparisons is when we identify ideas and facts according to the *level of social analysis* (individuals, groups, organizations, etc.). In this instance, we are comparing across the same or different levels. For example, we can compare the idea of norms that exist within a department to the norms that exist within an entire company.

Similarly, we can make comparisons when we note the level of an idea's abstraction (see Figure 3.1) or where an idea lies along the continuum of certainty (see Figure 3.2). For example, we can note whether our ideas are more concrete (lower down the ladder of abstraction and thus providing more characteristics), which aids our ability to find verifiable evidence in the case. When we make note of whether our ideas are supported by facts, inferences, speculation, or assumptions, the greater our ability to sift through information in the case and to seek the facts for understanding the case.

We are constantly comparing in other ways too. It is common to compare the behavior and reactions of some case characters to:

- other case characters;
- our own comparable experiences;
- similar persons in our organizational experience; and even
- managerial heroes in books and the business press.

Eventually, having prepared and discussed many cases, we can usefully compare across the various cases the managers and other characters we find, and seek what seem to be useful cross-situational rules of thumb.

In some case work, as in everyday life, we compare. We compare ideas to facts, ideas to ideas, and facts to facts. Why do we do all this comparison? Because the more comparisons we make, the more we understand about situational reality and how things happen there.

WHY ARE CONTEXTS AND DETAILS SO IMPORTANT?

In Chapter 3 we were reminded of how commonsense beliefs, fuzzy ideas, intuition, unfounded universal principles, and high levels of abstraction hinder clearer thinking because each clouds over the particulars of specific, always somewhat unique, situations. Talking and thinking in general terms is much like remembering. We never remember everything, hence we overlook some things, and sometimes the overlooked specifics can be the important things.

Details enable us to stay focused on situations, on the complexities that are the reality of all situations. Focusing on details assists us in staying *descriptive,* thus keeping our biases out and reducing the very human proclivity to attribute, speculate, and assume. For example, this sentence appears in a classic Harvard Case, "Joe Longman is a red-haired Scotsman." While descriptive, these two features of Joe really do not tell us much about him, and unless we are careful, we may believe that Joe has a fiery temper because of his Scottish heritage. Such an attributed speculation may lead to other misinterpretations of Joe and his behavior.

Contexts enable us to appropriately apply our knowledge (a statement composed of two or more ideas and how they are related) and our conceptual frameworks. *Contexts* help make sense out of details just like conceptual frameworks make sense out of cues. For example, annoying airport security checks become acceptable if terrorists have been hijacking airplanes. Additionally, we understand that consultative, employee-sensitive, supervisory behavior may be abandoned when a fire breaks out in the workplace. Favorite practices simply do not always work in all situations. Thus, context is important.

Contexts and details are important because, as the cases in Part III will show over and over again, we live and work in specific contexts with all of their details.

WHAT PART DO EMOTIONS PLAY?

Much managerial advice states that managers should keep emotions out of business affairs. Managers should strive to be rational and analytical in their thinking, focusing on what is objectively observable. Such advice assumes that we can control our emotions and that emotions somehow are neither real nor important. In many organizations, emotions are taboo, not to be talked about. Of course, if we don't talk about emotions we tend to overlook them and even dismiss those we feel or see.

It takes very little honest reflection, however, to realize that emotions are ubiquitous. We all have some emotions all of the time. National cultures, organizations, and occupations all vary in whether emotions are acknowledged and may be utilized in our thinking. Psychologists focus on emotions, accountants feel satisfaction upon solving difficult tax issues, service businesses know that the feelings of their service providers are reflected in customers, Marines feel pride in the Corps, new parents lovingly cuddle their infants, etc. Emotions are part of being human and social. Whether as moods (e.g., "waking up on the wrong side of the bed") or reactions to events, emotions influence our thinking—especially strong, positive and negative emotions such as ecstasy, joy, love, fear, anxiety, and anger. Strong moods and emotions, in general, simplify our thinking by highlighting some facts and exaggerating contrasts among facts. When we are upset, emotionally we become defensive and resistant.

The previous paragraphs suggest that in our case work we should pay attention to emotions. On the one hand, we need to pay attention to case information regarding the felt and displayed emotions of the case characters. What are the group or organizational rules/norms about showing emotions? Are case characters over or underreacting emotionally and why? Do positive or negative emotions prevail and why? Are case characters sensitive to their own feelings and the feelings of others? It is useful, too, to pay attention to our own emotions as we work with cases. If we are aware of our own strong emotional reactions to specific case facts or circumstances, we can more likely keep from thinking simplistically about the case situation or projecting our own feelings onto case characters. The suggested rule of thumb for case work is "be empathetic not sympathetic"—appreciate how case characters are feeling, not feel as they do.

Also be forewarned about the typical pattern of emotions you might experience as you discuss cases. You may progress through at least three discernable phases. At first, feelings of confusion and even helplessness may set in as you discover your inability to think of everything that your classmates can think of. Listening to others bringing up all sorts of interpretations and arguments you haven't thought of can be discouraging. Eventually, a second phase occurs, that of accepting easily and without distress the need and the satisfactions of cooperative help. Accepting the good work of others and building on it can lead to feelings of competence and even pleasure. The final phase is when you come to recognize that the instructor doesn't always or necessarily know the best or right answers and that others can present and hold contrary views of what is situationally feasible and valid. The feelings associated with abandoning the fear of disapproval and/or the search for an authoritative crutch are the positive feelings of one's own growing intellectual prowess and maturity. These feelings come with your increasing competence and confidence in case work. The phases and emotions just outlined are not peculiar to business case courses. They have been reported in other case system professional education, that is, in law, medical, social work, and teacher preparation programs.

WHAT IS TOUGH-MINDED SENSEMAKING?

This question weaves together sensemaking and tough-mindedness, both discussed previously (sensemaking in the Section "How Do We Make Sense of and Learn from Experience?" in this chapter and tough-mindedness in the Section "What Is Tough-Mindedness?" in Chapter 3). Together they refer to careful, fact-based thinking and judgment using appropriate conceptual frameworks. Until we have prepared and discussed a number of cases, however, the last sentence will probably not be fully appreciated. Becoming a tough-minded sensemaker means losing one's naïveté. It means you no longer unquestionably accept the general, context-free, naïve beliefs that are touted as managerial advice or wisdom as being correct. These beliefs include such ones as:

- Bosses know best because they are more rational and they know the most;
- Employees have to be told what to do and are motivated only by money;
- The only relationships among people at work that matter are defined by the organizational chart; and
- Everyone inherently resists change.

The ideas contained in these beliefs are seen, as one becomes a tough-minded sensemaker, as being too abstract to be helpful. They do not take the context (situation) into consideration and thus are unlikely to aid in clarity and accuracy.

Tough-minded sensemaking in life and in case work is a combination of attitude, skills, and knowledge, all in the service of effective action and learning. We need to expose ourselves to unfamiliar, even new situations; be curious about them and open to their unexpected discrepancies, puzzles, and surprises; be bothered enough to actively seek new facts and entertain new ideas; to think about both familiar and unfamiliar situations as clearly, systematically, and thoroughly as possible; and be ready to change our minds. This way of being, as we have previously stated, is neither quickly nor easily acquired. It takes repetitive real work over considerable time. Be patient with yourself.

Summary

This chapter began to sketch what learning from case work entails. We hope that the earlier chapters of Part I on getting the feel of an actual case, our discussion of what constitutes a teaching case and the case method, and the several reminders for clearer thinking, have paved the way for this chapter. Learning from case work, as we have read, is cyclical, comparative sensemaking with conceptual frameworks that bring our attention to the contexts, details, and the emotional aspects of the situations we encounter. The text and ideas of this and prior chapters are worthy of being reread many times. They will be appreciated as we gain experience with case work.

In Part II of this book we will describe an approach for preparing cases for class discussion. Following this approach over and over in preparing a series of cases will provide another way of understanding what we mean by becoming a more tough-minded sensemaker who learns from case work.

PART

II

Preparing Cases for Discussion

Another basic point in teaching through cases is the careful, step-by-step analysis of case facts as a prelude to discussion. Many students are tempted to read cases through quickly as a kind of story and then to engage in a rather haphazard, easygoing "bull session," so general and abstract to be of little value.

—GLOVER AND HOWER

How long should I spend preparing? What am I supposed to do when I get to the end of the case and say to myself, "So what?" How many times should I read the case? . . . These are common questions students raise in wrestling with case preparation.

—ERSKINE, LEENDERS, AND MAUFFETTE-LEENDERS

One of the most difficult issues instructors face in teaching a subject by the case method is students' lack of a consensual approach for analyzing and resolving situations. That is, students vary widely in the nature, explicitness and logicalness of their approaches to problem solving, decision making and planning.

—E. HOGAN

Successful managers (someone responsible for coordinating the activities of others to accomplish organizational goals) acquire competencies (combinations of knowledge and skills) about many things—about managing, about the business, about the work situation, etc.—and they learn to invest their time, energy, and attention in many ways as circumstances warrant. Much as we might wish it were so, there are no universal principles or general how-tos which, if slavishly followed, automatically guarantee success in all situations. *The reality is that every manager and every situation at a point in time is in some ways unique.* Nevertheless, observation of successful managerial practice lets us note some commonalities, such as:

- Successful managers are usually well informed about their current situation and their anticipated circumstances. They get and stay well informed.
- Successful managers stay alert to those aspects of their ongoing situations that present current difficulties or are likely to produce difficulties in the future.
- Successful managers ensure that appropriate choices for preventative and corrective actions are made in a timely and effective manner. They act to enhance performances as well as contribute to the well-being of the organization, its members, and its resources.

While this list might be extended, it is clear that successful managers are both thoughtful and active. But, you might ask, how?

While some managers prefer to act intuitively and some difficulties are so familiar that unconscious judgments, decisions, and habitual actions based upon experience suffice, most difficulties are unfamiliar, complex and encompassing, or so important that a more thoughtful approach is preferable. The presumption we make here is that the more thoughtful we can be about our current situations and anticipated circumstances, the less naïve, biased, and prone to error we will be. In the following chapters, we present a general, yet systematic, approach for understanding the organizational situations we find ourselves in (or read about) and for coming to and taking (or recommending) appropriate action in them. Careful attention to each step in the process is advised—for each step is an important foundation for those that follow.

5

Preparing Cases, Steps 1–3: Initial Work

Knowledge is the beginning of practice; doing is the completion of knowing. Men of the present, however, make knowledge and action two different things and go not forth to practice, because they hold that one must first have knowledge before one is able to practice. Each one says, "I proceed to investigate and discuss knowledge; I wait until knowledge is perfect and then go forth to practice it." Those who to the very end of life fail to practice also fail to understand. This is not a small error, nor one that came in a day. By saying that knowledge and practice are a unit, I am herewith offering a remedy for the disease.

—WANG YANG-MING (CHINESE PHILOSOPHER, 1472–1529)

Management, like mass transit, is only noticed when it is bad.

—EVERETT SUTERS

Chapter Objectives

▪ Introduce a semi-structured approach for preparing cases for classroom discussion.

▪ Describe and provide examples of the initial work of case preparation, which consists of getting familiar with case information, listing symptoms of possible difficulties in the situation, and listing probable goals of case characters and organizations.

▪ Begin to appreciate both the real effort involved in good case preparation and some of the errors overcome by careful initial case preparation work.

We begin with an action-focused case (see the Section "What Types of Teaching Cases Are There?" in Chapter 2 for the definition) and request that you read it once somewhat swiftly and then again *very carefully*. This case will be referred to over and over again in this and the next three chapters.

THE JENNA'S KITCHENS CASE[1]

Jenna's Kitchens Inc. was a rapidly growing, regional chain of family-style, franchised restaurants offering American and California-style, mid-priced cuisine. Throughout the states of Washington, Oregon, Idaho, and the western parts of Montana, Jenna's Kitchens, with their "ranch style" interiors (lots of plants, brass fixtures, rough boards, gingham curtains, etc.), unique salad and dessert bars, and bakery sections, had enjoyed increasing customer acceptance. Typically situated on the major highways near the edge of the city or town, Jenna's Kitchens all had excellent parking and a distinctive, carefully maintained floral garden surrounding each restaurant. They were known as the cleanest restaurants of their type in the Pacific Northwest. The company purchased each property and built the restaurant, leasing it to the franchising owner-manager.

The success of the company was generally attributed in part to its technically competent buying and regional warehousing and distribution, but especially to unusual skill in negotiations with purveyors and bankers, and to a continuing "all out" advertising program. Jenna's Kitchens had achieved some fame in Pacific Northwest business circles for its willingness to spend freely on manager and employee training, and on promotional activities, as well as for having only women in its managerial ranks. Over the years, profits had grown, but by no means in proportion to the expanding scale of operations.

While the company paid salaries, wages, and benefits in line with those of its competitors, many of its employees, franchisees, and district managers had been attracted away from them to Jenna's Kitchens. Most members of Jenna's Kitchens regarded their jobs as desirable in comparison to similar restaurant jobs, and as carrying with it considerable prestige. Employee turnover in the restaurants and the whole company was low, and few people left of their own accord. While the company was not ruthless in its handling of inept employees, employee relations were, as one executive phrased it, "Firm. People take care to see that their work is a bit better than satisfactory."

Jenna and the other women, who had founded the company nearly 10 years before, still retained positions in top management in the winter of 2000. The five regional managers, all women, who worked directly under this home–office group, as well as franchisees throughout the entire chain, frequently commented on Jenna's energy and enthusiasm. Her infectious aggressiveness and attention to detail was said to have permeated all parts of the chain.

The top management group determined corporate strategy and major policies, managed the company's finances, selected new outlets, and negotiated with new franchisees and suppliers. They delegated considerable authority in the actual operations of the company to the regional managers, and gave some weight to their regional managers' views on broad policy matters.

Judi Singleton, Regional Manager

During the two years she had been with Jenna's Kitchens, Judith ("Judi") Singleton, regional manager of the company's Inland Empire region (comprising eastern Washington and northern Idaho), attended many business meetings and not a few pep rallies at the home office in Portland, Oregon. Scarcely three weeks went by that she did not receive a personal visit from

---

[1] Reprinted with permission from Teri Tompkins (Ed.), *Cases in Management and Organization*, Prentice Hall Publishers, 2000. The company's name and the names of all case characters have been disguised.

some executive from the head office. Judi Singleton usually used these visits to talk through some action she was planning on taking. Lately, no doubt because of the lingering recession however, these contacts had held what generally amounted to pressure for increasing sales volume and injunctions to keep expenses down. Singleton responded negatively to this pressure to cut costs and expressed herself openly, both to her superiors and to her own staff. Jenna's, she asserted, was getting to be as bad as the large national restaurant chain where she had formerly been employed.

The Inland Empire regional office was located in one of the newer office buildings in the center of Spokane in the vicinity of the better hotels, shops, and theaters. It was considered a very nice location, with many potential tenants waiting to lease in the area. The lease on this suite of offices was nearly $35,000 a year, and renewal of the lease, which was about to expire, would be at least $45,000. In addition, the regional office had several expensive direct telephone lines to the company's warehouse and shipping terminal. This facility, which consisted of a large warehouse with cold storage lockers, packaging equipment, mechanized revolving inventory systems, truck and railroad docks, and so on, was located in an area of light manufacturing firms, petroleum distributors, warehouses, and wholesale firms, all grouped along the Spokane River a couple of miles to the east of downtown.

Moving the Regional Office

The top executives of the company had stated on several recent occasions that they thought Judi Singleton should move her regional office from the central, downtown location into a portion of the warehouse in order to reduce costs. Singleton had been clear in her opposition to moving the regional office, and top management, in accordance with its custom of giving latitude to its regional managers and respecting their judgement, had been reluctant to force the issue. On a recent visit, however, the president, Jenna herself, had once again indicated what Singleton thought were very strong feelings about such a move. Singleton, finally, had agreed.

The warehouse had previously housed the regional office when the region was first established. After the downtown office suite was leased, the warehouse offices remained largely vacant, although still in good state of repair. In anticipation of being reoccupied, Judi had the warehouse office totally repainted, soundproofed, carpeted, given new lighting and otherwise renovated. At the beginning of April 2001, the 20 regional office employees and Judi Singleton moved into their new quarters.

Within a few weeks after the move to the warehouse, a noticeable unrest developed among the office personnel. Sensing this, Judi Singleton was seriously concerned. This new climate, in which lack of enthusiasm and strained relations were noticeable, was totally opposite from that which she had known during the past two years. All joking and kidding, in which the whole office had previously taken part, had disappeared; the performance of the whole office seemed lackluster and lethargic; even Singleton's direct reports had stiffened in their relations to her. For example, the inventory control manager frequently complained about being swamped with work, and seemed always to be behind in his record keeping. The accountants and credit department personnel found it hard to keep up with their work, and voluntarily began to shorten their lunch hour to resume work. In general, the work of the office was behind the standard of promptness that had prevailed before.

The office workers' efforts not only reflected their attitude, but they continually complained about such things as the time they wasted in driving to work, the noise and blowing dirt in the area, and the inconvenience of having to bring their lunches to work or eat at nearby "greasy spoons," and they did not like to park in the warehouse lot among the pickup trucks and 4×4s of the all-male warehouse crew. Although no one in the office had actually quit, several had come to Judi requesting higher wages or had talked among themselves about finding better employment.

Judi Singleton thought about these complaints and the facts of the situation carefully, more than once discussing them with her husband. She discounted many of the complaints. She had made no changes in the organization structure or of personnel. All work related procedures and systems were as before. The office equipment was the same. The jobs were substantially the same as before the move. Several jobs, in fact, had been simplified in that office members could now take up many problems directly and personally with the warehouse crews, whereas before they often had to spend a lot of time in lengthy telephone conversations or on inconvenient visits to the warehouse.

Judi Singleton believed that the refurbished offices, because of the carpeting and sound-proofing, were not as noisy as the former ones. She remembered how the street noises, especially in the summer months, had welled up from the busy intersection that her office had overlooked. All office workers also now had free parking at the warehouse, whereas before they had to pay up to $80 a month for a parking space several blocks from the office. To avoid the rush hour congestion, the regional offices of Jenna's Kitchens now opened and closed a half-hour earlier than the warehouse crew and the surrounding industrial firms. Judi Singleton believed that, with this early closing, her office staff had a least an hour to shop or do errands in the city before stores closed. Singleton, along with some of the office staff, often had her lunch at either June's Café or The Diner where the food was wholesome, well-served and inexpensive, although the clutter of dishes, jukebox music, and truck driver chatter contrasted with the typical mid-town restaurants.

Responding to the Complaints

The pressure for wage and salary increases, however, continued. Judi Singleton resisted for nearly three months because Jenna's not only paid competitive wages, but also because she was concerned that any increased salary costs might offset the savings from the move. Yet there was the felt risk of losing efficient, experienced people at a time when business was increasing, and competent personnel were still hard to find. As the morale of the office continued to deteriorate, the pressure for wage increases mounted, Judi Singleton concluded there was no alternative but to raise the wages and salaries of the office personnel. Because she felt that the company shouldn't raise the wages of its office personnel without raising those of the warehouse crew, she proposed to the home office that an increase be granted to the whole regional organization. After considerable delay, the top management of Jenna's accepted Singleton's proposal.

After the increase was announced, there was very little talk in the office about wages and salaries. Instead, the office workers seemed to spend even more of their work day complaining about working conditions and about the "blankety-blank company." Morale continued to decline. The warehouse supervisor reported to Judi Singleton that the office situation was spreading to his crew, who had begun to talk about the company "going to the dogs." This surprised Judi, and concerned her, since the warehouse crew had always been loyal and efficient. She also knew that, despite the recession, in the previous year, the sales and profits of Jenna's Kitchens had reached all-time highs. Her own bonus, reflecting earnings, was the largest of her career.

The "penny-pinching" of the head office bothered Judi, especially after overhearing one of her managers say, "Jenna's no longer pushing ahead. How can we be competitive with nothing but retrenchment? The company's about to go the way of all the rest of the big chains." She couldn't move the offices back to downtown, and having just raised wages, Jenna's top management was not about to raise them again. Yet, something had to be done, and soon.

BECOMING FAMILIAR WITH A CASE

 **Step 1**

The first activity of *preparing a case*, which is obvious but yet often underappreciated, is to acquire a thorough familiarity with the situation in the case. If we are already in the situation it is easy to assume we are "familiar enough" with it. This is seldom so simply because our current duties and recent behaviors mean that our attention has been focused on some things more than others. Taking the time to consciously review our situation in detail and follow up by investigating that which has been out of attention is almost always helpful. If we are new to the situation, acquiring familiarity simply means carefully learning about the place, persons, activities, events, and so on. This is usefully done in at least two stages—an initial familiarization with the general situation, that is, the flow of the "story" so far, who is involved, what they do, where, how, and so forth. This takes time. There is usually a lot of information to absorb! This is why we ask you to read a written case more than once at the outset of preparation. A second stage to becoming thoroughly familiar requires us being proactive with the available information, as follows.

Information Quality

It is usually helpful to sort what seems to be the important information as to its *quality*: to be clear about its degree of *verifiability* and where it lies along the "continuum of certainty" (introduced in Chapter 3). Recall that information that is discovered by an idea and is verifiable, that can be seen or heard by two or more people, is a *fact*. Information that represents your or someone else's judgment made on the basis of some supporting evidence is an *inference*. Information cued from the situation but whose verification is not possible is a *speculation*. Finally, information that is independent of any verifiable clues or evidence and arises entirely out of your or another person's mind is an *assumption*. In becoming familiar with a situation, we will usually acquire all of these types of information. Of course, facts are preferred over inferences, inferences over speculations, and speculations over assumptions. Knowing the different types alerts us to seek facts.

The Jenna's Kitchens Case is replete with facts, some quite obvious such as the move from downtown to the warehouse or the wage increase in July. Others are less clear but are still facts, since they are potentially verifiable, such as "the pressure for wage increases mounted" or the "warehouse crew had always been loyal and efficient." The case has many inferences too, such as lowered "morale," "climate," and "noticeable unrest" (all abstract terms, but based on information). An example of an assumption is contained in Judi Singleton's belief that the "company shouldn't raise the wages of the office personnel without raising those of the warehouse crew."

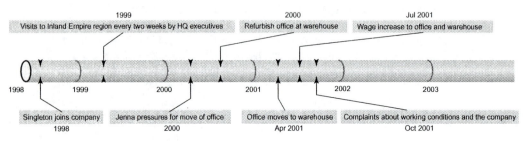

FIGURE 5.1   Time Line for Jenna's Kitchens Case.

Time Line

Familiarization with a situation or case is also aided by clarifying *when* incidents, events, or activities occur. We can do this by ordering such information chronologically or, usually better, by noting such information along a time line. A time line for Jenna's Kitchens is shown in Figure 5.1.

Levels of Social Analysis

Another useful aid for familiarization is to examine the situation in terms of several social entities, that is, at the individual, group, unit, organization, community, and societal levels of analysis as deemed relevant. In addition, examining the relationships within and among these entities as shown in the matrix shown in Figure 5.2 is also quite helpful.

	Individual				Community/
	A	B	Work unit	Organization	society
Individual A Judi Singleton	1	2	3	4	5
Individual B					
Work unit Office workers Headquarters' executives Warehouse crew			6	7	8
Organization Jenna's Kitchens				9	10
Community/ **Society** Spokane					11

FIGURE 5.2   Levels of Social Analysis in Jenna's Kitchens Case.
Shaded areas duplicate already numbered areas in the table (e.g., shaded area below box "9" is equivalent to the relationships depicted in box "10" since this shaded box represents the relationship between the community and the organization, the same of box "10").

In Jenna's Kitchens, we can notice information about all of the social entities at the various levels of analysis. At the individual level of analysis, we have Judi Singleton. At the work unit level of analysis, we have the office workers, headquarters' executives, and warehouse crew. At the organizational level of analysis, we have the company itself, Jenna's Kitchens. And finally, at the community or societal level of analysis, we have the city of Spokane.

Similarly we can note information for many of the cells of the matrix. For example, in cell 1, we can think about Judi's thoughts (within Individual A), and in cell 2, we can think about Judi's relations with other individuals (Singleton's direct reports had stiffened in their relations to her). In cell 3, we identify the relationship between Singleton and one or more work units, like her relationship with the company's headquarters in Portland. In cell 4, we can analyze the relationship between the company and individual employees. As noted in the case, the handling of employees was described as "firm." For cell 5, we can note the relationship between Jenna and the community of purveyors, as characterized by Jenna's skillful negotiations with purveyors and bankers. For additional familiarity, we can note that in cell 6, which represents the relationship between work units, the communications between the office workers and the warehouse crew was supposed to have been improved following the move. In cell 7, we can think about the relationship between the Inland Empire region and the company, and in cell 8, we can note the relationship between the regions and franchisees. Finally, in cell 9 we can think about the company's relations with banks, and in cell 10, the company's "fame" for spending freely on training (cell 11 is not applicable to this case). When we further note the amounts of information by entities or cell, we see that the most is about two entities—individuals (Judi, Jenna) and work units (office workers, headquarters, warehouse crew)—and cells 1, 3, 4, 6, and 7.

Organizational Chart

Drawing an organizational chart, if not known or provided, can usefully order some kinds of information. Beyond the positions and reporting relationships usually portrayed by such charts, we can also embellish them with the names of position incumbents, their ages, length of time in their positions, and any other details we know about the people and/or their positions (see Figure 5.3).

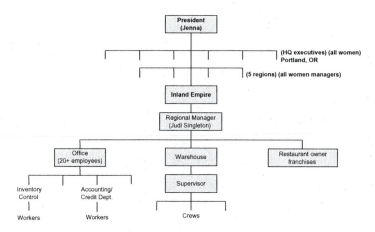

FIGURE 5.3   Organizational Chart for Jenna's Kitchens Case.

Our Feelings

One kind of information often overlooked as well as underappreciated in gaining situational familiarity is our own feelings. As we learn about situations, feelings do occur. Whether these feelings are positive or negative, focused or diffuse, it is important to note them because they may color our thinking about the situation as well as simply be significant facts in their own right. Knowing your feelings allows you to be somewhat more objective.

LISTING SYMPTOMS—WHY NOW?

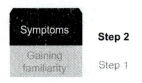

| Symptoms | **Step 2** |
| Gaining familiarity | Step 1 |

The next activity in this approach is to carefully prepare a listing of the apparent symptoms in the situation. A symptom is any indication that something is not as you or someone else thinks it should be. Symptoms are indicators that there may be more basic, more pervasive issues or difficulties in the situation. For example, think of the last time you visited a physician because you felt sick. In response to the doctor's query "what's wrong?" you told her that you had a headache, a temperature, swelling under your arms, and a red rash. Those were the symptoms, not the disease or illness that causes them.

 Symptoms

A symptom is any indication that something is not as you or someone else thinks it should be. It is an indicator that there may be more basic, more pervasive issues or difficulties in the situation. Symptoms are perceived inconsistencies, surprises or oddities in the situation, and behaviors, actions or outcomes that are over or under expectations or standards.

We strongly advocate listing symptoms right after situational familiarity and before any other sort of preparation for several reasons:

- So we won't be tempted to correct or solve symptoms when there may be more basic or underlying issues. For example, taking aspirin can alleviate one's headache but only temporarily if the headache is a symptom of a concussion.
- Symptom-listing delays making premature assessments or evaluations of what's important or at issue in the situation before we've done a careful analysis of it, that is, before we thoroughly understand what's going on.

- Listing symptoms also reminds us to be more tough-minded, that is, to always be a touch skeptical of the obvious and to seek more and better facts before we move to action.

And, as we will see in Chapter 6, symptoms often provide cues for what ideas and/or models we might adopt for our analysis.

Why do we list symptoms in a case?

- So we will not be tempted to solve symptoms
- To delay making premature assessments or evaluations
- To remind us to be more tough-minded
- To give us clues regarding ideas or models useful for analysis

---

Let us emphasize the usefulness of a skeptical attitude as you begin your initial work in case preparation. We never dive into a river pool until we have ascertained there are no rocks. With cases, as with our own lives, we want to work on the real issues—that is, we do not want to waste time or go down the wrong path alleviating symptoms rather than tackling the underlying root causes.

A listing of symptoms will include any perceived inconsistencies, surprises or oddities in the situation, and behaviors, actions or outcomes that are over or under expectations or standards. It is also useful to note who seems to be impacted or bothered by these indicators. Always list as a symptom a statement by any person in the situation that there is a "problem." Such utterances often indicate some more basic issue or difficulty. The symptoms listed may or may not seem related. Don't worry about it. Symptoms, remember, are *indicators* and subsequent work will uncover which are critical or really worth doing something about. The important thing for this activity is a thorough listing of symptoms.

In Jenna's Kitchens, we can list the symptoms by the three major, natural periods of time since the case occurs over considerable time. These naturally occurring time periods include the period before the office workers were moved to the warehouse in April, the period from the move until the July wage increase, and the period from July to the end of the case. Figure 5.4 lists symptoms in each of these three periods.

For example, we see that Singleton's initial resistance to moving the office was clearly echoed by the office workers themselves. We also can easily see that the wage increase stopped only complaints by the office workers about wages, but a new complaint—about the company—appeared. Interestingly, in the third period, the warehouse crew began to complain too, echoing dissatisfaction about the company even after the crew members received a wage increase.

Pre-move	Post-move to wage increase	Wage increase to end of case
Singleton:	*Office workers:*	*Office workers:*
"Responded negatively to this presence and expressed herself openly, both to her superiors and to her own staff"	"Noticeable unrest" • Joking and kidding had disappeared • Office performance seemed lacklustre and lethargic • Singleton's direct reports stiffened in their relations with her • Accounting and credit personnel behind in their work • Office promptness slowed • Complaints about parking, lunch, driving to work, noise, and dirt • Requests for higher wages	Complain about: • Working conditions • "Blankety-blank company" Morale continues to decline *Warehouse crews:* Complain about: • Company going to the dogs

FIGURE 5.4   Symptoms from Jenna's Kitchens Case.

LISTING GOALS—WHY NOW?

Next, our approach requires us to get as clear as we can about the multiple goals in the situation. This means creating several lists, each one a list of the major goals held by the major entities in the situation—typically for each of the central characters, any work units, groups or teams, and the organization. This will seem like, and often is, an arduous task, but it is essential because, as we will appreciate later in Chapter 7, identifying these goals is the basis for clarifying basic issues and conducting a thorough diagnosis.

Listing goals, however, is seldom easy since most goals are not publicly stated, written, or otherwise readily accessible. Do list those that are known. Also, list all those relevant goals that can be reasonably inferred from the other factual information available or that reasonably would exist. This will feel awkward for the first few cases, but practice will help. The trick, as always, is to be thorough.

In Jenna's Kitchens, the case tells us about some goals as well as lets us infer goals for several pertinent units of analysis, including the company, the Inland Empire region, the regional manager Judi Singleton, the office workers, and the warehouse crews. Figure 5.5 lists the goals for these units of analysis.

The Company	The Inland Empire Region	Judi Singleton	Office Workers	Warehouse Crews
Profit	Sales volume	Autonomy as manager	Pride in the company	Income
Growth	Lower costs	Bonus	Good boss	Keep distance from regular managers
Reputation	Low turnover	Good relationships with headquarters	Job security	
Invest in promotion and training	Attractive jobs	Maintain morale	Income	
Distinctive appearance e.g., flowers			"Prestige" working conditions	
Careful buying				
Attention to details				
Delegate authority to regional managers				

FIGURE 5.5   Goals from Jenna's Kitchens Case.

Summary

In this chapter we have indicated what is entailed in the initial work of preparing cases for discussion. There are three, ordered parts: first, becoming thoroughly familiar with the information about the situation; second, listing the symptoms of more basic, underlying issues or difficulties; and, third, listing the goals of all relevant persons and social entities as a basis for the eventual diagnosis of what action might usefully and feasibly be undertaken. Listing symptoms and goals will not only deepen your familiarization with the case, but will also create some need on your part to more fully understand the case.

This initial work is seldom easy. It requires time, attention, and energy to be careful and thorough. Many of us will want to shirk the real work outlined in this chapter. Nevertheless we must give this foundational work our best effort. We wouldn't want to erect a hotel, for example, on a flimsy foundation.

Perhaps we have begun in this chapter to appreciate even more things that most of us probably already knew. We probably already knew that it is silly to rely upon a surface sense of a situation, or just the information that happens to catch our eye, or to simplistically jump to action that reflects surface issues rather than more basic issues, or to assume there is only one or a few goals in a situation worth paying attention to.

In Chapter 6 we move forward to understand the situation with which we are now probably pretty familiar.

Preparing Cases, Step 4: Analytical Work

Conception without perception is blind, while perception without conception is empty.

—JOHN DEWEY

Chapter Objectives

- Describe and give an example of how to do a case analysis, which provides a systematic understanding of a case.
- Demonstrate the necessity (and the effort involved) in doing a careful, thorough case analysis.

With situational familiarity, recognition of symptoms, and the identification of goals, the next step in our approach is to acquire a systematic understanding of the case situation, that is, to do an *analysis*.

WHAT IS AN ANALYSIS? WHY NOW?

The object of doing an analysis is to understand, as fully as possible, the situation where symptoms have occurred and how it got that way. That is, why are the symptoms occurring? Why are things happening the way they are in the case? Analysis is more than using ideas to label case information, although such labeling (really fact identification) is a part of analysis. Recall the Section "Peeling the Onion—Looking Closer, Seeing and Understanding More" in Chapter 1 where we began to "peel the onion" with the Boyd's Catering Case. There we began to suggest what the information in the case meant. An analysis goes further—much further. By doing an analysis, you not only explain *what* is happening, but hopefully *why* it is happening.

We can see how this works by using the analogy of the "patient workup" done by a doctor. A patient with symptoms that he or she does not understand goes to the doctor. The doctor carefully records the patient's symptoms, and then gathers additional information by

Analysis	**Step 4**
Listing goals	Step 3
Recognizing symptoms	Step 2
Gaining familiarity	Step 1

carefully examining the patient and perhaps doing some tests, as guided by his/her medical training of how the body is put together and functions. The doctor uses this complete "patient workup" as the basis for later diagnosis and therapeutic prescription. In cases and actual organizational situations, an analysis is equivalent to the workup.

An analysis has three general steps. First, we select those ideas, models and/or theories that we believe will aid us in understanding the situation (see the Section "Selecting Ideas for Analysis" in this chapter). Second, we carefully and systematically apply these ideas, models and/or theories to the situation. Careful application means both knowing what the ideas mean and using all of the models' and theories' ideas that one can. Systematic means applying the ideas, models and/or theories to all possible parts of the situation to explain why things are happening the way they are. For example, if we ask about one team member's status, we have to ask about the status of the other team members. The third step of an analysis is to order the facts obtained in ways that can and will help our diagnosis (see the Section "A Large Scope Conceptual Model for Analysis" in this chapter).

The criteria for doing an analysis have already been suggested: we need to be systematic and thorough. It will be tempting at times to substitute your intuitions for explicitly applying ideas, models, and theories. It will also be tempting to interrupt an analysis upon discovering what seems to be a plausible explanation for some key symptom(s). It is likewise easy to let our own preferences and emotional reactions influence our analysis. For example, we may erroneously assume that the people in the case (the case characters) think and act like we do.

The reason for being as systematic and thorough as possible is the same reason for doing an analysis now instead of pushing on to action: *a diagnosis without analytic understanding is likely to be wrong*. Imagine calling your doctor after noticing a dark blue line advancing an inch up your arm every hour (one major symptom of blood poisoning) and he or she tells you to take three aspirin and call back the next day. Obviously, his or her diagnosis is inaccurate given the lack of

Three steps of an analysis

1. Select ideas, models, and/or theories that will aid in understanding the situation.

2. Carefully and systematically apply these ideas, models, and/or theories—use them to explain why things are happening the way they are.

3. Order the facts obtained from the analysis in ways that will help our diagnosis.

analysis. The doctor did not take the time and consideration to examine your symptom and try to determine why you have it. He or she simply treated your symptom, rather than determining its underlying root cause. Analysis is for the concerned, the responsible, and the tough-minded.

SELECTING IDEAS FOR ANALYSIS

If all situations were very similar, then we would be able to simply provide "the" ideas, model(s), and/or theory(s) found most useful for analysis. Unfortunately, organizational situations and their managers vary tremendously and thus no standard analytic ideas/models/ theories will be appropriate for all managers in every circumstance. To be sure, some things do appear in most situations and ideas about these things will be analytically useful over and over. For example, it is rare that human relationships are not pertinent. Managers have superiors, peers, and subordinates, and all workers have co-workers. Ideas for understanding interpersonal relationships, therefore, are likely to be useful in nearly all cases. Nevertheless, we should presume each situation to be analyzed is, in some ways, unique, requiring us to select an appropriate set of ideas, models, and/or theories for our analysis.

Because the quality of our analysis will depend in part on applying the appropriate conceptual tools (meaning ideas, models, and theories), our initial analytic task is to decide which ideas, models, or theories seem to be useful for thinking through the situation. Clues for this task exist in the following:

Symptoms

Listed symptoms (see the Section "Listing Symptoms—Why Now?" in Chapter 5) are suggestive. They are about or reflect something, so we need ideas (or models/theories) about those "somethings" to look more closely into them. For example, a case may contain some information about a manager who behaves insensitively toward a worker. Think about Emily in the Boyd's Catering Case. This information suggests the *idea* of human skill, a skill that is considered by some to be one of three types of important managerial skills (technical, human, conceptual). Thus, we would examine the *information* in the case using the *idea* of managerial skills, and we would be systematic in applying this idea of managerial skills across all managers noted (i.e., Emily and Mrs. Boyd). Using the *idea* of human skill to frame or make sense of the information about a manager acting insensitively toward a worker provides us with a *fact* (*information bracketed or framed by an idea is a fact*). And fact identification, although not equivalent to doing an analysis, is, however, a useful *part* of analysis. Additionally, these ideas used for fact identification can be pushed even further in that we can use them to try to explain *how or why* things got the way they are in the case.

Goals

Listed goals (per the Section "Listing Goals—Why Now?" in Chapter 5) are, likewise, suggestive of useful ideas for conducting an analysis. If an organization's or subunit/team's goal or individual's goal is not being achieved or is overachieved, for example, we might select *ideas* about the things we believe help or hinder goal achievement, such as adequacy of resources, accessibility of technology, job design, worker ability, the supervisor's style, the reward system, and so on. Again, think back to the Boyd's Catering Case and the probable goal of leaving the business clean at closing. Toward the end of the case, this goal was not being achieved and we can use different ideas to try to determine what factors may have prevented the achievement of the goal. The idea of supervisory style, specifically Emily's style, seems to be more explanatory than the other ideas just noted.

Key Facts

As we become familiar with a written case or begin to think about a situation, we always have something in mind that alerts us to that information that "stands out." The "something" we have in mind is our *ideas*, although we may not be conscious of them. If we then ask ourselves what made us notice the information, we can consciously bring our ideas to the surface and then apply them systematically to the case, using them to find other facts. For example, in reading the Boyd's Catering Case, you may have noticed the information about how Emily came to work wearing whatever she wanted instead of the white shirts the girls had to wear. What may have made you notice this information are the ideas of symbols and rules: Dress is usually symbolic and there was a rule at Boyd's about white shirts. Thus, we might be prompted to select and use these two ideas to look for other symbols and what they mean (like Emily's stool), as well as for information about other rules and rule adherence.

How to select ideas, models, and theories for analysis

1. Look at your list of symptoms.
2. Lists of goals are also suggestive.
3. Study the key facts of the case for suggestions.

A LARGE SCOPE CONCEPTUAL MODEL FOR ANALYSIS

Experienced, successful managers often have in mind a set of more or less connected general categories of ideas that forms a *conceptual framework* they use for thinking about managerial situations like those found in cases. You may recall that a conceptual framework is a known set of ideas with most of the relationships (e.g., association or causation) among the ideas identified. Managers tend to unconsciously create these categories in their conceptual frameworks by grouping and ordering ideas. What might such managerial categories or sets of ideas look like?

To understand these categories of managerial ideas, we have to examine what "managing" is—that is, what managers do. *Managing, laid bare, boils down to having some intentions (i.e., goals, objectives)*, and using these intentions to pay attention to the situations to which they refer. That is, the intentions (goals and objectives) direct managers' attention. For example, if a manager intends to reduce turnover, then he or she is likely to pay attention to (observe, monitor, measure, etc.) human resource practices, employee satisfaction, and supervisory practices geared toward employee development. The manager will then compare his or her intentions/goals (to reduce turnover by 10 percent) to the actual situations (perhaps turnover has been reduced by only 3 percent) to assess whether the goals have been achieved. If they have not, then the manager modifies either the situation (tries to change HR practices, increase employee satisfaction, or modify supervisory practices) or the intentions/goals (change the turnover reduction goal to 2 percent), or attempts to learn about what is going wrong by improving his or her understanding of the situation. Managing, thus, is about:

- having some intentions/goals;
- focusing on the situations to which the intentions/goals refer;
- assessing whether the intention/goal is achieved; and then
- making modifications or learning; and
- doing all of this over and over again.

Characterized this way, managing, in essence, appears simple indeed. It becomes more complex when we ask such questions as: Intentions, objectives, or goals about what? Attention to what? What do we compare? What should be modified or learned, how much, and when?

A manager can attend to—that is, continuously acquire an understanding of—an almost infinite number of factors that influence organizations. Experienced, successful managers often have in mind a set of more or less connected general categories that they use as a template for thinking about an organizational situation. Such categories basically group and order ideas unconsciously unless, like you, they acquire them from articles, books, lectures, workshops, and courses and then they can be used explicitly. While there is an almost infinite number of specifics one can pay attention to, we think that there are nine general, generic categories of ideas (worthy of every manager's—and case student's—ongoing attention) useful for systematically identifying, examining, and understanding all the factors to which they refer in organizational life. These nine categories or sets of ideas make up the large scope conceptual model presented in Figure 6.1A and listed here.

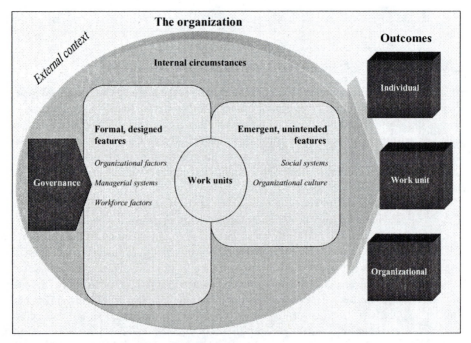

FIGURE 6.1A   Conceptual Model of How Organizations Operate.

There are two categories of ideas that refer to factors that act as constraints on management's intentions and actions and should be regularly considered and monitored. These two categories of ideas include: (1) the *external context* that the organization finds itself in and (2) *internal circumstances* within or about an organization that often impact managerial thinking, like the history of the organization and its physical setting, for example.

Another category of ideas is the organization's *governance*, meaning the people responsible for governing, managing and leading the organization. Managers, as leaders of the organization, design the organization according to their philosophy and vision. They design certain features of the organization, including what the organization should be like, what the employees should be like, and what the systems or procedures should be for guiding the organization.

These three sets of features of the organization are reflected in the fourth, fifth, and sixth categories of ideas that managers should and do pay attention to, and include:

- *Organizational factors:* managerial intentions that provide direction to an organization and coordination of its parts that are consciously designed, such as the mission and organizational structure (design) of the organization;
- *Management systems:* sets of patterned practices designed by management that link and integrate an organization's work force and organizational factors, such as human resource management systems and work designs; and
- *Workforce factors:* characteristics of the people and how many nonmanagerial members of an organization there are (also intentional and consciously designed), such as desired employee abilities and attitudes.

The *work units* of an organization, the seventh category of ideas, refer to where the organization's work is actually performed, and these work units are characterized according to their purpose, rules, ranking, etc. Like the formal, intentionally designed features of an organization (organizational factors, managerial systems, and workforce factors), work units will intentionally reflect the leaders' philosophy and vision, but may additionally exhibit some attributes that informally emerge or develop over time, such as informal rules, roles, and cliques.

In addition, the designed features of an organization (i.e., organizational factors, managerial systems, work force factors, and much of work units) have some consequences beyond those intended. These emergent features provide additional guidance for organizational members, such as the informal rules about what to do and what not to do, how to relate to one another, what is important and not, etc. These more widespread consequences of managerial intentions are captured in the eighth category of ideas, *emergent unintended features* (which reflect the organization's culture or "personality" and other informal, social attributes that influence organizational members' behavior).

Finally, all of the above categories combine to produce individual, work unit, and organizational *outcomes*, the ninth and final category of ideas.

This list of general, generic categories may initially seem a bit confusing until we see how they fit together and understand what each category is composed of. Figure 6.1B outlines our model and contains the following:

- where the governing dominant coalition usefully considers aspects of the organization's external contexts and its internal circumstances;
- the dominant coalition creates/designs overall organization factors, preferred workforce factors, and ties these together with a set of designed managerial systems which in turn are used to create the intentional side of work units;

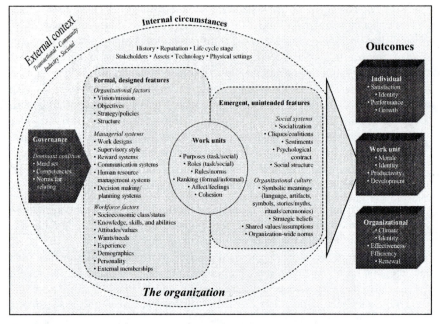

FIGURE 6.1B   Conceptual Model of How Organizations Operate (Expanded Version).

- some things emerge beyond the designed-in requirements however, both within work units as well as the organization as a whole; and,
- there are observable outcomes (some intended, some not) for individual organizational members, the work units, and the whole organization—and these outcomes, singularly and in combination, will sooner or later influence everything before them in the model.

With this overview, let us briefly examine each of these nine categories as shown in Figure 6.1B, the expanded version of the large scope conceptual model.

External Context

This set of ideas refers to four layers of factors that influence the organization from the outside, and that the governance of the organization considers and pays attention to (see Figure 6.2). These four layers include the following:

- a set of social groupings and other organizations that have *transactions* with the focal organization;
- the *local community*;
- the *industry* in which the focal organization operates; and
- the general *societal environment* that surrounds all organizations.

In terms of organizations that engage in *transactions* with the focal organization, there are those that provide inputs (those sets of organizations that supply resources, such as energy, money, materials, ideas, labor, equipment, regulations, etc., to the focal organization), and those that absorb outputs (those sets of people and organizations that accept the focal organization's products, services, wastes, gifts, etc.). Basic questions about these sets of input and

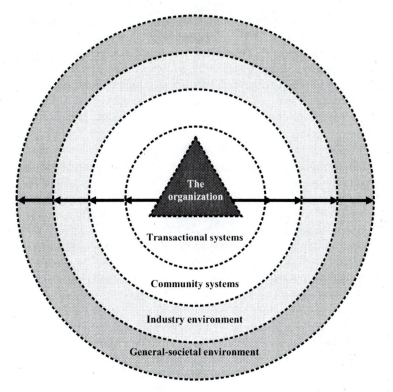

FIGURE 6.2   **External Context of Organizations.**

output organizations are: (1) How easy or difficult is it to acquire resources and sell services and products? and (2) How easy or difficult is it to know about these organizations? The first question reminds us that all organizations are dependent on other organizations. The second question reminds us that organizations exist under conditions of more or less uncertainty. A situation of either scarce resources or high uncertainty makes organizational functioning problematic and the manager's job more difficult indeed.

These input and output "transactional" organizations are embedded in and influenced by the local *community* and other organizations in the *industry* (including the competition). The local community and the industry affect transactional organizations and the focal organization primarily though the wealth of the community and whether it is stable or growing, and whether the size of the industry, the ease of entry into it, and its rate of innovation and change means it is stable, growing, or declining. Additionally, there is the general *society*, where features such as the health of the economy, the prevailing political climate, the dominant values of society, shifts in population, and the like, affect all organizations.

Internal Circumstances

The second category of ideas refers to a number of internal factors worthy of managerial attention because they tend to influence what managers will think and constrain what managers can and cannot do. These factors include an organization's history, reputation, life cycle stage, stakeholders, assets, technology, and physical settings.

First, there is the organization's own *history*, especially those notable events when the organization and its leaders were confronted with survival issues or times of major change. How these issues were handled and what actually happened often serve as lessons of how to handle similar issues in the future. Additionally, it is important to consider the organization's *reputation*, both internal and external. Since a positive reputation makes managing easier, managers strive to enhance it through all of their pronouncements and actions. People prefer to do business with and work for organizations viewed as good, fair, profitable, progressive, growing, etc.

Managerial attention is also usefully directed to the *life cycle stage* in which the organization finds itself. Organizations begin, grow, mature, decline, and end much as humans do. Where an organization is in its life cycle has an impact on what can be done. It is usually much easier to manage a growing organization, for example, than either a stable or a declining one. Another internal circumstance to monitor is the organization's *stakeholders*—those parties with a vested interest in the success of the organization such as owners, suppliers, customers, members, unions, the local community, etc. Not all stakeholders are equally important to an organization at various points in time, but regardless of their importance, they seek satisfaction with the organization. Managers who ignore the level of the stakeholders' satisfaction with the organization do so at their peril.

Yet another constraining internal circumstance is so obvious that it is often underappreciated: namely, the *assets* of the organization, including such tangible assets as property, buildings, fixtures and equipment, cash, and so forth, as well as intangible assets such as credit and patents, for example. Sufficient assets afford a manager much greater freedom in terms of what can be accomplished. Additionally, in terms of internal circumstances, there is *technology*, defined as those processes for changing inputs into finished products or services. Technologies are thus input-altering processes and things, like kitchens for restaurants, teaching practices for schools, information systems for human resources, etc. Questions of concern for management regarding technology are: How easily is it understood? How much has to be invested in it? How easy is it to replace or change? Last, there is the layout and spacing of the *physical setting* since settings strongly impact the movement of things, contacts, and hence communication among people, and signify who and what is important or not, for example, designated parking spaces, the location of the human resource office, whether there is an elevator for room service, etc.

Governance

Management itself deserves ongoing attention also. The *dominant coalition*, the third category of ideas that a manager can attend to, are those members of management who make the important decisions for the organization, such as decisions about what sort of business the organization is in, what the organization needs to do to succeed and grow, and how the organization's resources will be allocated. The dominant coalition tends to share a basic *mind set* or philosophy (values of what to strive for, beliefs about how to manage, and assumptions about what is the fundamental nature of human beings), and exhibit some mix of skills, knowledge, and attitudes known as *competencies*. Additionally, the dominant coalition (if more than one person) will tend to abide by an unwritten set of rules (*norms*) for how its members will relate to one another. The members of this dominant coalition, with assistance from other managers and staff advisors, and while taking the external context and the internal circumstances into consideration, will design and create the desired features of the organization (organizational factors, managerial systems, and workforce factors) according to its competencies and mindset—determining why the organization exists, what distinguishes it from others, and how it will be run.

Organizational Factors

The fourth set of ideas refers to organizational factors, those factors that provide direction to an organization and coordination of its parts. These factors include:

- the *vision and mission* of the organization,
- *objectives*,
- *strategies/policies*, and
- the formal organizational *structure*.

A *vision* is an organization's long-term goal that represents what the organization is striving to become, while a *mission* is a statement regarding what business the organization is in. An example of a mission statement for an economy hotel chain might be "To provide economy- and quality-minded travelers with a premier, moderate-priced lodging facility which is consistently perceived as clean, comfortable, well-maintained, and attractive, staffed by friendly, attentive and efficient people." An example of a vision statement for a health care company might be: "ABC Health Group, Inc. will be valued for its expertise in hospital management and its ability to positively impact the delivery of quality healthcare." (Note that vision statements are future-oriented, while mission statements are present-oriented.) Managers will intentionally recruit those people who are likely to contribute to the achievement of the organization's vision and mission.

Objectives (goals), along with strategies and policies and the formal organizational structure (patterns of jobs and groups of jobs), are organizational factors that formalize management's intentions about purpose, guidelines, and how the parts of the organization should be arranged, respectively. Many organizational objectives are defined in terms of outputs, such as services and products, or major indices of performance, like market share, profitability, and customer satisfaction. The objectives operationalize the mission, giving it a concrete form. For example, an organization might have as an objective to achieve a 97 percent customer satisfaction score during its next assessment. Objectives may and often do change over time as the organization's vision and mission for itself are modified by its experience.

Strategies are those broad plans for how the organization intends to satisfy its "key" stakeholders and fulfill its objectives. For example, the strategy for the above organization wanting to achieve a 97 percent customer satisfaction score might be to focus on employee training to ensure guest requests are completed accurately and timely. Another organization's strategy for achieving the same objective might be to focus on improving the furniture and fixtures. Each represents different strategies for attempting to fulfill the same objective. *Policies* are guidelines for making day-to-day decisions consistent with strategies.

Formal organizational *structure* is about how work tasks are arranged or grouped together and how these groupings are linked together vertically and horizontally through lines of authority, responsibility, formal communication, and control. Structure, in essence, says who does what with whom to achieve the organization's objectives. Organizational structures vary in several noticeable ways: (1) the degree to which objectives, policies and rules, positions, and operating practices are written down (known as the degree of formalization); (2) the degree to which decisions are made by top managers as compared to lower level members (known as the degree of centralization of decision making); and (3) whether jobs and/or work units are similar in form or not (known as the degree of standardization).

Workforce Factors

Every organization wants to have a workforce of the right size and composition so that organizational objectives are accomplished. Workforce factors, the fifth category of ideas that managers can pay attention to, are what members of the organization bring to their jobs and work units. Members come to the organization with several important attributes that are likely to affect how the organization operates:

- They come from a particular *socioeconomic class*.
- They have a certain *status* in the community.
- They possess certain *knowledge, skills, and abilities* and not others.
- They have particular *attitudes and values*.
- They possess specific *wants and needs*.
- They have more or less job-relevant *experience*.
- They differ *demographically* in terms of age, education, ethnicity, religion, etc.
- They have different *personalities*.
- They hold *memberships* in different organizations or associations outside of their work organizations, like in community, religious, and volunteer groups.

All these factors of an organization's workforce ultimately have an effect on the workings of the organization, affecting the types of additional training needed and the ways in which employees are supervised. Thus, managers intentionally try to recruit people with certain characteristics likely to contribute to fulfilling the organization's objectives. Since people differ in so many ways, finding and combining the right "workforce factor mix" is very important.

Managerial Systems

The sixth set of ideas represents management practices (systems) for integrating and coordinating organizational and workforce factors so that the organization's purposes are accomplished. In other words, managerial systems guide member behavior. Each managerial system can be designed in several ways, though ideally it should capture the essence and reality of the organization's workforce and organizational factors. There are six managerial systems, all individually as well as collectively very important, all of which have to exist for the coordination of work and workers. Each of these six managerial systems can be designed in several ways and managers consciously try to make all six systems consistent with one another. They include work designs, supervisory style, reward systems, communication systems, human resource management systems, and decision-making/planning systems.

The *work designs* (jobs/positions) can vary from a few simple, repetitive activities (simple jobs), to many complex task activities (job enlargement), to responsibility for planning the duration and sequencing of many complex task activities (job enrichment). *Supervisory style* can vary from one where the supervisor is constantly monitoring, correcting, and instructing subordinates to one where the supervisor is more empowering, encouraging both subordinate self-direction and inviting subordinate participation in job-related decisions. Supervisory style will, in part, reflect the work design.

Reward systems, another designed managerial system, can vary from those where an individual's monetary earnings depend only on the number of tasks accomplished, to those that include combinations of monetary rewards, benefits, and other forms of formal recognition that reflect a work unit's overall quantity and quality of productivity over a long period of time. These types of rewards represent extrinsic rewards, as opposed to intrinsic rewards, which are the feelings derived from the work itself, like feelings of accomplishment, contribution, and status.

Communication systems can vary from simple top-down systems that address just a few formal topics (like the giving of orders) to those where the information about everything flows in all directions, both formally and informally. They will vary also in terms of their intent to control workers and work (like directives and performance standards as opposed to mere suggestions). *Human resource management systems* are concerned with attracting, retaining, and developing workers (i.e., recruitment, selection, appraisal, training). They can vary from hardly existent (like in a family-run pizza parlor) to highly elaborated (like at Marriott Corporation). *Decision making and planning systems* can vary from those involving only top management to those involving everyone who is meaningfully engaged in any aspect of a problem or activity.

Management's choices about each of these managerial systems will reflect its perception of the workforce (how capable, motivated, etc.) and the nature of the organizational factors. If, for example, the organization is a high volume, limited-service restaurant where uniformity of product and swiftness of service is necessary, and the local labor pool is plentiful with young, inexperienced people, then management is likely to design simple, repetitive jobs, supervise closely, not share decision making and planning, utilize highly standardized recruitment and training procedures, rely on formal, top-down communications, and pay modest wages to individuals for time worked or number of products served. If, in contrast, the organization's goals could be accomplished only by highly skilled professionals, we would probably find a more flexible structure, enlarged jobs, decentralized decision making, free-flowing communications, development programs, and a more consultative, hands-off supervisory style. What is important is that these managerial systems are designed to be consistent with one another and supportive of the organization's vision, mission, and objectives. Observed inconsistency among these managerial systems (and/or the organizational factors and/or the workforce factors) invariably leads to confusion, poor performance, stress, perceived injustices, and dissatisfaction.

Work Units

The seventh general category of ideas is work units, our term for the organization's subparts, such as departments, staff groups, work teams, committees, and task forces. All of these work units will have features that have been designed by management, and that reflect the organizational factors, workforce factors, and managerial systems. Work units are conceived and implemented for several reasons: to accomplish the work necessary to achieve organizational objectives, to advise and serve other work-accomplishing units, to coordinate other work units, and sometimes to plan for and design/redesign other work units. Work units are characterized by their formal features, including:

- *Task purposes* (goals),
- Formal *roles and relationships* (which specify what members are expected to perform and how these roles are formally related),

- Work *rules* (what members are expected to follow to perform their role and relating responsibilities),
- Hierarchal *ranking* of authority and importance (which dictates who holds power), and the general ways members of the work unit are supposed to feel about the work units and their work.

All of these *intentionally* designed features, however, are usually paralleled by or co-exist with other characteristics that arise over time because not everything can or will be anticipated and designed. Common features of work units that *unintentionally emerge* over time (meaning they are not necessarily planned or controlled by management) include:

- Additional *social purposes*, meaning that the work unit develops reasons for existing that satisfy the social or relationship needs of the members beyond what are the task purposes of the work unit.
- Additional *social roles* that specify what members are expected to perform in the work unit "social network."
- *Norms*—the informal, unwritten rules that govern the work unit members' behavior.
- Informal *ranking*—members of work units eventually have a certain "status" within the unit that does not necessarily reflect their formal titles. Often these informal rankings are based on power and trust within the informal, social system of the work unit.
- Interpersonal *feelings* and influences that develop outside formal reporting relationships and/or lines of authority.
- *Cohesion*, the degree of affinity, liking, or "togetherness" that members of a work unit feel for one another.

These emergent, unintentional features of work units may end up supporting and enhancing the managerially designed formal features of the work unit, meaning that the informal social system that develops may actually help increase productivity, support the organization's objectives, and increase morale and development. However, it is also possible that the informal, emergent features of the work units that develop may run counter to the formal work unit. For example, a low-level waiter in one of the fine dining restaurants at a casino resort, although not high up in the formal ranking of the work unit, may exert tremendous influence and power over the members of the work unit because of his charismatic personality and prowess on the restaurant's baseball team. If management had decided to change the house brand of wine it pours due to a cost-cutting goal, and the waiter does not agree with the decision, he may be quite influential among his peers in getting them to tell guests not to order the new house brand of wine. In this example, the emergent work unit feature of informal ranking operates in a counter-productive manner toward fulfilling the cost-cutting goal.

Emergent Unintended Features

As just noted, because human organizations cannot be designed in every detail or every contingency anticipated, we can predict that some things in organizations, beyond the work unit level, will emerge that may not be intended. Emergent, unintended features, the eighth category of ideas for understanding factors influencing organizational life, reflect both *social systems* and *organizational culture*.

Several general social system features always emerge over time, including the socialization of members, cliques/coalitions, sentiments, a psychological contract, and a social structure.

Socialization represents how new members of an organization learn what to do, how to do it, how to relate to others, and what not to do from other members of the organization. Beyond the formal orientation and training that new members may receive, socialization speaks to the informal "initiation" of new members. For instance, when a front desk clerk is told by another more senior clerk not to worry about answering the phone using the script provided in training class because management never checks up on clerks, this is a form of socialization. The senior clerk is communicating to the new front desk clerk what *not* to do, and this bit of advice also helps the new clerk feel included.

Members who share similar self-interests sometimes band together to promote their interests; that is, they form *cliques and coalitions.* Another aspect of the social system, coalitions and cliques in organizations may be temporary or relatively permanent. They may serve a variety of interests, from providing social satisfaction to preserving occupational prestige, from promoting a change to preventing a change, from forming a car pool to getting rid of someone.

Social systems are also characterized by widespread *sentiments* (feelings) of various kinds that emerge over time about organizational practices. Members, for example, may gripe about lost benefits, get excited over a proposed merger, brag about their unit's reputation, whine about the lack of air conditioning, and so forth—all such behaviors expressing a positive or negative sentiment. Very common, general sentiments are about how loyal or personally committed members feel toward the organization.

As members of the work force are recruited and socialized, they also develop what is known as a *"psychological contract"* with the organization—an understanding of what constitutes a fair exchange between them and the organization for the work they do. For example, in exchange for their time, productivity, and loyalty, organizational members may expect certain levels of reward, job security, types of supervision, and working conditions. Organizational members judge the fairness of their organization in terms of whether it keeps its side of the psychological contract.

Inevitably, a *social structure* emerges which may or may not be consistent with the formal hierarchy of jobs. This informal social hierarchy or "pecking order" develops because power, social status, and trust, for example, may be acquired or reduced beyond that which comes from one's formal title, authority, and responsibility.

Every organization and subpart also develops a unique personality or *organizational culture*—shared values and beliefs that underlie an organization's identity. A variety of things, events, and patterned practices take on meanings beyond those intended by management. These cultural elements are symbolic in that they have meanings beyond conventional ones. Members invest *symbolic meanings* in elements of language, organizational stories, ritualistic practices, and particular artifacts, which serve to bind the members together, clarify ambiguities, and provide a common identity. Some things that hold symbolic meanings are company logos, office furnishings, size of work spaces, etc. Some are language related, like the symbolic meanings found in organizational stories and myths that teach what is important, and the organizational-specific terms and names that only members understand but outsiders do not. Other symbolic meanings are found in reoccurring events and practices, like retirement ceremonies, rituals of performance appraisals, and conventions about birthday celebrations or slacking off at the end of the work week.

Organizational cultures also share *strategic beliefs*, regarding, for example, what it takes to successfully compete in the industry, what the crucial operations are, how to change, the real differences between managers and workers, etc., and basic *shared assumptions and values* about time, basic human nature, reality, and the like. For example, an organization may believe that contributing to the community is important, and that human beings in general can be trusted. Additionally, organization-wide *norms* (unwritten rules) tend to emerge, and examples include norms like bringing one's spouse to the company picnic, encouraging friends to apply for open positions, and ways in which the top managers are addressed.

The shared meanings of organizational cultural elements serve to reduce ambiguities and bind members together. Attention to these various emergent, sociocultural factors provides management with signs of whether its formal, intentionally designed factors (for example, the human resource systems or communication systems) are perceived as fair and functional by organizational members.

Outcomes

What happens in organizations has consequences for individual members, for work units, and the organization as a whole. These consequences or *outcomes* represent the last general category of ideas to which management can and does pay attention. Some of these outcomes will be planned and intended, reflecting what the organization was trying to achieve as a whole, for its work units, and for its individual members. Other outcomes will emerge unintentionally. Whether intended or not, outcomes are indicators of how things are going in the organization. Less-than-desired outcomes usually attract managerial attention and action.

There are four types of outcomes that occur at each level of analysis (individual, work unit, organization), and each is a response to a question.

1. How do I (we) feel about the work situation? This is a question of *satisfaction* for individuals, also called *morale* when referring to work units, or *climate* when referring to the organization. Thus, an outcome of organizational life is the degree of satisfaction one acquires from one's job, supervision and the organization, and the level of morale or camaraderie that develops within a work unit. For the organization as a whole, a consequence of organizational activity is that a climate will develop where members more or less like coming to work.

2. How clear am I (are we) about who I am (we are)? This is a question of *identity*. Thus organizational life shapes and influences the identity of organizational members, work units, and the organization as a whole. Members want to achieve a more or less clear identity as to who they are in the organization, and what their roles and responsibilities are. Work teams as well want to and typically do acquire some degree of shared, common identity, as does the organization.

3. How much work is being accomplished? This is a question of individual *performance*, work unit *productivity*, and organizational *effectiveness* (which is the degree to which objectives are achieved) and *efficiency* (the ratio of inputs to outputs, which represents the degree of waste). Thus, another outcome of organizational life is that individuals and work units strive for specified levels of performance in their jobs, while organizations achieve certain production levels that either achieve or do not achieve specified production and waste goals.

4. Am I (are we) changing in positive ways? This is a question of *growth* for individuals, *development* for work units, and *renewal* for organizations. Through their employment, organizational members want to more or less grow as persons, and people assigned to

work units will more or less develop as teams. An outcome for organizations is that they will be more or less open to change and revival.

Positive outcomes for individual organizational members will probably contribute to positive outcomes for their work units, and positive outcomes for the work units will probably contribute toward positive organizational outcomes. Additionally, outcomes may and usually do, sooner or later, impact the other general categories in the large scope conceptual model for analysis (Figure 6.1B). For example, a highly dissatisfied individual may leave, prompting the human resource management system to replace him or her in the work force and possibly initiate management to rethink the work designs, reward system, etc.

USING THE CONCEPTUAL MODEL FOR ANALYSIS

The model for analysis just presented will initially seem overwhelming—there are so many ideas to understand and how they are grouped is probably unfamiliar also. Do not expect to comprehend the model and its ideas quickly. Do have reasonable expectations for how much work is involved to really "own" these ideas and be able to use them. You will have to reread this chapter many times. Do ask your instructor for clarifications and examples. After you use the model, or parts of it, over and over in case discussions, thinking analytically will become easier and easier. If you aspire to be a thoughtful, effective manager, you have to be analytically smart. This may not be easy, but it is necessary.

If managers continually stay informed about all the factors reflected in the nine categories of ideas of Figure 6.1B, they can compare what is actually occurring with what was intended and hoped for (what the goals or objectives were). If any of the actual outcomes are not the same as the intended outcomes (the goals were not met), managers begin to systematically ask what is out of line that might have caused the undesired outcome levels. Basically, *managers try to discover why things are occurring the way they are—which is exactly what you will do when doing an analysis of a case.* Thus, managers may ask questions about their organizations such as:

- Are the "constraints" (external context and internal circumstances) accurately understood and taken into account?
- Does the governance of the organization (dominant coalition) hold an appropriate mindset, have the right competencies, and enough quality relationships to fulfill its responsibilities?
- Does management hold a viable vision for the organization?
- Is top management, in fact, the dominant coalition?
- Are the organization's objectives, strategies and policies, and structure clear and reasonable given the context and circumstances?
- Is the right number of the right kinds of people employed?
- Are the managerial systems appropriate given the workforce members and what they are expected to do? Are these systems consistent with each other?
- Do the emergent sociocultural factors help or hinder intended practices?

When inconsistencies among organizational factors, workforce factors, work unit, and managerial systems are discovered, when they do not reasonably reflect constraints, or when emergent features do not facilitate the achievement of goals and objectives, managerial action is called for. What managers can do is modify one or more of those things under their control so that they are more internally consistent or lead to desired outcomes. Whatever aspects of an organization a manager selects to modify, every action taken should contribute toward the creation of a lasting high-performance company. Thus, management actions, small and large, unique or repetitive, should contribute toward building, for example, a positive work climate, a clarified strategic direction, a fair allocation of resources, an upgrading of the quality of management and other members, and excellence in operations and execution. Actions by managers, thus, are aimed at the fundamental tasks of all organizations— making major or minor internal adjustments, strategically realigning the organization to its constraints (both internally and externally), and preparing the organization for some anticipated future.

The types of questions that managers may systematically ask to identify causes of undesirable outcomes so that action may be taken are the same types of questions that you will ask when doing an analysis of an organization in a case. Remember that acquiring a deeper understanding (doing an analysis) helps one to take suitable action. Therefore, the fuller and more complete our understanding of a situation, the more likely our behavior in or toward it will be appropriate.

Cases have lots and lots of information to shift through. Ideas, however, let us notice factual information and let us assess the quality of case information. Ideas also let us order and compare case information. A set of ideas allows us to make sense of particular facts, and, sometimes, even lets us predict what may occur in the future.

Using the large scope conceptual model for analysis (Figure 6.1B), which is essentially just sets of ideas (and the relationships among them) that reflect the factors that influence how organizations operate, will help you achieve a full and complete understanding of the situation in a case—that is, to understand how it evolved. In most typical cases, an organization experiences one or more undesired outcomes, and your job as the reader of the case is to determine, after careful analysis and diagnosis, the appropriate action. Just as a manager may systematically proceed through all nine categories of ideas in the large scope conceptual model looking to identify what factors are out of line that may be contributing to poor outcomes, the reader of a case, in conducting his or her analysis, may proceed through the conceptual model, asking questions and attempting to identify why the situation in the case is the way it is. However, as suggested earlier in this chapter, rather than proceeding through all nine categories of ideas in the conceptual model, you may "target" your analysis by selecting ideas from the conceptual model as suggested by the symptoms, goals, and key facts of the case (see the Section "Selecting Ideas for Analysis" in this chapter).

As an example of using this method of analysis, think back to the Boyd's Catering Case. If we examine some of the symptoms for clues as to what ideas might be most useful for understanding the situation in the case, several come to mind, as presented in Figure 6.3. Once you have selected the ideas you will use for analysis, you must then gather facts from the case to help you understand why these symptoms are occurring. For example, how has Emily violated the norms? What impact does this norm violation have on the other employees? How has the work unit morale affected the employees' productivity, specifically, the cleanliness of the store? How has the perceived fairness of the human resource system, in terms of Emily's selection and training, affected the employees? These questions represent just a sampling of those that can be surfaced using a few ideas from the conceptual model as suggested by the symptoms of the case.

Selecting Ideas for the Boyd's Catering Case

Symptoms	Suggest	Ideas
Emily brings a stool up from the basement and sits.	▶	Rules/norms, roles, shared values/assumptions
The store is left less clean.	▶	Rules/norms, work unit productivity
Some of the girls are considering leaving the store.	▶	Individual satisfaction, work unit morale, cohesion
The employees don't want to tell Mrs. Boyd about Emily visiting her friend next door.	▶	Work unit: affect/feelings, cliques/coalitions, cohesion
It is rumored that Emily is getting paid more than the other employees.	▶	Reward systems, ranking, communication systems, human resource systems

FIGURE 6.3   Selecting Ideas for the Boyd's Catering Case.

ORDERING FACTS

As you may recall from earlier in the book, information alone has no meaning. However, when information is framed by an idea (recall the washing clothes example in Chapter 2), it has meaning and is a fact. A thorough analysis, by way of using ideas to make sense of the abundance of information, will produce lots and lots of facts! Understanding a situation presented in a case—the goal of an analysis—requires us to make sense of a situation's facts, for some facts will inevitably be more pertinent, more important than others because of where they fall along the continuum of certainty (see Figure 3.2) and because they can be trusted to explain symptoms and outcomes.

There are many ways to group and arrange facts so that they can contribute to our understanding of what's really going on in a situation. You will want to use several from the following list.

1. *Order/array facts along a time line.* Be clear about the chronological order of the appearance of facts, especially activities, events, and the states of entities (see Figure 5.1). Which are earlier, which are later, when do facts appear, get altered, or disappear?
2. *Order facts according to their levels of analysis.* Which facts are associated with individuals or types of individuals, which are group level facts, and which are organizational, community, industry or societal? This way of ordering will tell us for what level(s) we have a lot or a few facts (see Figure 5.2).
3. *Order facts according to dependency.* Some facts exist or have meaning because of other facts. This is especially true for work activities, for example, when one person's work depends on another person doing his or her work earlier. Listing such dependencies or relationships can be helpful for understanding the case.

4. ***Order facts as intended or emergent.*** Determine *what* management intended to happen, that is, what management had hoped would happen, and if possible, *how* they had planned for it to happen. Then determine if it did happen and in the manner management had intended. Additionally, look to see what else may have occurred that was not planned.

5. ***Order facts as to whether they are static or dynamic.*** Some facts describe something at a single point in time (statically), like how a work unit is designed in terms of the tasks it performs and the reporting relationships it has with other units. Thus, the thing described is not changing. Other facts describe how something changes over time (meaning dynamically). Be alert that the models about most things may be static (how something is structured at a point in time) or dynamic (how something is modified over time) or both. For example, a *static* model about groups would describe the group composition (e.g., only line-level employees, supervisors and line-level, only supervisors, etc.) and its design or structure (e.g., servers carry food out of the kitchen for their own tables versus expeditors who carry out the food so the servers stay out on the floor). An example of a *dynamic* model of groups would describe how the group changes over time in terms of group dynamics and development. For example, the model might describe how various group members gain and lose power and status over time given certain circumstances, or how the group develops cohesion (solidarity) over time.

Most of the above methods for ordering facts may be combined or captured in large scope models such as the one in Figure 6.1B. Time is implied via the ideas of history (which occurs over time), emergent features (which evolve over time), and outcomes (which are produced over time). Levels of analysis are implied in ideas about the external context, organizational factors, work units, and outcomes. Dependency is implied in how managerial systems need to be consistent with each other and with organizational and workforce factors. Some ideas are described as intentions and others as emergent features. And static versus dynamic is implied, for example, in ideas of how work unit designs evolve, with informal features emerging (a dynamic process) versus the idea of organizational structure which reflects the ways in which activities in an organization are coordinated.

AN ANALYSIS OF THE JENNA'S KITCHENS CASE

In this section, we present a preliminary and partial analysis of the Jenna's Kitchens Case (see the Section "The Jenna's Kitchens Case" in Chapter 5). As suggested earlier in this chapter, the initial task when conducting an analysis is to select those ideas, models, and theories that seem to be useful for thinking about the case situation(s). One source for ideas, as stated earlier, is to look at the identified symptoms. With reference to the symptoms listed in Figure 5.4 from the Jenna's Kitchens Case, we can extract several ideas:

- Singleton's negative responses to headquarters' pressure and her direct reports "stiffening" in their relations to her suggest we think about *relationships.*
- The disappearance of joking and kidding (patterned but not required activities) suggest we think about *norms.*
- The many, many complaints of the office workers that probably refer to something other than their content suggest we think about *symbols.*
- Wage requests suggest we consider the *reward system.*

- Both warehouse and office complaints referring to working conditions suggest we think about the case's *physical settings*.
- References to the "blankety-blank company" and the company "going to the dogs" suggest we look at the *psychological contract* between employees and the company.

In addition, we can look at some of the key facts of the case to expand our list of possible useful ideas for analysis. For example:

- Jenna's push for reducing costs and Singleton's increasing wages to quell complaints by the warehouse crew as well as the office workers suggests we examine *beliefs*.
- That executives frequently visit the region, the dedicated telephone lines between downtown and the warehouse, the talk among employees, Singleton's consultation with her husband, and other facts suggests we look at patterns of *communication*.

While we could go on adding to our list of ideas, these are probably sufficient to at least begin an analysis. The "test" of their usefulness is whether they help us understand what happened after the move of the offices to the warehouse, and what happened after Judi Singleton gave everyone a wage increase. That is, do these ideas help us understand why the situation in the case is the way it is?

At the outset of the case we recall that the company has a certain "fame" and image as a desirable place to work, provides lots of training, spends on advertising, etc. Thus, we can surmise that the psychological contract was positive, meaning the exchange between the company and the employees was essentially one where the employees did good work in exchange for an upbeat, fair, and growing firm. After the move, the psychological contract seems to have changed. The company is perceived as cost conscious and that it implied that doing good work isn't a fair exchange anymore.

At the outset, Singleton's relationships were characterized by her relative autonomy, her influence with the executives, and her relatively close relations with her direct reports. After the move, all of these relationships were changed. These relationship changes are also confirmed by altered communications, especially within the regional offices (e.g., from office workers initiating contact with the warehouse via telephones to face-to-face interactions at the warehouse).

At the outset of the case we see that the office workers exhibited norms around shopping, lunches in downtown restaurants, parking in public parking structures, etc. After the move, the office workers cut lunches and ate in "greasy spoons," didn't joke much, and competed for parking with warehouse workers. In addition, Judi changed the office workers' work hours from later than the warehouse crew to earlier. And the physical setting of the office workers dramatically changed too, from an expensive office building to the warehouse space. All of these changes were likely to be symbolic in that they were probably perceived as reductions in *status*.

With Singleton finally consenting to the move from downtown to the warehouse, we see some of her beliefs come into play. First, Singleton had the warehouse office refurbished, compensating, she thought, for the loss of the nicer downtown offices. Second, she raised office worker wages in response to complaints and lowered morale, as a means of compensating for the altered working conditions. Third, Singleton also raised the wages of the warehouse crew, trying to be fair to everyone.

Stepping back from the specifics outlined above we can see on the one hand that the differential in status or prestige between the office workers and the warehouse crew was diminished by the move and many of the practices it altered, and on the other hand, that the wage increases to everyone (and not just the office workers) symbolically did not reestablish the former status/prestige differential. In other words, office worker complaints were truly symbolic.

While the above represent the beginnings of an analysis of the Jenna's Kitchens Case, be advised that there are other ideas that might have proved fruitful in helping us reach our higher level of understanding of the situation in the case. Discussing with other people their ideas gleaned from the case can be quite fruitful in that, inevitably, others will see and think of things that we did not.

Summary

The outcome of a thorough and systematic analysis is that we come to understand what a situation really is and what is really going on. By conducting a thorough and systematic analysis, we discover and appreciate particular facts, features, or factors that we are likely to have undervalued, even if we had a lot of familiarity with the situation. With an analysis, we discover key linkages in the situation and, more importantly, realize that current symptoms and other happenings are part of a complex causal network that reaches back in time as well as into heretofore unforeseen places. A careful analysis almost always expands one's initial focus, and we begin to appreciate how aspects of the situation somewhat removed from current symptoms actually play a part in what's occurring. The more thorough and systematic our analysis, the more complete our understanding.

A thorough and systematic analysis is plain hard work, and thus is often skimped on. The felt pressure of time as well as the overconfidence of some managers (and students) leads them to believe that they can and do understand well enough to take action without the careful identification, sifting, and ordering of facts. They mistakenly believe that familiarity alone is somehow sufficient. Unfortunately, the avoidance of a solid analysis often results in symptom fixing or other action traps (see the Section "Action Traps" in Chapter 8). While analysis is hard work, it is crucial work. To skimp or slight analysis is to court superficiality, blind spots, and bias.

As this chapter has emphasized, the bywords for analysis are "thoroughness" and "systematic." A careful, full analysis requires us to be "tough-minded," neither hard-headed nor hard-hearted, but rather fact-minded and somewhat skeptical of quick or easy understandings. It is only with a deep understanding that comes about because of analysis that we can reasonably expect to clarify the difficulties and issues in a situation—that is, to do a diagnosis, to which we turn to in Chapter 7.

7

Preparing Cases, Step 5: Diagnostic Work

You must first be on a path before you can turn and walk into the wild.

—GARY SNYDER

Chapter Objectives

- Demonstrate how to do a diagnosis by describing and exampling the process of identifying problems, predicaments, and goal gaps.
- Increase your appreciation of the differences among problems, predicaments, and goal gaps so as to examine appropriate action possibilities.

WHAT IS A DIAGNOSIS?

Diagnosis is the process of identifying and clarifying the real difficulties in a situation, and prioritizing those that need immediate attention. These difficulties are believed to be more basic, and underlie or cause the more easily noticed symptoms. They are believed to be the root causes of the symptoms. In medical practice, diagnosis takes place when a doctor determines and names an illness or disease. In business situations, diagnosis involves comparing goals and intended practices to what has and is really happening, and determining what requires managerial attention and perhaps action.

Under the pressure of time, it is tempting to rush to action. After all, something seems to need action or there wouldn't be any symptoms. In part, the approach we are presenting—with careful attention to first enhancing our familiarity with and, second, deepening our understanding of the situation—is intended to help us resist attempting action before we're really ready, or before we've even decided what is the real "problem." Focusing on problem solving before problem identifying is likely to be a waste of time at the very least, and harmful at the worst.

Diagnosis	**Step 5**
Analysis	Step 4
Listing goals	Step 3
Recognizing symptoms	Step 2
Gaining familiarity	Step 1

IDENTIFYING PREDICAMENTS, PROBLEMS, AND GOAL GAPS

In our society and especially in business we tend to use the word *problem* rather loosely. As we have seen in the Section "What Are Key Lessons from Semantics for Case Work?" in Chapter 3, however, we need to guard against unclear word usage. We'll use the word *problem* in this book, but we give it a restricted meaning.

In the initial steps of our approach to preparing cases, we are concerned with becoming well acquainted with the information about a situation, listing symptoms, and then carefully listing goals for all significant actors and social entities. The importance of listing goals is straightforward and critical for diagnosis. When we do a diagnosis, we use goals to identify three types of basic difficulties. First we look for predicaments. A *predicament* is an inconsistency among goals—an inconsistency within a person's goal list or when the goals of two or more persons or social entities are incompatible. For example, a female employee may want to become the CEO of an organization, but also homeschool her children. Most likely these two goals are inconsistent—she cannot accomplish both of them at the same time, and thus she has a predicament. Another example of a predicament is when an individual's goals do not fit with his or her work group's goals, like when an employee of a self-managed work team wants to lead the team exclusively, but the team likes to rotate or share leadership among the various members. These goals are inconsistent or conflict in that both goals cannot be achieved at the same time.

In doing a diagnosis, we also look for problems. A *problem* is any discrepancy between a goal and what is actually being achieved. Problems thus refer to overachieving or under-achieving a goal. For example, an organization may have a goal of achieving 97 percent or better on a customer satisfaction survey, but scores only 92 percent. An example of a problem due to over-met goals is when an employee has a goal of using the employee cafeteria for breakfast every morning, and ends up spending more than his or her allotted time in the cafeteria.

Finally, a diagnosis also includes looking for goal gaps. A *goal gap* is simply when a person or social entity does not have a clear goal or a goal at all when it is reasonable to have one. For example, when a business organization apparently does not focus on maximizing profit, that organization would appear to most of us to have a goal gap.

To summarize: if there is intergoal inconsistency, there is a predicament; if a goal is not being achieved, there is a problem; and if a goal isn't clear or doesn't exist when it should, there is a goal gap. Be forewarned, most situations seldom contain just one predicament, problem, or gap.

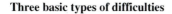

Three basic types of difficulties

Predicament	Inconsistency among goals, either within a single entity/person or between persons/entities
Problem	Any discrepancy between a goal and what is actually achieved
Goal gap	When a person or entity does not have clear goal or a goal at all

While it is common for one to identify several predicaments, problems, and/or goal gaps during his or her diagnosis, this does not mean that they all require managerial attention. Some perhaps simply can't be rectified; others may not be readily dealt with until later, etc. Managers usually have to focus on those issues of real concern. So, with predicaments, problems, or goal gaps identified, the next step in a diagnosis is to prioritize them. While any number of criteria may be used, such as impact on market share, profitability, morale, cost containment, innovation, shareholder value, etc., three generic criteria for prioritizing should always be given serious consideration: *time*, *importance*, and *action feasibility*. Essentially we ask three questions of our listing of predicaments and/or problems and/or goal gaps:

1. *Time priorities:* Which must be dealt with immediately?
2. *Importance priorities:* Which detracts from overall performance?
3. *Action feasibility priorities:* Which can be dealt with given existing competencies and resources?

Answers to these three questions help us prioritize the predicaments, problems, and goal gaps most in need of attention.

A DIAGNOSIS OF THE JENNA'S KITCHENS CASE

In this section we present a preliminary diagnosis of the Jenna's Kitchens Case (as presented in the Section "The Jenna's Kitchens Case" in Chapter 5). Let us begin by studying once again the lists of goals provided in Figure 5.5. With these goals clearly in mind, we can examine them in terms of what we know to be the reality at the end of the case, given our familiarity with and analysis of it. We are looking for goals that are noticeably overachieved or underachieved (a problem), any inconsistencies between two or more goals (a predicament), and any goals basically unclear or missing, when we would reasonably expect one based on what we know about the case (a goal gap).

Problems

The list of company goals has just one that may be becoming a problem: reputation. From what we know, both office workers and the warehouse crew are complaining about the company. The list of regional goals holds one clear problem—the goal of having attractive jobs is

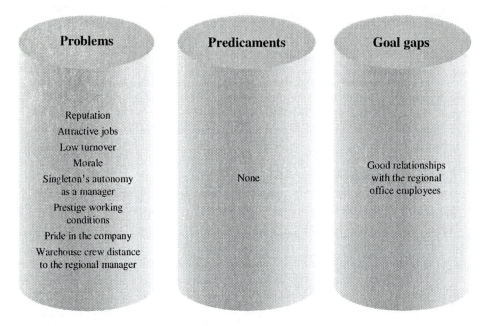

Problems	Predicaments	Goal gaps

Reputation
Attractive jobs
Low turnover
Morale
Singleton's autonomy
as a manager
Prestige working
conditions
Pride in the company
Warehouse crew distance
to the regional manager

None

Good relationships
with the regional
office employees

FIGURE 7.1   Diagnosis of Jenna's Kitchens Case.

not being met. Another of the goals—low turnover—may become a problem if things do not change. Of Singleton's goals, there is one clear problem of maintaining morale, and one possible problem regarding Singleton's autonomy as a manager, since she felt forced to move the office to the warehouse. Turning our attention to the list of office workers' goals we see two problems: (1) they no longer believe they are experiencing "prestige" working conditions since they lost their downtown, swanky office; and (2) perhaps somewhat related, their pride in the company is going down. Finally, one of the warehouse crew's goals is not being met because at the end of the case the crew is both physically and (probably) psychologically much closer to the regional manager (see Figure 7.1).

Predicaments

Interestingly there do not appear to be any inconsistent goals either within the five lists of goals or across the lists.

Goal Gaps

When we examine the lists of goals for goal ambiguity, we should remind ourselves that most have been inferred and hence any ambiguity may be in the way we have stated them. Attractive jobs, managerial autonomy, pride in the company, prestige working conditions, and distance from the regional manager, for example, are all stated fairly abstractly. While it is a judgment call, let's presume they are reasonably understood by the relevant parties. What goals might be missing? Here we have to be constrained by what we know of the situations and not attribute goals unwarrantedly. Only one gap suggests itself: namely the reasonable goal attributable to Singleton—good relationships with her regional office employees.

Given our understanding of the circumstances and events at the end of the case, four problems and one gap seem to be relatable: the company's goal of having attractive jobs, Singleton's goal of maintaining morale and her gap of having good relationships with her employees, and the office workers' goals of having pride in their company and prestige working conditions. This set says, in effect (as our symptoms and our analysis have already suggested), that the underlying issues have to do with the office workers' perceptions and resulting feelings about their deteriorating circumstances and what Singleton has done/not done for them that is reflected in her current relations with them. Additionally, the two problems involving pride in the company and prestige working conditions are assessed by the office workers comparatively against what they know of other office workers, against what they had experienced before the move from downtown, and against the warehouse crew. In a phrase, the office workers likely believe that they have lost comparable status. And Singleton, their manager, was largely responsible for this status loss. It seems that something must be done quickly! But what? And by whom? We will consider what actions to take in Chapter 8.

Summary

If diagnosis is the comparison among goals and between goals and what actually has happened, we can appreciate the importance of the initial work involving becoming familiar with the facts of the case, recognizing symptoms, and especially carefully listing goals (as described in the Section "Listing Goals—Why Now?" in Chapter 5), and a thorough analytical understanding (as detailed in Chapter 6). The process of diagnosis is composed of two quite distinct subprocesses: first, identifying predicaments, problems, and goal gaps, and second, prioritizing them. Also, diagnosis, like all of the work leading up to it, asks much of us. Like all prior steps in our approach, diagnosis requires considerable tough-mindedness—being thorough, being factual, and judgmentally careful.

Preparing Cases, Step 6: Action Planning

Everyone who's ever taken a shower has had an idea. It's the person who gets out of the shower, dries off, and does something about it who makes a difference.

—NOLAN BUSHELL

Chapter Objectives

▨ Provide an explanation of the purposes of possible action recommendations.

▨ Define the criteria for action selection.

▨ Describe and provide examples of the process of action planning.

WHAT IS ACTION PLANNING?

The last step in the case approach we advocate is called *action planning*, although, as we will soon see, it involves many substeps and more than just planning. In general, *action planning* refers to the steps we take to rectify a situation in a case. Action planning also refers to the steps necessary for finding or inventing appropriate actions (sometimes called interventions), choosing one or more of them, scheduling their implementation, and assessing their effectiveness. Action planning is thus analogous to the therapeutic stage of medical practice. After a diagnosis a doctor prescribes some action to bring a patient back to health, using, for example, rest, drugs, and/or surgery. If a diagnosis of predicaments, problems, and goal gaps reveals *what* desirable managerial action might usefully focus on, then action planning shifts our attention to *how, when,* and *where* to implement—and *who* should be involved in implementing—effective action.

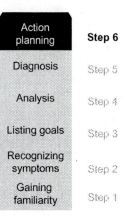

Action planning	**Step 6**
Diagnosis	Step 5
Analysis	Step 4
Listing goals	Step 3
Recognizing symptoms	Step 2
Gaining familiarity	Step 1

ACTIONS THAT RECTIFY, COPE, PREVENT, AND ENHANCE

While we already understand that managers take action to see that appropriate things get done in a timely and effective way, let's ask more specifically what good action plans might accomplish. Managers will, whether they are conscious of them or not, have one or more of the following objectives in mind as they plan for action:

- *To rectify:* Actions that solve a problem or correct a predicament or goal gap; in other words, to fix something.
- *To cope:* Actions that keep a situation from getting worse than it is either in the short or long run.
- *To prevent:* Actions that keep an undesirable situation from occurring again.
- *To enhance:* Actions that will make an acceptable situation even better.

Almost all situations that call for action are more complex than they seem at first. Symptoms, we recall, are indicators that something more basic is really going on. Usually, they point to several more basic or underlying difficulties (predicaments, problems, and goal gaps) as identified in our diagnosis. Thus, every action is likely to have several consequences. While there may be some immediate pressure to solve and cope in the short run, managers also want their actions, whenever possible, to prevent and/or enhance situations over the long run. Ideally, therefore, managerial action will simultaneously rectify most difficulties, prevent further deterioration, and enhance the situation in the future.

CRITERIA FOR ALTERNATIVE ACTIONS

How do you figure out what action to take? In recommending action for one or more case entities, similar to deciding what to do in the situations you face, you must always tailor actions to the specifics of the situation because every situation is in some ways unique, and the configuration of predicaments, problems, and goal gaps at a point in time is also unique. Nevertheless, even custom-tailored actions can and probably should reflect a small handful of generic selection criteria (general action criteria applicable in all or nearly all situations).

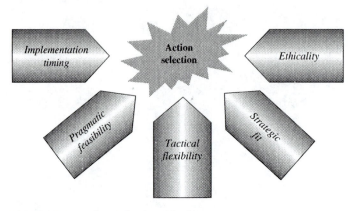

FIGURE 8.1   Action-Selection Criteria.

We suggest five generic, *action-selection criteria* to be used in combination and that ultimately influence the action selected (see Figure 8.1):

- *Implementation timing:* Must action be taken immediately? Or, can it be delayed somewhat? Or, is it best enacted over a period of time?
- *Pragmatic feasibility:* Does the action-taker have the interest and competence to take action? Are there enough appropriate resources available in support of action? Will others likely to be impacted by the action be receptive to it?
- *Tactical flexibility:* If this action is unsuccessful, will taking it eliminate most or all of the other alternatives from consideration?
- *Strategic fit:* Is the proposed action consistent with the general mission and direction of the whole organization?
- *Ethicality:* In the society, culture, community, and organization where the action is to be implemented, is it ethical? Is it understood as the right thing?

Beyond these five criteria, the situation may suggest or demand additional criteria that are important and appropriate for the given predicaments, problems, and goal gaps in a case. For example, you may consider taking a particular action because it:

- eliminates symptoms
- has the fewest negative side effects
- is the most cost-effective
- is practically guaranteed to be acceptable by stakeholders
- enhances the organization's image
- is legal

STEPS OF ACTION PLANNING

Action planning begins by specifying the *criteria* we will later use to evaluate the various alternative possible actions we might take. Regardless of which criteria are specified, it is important to *prioritize them at the outset of action planning* so when it comes time to select a sequence of actions we are not tempted to shift criteria so as to select a prior favorite.

With action criteria specified, we then have to find/generate one or more, usually several, possible actions that would rectify, cope with, prevent, or enhance the current situation characterized by the predicaments, problems, and/or goal gaps previously identified. Finding *action alternatives* means that we usually first search within our own experience of actions. Taking no action should always be one action alternative considered; some situations will self-correct if left alone. For example, think about when you were a child and your mother caught you playing when you were supposed to be doing your homework. Often, all your mother had to do was look at you; no further action was required since you were likely to self-correct on your own.

If we don't find plausible alternatives by searching from our own experience, we go on to search the experiences of others, typically by asking and reading. If our search, thus far, does not locate any appropriate possible action alternatives, we have to invent some. *Invention* here means either simply modifying some already known action to become more feasible, or simply combining parts of known alternatives into a new one.

Finding action alternatives, while essentially a creative activity, can be enhanced by proceeding according to the following three steps:

1. First, ask what the action-taker *can do*. List every action that you can think of, serious or silly, conventional or far-out. The more the better! Don't evaluate them; just list them for right now. Doing this playfully can enable you to escape your implicit preferences and habits of mind, as well as narrow conventional thinking.

2. Next, predict what the action-taker *will do*. You probably know enough about the action-taker from studying the case to make a pretty good estimate of how he or she or they are likely to act. If not, analyze them more carefully—the case always holds some cues. Don't overlook their beliefs, values, attitudes, needs, emotionality, or past behavior. If the action-taker(s) has/have previously not managed well, his/her/their predicted action alternative alerts you to the possibility that these action alternatives may not be good choices.

3. Finally, given the list of possible action alternatives from your "can do" list and the possible action alternatives from your "will do" list that you did not eliminate because the predicted action was considered to be poor because it was from one of the not-so-smart action-takers in the case, create two or more action alternatives the action-taker *should do*. Make sure to keep in mind the important criteria that you have chosen for evaluating your action alternatives (as described in the Section "Criteria for Alternative Actions"). In any given case, it may be crucial to take action swiftly. You'll also need to decide whether rectifying (solving), coping, preventing, and/or enhancing are most desirable. Forcing yourself to prescribe two or more feasible action alternatives will usually prompt more creativity than if you develop just one alternative.

Steps for generating action alternatives

1. List what the action-taker *can do*.
2. List what the action-taker *will do*.
3. List what the action-taker *should do*.

Consciously inquiring into the probable and possible positive and negative *consequences* of all of our action alternatives on our "should do" list is another way of making choices among them. We ask ourselves, in light of our analysis of the situation:

1. What would happen if this action were implemented?
2. Will this action prevent future difficulties like those currently faced by the organization?
3. Is this action relatively consistent with how things are done in this organization?
4. How will this action contribute to the longer-run, well-being of the individuals, the unit, and the organization?
5. Is this action ethically appropriate?

Such questions sometimes prompt redesign or combining of the actions being contemplated. If we modify our action alternatives, we need to consciously question their consequences all over again.

Eventually, our feasible action alternatives are evaluated against the criteria specified at the outset of action planning and the probable consequences, and *one action alternative is tentatively chosen.* This choice, we must emphasize, will seldom either maximize or optimize anything given the multiple action criteria you have chosen and the reality of the situation in the case. Most often we "satisfice," that is, we accept the action that meets the minimal acceptable criteria. Additionally, a useful rule of thumb is to select an action that leaves other plausible alternatives available in the future, in the event the selected action fails.

With an action alternative selected, we next specify an *implementation plan,* that is, a time-ordered sequence of substeps that must be taken to fully implement our chosen action alternative. Implementation planning means specifying, in detail, who should do what, where should it be done, when should it be done, and with whom should it be done. Essential steps for implementing an action alternative also include making sure to acquire the necessary resources and assigning responsibilities. Who will initiate action? Who has to support it? Who will monitor it? Who will ultimately assess it (and when)?

The final question signals the final step in action planning: *assessment* of the actions taken. A plan should be developed for evaluating recommended actions that defines when the

Action planning steps

1. Determine and prioritize criteria for evaluating alternative possible actions.

2. Generate/find action alternatives.

3. Determine the probable and possible consequences for each alternative.

4. Evaluate alternatives against the criteria and the probable/possible consequences, and then tentatively choose an alternative.

5. Specify an implementation plan.

6. Develop an assessment plan for evaluating the recommended action.

evaluation will be done, how it will be done, and who will do it. Such evaluation is necessary both to follow up on whether the suggested action was effective and to continue to learn from our experience. Knowing what works well, not so well, and why helps us learn how well we have analyzed and diagnosed the situation, and how good a job we did in selecting the appropriate action alternative(s).

ACTION TRAPS

Creating an appropriate and effective action plan is obviously both very important and very difficult. It requires us to be tough-minded and thorough, and not rush more than necessary. Unfortunately, both the *myth* that a good manager should be decisive and tough and the *reality* that managers are very busy and continuously interrupted tempt us to skip and skimp on the hard work of creating good action plans. The felt pressures of little time and multiple, important tasks all too often lead to *action traps*: choosing simple, convenient, known actions that really do *not* help the situations now or later.

Some of the more common action traps to which you should be alerted are described here.

- "Hipshooting" is the use of either a habitual or favorite action plan—no matter what the current diagnosis of the case has shown. Sometimes case readers will go through the difficult and challenging process of fact identification, listing of symptoms and goals, analysis, and diagnosis, and yet will unthinkingly try to apply their "favorite solution" to the case situation. This may occur because after reading the case rapidly, the reader jumps to conclusions about what is wrong in the case and determines that his or her favorite solution will be appropriate, all before doing an analysis and diagnosis! One of the most common favorite actions of students to take for rectifying a case situation is to hire, fire, demote, or transfer one or more persons in the case who are central to the diagnosed predicaments, problems, and/or goal gaps. Another common favorite action is to throw more resources (like training) or technology (a new IT system) at the difficulty, or to modify job descriptions or the organization chart, or add controls. This common but mistaken belief is that if some action seems to have worked in the past, why not do it again unthinkingly? Of course, this type of thinking fails to consider whether the current situation is similar to past situations, and it doesn't take into consideration the current analysis and diagnosis.
- Initiate the first reasonable course of action that comes to mind—in other words, "satisfice." Don't seriously consider more than one implicit favorite alternative action and don't carefully look at its consequences.
- Do what you think the big boss or some management hero would do.
- Do whatever seems to be necessary to correct the big symptom or crisis at hand. Better yet, take some general action that is hard to criticize because it is so general, like more training, better communications, or the latest managerial fad (e.g., quality circles, 360° feedback, zero-based budgeting, Management By Objectives, etc.).
- Create and lock onto an overly detailed, multiple-step action plan and then "sell it" authoritatively so as to overcome any doubt or resistance.
- Simply widely share the issues and assume that others will either self-correct or take action. Alternatively, call meetings and trust that enough discussion will generate some acceptable action and the energy to accomplish it.

These action traps are unlikely to lead to the most appropriate or effective action plans. In fact, the action plans developed from falling victim to one or more of these action traps are, at best, likely to only temporarily alleviate symptoms or, at worst, may even trigger more or other symptoms and/or predicaments, problems, and goal gaps.

AN ACTION PLAN FOR THE JENNA'S KITCHENS CASE

In this section, we present a preliminary and partial action plan for the Jenna's Kitchens Case. Before we describe our action alternatives, recall some of the facts, symptoms, and actions taken by Singleton. After the move of the regional office to the warehouse, office worker complaints occurred, work deteriorated, and morale dropped. Singleton's response was to raise wages—for everyone. This action, based on Singleton's beliefs of remotivating via the reward system and of being fair to the warehouse crew, did not work. Office worker complaints changed content, morale continued to drop, and work did not improve. Singleton's action of raising wages, we now see, did not result from careful analysis but was focused on symptoms.

As of the end of the case, what should Singleton do, if anything? As she contemplates further action, she very likely should state criteria before action planning. What objectives is she trying to meet in implementing action, and what constraints is she facing? The situation seems to be urgent—she has to take action now. Whatever she does, it has to stop the deterioration of office worker morale, loyalty and commitment to the company, work effectiveness, and what her subordinates think of and feel toward her. Hopefully too, Singleton's action will begin to reverse these trends. The refurbishing of the warehouse office and the recent wage increase also suggest there are little or no funds available. Therefore Singleton's next actions probably have to be very low cost. A final criterion for Singleton's action planning is to not overly constrain future actions in case her current actions are not as effective as she wishes them to be (like the wage increase, which means she now can't do anything more with wages).

Our analysis and diagnosis have shown that at the end of the case Singleton has two action objectives: to somehow reestablish the status/prestige differential between the office workers and the warehouse crew, and to somehow regain a better relationship with her office staff. How to do this quickly, with minimal cost, is her challenge.

What actions are available to Singleton at the case's end? In Figure 8.2 we present three lists of action alternatives: what she can do, what she will do, and what she should do. You will no doubt notice that some alternatives from the "can do" list (and all alternatives from the "will do" list) are not desirable in that they fail to meet some or all of the action-selection criteria stated above, such as:

- Progressive discipline (cost-effective, but likely to further deteriorate the declining morale and productivity issues).
- Move the office workers back downtown (restores office worker status but cost-prohibitive).
- Take wage increase away from warehouse workers (restores status differential, but devastates warehouse workers' morale).
- Either Singleton or Jenna talks to office and warehouse workers (cost-effective, but unlikely to reverse the downward trend in morale, work effectiveness, loyalty and commitment to the company, and the subordinates' perception of Singleton).

"Can Do"

1. Nothing.

2. Use progressive discipline for those who continue to complain.

3. Introduce small, cost-free changes to increase status of office workers:
   • Change work hours for office workers
   • Enlarge and/or enrich office jobs
   • Conduct regular meetings of the office staff

4. Implement minimal-cost changes to increase the status of office workers:
   • Separate parking into two sections
   • Install an office–warehouse communication system
   • Enhance entrance to the office
   • Celebrate special events of office workers

5. Ask Jenna to explain to workers that no further changes can be made.

6. Petition Jenna to move office workers back down town.

7. Take away wage increases given to the ware house workers.

8. Talk to office and warehouse workers and stress that:
   • The company is growing, the competition is more intense, and the company needs to be conscious of costs
   • There will be no more salary increases
   • There will be no more changes
   • Every one needs to focus on his or her job

"Will Do"

1. Nothing for a while.

2. May then petition Jenna to move office workers back down town.

3. Eventually may talk to office and warehouse workers.

"Should Do"

1. Introduce small, cost-free changes to increase status of office workers:
   • Change work hours for office workers
   • Enlarge and/or enrich office jobs
   • Conduct regular meetings of the office staff

2. Implement minimal-cost changes to increase the status of office workers:
   • Separate parking into two sections
   • Install an office–warehouse communication system
   • Enhance entrance to the office
   • Celebrate special events of office workers

FIGURE 8.2   Action Alternatives for the Jenna's Kitchens Case.

Our list of action alternatives has been narrowed down quite a bit to two "should do" alternatives that include several small, low-cost, quickly enacted, symbolic actions:

• Change the work hours for the office workers. Have the office workers begin work after the warehouse crew and work later (white-collar workers conventionally start later and work later than blue-collar employees).

- Change those office jobs that have been simplified, perhaps creating appropriate, enlarged, and/or enriched jobs.
- Conduct regular meetings of the office staff where company and regional information is shared, and as appropriate, solicit office worker input for enhancing office practices.
- Separate the parking lot into two sections. Have the section closest to the office entrance reserved for the office workers. Also give each office worker a parking spot with his or her name on it (and not so for the warehouse crew).
- Install an office–warehouse communication system that is under the control of the office.
- Make the entrance to the office, but not the warehouse, look more appealing using potted flowers, a tasteful sign, etc.
- Celebrate special events of office workers, like birthday lunches downtown, catered parties on holidays, etc.

These actions all appear to meet Singleton's action criteria. All alternatives can be implemented rather quickly, and all symbolically differentiate the office from the warehouse and begin to add back signs of status for office personnel. These actions could help to halt and hopefully reverse the decline of office worker morale, work effectiveness, office worker loyalty and commitment to the company, and positively impact what Singleton's subordinates think of her. In terms of cost, the first three involve no cost outlays, and the remaining entail minimal costs. Finally, implementing these actions will not overly constrain any future actions Singleton may take in case these current actions are not as effective as she wishes them to be.

Now that we have determined that the criteria have been met, inquiring into the possible positive and negative consequences of all the actions on the "should do" list is another way of making a decision among action alternatives.

Many of the positive consequences have already been described, such as reversing the downward trend in morale and productivity. But what of the possible negative consequences? At the face of it, one appears plausible. Now that the warehouse crew has been influenced by the move of the office workers into the same building and has received a wage increase, Singleton needs to be tactful in her implementation of the action alternatives for the office workers so as to not make the warehouse workers perceive that their status is being lowered.

But now the question is: Which do we implement? We could choose the first set of actions that require no monetary outlay, or we may consider implementing both sets of actions, or we may consider doing individual actions over time. Two alternatives are to (a) do them sequentially, spaced over perhaps a four to six week time period, or (b) do as sets, perhaps the first set of three actions, then the next set. The second alternative probably will have the most impact. Also, Singleton can simply initiate each of these actions, or she can confer with office supervisors about them. Again the latter is suggested because of its potential for enhancing her relationship with her direct reports, one of her action objectives. By introducing these actions, with or without consultation by others, Singleton is likely to be perceived as a manager who is sensitive to and caring about her office employees' need to be a higher status, more prestigious group than they currently perceive themselves to be. Additionally, these actions will likely repair some of the disrupted psychological contract between the office workers and the company.

By planning to initiate these actions either in sequence or by sets, Singleton will be able to assess their impact and thus confirm or disconfirm the underlying issue of status differential as she moves forward. For example, if after implementing the first set of actions there is a positive impact, she may decide that it is unnecessary to move forward with implementing the next set of actions.

Summary

Action planning, like each of the other steps in preparing cases, requires time and care. To follow the steps of action planning (outlined again in the Section "An Outline for Preparing Cases" in Chapter 10) will initially seem overly time consuming, certainly a bother, and perhaps stifling. Experience has shown, however, that adhering to such a process will improve the quality of your managerial thinking, decisions, and action-taking recommendations. Your success in action planning will be a great reward. With repetition, you will enhance your learning and reduce the likelihood of having to repeatedly resolve the same difficulties again and again. This approach need not, perhaps should not, be viewed as strictly an individual process. Discuss with others who have read the case. Two or more minds usually are better than one—they can collectively know more pertinent facts, make better inferences, share the work of symptom and goal listings, bring more ideas to bear on and contribute to the analysis, etc. Working with fellow students in a regular and increasingly disciplined way is commonly expected. With practice, this approach gets easier and you will become more efficient. When you involve others, not only does the work get easier and the process more effective, but you can also enhance your learning about the process itself.

9

Preparing Iceberg Cases, Searching for Information

Chapter Objectives

- Focus attention on an important managerial skill: acquiring more and more relevant information.
- Provide some guidance about what relevant information is and how to search for it.
- Provide an example of an information search in an iceberg case.

THE IMPORTANCE OF INFORMATION SEARCHING

It is common in business, as in everyday life, to encounter from time to time a situation about which we are relatively uninformed. To understand a situation well enough to decide whether to act on it or leave it alone—and if we are to act, to decide what to do—means we have to seek information about it. All too often the information we possess is about specific incidents or singular events, and is typically out of date or mostly second hand or just the speculations or assumptions of others. We are uninformed sometimes simply because we are new to the situation or have been away from it for a while. Whatever the reason, we realize that we are to some degree uninformed and thus our understanding of the situation is incomplete.

Acquiring more and better information does not just happen—we need to proactively make it happen. Knowing what information to seek and how to acquire it is therefore an important, central competency of managers. Without enough of the right kinds of information, analytical understanding and thoughtful action planning are difficult if not impossible to achieve.

In the next section we provide a case, "The Central Catering Company," to demonstrate the information searching process. It is an "iceberg" type case. Recall that iceberg cases are relatively short cases that provide a description of one or, at most, a few incidents, events, perceptions, and/or opinions. Much of the other relevant information, such as historical, contextual, and other related information, is only hinted at, if given at all. We are using an iceberg case to help you learn how to search for information by seeing or finding ideas in the information provided, and using these ideas or sets of ideas to determine what, where, and how additional information might be useful, if acquired.

Please read the case twice so that you are familiar with it (as defined in the Section "Becoming Familiar with a Case" in Chapter 5): first swiftly to get a feel for the situation, characters, and prior action, and slowly on the second reading to appreciate the nature and type of information provided.

Now, imagine you are a case writer in the field of hospitality management and have made arrangements to gather the information necessary to write one or more teaching cases around the management group of the Central Catering Company located in a large western city. At the present time, the Central Catering Company is attempting to reorganize the physical layout of its Bakery Division. Your task is to understand any issues associated with this reorganization and write a case based on your research. Your general approach for conducting this information gathering includes interviewing the management personnel and observing the situation related to the reorganization.

After obtaining permission to do this research from the president of Central Catering Company, you have gone through the ceremonial duties of entering the company and have been introduced to the management group at a recent meeting. You have explained to them something about the process of teaching by cases and the general approach and some of the possible consequences of your research.

THE CENTRAL CATERING COMPANY CASE

Your first interview, which occurred by chance, has been with Robert Coleman, the head of maintenance. In answer to your initial, general question about the reorganization of the Baking Division facilities, he said:

> "The Baking Division is a real clique. I'd like that clique busted up. Those people won't share their ideas; I don't think that's right. Jim Gordon and George Norman know more about baking than anyone in the company, yet they won't share their ideas. We have to find some way to induce them to share their knowledge. I dislike cliques; ideas and feelings should be exposed. Maybe we ought to hire a consultant—he or she might get things out in the open and get the clique broken up.
>
> "Young Steve Sampson already has made the first move toward busting the clique by moving George to the other end of the office. That's what is needed, some young guy who doesn't know the system around here coming in and making these changes. Only he can get away with it. Then again, we have this other young kid, Tom Gordon. Tom would like to do some efficiency studies in the Baking Division, but they won't let him. Because of this problem, both he and Steve, with whom he has discussed it, are getting sore at the bakery people. This clique has got to be busted.
>
> "As you'll discover after you've been here awhile, everything has a history. The baking situation is not an exception. I'm one of the very few people in this company who is aware of the history behind most of our problems. It's not because I'm so much smarter than anyone else, but just because I've been here longer. The development of the bakery clique is a long story. I'll just cover the highlights.

"When Central was first established, they did catering just downtown. The company grew fairly easily in those days until we did all kinds of catering all over the area. For all sorts of reasons, but especially quality as well as cost management, we wanted to secure many of the basics we needed in catering. Since baked goods can often make or break a catering business, they decided at first to "lock up" the output of a local bakery. In time, however, they decided that we needed our own. This created a need for someone qualified in baking. They checked with some counterpart caterers on the west coast to see if they had anyone who could fill the job. None of those coastal outfits had anyone who'd risk moving here. A southern California firm suggested Sam Neely, their former head baker who at that time had a small business of his own in Tucson.

"Sam joined Central when Dave Soucie was the president. Dean Chapple and Sydney Boldt, who are not with us now, were powerful men in the company at that time. Dean and Syd ran the whole show; they didn't use any of this communication stuff. Sam formed an alliance with Dave Soucie which separated him from Dean and Syd. Things got so bad that those two guys would not talk to Sam. That was the initial separation which evolved into the Baking Division clique.

"For quite some time catering and baking were done in two separate facilities. During that time, anyone the catering people wanted to get rid of was transferred to the other building. That contributed to the separation. In retrospect, you might say that the catering group is also a clique. Heck, we have all sorts of cliques around here. But let me finish my original story. Management decided they wanted to expand and update the facilities and would bring catering and baking under the same roof. They brought catering and baking together, but it never worked. It didn't work because those darn baking people continued to be a clique.

"About three years ago another rearrangement was made which physically separated baking and catering. Bruce Berkely, whose idea it was to have them under one roof, was instrumental in this physical separation. That's roughly the history behind the baking clique.

"The main people in the clique are Sam Neely, Jim Gordon, George Norman, and Ted Burns. I don't know who the others are, I just keep track of the big ones. It's going to be interesting to see what happens in four months when Sam Neely retires. Ted Burns is going to take over the role of father confessor for the baking group. He doesn't know it yet, but I can see it happening. However, I think that clique is going to get busted. It will be a good thing for you to follow if you're interested in people and their behavior."

SELECTING IDEAS WITH WHICH TO SEARCH

This appears to be the type of situation that you had in mind for a case.

Your immediate task is to determine what additional information is needed for a case so that students could do an analysis, make a diagnosis, and create a plan for effective action.

- What would you like to observe? What would you be looking for?
- With whom would you like to talk? What would you ask them? For what would you be listening?

When we find ourselves in situations in which the readily available information probably represents just the tip of the informational iceberg (like in an iceberg case), we are likely to feel uneasy—too little information or too little good quality information means we cannot be as certain about what is going on as we would like. While we will never be perfectly informed about anything, more information is clearly better than less—for managing as well as case writing. While we may never have exactly the quality of information we would like, the more factual information the better. Information searching, therefore, is not only desirable, it is often a necessity.

Much casual information is too untrustworthy a foundation upon which to build an understanding of a situation. Rumor, gossip, allegations, attributions, biased opinions, and individual perceptions are defective in two ways. Casual information may or may not be relevant or representative until verified by information from other sources and/or placed in a broader informational set so that it can be understood within the context of other information. Even a symptom in an iceberg case has to be viewed skeptically if it came from just one source.

Planning for information searching entails figuring out what information to search for. The answer is partially found in some of the steps of case preparation. The second step in preparing cases involves recognizing symptoms (see Chapter 5). Attempting to find symptoms is a type of information search, and thus we need to keep our eyes and ears open for additional indicators that things aren't what they might or should be (new symptoms and the confirmation of known symptoms). Similarly, the third step in case preparation—listing goals—advises us to search for information about goals—stated as well as unstated (of individuals, work units, organizations, etc.).

Another answer to the question, "What information to search for?" is provided by the limited information found in iceberg cases. If we think of the limited information in an iceberg case as cues, they signal us to dig for more information using a broader, more systematic information search. For example, if a work unit is mentioned in an iceberg case, we would probably want to know about it. Based on ideas or conceptual models (like the one in Figure 6.1B), we would be prompted to find out about the work unit's history, purpose, members, structure, technologies, functioning, and so on.

If you recall, this process of information or facts leading us to think of ideas, which we then use to help us find and make sense of more information, was described in Chapter 3. There we described how pieces of case information can suggest one or more ideas that in turn prompt us to notice other information or its absence. Having ideas/models, thus, is essential for information searching. Your text and your instructor's lectures will no doubt provide you with ideas/models for much that will be of interest. It is important, however, not to overlook information. A very wide-scope conceptual framework, such as the one depicted in Figure 6.1B, may be used as a guide for the types of possible information for which to search. In considering what information to seek, a rule of thumb is to not only search carefully into the entities, actions, and relationships the case focuses our attention upon, but to always also search into whatever exists around them and existed before them.

How is information acquired? The answer for managers in business situations is the same as for you in your life situations. We observe, we overhear, we casually talk with others, we interview them, we examine available documents, and we take notice of physical indicators. Usually we employ some combination of these methods depending on what information we are after.

Both what information we can seek and how we can obtain it are constrained by the realities of the situation and the seeker's relationships. What is feasible must be factored into information search planning. How much time is available for information searching? What access do we have to the people, places, and activities of the situation? What kinds and amounts of information are desired, and what can or must we settle for? Given the answers to these questions, what methods are realistically likely to provide what we want? Information seekers need to be ever sensitive to their power and status vis-à-vis others as it affects candidness, attempts to influence, and the quality of relationships beyond the information acquisition.

SEARCHING THE CENTRAL CATERING SITUATION

It takes just a moment's reflection to appreciate that the Central Catering Case is comprised of a mix of Robert Coleman's (head of maintenance) perceptions, opinions, inferences, and judgments. Thus, all of the case's information is from one man's point of view. Even in just a few paragraphs, however, Coleman refers to several persons, events, places, work units, and relationships extending over a considerable period of time. You as the case writer probably feel a bit confused by what Coleman has so quickly shared with you. It seems useful therefore to sort out and order (as per the Section "Becoming Familiar with a Case" in Chapter 5) what Coleman has said.

Coleman has noted two contemporary "cliques," one in the Catering Division (but he did not name any members) and the other in the Baking Division (naming Sam Neely as head and also Jim Gordon, George Norman, and Ted Burns). In addition, Coleman mentioned three other people. Two have made major decisions: Bruce Berkely was the first to put Baking and Catering "under one roof" and then three years ago physically separated them, and Steve Sampson recently moved Norman's office. Tom Gordon was the third person mentioned as one who isn't allowed to do efficiency studies in the Baking Division. Figure 9.1 portrays the information that Coleman mentioned about persons, cliques, and divisions. This

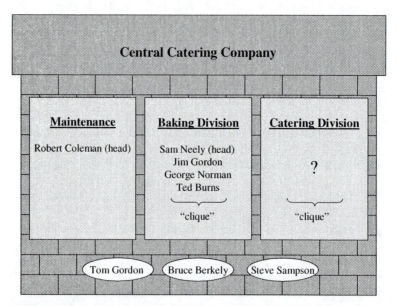

FIGURE 9.1 People, Cliques, and Divisions in the Central Catering Company.

information, of course, was embedded in what Coleman called the "history" of the situation. Ordering the events of this history by constructing a time line helps us see what Coleman believes are the key decisions and changes related to the cliques he asserts exist as well as the impending Baking Division physical layout changes. Figure 9.2 presents this time line of events.

Having ordered the information heard from Coleman, we now recall that we, as case writers, were interested in the twin foci of understanding the management group and the proposed changes in the physical layout of the Baking Division so that we could eventually write

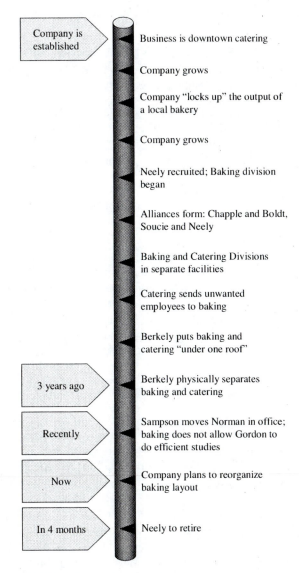

Company is established	Business is downtown catering
	Company grows
	Company "locks up" the output of a local bakery
	Company grows
	Neely recruited; Baking division began
	Alliances form: Chapple and Boldt, Soucie and Neely
	Baking and Catering Divisions in separate facilities
	Catering sends unwanted employees to baking
	Berkely puts baking and catering "under one roof"
3 years ago	Berkely physically separates baking and catering
Recently	Sampson moves Norman in office; baking does not allow Gordon to do efficient studies
Now	Company plans to reorganize baking layout
In 4 months	Neely to retire

FIGURE 9.2   Timeline for the Central Catering Company.

a teaching case. This means gathering information. But what information and how can we obtain it? Obviously we must plan (a) the verification of Coleman's information as well as (b) the search of information beyond Coleman's. Let's begin with verification and find out:

- If Coleman's alleged symptoms (Baking doesn't share its knowledge; Baking won't let Gordon do efficiency studies; that Gordon and Sampson are getting sore at Baking; the likelihood that the Baking clique is going to be busted up) are shared by anyone else, and if there are any other symptoms.
- If Coleman's alleged "cliques" are recognized by any others, and if Coleman's opinions about clique membership are verified by others.
- What are the positions and work units of Berkely, Sampson, and Gordon? Also are there work units beyond Maintenance, Baking, and Catering, and how are they formally related?

This list will verify much of what Coleman told us. However, now we require information about what these and other key players and work units do, how well they do it, and how they relate. We need to acquire information about:

- Managerial positions and their responsibilities, work unit objectives, how unit work is accomplished, type and modernity of unit technology, work unit (and key product) productivity, unit morale, and unit staffing and management in order to provide much of the needed contextual information to which Coleman's is linked.
- How the work units contribute to Central Catering's reputation and profitability.
- The company's aspirational ends (e.g., vision, objectives) and how to achieve them (e.g., strategies and policies, structures, how decisions are made and communicated, control and planning activities, and the like) in order to better understand the first two points of informational interest.
- Central Catering's markets, competitors, suppliers, labor pools, neighborhood, and storage and transportation to help situate (i.e., to place into context) much of the other information gathered as well as to learn about the company's physical facilities and work flows.
- How the work units are dependent upon one another (e.g., Catering using all or some of Baking's products, both Baking and Catering calling on Maintenance for equipment repairs, etc.) and how this is viewed by unit members and upper management.

As we go about acquiring all of the kinds of information mentioned earlier, we need to keep our eyes and ears open for information that cannot easily be directly observed or asked about. For example:

- All of the people mentioned by Coleman and probably most others will have feelings about the company's people, work and staff units, technologies, the work itself and its outcomes, social standards—just about everything. We need to learn about both positive and negative feelings, at least those that are strong and held by several people.
- Since all organizations and work units develop informal rules (about how to do things, relate to other people, judge what's important and what is not, etc.) we need to become informed about these and whether they are consistent with management-specified formal rules. People who know of and follow such informal rules will also be of interest.

A plan for what information to acquire as a case researcher will of course have to be flexible. It is hard to foresee beforehand exactly what will be needed and/or available. As information gathering proceeds, it is likely that some facts (idea-bracketed information) will suggest additional facts. Information acquisition is thus dependent on:

1. the ideas and models we carry into the situation;
2. the quality of the relationship between the case writer and organization members (enough trust to keep confidences); and
3. the ways information is gathered.

Much of the information desired about people's positions, work unit composition, overall organization structure, environmental factors, and similar "factual" matters can be acquired early on by interviewing just a few upper-level managers and asking to see recent company documents. Some information is readily obtainable through observation, for example, physical settings, work activities, technology, and work flow, which is easily confirmed and augmented by questioning associated workers or managers simply because most organizational members find it flattering as well as easy to talk about the descriptive aspects of their work and work place.

Much of the information we are interested in, however, is essentially somewhat more personal, involving people's perceptions, judgments, and feelings about how they are treated, other people, relationships among people and units, how well people do or don't do their work, and so on. Such information will come from talking with organizational members both through interviews and casual conversations.

After ordering the information obtained from our first interview with Robert Coleman and outlining the sorts of information we initially believe we require, how might our plan for our information searching look?

- First, by interviewing if possible the president, a financial officer, and a human resource officer, our information searching would very likely provide what we'd like to know about Central Catering's environmental circumstances, the firm's direction, strategy, resources, how it's organized, who's who, and so on.
- Second, Coleman might be reinterviewed to have him elaborate upon and provide specifics about most of what he said before. He will probably be easily induced to talk about other matters, too.
- Third, interviews with as many of the people Coleman mentioned would not only possibly verify what he has asserted but would allow us to probably learn much more about intraunit and interunit relations, including communications and work flow, perceptions about resources, technology, product amount and quality, and relative status, power and fairness. In these interviews a case researcher should also inquire into what seems to be working well and not so well.
- Then a small sample of upper managers and workers from all units can be interviewed about the current relationships between Baking and Catering, and what is believed to cause the strain, and what is likely to happen when Baking's layout is altered.

As information gathering proceeds, a case researcher will observe all along and probably reinterview people as new points of likely significance are brought up.

Summary

This chapter has focused on those situations (e.g., iceberg-type cases) in which we need more, different, and/or better information than we currently have, to better understand them and to determine whether taking action is necessary. Searching for additional information constitutes a very important managerial skill. While information searching probably goes on continuously at some level of consciousness, it is most often triggered by a perceived need for improved understanding. The keys to effective information searching are two: using appropriate ideas/models to guide attention, and using them systematically and thoroughly. The selection and use of appropriate ideas/models is an art that improves with practice and increasing experience, especially if we periodically reflect on how well our searches go.

10

Outlines for Case Preparation and Case Reports

Chapter Objectives

- Provide a summary guide for case preparation.
- Provide a guide for writing a case report.

This short chapter provides two guides. The first simply summarizes the case preparation approach that has been described in Chapters 5 through 8. Having already read about the six major steps of case preparation, we provide an outline of them as a quick reference in the Section "An Outline for Preparing Cases." Because students are sometimes requested to write a report of a case, in the Section "An Outline for a Written Case Report" we provide guidance for such a report—a generic outline as well as several helpful hints.

AN OUTLINE FOR PREPARING CASES

1. Gaining familiarity
   a. Describe, in general and over time, who does what, how do things happen, and where and when do events take place.
   b. Describe, in detail, any history and the current state of the places, persons, relationships, activities, tasks, and contexts of case events.
   c. Notice where case information lies along the continuum of certainty; also noting what most information pertains to.
   d. Recognize one's own emotional responses to aspects of the case.
2. Recognizing symptoms
   a. List all major, recent indicators that something is not as expected or desired by case characters and you (including any statements of "problems" by case characters).
   b. Note who in the case situations seems to be bothered by these symptoms.

3. Identifying goals
   a. List all the reasonably important goals of the major entities in the case, for example, central case characters, groupings, work units, organizations, and so on. Be sure to list all goals described in the case as well as all that can be reasonably attributed to major entities.
4. Analysis
   a. Select those ideas, models, and/or theories that seem useful for understanding the case.
   b. Carefully and systematically apply these conceptual tools to the case situations and circumstances.
   c. As new case information is revealed, cycle back through (a) and (b).
5. Diagnosis
   a. Identify relevant goal gaps.
   b. Identify major inconsistencies among goals (predicaments).
   c. Identify major discrepancies between goals and actual performance (problems).
   d. Prioritize identified goal gaps, predicaments, and problems as to urgency for corrective action and relative importance to the organization and/or key case characters.
6. Action planning
   a. Specify and then prioritize the criteria to be used to choose among action alternatives.
   b. Invent or discover possible and feasible action alternatives that detail specifically who should do what, when, and where.
   c. Carefully examine the probable positive and negative consequences of all action alternatives.
   d. Using the criteria choose the preferred course of action.
   e. Design a specific plan for implementing the preferred course of action. Include a schedule.
   f. Note a plan for assessing the recommended course of action, that is, how would one know whether it was effective?

AN OUTLINE FOR A WRITTEN CASE REPORT

Written case reports are asked of students for a variety of reasons: to give students practice in writing reports for actual managers, to test the quality of student preparation, to accompany a student presentation, and to evaluate a student's competency in case work. This section focuses on a formal written case report done by either an individual student or a student group. As opposed to a case class discussion or exam, a written report is distinguished by its thorough, rigorous analysis and recommendations as well as the quality of presentation.

A. Suggestions for effective report writing
   • *Review the assignment instructions.* Who is the recipient? Who are you as the writer? When is it due? Any length constraints? Any formatting considerations?
   • *Know the evaluation criteria that will be used to assess your report.* These typically will be some weighted combination of: clear identification of issues; thoroughness and soundness of analysis; reasonableness, range, and evaluation of alternative actions; feasibility and specificity of recommendations including action and implementation plans; logical consistency and linkage to case information; and the overall quality of the written report.

- *Work ethically.* Never copy or use another person's work without explicit acknowledgment. Do not contact the case company for more information or for what actually happened.
- *Plan carefully.* Part of planning for a written report means allotting sufficient time to do the preparation and writing. Budget your time cautiously. It is common to underestimate how much time it takes to do quality work. Begin early and keep to your schedule. The other part of planning, once your preparation is complete, is to outline the report (see "Case Report Checklist") and prepare any exhibits before starting to write. Remember: Reports are not creative essays. It can't hurt to ask your instructor if he or she will put a copy of a good report on reserve at your library.
- *Use an appropriate voice.* Case reports tend to follow business/professional conventions. Readability is always expected. When in doubt, write simply with clarity and accuracy. Brevity is usually appreciated. Use headings as signposts. Use short paragraphs and bullets as appropriate. Always clearly label and reference exhibits or appendices.
- *Review your written report very, very carefully.* Proofread the report at least twice. Be alert for typos, omitted words and sentences, misleading words and jargon, etc. Strive for professional standards. Try reading it slowly aloud—your ear may catch awkward phrasing or jumps in logic. Ask yourself if your report communicates persuasively.
- *Retain your notes from preparing the case as well as any preliminary outlines and drafts of the report.* These document your work and reasoning, and your instructor may ask to see them.

B. Organization of a written case report

While the structure of your report will depend on the nature of the case, report instructions, and your thinking about the case, it is likely to include the following parts—first presented as a checklist and then discussed part by part.

Case Report Checklist
1. Title page
2. Executive summary
3. Table of contents
4. Issues statement
5. Analysis
6. Alternative actions
7. Recommendations
8. Implementation plan
9. Exhibits/Appendices

1. *Title page.* Title pages are meant to help your instructor. A title page contains the following information (when possible ordered as your instructor wishes): the title of the case; the student's name; the date; the course title, number, and section; the instructor's name and title. The title page should be very readable, never crowded or "clever."
2. *Executive summary.* Business reports commonly are prefaced with an executive summary that is designed to serve as a compact summary for a busy manager, as a guide for the careful reader who wants to understand the report's overall direction

before plunging into it, and as a convenient reference for anyone who will use the report. It should succinctly (around 300 words) summarize your analysis and then focus on your key recommendations. We recommend writing the executive summary last, once you have written your report.

3. *Table of contents.* This page presents the sections and subsections of the body of the written report, including exhibits and appendices, and gives their page numbers. Many readers look closely at the table of contents to obtain a sense of the report's flow and completeness before reading the report. The table of contents should always be readable and accurate.

4. *Issues statement.* This part of your report states as clearly as possible the issues in the case (i.e., problems, predicaments, goal gaps) that require managerial attention. If there are multiple issues they should be ordered according to their importance, that is, major and minor. This part may defend the selection of underlying issues, with reference to symptoms.

5. *Analysis.* The analysis is the heart of the report. It is the platform upon which the eventual action-related recommendations will stand. It should convince the reader of the careful thoroughness of the report writer's thinking.

   If analysis depends on any assumptions—about important information not contained in the case—the assumptions should be stated at the outset. Be sure they are plausible and realistic.

   An analysis, in essence, is your reasoning about what is important in the case that results in the issues you have identified.

   An analysis is *not* simply a restatement of key case information. Rather it uses case information to justify the sequence of claims made in the argument about what has occurred that deserves managerial attention. An analysis may summarize key points in exhibits (tables or figures) or use bullets to list key points. Appendices should be used for evidence and arguments that are too technical or lengthy or only of peripheral relevance.

6. *Alternative actions.* All issues can usually be corrected and/or prevented by more than one course of action. This part of the report presents those reasonable, legitimate alternatives that link to your analysis.

7. *Recommendations.* This part begins by presenting the strengths and weaknesses of each actionable alternative, that is, evaluates each alternative in terms of some stated choice criteria. Probable positive and negative consequences should be noted. It is common to give less space to less-worthy alternatives and more to merit-worthy ones. One alternative should be selected and carefully justified by the end of this section.

8. *Implementation plan.* This part of the report states how, where, when, and by whom the recommended course of action will be implemented. How issues will be corrected and/or prevented in the future is noted here. Considerations of employee resistance, resource reallocation, potential major impediments, and the like may also be noted. Specificity always enhances one's argument.

9. *Exhibits/Appendices.* This part of the report includes any tables, figures, etc. you may have created for your analysis (for example, to summarize key points) or to present evidence and arguments that are too technical or lengthy or only of peripheral relevance to be included in the main body of the written report.

III

Cases for Discussion

A student of business with tact
Absorbed many answers he lacked.
But acquiring a job,
He said with a sob,
"How does one fit answers to fact?"

—Charles I. Gragg

The road to wisdom? Well, it's plain
and simple to express:

Err
and err
and err again
but less
and less
and less.

There is
one art,
no more,
no less:
to do
all things
with art-
lessness.

—PIET HEIN

This part of our book consists entirely of cases. Some are quite short; many are of moderate length, and some are fairly long. Case difficulty, however, is not correlated to length. The cases vary also in their descriptive detailing as well as their scope, that is, the number of events, characters, span of time involved, and so forth. All but a couple of these cases take place in hospitality situations—restaurants and other food service situations, hotels and other lodging situations, and situations where hospitable service occurs. You should note that although all the cases describe real events that occurred at real companies, the names of the companies and case characters in some cases are fictitious (as requested by the companies and people involved).

By working with these cases you will learn a lot about hospitality organizations, their managers, employees, and all sorts of hospitality jobs! Be forewarned that these cases are not intended to portray effective hospitality practices, for as we noted in the Section "Where Did the Case Method Begin? How Has It Evolved?" in Chapter 2, cases exist "to enhance discussion . . . in the service of thinking."

The cases that follow are of the three types defined in the Section "What Types of Teaching Cases Are There?" in Chapter 2, that is, iceberg cases, cases for analysis, and decision-focused cases. These are randomly distributed in Part III, because the cases are ordered alphabetically by title. Your instructor will determine which cases you will prepare and the order in which you study them. Case choices and scheduling is the prerogative of your instructor and based upon your course's level, the academic sophistication of your class, course objectives, the extent and nature of your class's work experience, and other factors.

Let us once more alert you to a common experience that may be yours as you go forward. Early case discussions may seem to be messy, to wander, to be inefficient, etc. They are bound to be! Don't get discouraged. You will gain experience and learn from repeated case work. As your case preparation improves, so will the case discussions. Remember that learning from case work is about enhancing your managerial thinking and competencies. Skilled practice is a lot more than knowing! So work hard, but be patient with yourself.

AU NATURAL RESTAURANT

It was 9:30 P.M. when David Wikes, owner-manager of the Au Natural Restaurant, poured himself a cup of coffee and sat down to rest at a rear table for the first time since coming to work at three that afternoon. David felt overly tired. It had been a busier evening than usual as the cash register would no doubt show. As he sipped his coffee, however, David's thought returned to the fact that he'd spent the whole evening filling in for a wait person who had quit unexpectedly. Besides being awfully tired, part of David felt frustrated for he knew that some important things had to be left unattended to when he filled in for his staff. On second thought, it was more than frustration, the feeling verged on anger—he'd been filling in a lot lately for employees who were late, simply didn't show up, or left without notice. Too damn much in fact! As David took another gulp of coffee, he saw customers had just been seated at his station. He made a mental note to insert an advertisement in the local newspapers and got to his feet.

THE BAGEL HOCKEY CASE

The Cafeteria for the Toronto Training Academy (TTA) was located on the first floor of the school's main residential hall. The cafeteria was open seven days a week. It consisted of a short-order grill, a salad and delicatessen bar, a soda fountain, and a hot-meals counter, although the latter was not operated on weekends. It was heavily utilized by the students and by others during the week for food and as a social center. On weekends its use was rather limited, since many TTA students were commuters and others left campus for the weekend. What business there was tended to come in spurts due in part to the use of the building for special workshops and other group activities.

During the weekend, the cafeteria employed a different crew of workers than during the week. All seven of the weekend employees were students except for the cashier, who was a housewife in her mid-30s. Two of the employees were attending high school; the senior student supervisor was from a two-year business college, and the remaining three workers were from TTA.

Ernie Slim, the senior student supervisor, had been employed at the cafeteria for four years, a long period of employment for the cafeteria, and had worked his way up from grill attendant to his supervisory position. He was a shy, friendly character who rarely worked directly with the public but spent most of his time in the back room making food preparations for take-out and banquet orders. Henry Delano, the junior student supervisor, was more personable with the customers, often standing and chatting with them. He spent most of his day walking around overseeing the other employees, sometimes helping them when they found themselves bogged down with orders, or working the grill and fountain positions by himself while others took breaks. Having had no previous experience before beginning the job, Henry was often forced to rely on employees below him to explain tasks.

Two male students usually worked the grill, and during slow hours of the day they were required to work in the dishroom. Two female students worked the fountain and deli bar and during slow hours bused cafeteria tables. The cashier's job only required her to attend the register and at the end of the day determine the total income. This position was always occupied (even during weekdays) by an older, more mature woman.

All worked under the general regulations of the cafeteria, which required that all employees be neatly and cleanly attired. Girls were to wear hairnets and blue smocks over skirts, while boys had to wear white work shirts and paper hats. Sideburns were not permitted to extend below the ear lobe, and beards were not allowed. Mustaches had to be neat and closely trimmed, not extending beyond the width of the upper lip. Good sanitary practices were expected of all employees, and the regulations included the statement: "Loud talking, singing, whistling, or horseplay will not be tolerated." A pay differential was established depending upon the individual's position, time employed, and whether or not the student had purchased a meal ticket. Weekend and weekday employees were on the same wage scale, and the pay range for grill and fountain employees was between the minimum wage and 30 percent higher, while the supervisors received double that of the employees. Except for the supervisors, the job was not considered a very desirable one; and, in fact, it had been a last-resort choice by every weekend employee.

Since the cafeteria was open from 12:30 to 7:00 on weekends, only one shift of workers was needed. All weekend employees worked on an eight-hour day and were allowed a half hour for dinner and given a 15-minute coffee break. These breaks were given at the discretion of the supervisors, but employees felt free to ask for them if they thought business was slow enough.

Scheduling, hiring, and firing were all done by the cafeteria manager, Mrs. Laraby, a middle-aged woman who had been manager for five years. She worked a 40-hour week, Monday through Friday, and rarely came into the cafeteria on weekends unless there was a special banquet to be set up. As manager she encouraged a relaxed working atmosphere but expected each employee to be responsible for his or her job and to strictly observe the regulations of the cafeteria. Although she was firm about what she expected of her workers, Mrs. Laraby was willing to listen to any problems encountered by the employees. As a result, they respected Mrs. Laraby and felt comfortable enough in her presence to joke with her, although they were careful not to whenever her boss was around.

Grill products were of the hamburger and hot dog variety; the fountain's main business was ice cream cones; the deli bar served salads, desserts, and cold sandwiches, most of which had been made during the week and were now in the "staling" process. All beverage machines were self-service. A customer passed down the food line and paid the cashier located at the end of the line.

During the weekends, no large quantity food preparation was done, leaving the large kitchen area desolate and open to all employees. This large back room was blocked from the customer's view by walls that separated it from the food area. (See Exhibit 1.)

All employees performed the essential tasks that their jobs demanded of them, but without much enthusiasm. The working atmosphere was extremely relaxed and lenient, and since the work was menial, there was a flexible setup in which almost everyone could operate in another's position. Frequently the fountain person helped out the grill individual, and vice versa. However, a large portion of the working day passed with only a few customers trickling in. There was little opportunity to converse with friends coming through the food line, as was commonplace during the weekdays. This left the employees with much idle time.

The employees were close in age and shared common interests. Many friendships were formed. Supervisors were treated as equals, and joked and fooled around with the others. In

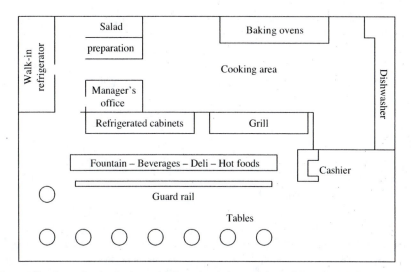

EXHIBIT 1   *Effective Behavior in Organizations* 6e; Cohen, Fink, Gaddon, and Willits; pgs 448–450.

Source: Reprinted with permission from A. Cohen, S. Fink, H. Gaddon, and R. Willits. *Effective Behavior in Organizations.* R. D. Irwin, Inc.

the back room (kitchen) as time allowed, the male employees—including the supervisors—often engaged in a game of floor hockey, using brooms as sticks and a stale bagel as a puck. The crew also participated in other sports. One was "baseball" played with a spatula and a hard-boiled egg. Another was "king of the eggs." This game was particularly popular with the female employees. The idea was to find the "king egg" in a batch of hardboiled eggs destined to be used eventually in egg salad. The game required two players. Each chose an egg, then one party held her egg firmly in one hand while the other person used her egg to hit the immobile egg. The player whose egg withstood the impact without cracking was declared the winner and continued to challenge any other potential players. Of all the games, only baseball ruined any appreciable quantity of usable food.

There had never been any crackdown attempts on this behavior, which occurred only on weekends when the large kitchen was not in use and there were no older supervisors or managers present.

Participation in these events was left up to the individual, but the usual participants included the three male student workers and the supervisor. The fountain girls took part in games such as the egg cracking less frequently, while the cashier never participated in any events but read during long intervals between customers. The general attitude of all employees toward these tournaments was favorable except, as a fountain employee put it, "when you get stuck doing all the work while the others are out back having fun." On occasion, when employees were engaged in these tournaments, business picked up in the food service area. Then, the one or two individuals left attending the fountain or grill were swamped with orders, finding it impossible to leave their jobs and notify the others in the back room of the customer influx. It placed a lot of pressure on these workers, and if this happened it meant that customers waited a long period of time for their orders.

One Sunday, during a normal midday lull, the three men and the supervisor were deep into a game of bagel hockey in the back room. The participants were totally involved in their fun and did not notice that there was an influx of customers, that the other attendants were overwhelmed at both grill and fountain, and that the cashier was busy at her register. On this particular occasion, Mrs. Laraby, the cafeteria manager, decided to pick up a book she had left in her office. Entering through the cafeteria, she first came upon the swamped employees; then proceeding to enter the back room, she discovered an exuberant hockey game in progress!

THE BAMBOO GARDEN

On Friday evening at the height of the dinner hour, all but one table was occupied in the dining room and only two seats were open at the sushi bar. A group of guests entered the Bamboo Garden and stood waiting to be seated. After a short while one guest went to the back of the restaurant, found the office, and asked the owner-manager, Sue Lee, if his party could be seated. Sue Lee then asked one of the waitpersons to seat the party. After several minutes, Kacey Wu, another waitperson noticed the new guests, and brought them menus and water. Shortly Kacey came by the table and took drink orders. Kacey then prepared the drinks and another waitperson served them as well as took food orders.

Fifteen minutes later Kacey noticed these guests giving her puzzled looks and looking at their watches. She asked them what was wrong and was asked why it was taking so long to get their appetizers. Kacey immediately went to the kitchen and asked one of the cooks, Heon Han, about the appetizers. Heon snapped, "I'm busy!" A few minutes later however Kacey saw that the appetizers were ready and brought them to her guests. Moments later another waitperson stopped by the table to inquire if the appetizers were satisfactory and was told they were "great" and "enjoyable." While clearing off a table, Kacey was told by Heon that the soup was ready for the party who had just been served their appetizers. She replied that she had to finish clearing a table and would be right back. While she did this another waitperson brought the soup to Kacey's table.

The next 30 minutes were hectic for everyone. Kacey was almost running to take care of several tables. She noticed that the hostess stand was not manned and that new guests were waiting. As she was seating these new guests, she noticed the original table was motioning for her. When she approached them they asked why only two of them had been served their entrees and two had not. Kacey apologized and rushed to the kitchen to ask Heon. He said he hadn't seen the check for the table. Kacey looked around the restaurant and saw it was still posted at the sushi bar. She grabbed it and took it to Heon. Kacey felt frustrated and worried. How would she explain to her guests why the entrees were taking so long? How much longer could she cope?

THE RESTAURANT

The Bamboo Garden was a new restaurant, open for just a few months, in an area of shops and restaurants close by the entrance to one of the colleges in a mid-size town in central Massachusetts. It served an array of Japanese and Korean dishes and featured a sushi bar. The

Bamboo Garden was open seven days a week. Lunch was served from 11:00 A.M. to 2:00 P.M. on weekdays and from 11:30 A.M. to 2:30 P.M. on weekends. Dinner was served from 5:30 to 10:30 P.M. on week days and from 5:30 to 11:30 P.M. on weekends. The restaurant was especially busy from 6:00 to 8:00 P.M. on Friday, Saturday, and Sunday. The majority of customers were the undergraduate and graduate students from the nearby colleges. In addition, local families and college faculty and staff dined there as well. Because it had recently opened, the restaurant had not received a liquor license but customers were permitted to bring their own alcoholic beverages with them.

The Bamboo Garden was decorated with Asian paintings and flowers, a pair of small self-contained waterfalls, and pots of bamboo. Japanese music played softly. Under dim overhead lights, the interior gave an impression of tranquility. The restaurant layout (see Appendix) was in the shape of a "U." Just inside the entrance, on the left was the sushi bar, and on the right several small tables. Back of the sushi area was a coat rack, the host stand, and the cash register. The kitchen, with the office tucked in one corner, occupied about half of the back of the restaurant. The main dining area, consisting of 20 two- and four-person tables, filled the remainder of the restaurant. Space between these tables was relatively narrow, prompting guests to shift their seats to accommodate passage by persons with disabilities.

MANAGEMENT AND STAFF

Sue Lee owned and managed the Bamboo Garden. She had worked in restaurants most of her life. She also owned and managed a small, mostly take-out restaurant called Korean Dining located just a block away from the Bamboo Garden. Korean Dining had existed for nearly eight years and was reputed to be quite successful. Sue Lee, at present, put almost all of her time and energy into Bamboo Garden. She did not speak English very well. Sue Lee's employees agreed that she was a friendly, even kind manager. When Sue Lee wanted something done, she usually made her requests politely with a smile. When the Bamboo Garden first opened, Sue Lee stood at the host's stand to greet and seat guests. After the first month, however, she spent most of her time in the office occupied with bills and purchasing and record-keeping of the restaurant.

Hannah Lee was Sue Lee's daughter. Hannah was a hospitality undergraduate at one of the nearby colleges. She worked at the Bamboo Garden, sometimes as a waitperson and when her mother was absent, as the manager. Because her English was good, Hannah often spoke for Sue Lee to the restaurant's English speaking staff. Her work schedule in the restaurant varied considerably, both due to her class schedule and her course work load. When in the restaurant Hannah was responsive to the questions of the waitpersons, however, she did not make decisions about the menu, pricing, or hiring and never attempted to tell the chefs what to do.

Heon Han and Kim Young were the kitchen chefs. They were both in their mid-thirties, recently emigrated from Korea, who spoke English with difficulty, conversing with each other, Sue Lee, and the sushi chef almost entirely in Korean. They were accomplished cooks and took pride in their work. Their food preparation was swift and consistently very good and they received numerous compliments from customers. Both Heon and Kim had worked at the Bamboo Garden from its opening. They always wore white chef hats and coats on the job. The kitchen was their "territory" and they ran it like they wanted. For example, while Sue Lee had instructed the wait staff to take out soup and salad immediately after an order was taken, Heon and Kim told the wait staff to take dishes out one at a time because guests should not be overwhelmed with too much food in front of them.

Tai Sung, the Sushi chef, was also a middle-aged Korean who spoke English reluctantly. Tai Sung wore a traditional Japanese robe. He was an expert in creating a wide variety of sushi and his work was always prepared very carefully. Tai Sung preferred to take his time with each dish to make it just right; since his sushi was consistently prepared perfectly, guests frequently commented that it was worth the wait.

The wait staff at the Bamboo Garden were all female college students. Most were Caucasian but a few were Chinese-American or Korean-American. The number of waitpersons on the floor varied by shift and day. During the week, one or two worked the lunch shift and three the dinner shift, while on the typically more busy weekends, two or three worked lunches and four or five served dinners. The pool of wait staff, all part-time, varied from 10 to 15 persons. The dress code for the wait staff was all black. There was also one dish person, Jose Gonzales, who was employed full-time. Jose spoke only Spanish.

OPERATIONS

Sue Lee made all of Bamboo Garden's business decisions, such as ordering food and supplies, negotiating with the building owner, hiring the staff, doing all recordkeeping, and mailing checks. When she thought that she needed to acquire more wait staff, Sue Lee would place a "help wanted" sign in the restaurant window. Her hiring criteria were a neat appearance, a "friendly positive personality," and a "bright smile." There were no written policies or rules for the restaurant. Sue Lee believed that the Bamboo Garden would succeed by serving "excellent food in an inviting atmosphere."

When a new waitperson was hired, there was a required three-day unpaid training period. This training was very hands-on. Waitpersons were not instructed in their duties or allowed to shadow anyone. Rather, they learned as they went, waiting on guests, cleaning tables, seating guests, calculating bills, processing payments, etc.

Upon completion of their training, the wait staff performed the same set of activities they had learned, from seating guests to processing payments. No tables or areas were assigned. During slow periods the wait staff filled their time cleaning, folding napkins, refilling soy sauce containers, lighting candles, and so on, as well as socializing a little. When the Bamboo Garden was busy, the wait staff could be observed moving swiftly all over the restaurant. Sometimes the wait staff was unsure which guests had been serviced and which required assistance. They did attempt to help one another by delivering food or drinks, asking if guests needed anything, and responding to guests who indicated they had a question, etc.

When the Bamboo Garden opened, the wait staff were paid a $13.00 hourly wage but received no tips or meals. All tips were given to Sue Lee who distributed them to the chefs. After a few months, the waitpersons complained and Sue Lee changed her waitpersons' compensation practices. At the time, all waitpersons received $3.50 an hour and a proportional share of all tips, collected by and distributed by Sue Lee. Meals were still not provided because Sue Lee believed that a three-hour shift was not long enough to warrant a meal.

APPENDIX: BAMBOO GARDEN LAYOUT

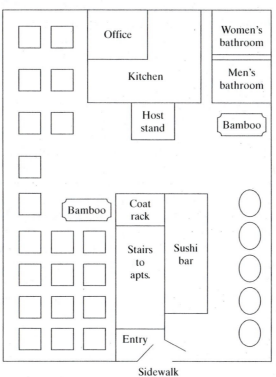

I'm an expert on bars, so I made this an easy place to drink. Customers can get a drink at the bar, circulate without stepping all over everybody's toes, play Pac Man, hit the juke. Like

BAR MANAGER

Why run a bar? If I weren't here, I'd be in someone else's bar from 7:00 'til midnight. This way I just recycle my money. And I always wanted my own bar, so when this one was put on the block, my partners and I came up with the cash. One hundred grand, and we've put a lot into it—about 20 grand—to fix it up. Knocked out some walls. Added this nice cedar bar and tables over there. Expensive? Yeah, but we used scab carpenters—$6.00 an hour—and we laid the floor ourselves. Good idea, this tile floor. Just mop it once when we close up, and that's it.

As for our target market, we shoot for the unmarrieds. They spend money; it don't mean nothing to them. Marrieds, they count every penny and don't travel. Singles, now they come in, spend a few hours, drink with their friends. And they'll drive to get here. If a place is popular, they'll drive 15 to 20 minutes to get here. Marrieds, they stick close to home, so get a place that's "in" with the singles and they'll pack the place every night, drive from all parts south of the city.

We keep this place pleasant, light, and airy. Open and loose, the way they like it. For example, see those potted plants hanging there? Good idea. Cheap, too. Spent less than $50 on all of them. Got some plants on sale at K-Mart and then rigged up some pots for them.

I'm an expert on bars, so I made this an easy place to drink. Customers can get a drink at the bar, circulate without stepping all over everybody's toes, play Pac Man, hit the juke. Like the juke? My idea with these large in-set speakers. Gives good sound without deafening you. And look at the counter here against the window. Nice place to lean on and look out the window—right? That's not half of it. Had the carpenters build this in front of the windows so that people don't go through them in fights. Nice little detail that saved us a window last week.

Fights? They come with the territory. We tell customers to take it outside or we'll call the cops and sign a complaint. Usually that works, but when it's off-duty cops, it can get hairy. We make sure to cut them off the next time they come in. We had some big Irish dudes—packers, loaders, steel men—come in a lot when we opened. You know, they like to drink a lot, arm wrestle, and fight. Geez, you and I like to sit here and talk; these guys like to fight. So they come in, drinking, fighting, and all that. How did we handle it? We didn't. All the other bars on the south side got together and banned them, so they thought we had too. Haven't seen them in a year.

When you run a place like this, you *got* to be here. You might not do a lot, but you've got to be here for whatever comes up. Like that broad who ordered a bourbon sour a few minutes ago. No way! I cut her off up front. She goes wacko with one drink, so we don't serve her. Some people can drink all night and be okay. Others you got to watch; one drink and they're crawling. Usually I leave that up to Kay or Norma. I stay out of the way. If someone is giving them too much grief, I step in and tell the fellow or gal to cool it or leave. That's my management philosophy. Let the employees run the place. They think it's their territory. That's fine with me.

You got to be cool with your employees, too. Take some ragging that you don't have to. Like last night I used Kay's keys to open up the stockroom. Then I took them home by mistake. Kay then has to ride with Mary; rather, she has to drive Mary's car, with Mary and her kid riding. Mary's kid keeps crying that it's too cold with the window down; it has to be down because the defroster doesn't work. So the window has to be up; the windshield fogs; Kay runs a stop sign, and a cop pulls her over. So I got to take some ragging for that. I just bought her a sandwich, and pretty soon we were all laughing.

Mainly I'm okay if I respect their territory. Like I use the pay phone up front and don't go behind the bar. Kay gets irritated if we go behind the bar. Like I said—her territory. My date last week went back behind the bar to make herself a cup of coffee. Kay hit the ceiling. Ragged on me for a week about that. I take it. It's her job; she's honest and good. Stands back there 6:00 'til 2:00 pouring drinks, on her feet all the time. It's dark and smoky, and at times it gets mighty heavy. Then Norma's in as a backup, and they've got to maneuver around each other. It's not a lot of fun, so I give them their space and let them handle their end. The job and customers tell them what to do, dictate the pace. So I stay off their cases.

Had one partner who couldn't keep his hands off the details. He was here from 5:00 'til 2:00 every night. Had to watch everything, money, beer, tables, customers, bouncers. Drinking too much, too. He was here for nine straight hours, making all the decisions, driving everybody nuts, plus himself. So he drank to calm down. We had to buy him out.

Sure, I use the stuff I learned in school, with some modifications. Take the EOQ (Economic Order Quantity) idea. In MBA school, we were taught that you order enough inventory so that carrying costs just equal the cost of lost sales. Well, I figure a more important factor into the model—cost of stolen inventory when you get robbed.

In this business, you also got to know a lot about PR. I always sit back here by the john, where I get to meet everyone. They come in, have a few drinks, and got to go to the john. I watch, see them coming, and call out their names. On a good night I see everybody two or three times.

And I buy free beer for our softball team when they win. Then for Friday or Saturday night I hire one or two of the beefier ones as bouncers. They're going to be here anyway. They think it's cool—drinking beer and being paid for it. If there's big trouble, all their buddies jump in to help; so actually I got seven or eight bouncers on my hands for the price of one or two.

I set this place up to run itself. The girls run the show, pour the drinks, handle the customers, decide what drinks—beer especially—to order. They got an advantage; guys are nicer to them than they are to males. If somebody gets too heavy, I ask him to leave, and if he doesn't, I call the cops. If a guy comes in with a motorcycle jacket on, I tell him to take it off. We don't want that in here. Prostitutes, I just throw them out.

I handle the exceptions, and I help the girls with their personal problems, or if a keg is foaming, say, and they get behind in something. They help me when I'm down. Exceptions on customers I handle—the loud ones, drunks, fights, off-duty cops. Too many off-duty cops in here. I don't like it; they always want some handout. Some are okay, but too many want handouts.

I do the planning, too. Do we add another bar? A kitchen maybe. I think I'll add some food, then maybe we can catch the dinner crowd. We're running a good operation here. Guess I learned how to run a bar by spending a lot of time in them. And friends down here have helped me and given me advice.

Who to target? Unmarrieds. Where to locate? Away from homes and in a place with lots of parking around. Where to buy booze on the side? Friendly liquor stores. See, the IRS looks at our purchases and extrapolates what our sales are. So I buy a few extra cases on the side and don't list them as expenses. For example, from a liter we get about 20 drinks. That's about $40. Helps to buy on the side.

Video games? Don't have to ask about them. The mob puts them in and takes good care of them. Nicest guys in the world. They count the money right here on top of the counter and give us 50 percent. How much of that gets reported to the IRS? Who knows? And they take good care of the machines. One broke last night at 11:30. A guy was here in 15 minutes to fix it. I'm not dumb enough to put in my own machines. They'd break up the place. It's their territory and not worth the risk. Besides, they're nice guys.

And payoffs. I had got all the information when I opened. Whose palm to grease. But that was old times. Can't pay off people anymore. Too bad; now we can't get anything done quickly.

A BELLMAN'S TALE

Glancing through the pile of mail and files his secretary had just handed him, Professor Simms saw the transcript from his recent talk with Steve Harlow. Seeing the transcript reminded Simms that Steve had an appointment with him early next week.

Steve Harlow was a soon-to-graduate senior majoring in hospitality finance. He had taken a management course with Professor Simms in his junior year, a course in which cases were discussed every other class meeting. Steve, Simms recalled, had been an average student until about the two-thirds point in that course when he had suddenly become very attentive and vocal. Simms had had his students write a paper in which they applied some ideas about organization and management to their personal lives. Steve elected to write about his recent marriage and had acquired several useful insights. After the course Steve had occasionally dropped by Simms' office to chat about career matters, their joint passion of fly-fishing, and Steve's experiences as president of the student finance club.

Professor Simms had been pleasantly surprised the week before, therefore, when Steve had come to his office asking if they might talk about Steve's job as a bellman at Dr. Brown's Inn located a few blocks from campus. Steve had said that he thought there might be a case in that experience, but mostly he just wanted to understand it better. Simms had suggested that he record the conversation, get it transcribed, and then they could later make sense of it, sort of like a case. Steve agreed. The tape recorder was started, and Professor Simms lit his pipe while Steve had begun to talk.

As Professor Simms began to read the transcript (see Exhibit 1), he realized what he should do in preparation for Steve's next visit. He should do what he would encourage Steve to do. First, let the transcript information suggest ideas; second, use those ideas to see related information, and, third, see those ideas as components of conceptual frameworks or models and let those guide the discovery of other information needed to fully understand the situation. Picking up a pencil Simms began to read the transcript again, numbering the paragraphs, underlining bits of information, and jotting idea words in the margin.

"To begin with there were several people who were extremely influential in my indoctrination. The first was Tom, a young bellman who enjoyed his job at Dr. Brown's. He had had one year of college but felt that this was a much better job than he could obtain any place else. He was impressed by the amount of financial benefits he received and was quite involved with the rest of the people working in other parts of the hotel. He played a lot of golf with them and afterwards drank with them, partied, and had a good time. He was the first to approach me to tell me about taking care of the bell captains or the service manager or anybody else there at the inn. His feeling was that if a bellman were to take care of Mr. Gates, the service manager, then everything else would be taken care of, and this is quite different from what some of the bell captains thought. A bell captain like J.B. Shrews would approach me seriously and, in kind of a joking manner, remind me to take care of the bell captains. His feelings were that they sat here on the bench all day and let the bellmen have the good bells. He was more full of bullshit and laziness than anything else. He himself had to give up some of his earnings to Mr. Gates.

"Mr. Hicks was another bell captain. He at first refused to take any money from me when I was working as a limousine driver because he felt I wasn't making enough to warrant taking the full amount. When I became a bellman, his immediate approach to me was that I had to pay an initiation fee or sort of go through a bellman's school, which actually involved no learning but it meant that I had to pay some each month to him and he would share it with the other bell captains. He quit a job as a salesperson at another major downtown hotel to become a bell captain at Dr. Brown's Inn. He felt that he could receive more money in his present position and that he wouldn't have to travel and be away from his family as much. This was important in his life. When he did start taking money from me when I was a bellman, it was only to get off on days that I wanted to trade, and $5 was the standard fee. Also, J.B. would take this amount as a standard. Later on, when I had worked there for several months, J.B. met some friends of my grandparents in Palo Alto and they explained to him that my grandparents were very wealthy people, according to them, and they wondered what I was doing working in such a position. After this he came back and raised the price for my days off to $1 an hour, and this sort of ruined the impression that I had tried to create, and in fact had been creating, that I was just a hungry student trying to make enough money to support my wife and child.

"One of the old men there, Patton, had been working as a bellman all his life and had worked at all sorts of hotels. Back in the period when bootlegging was quite common he often made $200 or $300 a night. He never gave up any money to the bell captains and consequently he never got other than his regular day off.

"Stubby, another older bellman with much experience, thought that the bell captains had the wrong way of letting people off—they let them off on their ability or their desire to pay rather than off on the basis of who had been off lately. This whole operation is contrasted against the other major downtown hotels where most of the people worked before Dr. Brown's Inn opened. Down there all the bellmen would line up before they would go on duty. The bell captain would walk behind them and inspect. Then, as he would walk in front inspecting them, each man would hand the bell captain $1. On special occasions such as the Texas-Oklahoma football weekend, they would have to hand him $5 or $10. This would be when they went on duty and when they came off duty.

"Mr. Gates, the service manager, is a quiet, calm, smooth operator and very intelligent and sensitive to what most of his employees want. If a bellman wanted something done the best thing to do was to go to Mr. Gates. If my schedule changed where I wouldn't be able to go to work for a couple of days, or at least I would be late and needed one extra night off, I had to go to Mr. Gates and take care of him. He would make it all right with the other bell captains. His approach to getting money was to just take care of us every once in a while—to sort of remind us in a more joking manner, but he did expect it.

"Another old-time bellman working at Dr. Brown's Inn was Phil. Phil gave up money occasionally to get off and also took care of the bell captains in other instances. He had a free hand in just about whatever he wanted to do. If his outside interests were demanding of this time, the bell captains would see that he got time off. In his operations, Phil needed to use the telephone quite a bit and would often have people call him there at work at the bell captain's phone. This was all taken good-naturedly, and we often answered the phone with, 'Phil's answering service.' After a while, about three or four months into the football season, the bell captains got tired of it, and started keeping track of how many calls Phil got in a night. Nothing really ever became of it but they didn't appreciate him using the phone quite as much as he had been.

"Phil was also good if someone would not tip you, or especially when I was a limousine driver, I would stand up at the front of the desk and wait for my passengers to tip me after I carried their bags in for them. Often, it looked like they wouldn't. Phil would come up and comment, 'That's all right, he makes $1 an hour. He's right here.' When someone else would start to walk away carrying their own bags, he would walk up behind them and say, 'Ah, there goes another ex-bellman,' and he had an amusing way of insulting people where they would take action and tip someone without really being offended, sort of a rare talent in that respect. Actually, his actions may not have been so offending as they reminded people that he did work on tips. I don't think that people realized that we got just $3 an hour and were solely dependent on them.

"When I first started taking care of the bell captains, I was rather hesitant and had the feeling that they made this attempt to get me to give them money, trying to develop a more or less sucker out of me or someone who would do this regularly for them. It was only after I had been there quite a while that I realized that everybody else was taking care of them and that I would make some difference in the way things were. Often I would be called on before I started paying, 'to take a last' which means going out to change the signs in front of the hotel or deliver packages to someone's room when they weren't there and there was no prospect of receiving money from them, or something like this. After I started really taking care of the bell captains, things were running a little more fairly.

"J.B. had a favorite trick in that he would make someone work on their regular day off and then later in the week when things would be slower he would make them pay to get a day off that week. Hicks, another bell captain, wouldn't do this. He would try to be fair about things like this. Once on my day off (it was the first day off I had had in a couple of weeks), I wasn't real sure if

(EXHIBIT 1 *continiued*)

he wanted me to take it or not, so I called in about an hour after I was supposed to be there to make sure that everything was going okay and see if they needed some more help. I didn't realize it at the time but this was something that he really appreciated. He said it quite a bit later. I remember I made a mistake one night with Hicks. He told me to have my shoes shined and I said, 'Okay, I'll have them shined right away.' He said, 'You'll have them shined?' I said, 'Yes, sir.' He then lectured me on how much better it would be for me to shine my own shoes and I wasn't too good to do this. This was after my grandparents' friends from Palo Alto had already talked to him. I not only shined my own shoes but in that particular instance was going to go down to the barbershop in the basement to have them shined.

"Whenever we would take care of J.B. and Hicks would hear of it, he would of course want to be taken care of himself. Often we would buy J.B. a pint of whiskey and expect to be let off early for the next week. Say we usually had to work until 11:00 or so, sometimes stay over until the crowds had quieted down at maybe 12:00 or 12:30. Well, if we brought him a pint of whiskey he might let us off at 10:30 before the night bell captain got there. Often, I'm afraid, Hicks was disappointed on that score.

"J.B. was always the greedy one, anxious for all sorts of money. During the Texas-Oklahoma weekend when seats to the game were at a premium, he bought some tickets from the doorman, assuming of course that they were both together. When he tried to sell them for about twice the price that he had paid for them, which was quite high, he found out that they were in opposite sides of the end zone. This sort of upset him for a while. He tried to get his money back from the doorman who refused.

"Stubby was a good bellman when he was working. He was a very smooth operator and knew how to handle people well, but he was an alcoholic and about two or three times a year he would take off for a week or longer and just stay drunk the whole time. He was quite wealthy as his parents had left him a farm which had sold for a good deal of money. One time he came by in a pickup (that he had gone out and paid for in cash) with a chauffeur driving him. He had been drinking for about a month this time and his teeth were black. Everybody went out and talked to him and told him to hurry up and come back. About a week after that he showed up at work as if he had never missed a day. He never talked about his experiences or anything else. He just worked and joked along with the rest of us.

"Everybody showed a good deal of interest in the studying I did around there. Often at night I would try to do my homework in the back room where everybody smoked and drank every once in a while. They were always trying to learn what I was doing, what I wanted to do, and what the practical applications of my studies were. They seemed very concerned with this and had the general feeling that more can be learned in the real world of business, in contact with people, than in school. This is probably true for them as they would see college graduates coming out making quite a bit less than they would. It was always the butt of humor."

EXHIBIT 1

BETA BETA FRATERNITY

Tom Carson interrupted unpacking his suitcase and sat on his bed. The fraternity, at 3:00 P.M., was quiet. Tom looked around his room, a single since he was a senior and the house steward. He was a day late in returning from spring break and had lots of schoolwork to do and he needed to call his coach. He also guessed that his girlfriend Debbie would expect to see him after her Chemistry Lab. Tom found it hard to concentrate on all that he should be doing; his mind was whirling about what he had just learned about the cook's replacement. "That damn Maureen," Tom thought, "And who in the hell is Kevin?" Sighing, Tom leaned back on the bed. "What a mess. How could it have happened? What should I do?" Tom began to reminisce.

RUMOR AND REALITY

Waiting for his pack and suitcase to come out on the baggage carousel, Tom felt a hand on his shoulder and heard George, a fraternity brother, say, "Hi guy, how are they hanging? I almost didn't come home from Fort Meyers. It was my kind of place—sun, babes, and beer every day. It's going to be hard getting back into the old grind." Tom smiled and nodded. He had spent most of his break interviewing for a job after graduation. He said, "Yeah. What's the news at the house?" George laughed. "I guess you haven't heard; Maureen's quit. I hope there's dinner tonight." Tom blinked. As Beta Beta's Steward, one of his main duties was to manage the kitchen, food purchasing, and, of course, the cook. Seeing Tom's reaction, George went on, "Well maybe it's just a rumor. I also heard we have a guy cook now."

As Tom walked up the steps of the Beta Beta house, two brothers came out. Tom asked about the rumor about Maureen and was told it was true. At that very moment, a car backed out to the driveway of the fraternity next door. Maureen was at the wheel. Seeing Tom she pulled her car back up the driveway out of sight.

Dropping his luggage in the front hall, Tom reached for his mail. On top was a handwritten letter dated five days previously. It read,

---

Dear Tom:

I have made a decision to except a position offered to me elsewhere, therefore I won't be returning after spring break. I'm sorry to do this, however, I feel this is best for me. I don't feel I have been appreciated, and have received the cold shoulder for the last few weeks. I have been expected to do duties that really should be those of the brotherhood. (Pots, dishes, clean up, mopping the floors, etc.). S.C. will be sending you resumes of acceptable chefs and I will be leaving my keys with them. I wish you only the best.

Very Truly Yours,
Maureen

Feeling stunned, Tom only slowly became aware of the whistling coming from the kitchen. Going there to investigate, he saw a man not much older than himself wearing a long white apron working at the stove. Tom said, "Who are you?" Turning with a wide grin the man replied, "I'm Kevin. But don't ask, there's no snacks. Save your appetite for dinner. It'll be really tasty tonight, if you like chowder, slaw, stuffed flounder and pie and ice cream." Tom opened his mouth and shut it. The kitchen smelled wonderful, and wasn't that fresh baked bread on the counter? Tom smiled, backed out of the kitchen, and headed upstairs to his room.

COOKS

Six years ago, Jackie and Anna were Beta Beta's cooks. Jackie made lunch and Anna cooked dinner. Their shifts overlapped and they helped one another frequently. They became best of friends. Over time, however, the quality of food steadily became poorer and complaints from the brothers increased. One evening the house president found cigarette ashes in his stew. Soon thereafter a brother saw Anna drop a scoop of ice cream on the floor and then put it in a dish to be served. These and other similar incidents finally prompted a special house meeting at which it was decided to fire Anna. Jackie stayed on as the full-time cook. For awhile meals were tasty and on time. After a year or so, however, more and more of the meals came out of cans and jello was the dessert at least half the time. Jackie could be found drinking coffee, reading the paper, and talking to her friends on the telephone almost anytime during the day. The Steward at that time, Mike, also determined that Jackie had for some time been getting a kickback from the food purveyor as well as taking kitchen supplies and food home regularly. Jackie's contract was not renewed for the following year.

That summer, John, the new Steward, had the responsibility of finding a new cook. Within a week, John found Maureen. Maureen was a very experienced cook. She had just finished a three-year position as cook at a prominent campus sorority. She was in her late fifties, widowed, with two grown children—one who lived with Maureen along with her two children. Maureen had lived in the town since her own children had been born. John used to say that Maureen reminded him of his aunt. Cautious because of Jackie, John called the house Steward at the sorority Maureen had worked for and asked why she had left. He was told that they believed that Maureen was skimming off the kitchen budget and stealing supplies but couldn't prove it. John decided to give Maureen the benefit of the doubt and hired her.

Maureen started cooking at Beta Beta in mid-August last year when some of the brothers gathered to do some annual painting and yard work in anticipation of the fall semester and rush week. After Anna and Jackie, hopes for Maureen's first dinner were modest; however, the brothers were impressed. The entrée was great, and the dessert even better. And, to everyone's surprise, meals remained tasty the rest of the semester. The food was so good that often one or more brothers would help Maureen clean up after dinner. John was relieved. His relationship with Maureen, however, puzzled him. She seemed hypersensitive to him, viewing any suggested change in procedure as criticism and would not tell him of any kitchen-related problems unless he probed.

TOM'S TURN

With the start of the spring semester, Tom was elected to be Steward. As there was nothing written down about the Steward's responsibilities, for the first few weeks Tom often went to John for advice. Since the meals continued to be good and Maureen didn't initiate any conversations with him, Tom only occasionally talked with her. A few times Maureen told John about her kitchen problems and John relayed them to Tom who would do whatever was necessitated.

In the third week of February, Maureen left a note for Tom that she needed to speak with him. The cook at the fraternity right next door had been arrested, and Maureen had agreed to fill in as their cook. She assured Tom that she could do this in addition to her Beta Beta job and that this was a temporary situation of only two or three weeks until a replacement could be hired. Tom acquiesced but told Maureen that he would ask her to stop cooking next door if Beta Beta's food quality declined.

Three weeks later at the weekly Monday evening chapter meeting, Tom got an earful. Brother after brother complained about the poor food, seemingly getting poorer every day. They told Tom that Maureen was hardly ever around, the kitchen ran out of some drinks and food, dishes, cutlery and cooking utensils weren't clean, she didn't take out the garbage daily, and on and on. The most frequent complaint was about eating off paper plates and drinking out of paper cups. The house treasurer added that those paper supplies "cost a bundle." After the meeting, Tom went upstairs to the kitchen but Maureen had already left.

Tom's interview schedule for spring break was so full that he left a day later. He thought that by the time the break was over that the neighboring fraternity would surely have replaced their cook, Maureen would be rested up, and everything would be back to normal for the rest of the semester. Before he left, Tom did leave a note for Maureen saying he was leaving and how he might be contacted. In addition he noted that if she had any questions or concerns that she should talk with John, the previous Steward. On his last class day, Thursday, John approached Maureen just after lunch during clean up. He told her that "all the brothers think that your meals are slipping and it's time you did right by them!" Maureen's eyes teared but she said nothing.

KEVIN

Beta Beta's recent past president, Will, remained in residence during the Spring Break. One day he noticed Maureen collecting her personal things in the kitchen and asked her where she was going. She told Will she was quitting, had just put a letter in Tom's mailbox, and was leaving as soon as she could. Will, unable to contact Tom, decided that immediate action was required. He got in his car and went to the Hospitality School on campus. Soon locating a Food's instructor, Will outlined Beta Beta's plight and asked how he might contact available cooks. To his surprise and delight the Food's instructor reached for his telephone. Within just a few calls, Will was in contact with Kevin Jacobson a recent graduate of the Culinary Institute of America. After listening to Kevin explain his experience and say he could begin in three days, Will outlined the job (including an alumni banquet at the end of the first week after spring break) and offered Kevin the position as Beta Beta's cook. Kevin accepted, and asked Will to find him a room.

BOSNIAN RESETTLEMENT (A)

Although he was happy to be eating someplace other than at the hotel today, and he had to admit the food was very good, Gordon was bothered by his thoughts. Should he or shouldn't he get involved? He wasn't at the World Relief luncheon in an official capacity, although

Hotel Inter-Continental Chicago could potentially stand to benefit from his activity. Gordon truly believed that World Relief's work with the Bosnian resettlement program was the right thing to do.

The horrors the Bosnian people were facing were tremendous. He wondered what it must be like to go to work one day and come back and find your entire community has been blown apart. Then the next thing you know some relief workers are putting you on a bus and taking you to the airport, and bang!—you're in America. The World Relief speaker was explaining that in some cases it literally happened that quickly.

Gordon knew the resettlement program could use all the help it could get. Plus it would be a great humanitarian gesture on behalf of the hotel if he offered to take Bosnian placements. The speaker was asking anyone interested in helping World Relief to drop off his or her business card on the way out. As Director of Human Resources, and having been at the property since it opened, Gordon knew the history of the hotel and the labor supply fluctuations it faced. Turnover in housekeeping was high, between 50 and 60 percent, and he was having increasing difficulty filling the positions. So why not bring some Bosnians in? Gordon began to reach for his business card and then hesitated. Even though he was empowered to make the decision and he knew Mr. Rice, the General Manager, would back him up, Gordon was still ambivalent about whether or not he should get involved, and even more importantly, whether he should get the hotel involved.

GORDON SUTHERLAND

Gordon hadn't planned on a career in human resources and the hotel business; he just seemed to fall into it. He went to school for architectural engineering and was happy to land a job with an engineering company upon graduation. Within a year, Gordon was offered a position to recruit and train engineers. He accepted the position only because he would then know how personnel officers worked and how to get jobs in the future. Having accepted the job, he quickly fell in love with human resources and had been in it ever since.

Gordon eventually left the company because it was in financial trouble and he knew it. His brother had an interior design and carpet installation business and he'd had wanted Gordon to go into business with him. They worked together for about a year, but Gordon missed human resources, so he began looking at ads in the newspaper and saw one for a benefits position at Westin Hotels. He was familiar with training, recruitment, and employment from the engineering company, but he didn't know the benefits side of human resources. He responded to the ad anyway and said "Look, even without benefits experience, I'm very good." But, the Westin was looking for someone who would meet certain criteria and according to Gordon, they thought he was crazy for applying. However, within two weeks Westin called him back and offered him the job.

After working at the Westin-Chicago, Gordon helped open the Westin-O'Hare, went back to the Westin-Chicago as Director of Human Resources, and then was asked to look at opening the Swan Hotel in Orlando—a Westin property. At about this time, Inter-Continental Hotels & Resorts (ICH&R) contacted him about opening two hotels in Chicago. Gordon had received a recommendation from a friend previously with Westin but who was now at the Inter-Continental corporate office. Since Gordon had never actually managed human resources for two hotels before, he thought it would be exciting. He accepted the position, not fully aware of the challenges that lie ahead.

INTER-CONTINENTAL HOTELS & RESORTS

Established in 1946 as a subsidiary of Pan American World Airways, ICH&R managed Hotel Inter-Continental properties, 4- and 5-star hotels located in business centers around the world; Forum Hotels, established in 1972, featuring the same 4-star level of service as Hotel Inter-Continental properties, but differing in room size, amenities, and furnishings; and Global Partner hotels, established in 1993. Global Partners were first-class small hotel chains or independent properties in other cities that complemented the Inter-Continental or Forum brands and were marketed, sold, and provided the same reservations services as Inter-Continental and Forum Hotels. However, Global Partners retained their independent status and received no management, financial, or franchise support. The program offered ICH&R representation in strategic locations and the advantages of franchising without a franchise.

ICH&R was purchased by Saison, a Japanese retailing and travel conglomerate in 1988, from Grand Metropolitan, a leading UK leisure services group who owned the hotel company for six years. In 1990, the company was ranked fifth among hotel companies in terms of geographical spread, and in 1994, they opened 29 new hotels. In 1996, Inter-Continental Hotels and Resorts managed more than 170 hotels in 67 countries.

TWO HOTELS, ONE COMPANY

In the late 1980s, ICH&R acquired two connecting properties in Chicago. What was to become the South Tower of Hotel Inter-Continental Chicago in March 1990, was originally constructed in 1929 as the exclusive Medinah Athletic Club for members of the Shriner Masonic Order. It was lavishly adorned with painted ceilings, sweeping balustrade staircases, arched entries, inlays of marble, intricately detailed bronze and brass highlighting, and masterpiece murals and friezes. The Medinah Athletic Club housed a running track, gymnasium, boxing ring, bowling alley, and its renowned Junior Olympic size mosaic-tiled swimming pool located on the fourteenth floor and accented by a two and one-half story vaulted ceiling. At the time, no one had ever built a pool that high up in a building. Due to its enormous weight, the pool was held up by a bridge girder.

The beautiful building had to be sold when the Athletic Club went bankrupt within five years of opening due to the stock market crash. Over the years, the Club had become an apartment building as well as various hotels. It even sat empty for a few years. In the 1960s, Sheraton took possession of it and then Radisson. It was at this time that the North Tower was added, providing 500 additional rooms to the 300 rooms in the South Tower.

The South Tower, having been built in 1929, had become shabby over the years, and the different hotel companies that occupied the once majestic Athletic Club chose to cover up rather than repair the lavish appointments. Murals and frescos were painted over; dropped, false ceilings covered painstakingly painted ceilings; and drywall and paint covered arched entries and entire rooms. When the North and South Towers were acquired by ICH&R in the late 1980s, the company took great strides to restore the building's splendor by bringing in Lido Lippi, an artist who worked on the restoration of the Sistine Chapel, along with the crew who restored the Vatican.

This was not ICH&R's first restoration. Over the past decade, the company had restored 20 buildings. Prior to opening each hotel, the company conducted extensive studies to ensure that each property's architecture and design harmonized with and reflected the cultural heritage of the host country and local area. ICH&R thought there was no better way to reflect the Chicago flavor than to restore a truly historic Chicago treasure.

The rooms in the North Tower were too small to meet Inter-Continental 4-star standards. Rather than undergo the enormous and expensive redesign of rooms, and since already being deep into the restoration of the South Tower, the company decided to make the North Tower a 3-star, business class, Forum Hotel. Although Forum Hotels featured the same level of service as Hotel Inter-Continental properties, they typically had smaller rooms, simpler décor and an informal atmosphere. The Forum Hotel was opened in October, 1989, and five months later Hotel Inter-Continental Chicago opened in March, 1990.

According to Gordon Sutherland, operating the two hotels was a challenge:

> Not so much for the employees as it was the guests . . . I think the most confusing part was for the guests and for the sales department. You had a combination of almost 850 rooms. One was 300+, the other was 500+, so if a group needs 600 rooms you could actually take them, but now you have to explain, there's two hotels, with two front desks, but it's really the same location, it's really one company, and it was really kind of confusing. No one had ever done this concept before so we didn't really know a lot. We felt our way thorough it. We opened the Forum first and pre-opening is a lot different than when a hotel is actually operating, so we opened the Forum and while we're trying the service and staff of that hotel and training the employees, now I have a second hotel to open. So, now we start a whole mass recruitment process for the second hotel while running the first hotel.
>
> But, for the most part it worked pretty well. I think some of the things we learned through evolution. We had two different front desks, two different uniforms and so when one hotel got very busy and the other wasn't, we'd have the agents run down, change clothes, get into the other hotel's uniform and go to the other front desk and check in guests. Then, after a while we realized that we probably should have gotten the same uniforms, then employees could just go back and forth. So, a lot of things kind of happened as time went on.

ICH&R was very decentralized and their philosophy was to allow each hotel to operate with minimal corporate intervention. Decisions at the property level were based on the regional area. Because of the relatively few corporate international guidelines or standard policies and procedures, Gordon and the rest of the management staff were permitted to be very creative and learn as they went along.

In the beginning, the Forum property did well, charging $69 a room, an incredibly low rate on ritzy Michigan Avenue. Hotel Inter-Continental Chicago, however, staggered along with other luxury hotel properties due to the recession. After approximately two years, the economy began to recover and guests were staying in the Hotel Inter-Continental Chicago property (the South Tower) and the Forum property (the North Tower) was half empty.

Although the Forum room size had been considered too small for ICH&R standards, the decision was made to upgrade the North Tower rooms with better furnishings and marble bathrooms. Additional amenities were added as well, and in August 1994 the renovation was completed, and the rooms in what was the Forum Hotel were now considered standard rooms in the Hotel Inter-Continental Chicago. No longer any confusion for the guests, the sales department, and the other employees.

And somehow they all got through it, Gordon thought. Fortunately for him, Gordon had been in the city and the hotel business for so long that he was able to put together a good management team. Since ICH&R was not well represented in the U.S. market, when they opened the Chicago property, they brought in people from Westin, Hyatt, Marriott, and Inter-Continental international properties—a very diverse group in terms of hoteliers. Gordon's Director of Training, Chris Taylor, had come from the Westin where she had worked with Gordon for many years. And she had stuck through it all at the Inter-Con, and to his benefit, many of the management team were still there. Even turnover in other areas of the hotel was low (42 percent) compared to other hotels in the area. The laundry staff was almost the same as had opened the hotel in 1989, almost six years ago, and considering the hot and humid working conditions, it was an accomplishment to keep staff in that department. Turnover was also low in the accounting department, as it was among the secretarial staff, but in housekeeping it was still high.

And now he had an opportunity to do something about it by bringing in Bosnian placements to work, possibly in the housekeeping department. But it was a risk.

BOSNIAN RESETTLEMENT (B)

As Gordon Sutherland handed his business card to the World Relief Bosnian Resettlement coordinator, he suddenly wondered what he was getting himself into. He thought to himself, "You just don't go out and hire a bunch of Bosnian people who don't speak English and aren't familiar with the American culture and expect everything to work fine." It would be an incredible investment in terms of training and effort. "And what do I know about the Bosnian culture?" Gordon thought. "How am I going to help these people make a transition from a war-torn country? What problems are we going to face?"

As Gordon Sutherland thought about the World Relief Bosnian Resettlement program and the Bosnians he had decided to hire, he suddenly had a flashback to a similar situation. Two years ago Gordon had attended another of the World Relief's luncheons, this time for the Tibetan resettlement program, and had agreed to the placement of Tibetans in the hotel. He thought everything was working out wonderfully until one of the Tibetans left for Minnesota for religious reasons and within a matter of two or three months, all the other Tibetan placements had followed. They had been at the hotel for less than a year. What a disappointment that had been.

After all that preparation, after all that training, after all that translating, after all those English-as-a-second-language classes, after all of that, the Tibetans had left. Now he had to consider what to do with the Bosnians. Would the hotel make an investment in training and transition just to have them leave again? And what if they did leave? Would it be any worse than what was happening now with turnover?

Gordon believed that Americans were getting to the point where they didn't want to do anything, particularly the physical kind of work involved in housekeeping. People from other countries seemed to have a stronger work ethic, and because productivity was so important, he felt it was a good economic decision as well as humanitarian decision to go after a work force that he thought would be more stable. He would gladly accept the difficulties in terms of language skills in order to get employees with a good work ethic who would produce.

Hiring competent and motivated employees, or members as they were called at Hotel Inter-Continental, was one of Gordon's most important duties. And he took it seriously. His philosophy communicated this value:

> I tell a lot of managers that if one day all of the managers got upset with the company and walked out, the company would still operate. But, if all the employees got up and walked out, we'd shut down. My philosophy is that the people who really make this thing happen are the employees, not the managers. Our role is more of a coaching, empowering kind of role. And, that philosophy has extended . . . I mean, we practice what we preach. The healthcare benefits are identical for the managers and for the employees. And, those are the people who really make it happen. So, we look for managers that believe that if they take care of their staff, their staff will take care of the guests. And, the managers who have a problem with that have a very difficult time here.

He couldn't help but remember the Tibetans and how they had left. Although the Tibetans said they were leaving for religious reasons, Gordon could not help but wonder whether he could have prevented them from leaving. Would the same thing happen with the Bosnians he decided to hire? What if they left in a couple of months? Had he made the right decision? Oh well, Gordon thought, he didn't want to second guess himself now. To him, life was a gamble, and with the luck he had been having with Americans, why not take a chance?

BOSNIAN RESETTLEMENT (C)

Gordon wondered how he was going to convince Chris Taylor, the Director of Training, that the Bosnian placements in housekeeping were worth the risk. Although she thought hiring Bosnian refugees was a good idea, she was still concerned. Some of the Bosnians were teachers, lawyers, and doctors, and Chris was afraid that once they learned English they would leave the hotel for other employment.

Gordon tried to explain.

> Yeah, yeah, but you know that's okay because housekeeping is traditionally the high turnover area in this industry anyway, and I don't think that this group, because they have a pretty good background, is going to leave until they really understand the language. So, if we lose them in 12–18 months, that's okay. But, I hope that we'll lose some of them to other departments. In the meantime, it's stabilized the turnover in housekeeping, so we're okay.

It seemed like years ago when Gordon was at the luncheon for World Relief. He wondered why he had hesitated about giving his business card. Turnover in some areas of the hotel had been high, like in the restaurants, because the servers they hired were from schools and depending on semesters and graduations, the hotel lost them. And, in housekeeping, yes, in housekeeping, turnover had been very high. But with the influx of Bosnians they had decided to hire, turnover in housekeeping had been reduced quite a bit. The department had been transformed from one that was predominantly African-American and Hispanic to predominantly Bosnian. There had been some complications with the Bosnians not speaking English, so English-as-a-second-language (ESL) classes were started, but overall, Gordon felt the program had worked out pretty well.

Of course, bringing the Bosnians in hadn't been easy. The kind of training the Bosnians needed was costly to provide, so Gordon had made the hiring contingent on getting some support from World Relief. Gordon summed it up this way:

> What we did was, we said we're willing to work with you [World Relief] and we have positions for the people resettling here. However, here's our criteria if we want to work together. So we made it clear that if you're going to work with us, then we want you here for the initial two week training program; we want you to understand. And, we had the replacement counselors come in and we showed them the work area, what the company's expectations were, and job descriptions. So, they knew what our philosophy was, how the building was laid out, what the rooms looked like. They understood exactly what was what. Then, during the first training phases the counselors were here translating during training. We gave them our written materials and they translated for the Bosnians.

The Bosnians were hired 10 to 20 at a time, and one or two placement counselors would come every time a group was hired. Gordon remembered fondly the orientation for the first group of Bosnians. He remembered speaking to them, smiling and talking, and then pausing, and the translator would speak and the Bosnians would respond. The orientation just went on forever and ever it had seemed like to Gordon. The first training classes were mostly show and not tell because of the language situation. But they picked it up. And it was neat, he thought, really, it was a good feeling.

Of course there were some problems that arose when a Bosnian housekeeper was in a room cleaning and the guest returned. Gordon hadn't fully anticipated the degree to which this would cause problems, so he immediately accelerated the ESL classes. He looked to recruit a Bosnian supervisor who was bilingual as well. Much to his delight, two of the Bosnian room attendants had excelled in their English language classes and consequently, had become quite fluent. In addition to the bilingual supervisor he hired, Gordon now had three people who worked with the Bosnians.

Gordon certainly hadn't anticipated the problem associated with cultural differences in terms of personal hygiene issues either. According to him, "there were many challenges in the beginning." The Bosnians found that Americans were obsessed with body cleanliness, since in their culture, and in many others, someone else's smell was not offensive. However, guests at the hotel did not feel the same way, so Gordon quickly brought in the World Relief placement counselors and had them communicate the problem to the Bosnians. For the first few groups of Bosnians hired, personal hygiene continued to be an issue. But even that had changed as the Bosnians got indoctrinated into the United States and its culture.

The first group of Bosnians employed at the hotel went back to their new community in Chicago and began talking to other Bosnians about the hotel and the work. They were, for all intents and purposes, training their friends at home over the dinner table and over cocktails. By the time their friends were hired by the hotel, they already knew what to expect when they started their jobs. In addition, the newly hired employees would be helped by their Bosnian friends who had been working at the hotel for awhile. Gordon felt the hiring and transition worked well.

The number of Bosnians in the housekeeping department had risen to 70 out of a total staff of 135. Of the remaining housekeepers, the next largest group were Hispanic, African-American, and then a mix of white, African, a little bit of Vietnamese, and Chinese. Gordon liked the mix of people and was careful to maintain cultural diversity. He didn't want the house-keeping department to become 100 percent Bosnians because he feared the perception that being Bosnian was a criterion to get into the department. Plus he feared culture clashes such as what happened with the incentive program in housekeeping. Gordon explained it as follows:

> We have an incentive program in housekeeping called Star Achievers, where the room attendants are graded on their performance for the cleanliness of the room. We just instituted this program about 3 or 4 months ago, and there's an incentive that room attendants can make a certain amount of money per hour. Over the course of a month, if their inspections are 90% or higher, they get a 27¢ per hour increase and that increase remains in effect until their ratings drop below 90%, then it goes back to the regular rate of pay. And, for the first group of star achiev-ers, I think it was 5 out of 6 were Bosnian. And then there were some comments about that, oh, it's unfair treatment, the Bosnians are getting all the raises. But, the supervisors doing the grading of the rooms were non-Bosnian.

Other hotels in the downtown Chicago area soon heard of Hotel Inter-Continental Chicago's success with the Bosnian resettlement program and decided to take Bosnian placements as well. Their results, however, did not match the success at the Inter-Continental. Gordon hypothesized about why the other hotel's efforts to hire Bosnians turned out to be disasters:

> I think the difference is, they didn't give them support systems that were needed. To do something like that, you really have to have strong support systems. You need to have a good relationship with the agency and make sure those placement people are involved with the day to day training in the beginning. English-as-a-second-language classes are to start immediately as a pre-requisite to hire. Some of the other hotels had found out that we were successful and wanted to get on the band wagon and they just hired a bunch [of Bosnians] and it didn't work.

Although he had to admit the program wasn't without its difficulties, Gordon was quite pleased with the results of the Bosnian resettlement program at the hotel. Not only was it a great humanitarian gesture on behalf of the company to help the resettlement of people who had gone through such a traumatic experience, but at the same time, it was also beneficial to the company. He commented:

> What you really need to see now is the difference between when the first group of Bosnians came in and now when you walk through the halls you hear them say "Hi, Mr. Rice. How are you?" I mean, that is so neat to see. We haven't promoted any out of housekeeping, but we know we're just months away from the first group being promoted to some higher level positions, possibly in banquets, room service, valet, or the laundry area.

THE BOX TREE*

This was such an unbelievable time, Gila Baruch thought. She made it through difficulties she could not even envision. As the new owner of the Box Tree restaurant and hotel, she had settled the longest restaurant/hotel strike in New York City's history. Now it was time to take the next step. Tremendous challenges were still ahead. After more than four years of bitterness, bad blood, and raucous picketing, she had no choice but to take back the seven strikers who wanted to return. She had vivid memories of these same people hurling insults at customers as they tried to cross the picket line to dine. The memories of the dirty tactics they used to undermine the restaurant were still very fresh for her and those who crossed the picket line to work. Was she supposed to pretend that nothing ever happened? How would the replacement workers who helped her get through the strike feel about working with the former strikers? What could she do to get them all pulling together to reclaim the reputation the Box Tree once had? The restaurant, and her investment in it, which included over four years of time and energy devoted to managing the restaurant through the strike, depended on it.

THE RESTAURANT

The Box Tree was a fine dining restaurant and hotel located on 49th Street in the shadow of the United Nations building. When its workers went out on strike in December 1993, the Box Tree had been in existence for 20 years. Known for its five-course prix fixe meals, priced at $86 per person without beverages, tax, or tip, the Box Tree was anything but typical in terms of its concept, service, and décor.

With only eight tables and twenty seats in the main dining area, the restaurant was quite intimate. A few steps down from street level, one entered a foyer/reception area. In addition to the podium where the reservation book and phone were located, there was a seating area with several overstuffed armchairs situated around a fireplace. The entire first floor, consisting of the reception area, a bar/lounge area used for dinner on busy nights, and the main dining room, had walls painted a dark evergreen. The ceiling was steel blue, and the wainscoting was gold. All the rooms were filled with antiques, mostly of dark, rich woods, and each had a working fireplace. The bar, which was stunning, was mahogany and was replete with sterling silver service ware.

Upstairs, through the lounge area, were three private dining rooms. Each room had a working fireplace and distinctive decoration. The "music room" was at the head of the stairs on the right, and seated up to 14 people. The music room was quite formal and had a long, rectangular table. To the left of the landing was the "blue room" which accommodated 12 to 14 people around its large, round table. The blue room was considered the "power room". It was frequently booked for lunch and/or dinner meetings by high-level executives and government officials. Past the blue room was the "gold room" which had a Versailles feel. The artwork and furnishings were magnificent—very formal and very French. The feeling in this room was one of opulence, from the crystal and gold chandeliers to the detail work on the ceiling and walls, all painted in gold leaf.

The three floors above the private dining rooms, and the top four stories of the adjoining brownstone, housed the Box Tree Hotel. The hotel had 13 rooms, each with a king bed and private bath. The rooms were appointed with antiques, fine linens, Chesapeake china, and all the amenities one would expect in a luxury property. The attention to detail was incredible and the owners spared no expense—the china soap dish in each bathroom wholesaled for $45. In 1996, the rooms sold for $240 per night.

For years, the Box Tree served the crème de la crème of New York society, from CEOs to politicos like the Kennedys and Kissingers. Though they visited occasionally for simple, intimate dinners, these power players were known to hold small private functions for family and friends, and mostly lunch or dinner meetings. The dining areas afforded enormous privacy. This privacy, the restaurant's pricing structure, and its exclusivity, made it the perfect place for society's power players to meet and do deals.

The service staff worked in teams of a captain and a waiter or two. Rather than typical American service, more formal service was the standard. Diners did little themselves save chewing and swallowing. The service staff guided the diners through meals that were culinary and gustatory experiences. Despite the high degree of server–customer contact, the formality of the service and the skill of the staff provided diners with great privacy.

THE OWNER

Augustin V. Paege conceived and built the restaurant. A few years after he moved the Box Tree to 49th Street he bought an adjoining brownstone, renovated it and the rooms above the restaurant, and opened the hotel. Paege, a Bulgarian-born multi-millionaire, was an absentee owner who spent most of his time in Europe. Although he certainly wanted to—and did—turn a profit on the restaurant and hotel, in some respects it seemed they were little more than creative outlets for him. He was an artist for whom the creative process held much more interest than day-to-day management. Paege hired people to "mind the store" for him. Two or three times a year, he visited New York and the Box Tree, and occasionally he called to check in. However, he never asked to see financial statements and did not inquire about the restaurant's operating results or its operations.

In 1992, the year prior to Gila Baruch's arrival as comptroller, Paege's cousin managed the operation. It was Paege's cousin, just prior to her own departure, who hired Baruch. Once Baruch arrived in late August 1993, management was by committee, with no one person overseeing the entire operation. She was responsible for all the restaurant's and hotel's financial matters, the chef was responsible for the day-to-day management of all back-of-the-house functions, and the maitre d'hotel ran the dining rooms.

GILA BARUCH

Bulgarian born, and raised in Israel, Gila Baruch spent the better part of her adult life in the United States and Europe. She began her financial career as the assistant to one of New York City's most prominent jewelers, Fred Leighton, and through people she knew socially, began working in restaurants. However, other than her experience as a customer in many of New York's finer restaurants, Baruch had no restaurant management experience. Though she never had the formal title until her position at the Box Tree, she had a comptroller's responsibilities in the various restaurants in which she worked.

Baruch was a partner in a restaurant called Jezebel prior to joining the Box Tree. One of New York's hotspots, Baruch frequented this upscale soul-food restaurant over the years. After becoming part of the Jezebel "family" of regulars, Baruch was almost like a working customer. She helped her good friend Jezebel, who owned the restaurant, out in the front-of-the-house if she happened to be there on a busy night.

After much discussion over a period of years, Baruch and Jezebel decided to partner on a new Jezebel location—in Paris, France. As with her previous restaurant work, Baruch operated mostly behind the scenes, handling the financial aspect of the business. With a French partner, they opened and operated successfully for two years. Success in restaurants, however, could be peculiar. Jezebel was full almost all the time but somehow it was not generating enough revenue to be profitable. Baruch and Jezebel discovered that their French partner was swindling the restaurant by conspiring with its suppliers and bleeding the restaurant's profits. The suppliers were overcharging the restaurant, and the partner was collecting kickbacks. Rather than fight him in the courts, Baruch and Jezebel closed the restaurant and returned to New York. Weeks later Baruch was on salary at the Box Tree, working as the restaurant's comptroller.

The Strike at the Box Tree

Gila Baruch had been working at the Box Tree approximately four months. As she walked toward the restaurant on that cold, December day in 1993, she saw a crowd in front of the Box Tree—they were making noise and chanting "Boycott the Box Tree!" As she got closer, Baruch recognized the faces of the people in the crowd and saw that many of them were holding large placards. The hourly employees at the Box Tree were on strike.

Baruch did a quick head count. Thirty-one people were on the payroll at the Box Tree, and she counted at least that many people on the picket line. The placards many of them held indicated the union was behind the strike. Baruch figured HERE (Hotel Employees and Restaurant Employees Union) must have recruited picketers who were not even Box Tree employees. She crossed the picket line as the hourly employees shouted at her, calling her names. "The first thing I did when I got downstairs to the office was to call the owner, Augustin Paege, in Europe. He had to be alerted as to what was going on."

Why the Strike Began

Many New York City restaurants and hotels were unionized, and the Box Tree had become a target of Local 100 of the Hotel Employees and Restaurant Employees Union. It was not entirely clear why HERE was so interested in such a small operation, though a fair number of small- to medium-sized, high-end operations were union shops. Possibly, because of its pricing and high-profile clientele, including politicians, the union saw the Box Tree as an opportunity to garner at least local press and for the Box Tree to serve as a catalyst for unionizing many other smaller operations. According to Brian McLaughlin, the then president of the New York City Labor Council, "Even though this is a small struggle by labor standards, it's symbolic. What we have here with the Box Tree is a typical situation where, in a place where affluent people gather and that's doing quite well, management is not doing the right thing" (Goldberg, 1995).

Until the late 1980s, the Box Tree's service staff had never been interested in unionizing; workers had always made a very good living. For those who were nontipped, hourly workers—the cooks, dishwashers, and the housekeepers on the hotel side—the union was promising insurance coverage and higher wages. These workers felt they had much to gain from union representation. However, it took an inadvertent misstep by the owner to rally the service staff and get most everyone thinking pro-union.

Baruch recounted that:

> . . . the owner had a system. He was very shrewd, but probably unknowingly, he made a mistake with the system. Essentially, the system kept payroll costs low by providing everyone in the front-of-the-house with a cut of the tips. The restaurant pooled tips and distributed them based on a point system. The captains got six points and waiters received four. There were no bussers. The hourly wages paid for each position were the minimum allowable. The problem started when the owner decided to cut costs by not having a full-time manager. He changed the tip distribution to include the maitre d' and even gave the chef points. The staff felt the owner was stealing their money. He was saving nearly $100,000 in payroll; but without thinking about it, he made problems for himself. The service and kitchen staffs suddenly united against him.

Employees voted to become unionized in 1990, but HERE was never able to negotiate a contract. According to Baruch, Paege thought the restaurant was too small to be unionized. He thought having workers who would be more concerned with the specifics of their positions according to a union contract than with providing top quality service would make managing more complicated. The fear was that workers would start saying, "that's not my job." Ultimately, the lack of a contract coupled with the continuation of conditions and practices that led to unionization led the workers to strike on December 16, 1993. All the Box Tree employees, with the exception of one cook, one maid, and a butler, went on strike. According to Baruch, these three employees "Were not into it. They didn't care. They all needed their jobs."

As a result of the massive walkout, no one was running the restaurant. Baruch remembered:

> From the day they walked out, it fell on my shoulders. I thought about not taking the responsibility, but it was around Christmas time and we had two weddings that weekend—I couldn't do that to the brides. Once I was in it, I was determined to see it through. There was a lot of adrenaline from the fighting. What got me through was being able to blow off steam at the gym. This was my release.

Life During the Strike

Even though she had been working in restaurants for some time and had been a part owner of one, Baruch's role had been primarily financial. She had never managed day-to-day operations, a task that became increasingly difficult as problems cropped up. However, Baruch instinctively knew that closing the doors would be the Box Tree's death knell. Somehow, she would have to staff a restaurant and small hotel on a moment's notice—at the busiest time of year. The restaurant was fully booked that first evening of the strike and through Christmas with private parties. The reservation book was full with a-la-carte reservations for the season as well. The hotel had scheduled a wedding in three days. Baruch felt she could not simply call the bride to apologize, saying the workers were striking. Calling on friends and colleagues for referrals, Baruch pieced together a staff to get her through the near term. She managed to find professional waiters and captains willing to cross the picket line, and was willing to make do with less than perfect service until things settled down and people learned the systems. She even borrowed her friends' and neighbors' maids to help keep the hotel open. Baruch believed that as long as she "created the show, everything was kind of normal."

Having gotten the situation under control enough to keep the doors open, Baruch updated Paege. She recommended for the first of several times over the next few years that he meet with the union leadership. He adamantly refused to recognize the union. There would be no negotiation. Once he knew the Box Tree was still doing business, albeit not quite as usual, Paege was content to let the strikers continue. He believed they would ultimately give up rather than spend the winter on the picket line.

Baruch continued to run the Box Tree with the temporary staff becoming permanent. Though their numbers dwindled significantly, the strikers remained out front every day for over four years. "Snow, sunshine, rains, winds—they didn't miss a day." According to Baruch, the strikers stopped at nothing in their efforts to chase away business and make life difficult for Box Tree employees and customers. Business dropped off by about 40 percent because of customers' reluctance to cross the picket line. It was not necessarily a pro-union stance—customers just did not want to subject themselves to the picketers' verbal abuse. When people called to make reservations, Baruch warned them that there were picketers out front; they were essentially told "if you want to cross the picket line, fine, we would be happy to serve you." Baruch knew that she could not have people pull up in limousines without knowing they would find a picket line waiting for them.

According to Baruch, and Abby Sims, a residential neighbor of the Box Tree, strikers called the women who came to dine "whores, bitches, and other words like that." When the women, or their dinner companions, responded to the strikers, the strikers in turn said things like "Hey you #&%*ing old bag, if I looked like you I wouldn't open my mouth." *The New York Times* reported that:

> . . . strikers on the picket line carried cellular phones and arranged for potential Box Tree patrons to eat instead at Lutèce or Café des Artistes. The union telephoned companies that had reserved party rooms at the Box Tree to urge them to cancel their parties. . . . Some workers who crossed the picket said the picketers . . . sometimes dropped dog feces in front of the restaurant.

Sims noted that the Box Tree had a tuxedoed employee outside greeting customers during the strike, attempting to shield them from the picketers.

In the early days of the strike, other neighbors, both quite noteworthy, were open in their support of the union. Both Katharine Hepburn and Stephen Sondheim, owners of neighboring townhouses, were upset with Paege's expansion into the second townhouse. The street was disrupted by the construction, but what was worse was that the private garden shared by a group of townhouses on the block was made less private by the presence of the Box Tree hotel. Hepburn occasionally sent cocoa to the strikers that first winter, and even permitted them to use the bathroom in her townhouse. Sondheim joined forces with the union by opposing Paege, who sought permits for the construction already underway on an adjoining restaurant space he purchased and additional construction he hoped to undertake, adding two floors to the hotel (Howe, 1994).

Near the end of the strike's second year, the union filed charges with the NLRB, saying the "Box Tree refused to bargain, coerced workers, obstructed the union, and harassed it." In addition, the union acted as a whistleblower, encouraging various government institutions to examine the Box Tree's practices.

Health inspectors found it operating without a license and cited conditions "conducive to vermin." Buildings officials issued zoning and safety violations for apartments converted to a hotel, illegal construction and demolition of a load-bearing firewall. State Labor Department officials ordered repayment of $92,000 in tips and overtime. Federal labor officials ordered the rehiring of two workers fired for union activity (Lambert, 1995, p. 21).

Baruch said the visits from City agencies were a routine occurrence:

Every day, every second day, another inspector from another bureau was here. Because the union called those departments—the fire department, the health department, the building department, the labor department. Forget the labor department. I have an audit now for back pay from all this.

Here's another example. When [Paege] opened this hotel he didn't apply for permits at all. It's a little hotel, you know, up in the building. Because everything he had done here, was done along the way. He purchased the building. And, he had the restaurant and tenants upstairs. So, some of the people that used to come to eat here said "wouldn't it be fun? Ah, the way we feel now we'd just go upstairs and . . . ," whatever the story was. Just because of the ambience. So, it gave him an idea [for the hotel]. He just opened those rooms and he never went for the permit.

In actuality, after Paege's instruction to convert the residential units, it was his then manager who oversaw the development of the hotel, and failed to execute on the required permit process. As with the payment of all appropriate wages (overtime and otherwise), taxes, and fees, Paege simply assumed his managers through the years had done what was legally required of the restaurant. In describing to a reporter how the Box Tree had operated prior to her arrival, Baruch stated,

> *"Paege is an absentee owner . . . He has been an absentee owner since the beginning, but he had managers who were not familiar with government requirements and who failed to alert him to problems."*

Baruch further stated:

And what do I know? This was an established place. It's not like it's new and you're part of the thing and you know what [they've] done and what [they] haven't done. The building department asked me what was upstairs and I said "we have rooms." They asked "are they transient?" I said "yes" and then I realized that I'm in trouble because I saw it wasn't transient on the C of O (certificate of occupancy). But, we used to pay the taxes for hotel occupancy to the city. So it's kind of a Catch 22. On one hand, [the City is] taking the money [and taxing us as if we are a hotel] and on the other hand, [the City says we] can't operate as such.

So, the city can force you to get a proper C of O. To have the proper C of O you have to do certain things involving the fire department. They coincide with the logistics of whatever you should and shouldn't have. In the meantime, I'm still open, paying hotel tax, and I never got the paperwork. It's still not legal. I paid a lot of fines. I went in and out of courts for the past four years, and I'm still in business.

The union's use of hardball tactics led Paege to dig in his heels further. As noted in HERE's NLRB filing, Paege fired back with a slander and defamation lawsuit in which he sought $1.7 billion in damages. This suit was the source of the harassment alleged by HERE. The NLRB judge refused to hear the case, declaring the suit frivolous (Prewitt, 1996). Paege also attempted to wage war in the press over a period of years. In a *New York Times* interview he paraphrased the famous line spoken by Emile Zola during the Dreyfus trial in France. He said

> *"This is not just a little restaurant thing, this is 'j'accuse' . . . This is not about hamburgers. This is about ideology."*

Paege, the Bulgarian multimillionaire, painted himself the underdog in this fight. He claimed that U.S. labor unions and their "13 million soldiers are looting and raping the country." In describing the union's whistle-blowing tactics, he was quoted further, saying

> *"For me, they're fascists because I can't see much difference between Kristalnacht and what they're doing to me for the last two years. The last two years have been Kristalnacht for me."*

Kristalnacht was the night the Nazis smashed nearly every window in every synagogue and Jewish-owned business in Germany in the beginning of WWII.

Amazingly, through all the trials and tribulations the Box Tree went through over the course of the strike, the restaurant operated in the black. Even with the fines and legal expenses, and the reduced revenue, the restaurant broke even. The results heartened Paege, and they fortified his resolve. He stuck to his principles and refused to bargain with, or even acknowledge, the union. Paege believed the financial results, particularly under these trying circumstances, indicated that the restaurant was in capable hands. He hardly ever heard from Baruch, and frankly, according to Baruch, he liked it that way. He was "hands off" when times were good, and he certainly did not want to change suddenly.

The Beginning of the End

Baruch thought she had handled everything the union could throw at her through the first three years of the strike, and she had. There were at most a handful of picketers outside the restaurant each evening. The clientele and the neighbors had become so accustomed to their presence that the picketers seemed to be having little effect. Baruch thought HERE chose its next tactic out of desperation. "How many more inspectors can they go through?" she figured.

According to Baruch, HERE began sending underage people into the restaurant to dine, and more important, to drink. The staff was not accustomed to serving such a young clientele and, because the HERE insiders looked older, at least in their early 20s, no one asked for proof of age before serving alcohol to them. Further, when caught serving minors, the Box Tree could not dispute the stories the young men posing as customers told. They were all cadets at the New York City Police Academy (Greenhouse, 1997). After a few violations and $1,000 fines issued by the State Liquor Authority, the staff checked the identification of everyone who looked even close to being underage.

Next, what Baruch characterized as the union's sting operation moved into the hotel side. A second, separate liquor license was required in order to serve alcohol in the rooms. The Box Tree did not have such a license. A couple checked in. They claimed to be celebrating some occasion. They requested and received a bottle of champagne in their hotel room. According to Baruch, "they took pictures, the whole shebang. It was a setup."

The holder of a liquor license issued by the New York State Liquor Authority (SLA) must renew it every three years. Typically, the renewal paperwork was sent to the restaurant and the process, provided nothing outrageous occurred over the previous license period, was relatively perfunctory. The SLA did not revoke licenses or decline renewal applications unless something was seriously wrong.

Baruch, knowing the Box Tree's license was up for renewal, was expecting the paperwork from the SLA. It never came. She called the liquor lawyer the Box Tree used—reputed to be the best in the City—and expressed her concern. He suggested it was probably in the mail, because in his experience, the Box Tree's violations were not serious enough to jeopardize a license renewal. The attorney indicated that Baruch should call Albany (the SLA's main office location) to inquire after the paperwork if it would assuage her. Baruch's call to the SLA had the reverse effect.

The clerk Baruch spoke with asked for the restaurant name and license number. After putting Baruch on hold, the clerk came back on the line and said "I'm very, very sorry but we have a big sign on the computer. 'No liquor license for the Box Tree.'" It was November 1996, and the holiday season was once again around the corner. Without a liquor license, Baruch thought, it would not even be worth keeping the doors open. How could the Box Tree expect people to pay $86 a head to dine (and even more for the private functions) and not be able to order wine with dinner?

Baruch was to appear with the liquor attorney at an SLA hearing to discuss the restaurant's violations. The hearing was to take place after the license expired—too late to do anything about the renewal. Baruch called the liquor attorney immediately upon hanging up from her conversation with the SLA clerk. He cautioned her to be vigilant about potential future violations and told her he would do what he could. The attorney was successful in moving up the hearing date. He and Baruch hoped all would be resolved in time to renew the license.

Baruch described the hearing this way:

> We walked into the hearing and, to our dismay, there were about seven or eight people, one from every single bureau. Liz Holtzman, Mark Green, Roy Goodman—you just name it, every politician was there. If you remember, this past year was election year. Every single representative was in this hearing. Little did we know it was for us. We said "What the hell was going on here?" So many people. And, the union representatives, naturally, and my lawyer, all there. Each one of them got on the podium and said, "No liquor license for the Box Tree." Apparently the union said [to the politicians], "Listen, you want the vote, you've got to do this for us." I couldn't believe this was happening. So, the Liquor Authority said, "No license."

The Box Tree's attorney went to Federal court, which granted a stay, enabling the restaurant to continue serving alcohol on its expiring license. The stay was to last until the court could hear the matter with the restaurant and the SLA presenting their cases. After approximately a year, the court held the hearing. At the hearing, convinced the case was too politically charged, the lawyer predicted the Box Tree would lose the appeal. He had a suggestion though—an idea he believed would provide the Box Tree with its only chance at a liquor license. The attorney suggested that Baruch call Paege at his home in Paris and present him with two options: Paege could either close up shop or sell the restaurant to Baruch. The plan to sell the restaurant was viable because New York State liquor licenses belong to the person, not the establishment. There was no reason to believe Baruch could not get a license to sell liquor at the Box Tree.

In order to reduce the political pressure and enhance the Box Tree's profit potential, the attorney also suggested Baruch settle with the union. If she became the owner and welcomed the union in, he believed the politicians and the SLA would have to reward her by letting the license through. So, a little over four years after she first walked through the Box Tree's front door, Gila Baruch owned the restaurant through a lease agreement with Paege.

A New Beginning and New Challenges

As part of the settlement with HERE, Baruch had to rehire any strikers who wished to return to the Box Tree. Seven people chose to return, four in the kitchen and three in service positions. The restaurant had to reinstate all seven with seniority, which meant they got the choice schedules. However, Baruch was adamant about not firing anyone hired during the strike. She wanted to reward the hard work and loyalty they showed her. People would have to work a four-day workweek until the Box Tree rebounded and volume picked up. Demand, she hoped, would solve her overstaffing problem.

However, it really was not that simple. She was tired and angry after the four years of battle with the union. Now she had to welcome back the returning strikers, the same people who had make her life a living hell. On top of that, the replacement workers who had seen her through four years of very bad times, the people to whom she owed her sanity, now believed they would be second-class citizens. According to Ned Goodman, who was the maitre d' during much of the strike, tension was inevitable now that strikers were returning to work. He noted that,

> *"Given the language they used, the animosity they showed toward the clientele and all of us who stayed on working, it will be difficult for us to cooperate with them."*

With all the terrible things that went on during the strike, would people be able to forget and move on? How could she ever restore the once sterling reputation of the Box Tree? How could Baruch get these two groups of employees working as one to produce the great food and service for which the Box Tree had once been known? As these questions raced through her head, Baruch knew that unless she found the answers, she would lose her investment in the Box Tree.

References

Goldberg, C. Tiny strike at restaurant has epic tone. *The New York Times,* December 1995, sec. 1, p. 25.

Greenhouse, S. Restaurant's liquor license suspended. *The New York Times,* March 1997, sec. B, p. 3.

Howe, M. E. Neighborhood report: East Side. *The New York Times,* January 1994, sec. 13, p. 6.

Lambert, B. Neighborhood report: East Side; Rulings rain on Box Tree. *The New York Times,* October 1995, sec. 14, p. 21.

Prewitt, M. 1996, September. Three-year Box Tree labor strike marches on. *Nation's Restaurant News*, 30(38): 104.

THE CABINET TEAM

On November 4, before the first year graduate hospitality marketing class, Lynn excitedly came up to Madeline and Minalie and exclaimed, "I've been given the okay to switch groups. I'd like to join your group!" Madeline mentioned that this should be discussed with Keith. After the class, The Cabinet team, Minalie, Madeline, and Keith[1]—met in the Hoffman Hall Lobby.

MADELINE: Professor Nordstrom is letting Lynn switch groups, and she wants to be in our group. Keith, what do you think about this?

KEITH: Isn't it too late in the semester? I mean, aren't we starting the group case this weekend? What can she contribute at this point?

MINALIE: I don't see what the problem is. I think that she would be an asset to our group. Another group member is what we wanted all along, isn't it? I'm surprised that we are even having a discussion about this.

KEITH: But, that was a month ago. I think it might be too late now.

MINALIE: I don't see how adding her would harm the group. Another person's viewpoint is just what we need.

Lynn A. Barrett: 24 years old; received her B.S. in Business Administration— Entrepreneur Program, from the University of Southern California. Prior to entering the Masters in Hospitality Management (M.H.M.) program at Cornell University, she worked as a contract analyst for the Northrop Corporation in Los Angeles. Her M.H.M. emphasis is real estate/finance, and she is currently involved in the startup of a real estate service company.

Minalie Chen: 24 years old; received her B.S. in Business Administration with a concentration in finance from Boston University. Before entering the M.H.M. program, she worked for two years as a financial analyst in the Corporate Profit Planning department at Data General Corporation. Her M.H.M. emphasis is Finance/International Business. She currently works part-time in the Career Services office while attending Cornell full time.

Keith A. Horton: 24 years old; graduated from Arizona State University in Tempe, Arizona with a B.S. in Accounting. Before entering the M.H.M. program at Cornell, he worked as a financial analyst for 15 months and as a sales representative for nine months with a time-share firm, both in Minneapolis. His emphasis in the M.H.M. program is Marketing. After graduation, he plans to work in sales and eventually own a resort business.

Madeline Wong: 23 years old; received her B.A. in Fine Arts from the University of California, Los Angeles, in March a year ago. Prior to entering the M.H.M. program, she worked at a major advertising agency for a year. Her emphasis in the M.H.M. program is Finance and Marketing. Upon graduation, she would like to continue her career in advertising for a major hotel chain.

EXHIBIT 1

---

[1] Exhibit 1 provides some background information about members of The Cabinet.

MADELINE: I agree with Keith. Maybe it is too late in the semester. I'm also concerned about our relationship as a group. The three of us have always gotten along really well. I don't know what would happen if a new member joined now. We would have to form, storm, and norm all over again. I just don't want any group conflicts right before we write our case.

MINALIE: I agree that we have a really good team, and that we all work well together, but I think it's worth the risk to have an even better team. Oh, there's Lynn; let me go get her.

When Keith and Madeline expressed their concerns to Lynn about adding a new member at this time, Lynn was very surprised. Based on previous interactions with group members, she had assumed that there would be no problem with her joining. Minalie was also surprised for the same reason. At this point, Keith left for class. Minalie, Madeline, and Lynn continued the discussion, until it was evident that emotions were running high and a decision could not immediately be reached. Lynn stated her concern that she needed to have a decision soon. Minalie told her that she would confer with Keith and Madeline and get back to her that night.

Walking to the library, Minalie told Madeline her reasoning for having Lynn join the group. After listening to her opinion, Madeline said that she would vote Lynn in, but Minalie should talk to Keith first. Minalie then asked Madeline that if Keith voted no, would that change her vote to no? Madeline just shrugged.

Minalie called Keith later that evening to discuss the situation. During the conversation, Minalie restated her reasoning for adding Lynn to the group. Keith listened to her voice, as he would later say, her adamant opinion for 15 minutes, but reiterated that he still had reservations, and would like to think about it some more. He would call her back. Minalie said that she would respect the team majority vote. After a telephone conversation with Madeline, Keith called Minalie back and told her they had agreed that Lynn could join the group.

Minalie telephoned Lynn that evening with the group's decision. Lynn expressed her concerns over the group's difficulty at reaching a decision, citing her informal participation with the team in the past (she had sat with them in class several times) and previous discussion on the possibility of her becoming a member, and her reasons for anticipating a smooth transition into the group. Minalie assured Lynn that the difficult decision was not based on personal reasons, but that the key concerns were timing and the possible disruption of the group's cohesion. Minalie reassured Lynn that the team felt that her addition would be a positive experience and that a meeting of the newly formed Cabinet Team was scheduled for the following day.

THE FORMATION OF THE TEAM

Anticipating that team work would be a vital element of the marketing class, Minalie and Madeline had began in the second class meeting to discuss their desire to work together due to their similar schedules and personal goals for the class. Madeline and Lynn also discussed their backgrounds with each other. Prior to the class formation session, near the end of the second week of the team, Minalie had also talked with Lynn about forming a group. Both had a desire to work with one another because of the type of experience each had had with case work and prior classes like this one.

At the fourth class meeting on Thursday, Dr. Jenna Nordstrom, Professor Nordstrom's wife, was substituting for him. She had the class continue with the 10-minute getting acquainted sessions which Professor Nordstrom had initiated in earlier classes. Lynn and Minalie spoke together for a second time. Minalie was especially interested in working with Lynn because in a prior class exercise, when describing her positive qualities, Lynn had mentioned that she had done a lot of reading in analytical consumer behavior.

During another exercise in the class, Keith approached Minalie. In their discussion, it was noted that they had identical schedules. Keith believed that Minalie's prior casework experience would be beneficial to a team. Lynn joined Keith and Minalie in their discussion. Professor Jenna Nordstrom then instructed the class to form teams, stipulating that each team must have at least one female member. The gender ratio, on that day, was such that only one group could have two females. Lynn turned to Minalie and Madeline and said, "Oh, I assume you two want to work together." Madeline replied, "Yes." Lynn left to join another team. Keith then went up to Minalie and Madeline and said, "I'd like to work with you." Thus, the team was formed.

FIRST TEAM TASKS

The members of the class arranged themselves in their new groups. The professor instructed the teams to decide on a name, to formulate initial rules for themselves, and to discuss a short sales management case. The decision of the team name did not come easily. Keith immediately suggested "The Raiders" which was promptly rejected by the other two members. Minalie suggested that a more positive and serious-sounding name such as "The Winners" would be more appropriate. The team continued to brainstorm until Minalie proposed "The Cabinet," which was subsequently adopted.

The next task was to formulate team rules, and the following were chosen: (1) a member must give notification if he/she cannot attend a meeting, (2) members must be on time for meetings, (3) members should be prepared for class, and (4) the majority rules.

The team then reviewed the case and wrote a list of symptoms. During the discussion, the team discovered that they shared similar viewpoints on the case.

THE FRANK MASON CASE

Early in the next class, team managers were given work orders by Professor Nordstrom to take back to their teams. The Cabinet had not selected a team manager. Minalie volunteered to get their team's task. The Cabinet's specific task was to describe Frank Mason's and Ed Nolan's assumptions in the "Frank Mason: Marketing Manager" case and relate them to the three sets of managerial assumption in a class handout.[2]

Each member of the team took notes as the team came up with case information suggesting first Mason's and then Nolan's assumptions. After a few minutes, Keith stopped writing, stating that he could not keep up with Minalie and Madeline's note-taking. A few minutes later, Madeline too, dropped out. At that point, Minalie jokingly said she would drop out also, but quickly added that since she was "today's manager" she was ultimately responsible for the task and would take notes of the discussion.

In discussing each case character and relationship to the Miles' model, Madeline suggested that they use ABX Theory, which later the team members would jokingly call "Madeline's theory," due to her frequent use of this theory.

---

[2] The handout was taken from Raymond E Miles' (1975). *Theories of Management*. New York: McGraw Hill.

At the end of class that day, Keith mentioned to Minalie that he wanted to meet before the next class period to discuss the next case, but he was hesitant because he was not the manager. Minalie said he should suggest it to Madeline who she thought they should make the team manager. Madeline joined the group after talking to Jim, another class member, about their statistics homework. Keith then asked Madeline if she would be their team manager for the next week and if the team could meet before the next class period. Madeline had no objections, and it was decided that the team would meet at 1:00 in the graduate lounge before the next class.

THE REJECTION EXERCISE

Madeline, Minalie, and Keith arrived at the same time in the student lounge. They sat down at a table to discuss the case. Before they got down to business, Minalie and Madeline talked about the Bruce Springsteen concert that Madeline had attended the previous night. After about 10 minutes, Keith suggested that the group begin discussing the case. Madeline apologized for not being very prepared to contribute much to the case discussion, as she only had time to read the case once. Madeline then volunteered to take notes. Keith and Minalie spent the majority of the time trying to understand how the manager's role and skill matrix fit with the marketing function of the case.

In class that day, Professor Nordstrom assigned a rejection exercise to the teams. He asked the groups to reject one team member based on any criteria they chose. Madeline stated that since she was manager that week she could appoint herself to leave. She also felt that since she was less prepared, her contribution to the case discussion would be minimal. Minalie and Keith agreed with her reasoning and said goodbye.

Madeline and the other "rejects" formed a separate group to discuss why they were rejected from their respective teams. Shortly thereafter, the professor assigned each of the "rejects" to different groups. Madeline was assigned to the Sigma Team consisting of Neil, Jennifer, and Bruce. Jennifer, the team manager, told Madeline the circumstances surrounding Mike's rejection and then filled her in on the Sigma Team rules. The team had mandatory meetings before each class in which each member was required to be prepared and to participate. Occasionally, they would rate each other's performance. Madeline was surprised at how formally the Sigma Team was structured.

At the end of class, Keith and Minalie welcomed Madeline back into The Cabinet. Madeline recounted her experience with the Sigma Team and suggested that The Cabinet adopt a more formal structure. Minalie said she did not like the idea of rating members, and did not think The Cabinet needed such a formal structure due to its small size. Keith agreed with her, but stated that the group did need to meet more often. Everyone consented.

A SATISFYING CLASS SESSION

Professor Nordstrom assigned the task of constructing two scientific statements about marketing managers using a form he explained. Minalie came up with the first example. Madeline then came up with a statement that Keith and Minalie said was very good but that it could use some revision. After discussing it, the group came up with the statement, "If a manager's preference for variety is high, and the variety of the task is high, then the manager will be satisfied and productive."

Each team in the class put its statements on the board. Minalie made comments about several of the other groups' sentences that showed their flaws. Jokingly, other class members stated they would attack The Cabinet's sentence when Professor Nordstrom read it aloud. Jim, a member of the Tigers, stated The Cabinet's second statement was good, but added, "all other things being equal" and smiled and winked at the group. When class ended, members of The Cabinet spent several minutes socializing with other class members.

A VERY SMALL GROUP

At the beginning of the next class, Professor Nordstrom called a manager's meeting which Madeline attended. The managers listed on the board the goals of the "Shawnut Corporation" case. The managers then returned to their groups to spend 45 minutes in discussing how the case characters and work groups in the marketing department met those goals.

Madeline joined Keith in the back corner of the room and told him that Minalie could not make it to class that day. Madeline explained the task and she and Keith worked until a second manager's meeting was called. The managers regrouped in the front of the room. Professor Nordstrom asked them to spend a few minutes discussing among themselves but in front of the class how to present the case to him. Later, he asked the managers if their team members had been good consultants, and whether their colleagues had understood the case well enough to step in for the manager. Madeline was the first to respond, and confidently answered yes to both questions. After class, Keith told Madeline that he was proud of her.

GROUP DEVELOPMENT

"A Framework for Analyzing the Marketing Function" by Michael McGrath was the model to be read and understood for the day. The Cabinet felt it was very well prepared for class, and the members helped each other fill in any holes in their understanding of the model.

Following the class discussion of the McGrath model, the group was given an opportunity to "step back" and look at how they worked together. This was done by analyzing four roles within the group: (1) communication; (2) decision making; (3) task; and (4) social. Madeline said that Minalie and Keith tended to interact with each other more than with her. Minalie and Keith concurred, and Madeline pointed out that this may be true because she had been less vocal. The decision-making role was believed to be equally shared by all.

The task and social roles were more difficult to assess. As a general rule, all members expected whoever the manager was to coordinate any group meetings. As for social roles they believed all played them all the time.

After the group completed its evaluation, Professor Nordstrom posed two questions: (1) Is your team willing to add a member? and (2) Is your team willing to allow a member to leave? The Cabinet answered yes and no.

THE MIDTERM PROCESS

Several classes later, Professor Nordstrom gave the class information about the midterm he would be passing out at the next class session. Keith was late for class and missed what was said. After class he told Minalie he had already asked Madeline what the professor had said regarding the midterm, but that he wanted to hear what Minalie had to say also. When Minalie mentioned that Professor Nordstrom wanted the class to bring all the course materials to the review session, Keith exclaimed, "Oh, Madeline didn't tell me that!" When Minalie saw Madeline later, Madeline asked her if Keith asked her what was going to be on the midterm. Minalie said yes. Madeline commented, "So, Keith had to ask you too!" Lynn had come up to the group after class, and said that she very much wanted to join The Cabinet to discuss the midterm. Everyone said that would be fine.

On Thursday, October 17, Professor Nordstrom handed out the midterm questions to the class and said that individual responses would be due at the beginning of the next class on Tuesday. After entertaining several clarifying questions, he left. Madeline, Minalie, and Lynn, who were seated next to each other, began discussing the content of the midterm. Keith was sitting in his usual back corner, and began talking to Matt who was seated next to him. A few minutes later, Keith joined Minalie and Madeline who were now talking with other class members about the exam. The Cabinet members discussed meeting, and since all the members had other midterms to study for on Saturday, they decided to meet on Sunday. At this point, Lynn asked again if she could join their meeting. There were no objections voiced.

On Sunday morning, October 20, Minalie called both Keith and Lynn and discussed the midterm questions with them before heading to the library to meet with Madeline. That afternoon Minalie called Jim to see how he and his team were faring. Madeline had called Keith that morning to ask him if he wanted to meet between 7:00 and 9:00 that evening at his apartment. Minalie was invited to join them, but she said that she had no way of getting to the south hill. During the midterm discussion, Keith did not agree with Madeline's interpretation of one of the questions, so Madeline suggested calling Professor Nordstrom at home for clarification, which they did.

On Monday morning, the 21st of October, The Cabinet, along with Lynn, met at 11:00 A.M. in the school lobby. When they arrived, they found several other class members already discussing the midterm. The other students asked The Cabinet to join them but Lynn and Keith left to discuss the exam in the Engineering Library. Minalie and Madeline continued talking with the other students.

Neil and Mike joined Minalie and Madeline for lunch as the intense discussions about the midterm continued. The whole marketing class was very keyed up about the upcoming exam and there were substantial conversations among the teams in the class.

THE ELC

A marketing class meeting at the Experiential Learning Center was held in late October. The ELC was equipped with video, sound, and various other recording systems. On this day, all teams were videotaped as they performed their work. Keith acted as the self appointed manager. As The Cabinet moved to their "recording studio," Keith asked the professor to elaborate on the task. Now assured of the job, Keith explained to Minalie and Madeline that they were to compare and contrast the styles and effectiveness of three marketing managers of three different cases they'd already discussed. Keith assigned Madeline to be the note-taker. She reluctantly agreed, as it had become a standing joke that Keith always avoided note-taking.

Following the team's completion of the task, the group watched the videotape replay. Minalie and Madeline were quite critical of their own mannerisms and general appearance. "Put your hands down!" yelled Minalie to herself on the screen. "I look terrible," said Madeline. Keith commented that he sounded different on tape. By reviewing the tape, the group was able to see themselves work and to evaluate the visual feedback. Additionally, Professor Nordstrom had given Keith a team member feedback form to be independently filled out by each person after watching the tape. An average of the team responses is presented in Exhibit 2.

Three items were of particular interest to the group. First, acceptance of minority views was the only item rated below five. Minalie pointed out that when two members strongly agreed on an idea, the minority view was frequently ignored. Her comment was accepted by the group, and it was agreed that this was an area that needed improvement. Secondly, cohesion, participation, and communications ranked at the top of the scale and the group members were proud of how this had evolved over time. In conjunction with these ratings, membership growth was also rated near the top of the scale. All members agreed that this was the result of more scheduled meetings to discuss cases and the increased social interaction among team members.

As class ended that day, Professor Nordstrom asked The Cabinet if they thought they needed a consultant (where the professor would act as a consultant to the team). Without even asking Madeline and Minalie, Keith replied, "Definitely not."

THE NEW CABINET

On November 5, the first meeting of the "new" Cabinet with Lynn was scheduled for 1:00 in the student lounge. Lynn arrived a little early to find Madeline waiting to speak to her alone. Madeline expressed her concern that Lynn understand what had happened the previous day when she had requested to join the group. She assured Lynn that she was happy to have her in the group. Lynn told Madeline that she hoped she had not caused too much disruption in the team, and had been upset because she had been looking forward to working with Keith, Madeline, and Minalie.

Keith and Minalie then arrived, and Lynn was briefed on the team rules. Discussion of the "Sturdivant Hotel" case was begun by Madeline, who asked the question, "Should the company change their marketing strategy?" Keith adamantly said no. There was a heated argument regarding this question with all team members participating actively. This continued until class time.

Two days later, the group met again in the student lounge prior to class to discuss the assignment. When Lynn arrived, Keith and Madeline were sharing a table and talking with other students. Minalie arrived shortly thereafter, and the group continued the light socializing among themselves. Keith finally suggested that it was time to take a look at the assigned case and opened with his ideas about the week's reading.

After a short discussion, the group turned to the topic of The Cabinet team case they were to write (see Exhibit 3). It was agreed that writing would begin on Saturday. Keith offered his apartment as the meeting place and suggested that everyone come in one car since parking could be a problem.

THE FIRST GROUP CASE MEETING

Saturday morning at 10:30, Minalie and Lynn met at Madeline's apartment and the three went to Keith's apartment together. The group quickly got to the task at hand with Madeline presenting her idea for the organization of the case. The group discussed the

Instructions: Circle your responses to each item. Do not sign your name.

1. Adequacy of mechanisms for getting team feedback:
   Poor   1   2   3   4   5   6   Excellent

2. Adequacy of decision-making procedures:
   Poor   1   2   3   4   5   6   Very Adequate

3. Cohesion:
   Low   1   2   3   4   5   6   Optimal

4. Acceptance of minority views:
   None   1   2   3   4   5   6   High

5. Use of member resources:
   Poor   1   2   3   4   5   6   Excellent

6. Communications within team:
   Unclear   1   2   3   4   5   6   Very Clear

7. Goal acceptance by members:
   Not Accepted   1   2   3   4   5   6   Accepted

8. Flexibility of team procedures:
   Not   1   2   3   4   5   6   Very

9. Sharing of leadership function:
   None   1   2   3   4   5   6   High

10. Feelings of team members:
    Unexpressed   1   2   3   4   5   6   Freely expressed

11. Participation:
    A few dominate,   All get in, all
    some not listened to   1   2   3   4   5   6   listened to

12. Trust level in team:
    Very low   1   2   3   4   5   6   Very high

13. Diagnosis of team problems:
    Problems ignored   1   2   3   4   5   6   Problems always
                                                     raised and dealt
                                                     with carefully

14. Membership growth:
    Members in rut   1   2   3   4   5   6   Members changing
                                                     and growing

15. Overall team effectiveness:
    Low   1   2   3   4   5   6   Excellent

EXHIBIT 2

Date: September 5, 2000

To: Student Teams of Marketing Management 520

From: Professor Nordstrom

Subject: Writing a case on your team experience

1. Your team is to write a descriptive case about your marketing team over the course of this semester. It should begin when your team was formed and run up to early December. It should include enough specifics so that someone could analyze the team's structure, team's processes, and the team's development over time.

2. I will be happy to consult with your team on this project. I can be most helpful if you present me with a draft copy to look at.

3. The final draft of your case is due, in class, on Thursday, December 5.

EXHIBIT 3

pros and cons of the idea and agreed that Madeline's suggestion would be the best way to present the case. The discussion continued and decisions were made concerning the details of the paper, including the presentation of exhibits, the typing task, and the estimated completion date.

After a break for take-out Chinese food, the group began work on a detailed outline. Events were recounted and decisions were made as to their significance to the case. After reviewing the outline, the group went to Lynn's apartment to begin typing the paper into her computer because Keith's roommate had come home. After many revisions, the first section of the case was completed. It was 7:40 P.M. and the group "called it a day." Each member expressed excitement about the way the case was shaping up.

DELEGATION OF THE CASE WRITING

On Thursday, November 14, The Cabinet met at 1:00 in an empty classroom to discuss how to delegate the writing of the rest of the case. Immediately, there was a disagreement. Madeline suggested that Minalie write about the team formation process, and Lynn write about The Cabinet at the point she joined the group. The group processing (the day in the ELC) section would be divided among Minalie, Madeline, and Keith. Lynn nodded in agreement. Keith and Minalie had some objections. They raised the question of how the paper would flow if the members wrote their sections independently. Then followed a heated discussion about the style of writing the case until Madeline and Lynn explained that they would all review and edit all sections together for the final draft on Saturday, November 16. At that point Minalie and Keith agreed stating that it had not been clear that the whole team would do the final writing all together. At this time, the rest of the class filed into the classroom commenting on the intensity of The Cabinet's meeting.

ANOTHER CASE WRITING DAY

Lynn arrived at Madeline's apartment Saturday, November 16, at 10:00 A.M. Expecting the rest of the group to arrive soon, they began revising the rough draft of the group case. Keith arrived shortly thereafter, and Minalie telephoned to say that she had a bad case of stomach flu and would come as soon as she was feeling better.

Madeline, Keith, and Lynn started editing each other's sections. When Minalie arrived at noon, she was given a copy of the revised first section for her approval and input.

The team members continued to edit each other's sections until Keith left to pick up a friend at the airport. Madeline, Minalie, and Lynn drove to a nearby delicatessen for lunch.

After lunch, the group reconvened at Madeline's apartment, and the editing session continued. During this time, there were differences of opinion on writing styles between Lynn and Minalie. Lynn wanted to delete paragraphs that Minalie thought were important, and a 20-minute argument ensued. Finally, they compromised.

THE FINAL DRAFT

On Monday, November 26, The Cabinet members met after their marketing class to arrange a meeting on Sunday, December 1, to write the final section of the case.

That Sunday, Madeline and Minalie called each other to arrange a meeting time. Minalie and Madeline both tried calling Lynn, but she could not be reached at home. Madeline then called Keith who said that he did not want to meet, because he had too much work to do. Since Lynn was supposed to write the final section, the group did not meet.

In class on Tuesday, Madeline told Keith that Minalie had cancelled her plans on Sunday so she could meet with the group, and that she was irritated that the meeting did not take place. Keith then stated that he had never agreed to meet on Sunday. Madeline disagreed, and a short argument followed. Later that day Madeline gave Minalie the last section of the case that Lynn had written. Minalie and Madeline reviewed the section together and felt that certain key points were left out. They told Keith and Lynn their concerns and offered to rewrite the last section and to format the final copy. Keith and Lynn agreed.

As the marketing class assembled on Thursday, December 5, The Cabinet gathered to sign their names to the cover of their team case as required before being turned in. When Professor Nordstrom asked for the cases, Madeline took The Cabinet team's case to the front of the class. As she handed it to Professor Nordstrom she commented, "I never want to see that again."

THE SURPRISE

On the next-to-last class meeting, Professor Nordstrom handed the cases back to each team. He said that at the end of class he would distribute his evaluation and comments on the case. He then said that this class session would be devoted to a graded team analysis exercise. Teams were to utilize the next hour and fifteen minutes to write a report based on their team case following a guide sheet he handed out (see Exhibit 4). Professor Nordstrom cautioned that only the facts in the written case were relevant in this assignment.

Date: December 12, 2000

To: Student Teams, Marketing Management 520

From: Professor Nordstrom

Subject: An analysis of your Team Case

1. Today, in class, your team is asked to write an analysis of the case that you wrote on your team's experience this semester.

2. Your analysis should include, but not be confined, to the following:
   a. Describe your team formation and acquaintancing activities.
   b. Describe—both early in the semester and at the end—how your team made decisions and communicated with each other.
   c. Describe your team's status and how it affects its structures (figures OK here).
   d. Describe the task and social roles of members over time.
   e. State and explain three changes in how you worked together that would have improved your team's performances.
   f. Briefly describe how you went about doing this report.

EXHIBIT 4

CASINO GRANDE

In the early afternoon of June 20, 1992, as Roger Parks, the reservation manager of Casino Grande was packing his briefcase to go out of town to a hospitality association conference, Randolph Jackson, the General Manager, called him into his office and the following conversation ensued.

JACKSON: Damn it Roger, didn't I tell you to talk to those two girls about getting to work on time? All they do around here is drink coffee. I guess I'm going to have to install martial law around here. They both recently got raises, too; who do they think they are, anyhow? You tell them in no uncertain terms that if they don't shape up, we'll give them the sack. We can still hire people who follow the rules.

PARKS: Whoa back! What's going on? What in the heck are you talking about?

JACKSON: Don't pretend with me. You know just what I'm taking about—it's those two girls, Kane and Palumbo. I saw them come into the employee cafeteria this morning at 8:00 and they were still there when I left at 8:20 to come upstairs. They couldn't have gotten to their desks until 8:30 or later! Then, at 10:30 they were back down there for coffee—I saw them with my own eyes! They're just going to have to shape up. Other people have noticed as well. Why, Cooperider (Housekeeping Assistant Manager) mentioned it just the other day. Why on earth didn't you talk with them like I told you to do?

PARKS: Cool it, Randy. I did talk the whole thing over with Marshall, and she talked with the two women. She told me later that she had, and said the women had agreed to do better from then on.

JACKSON: Posh, they aren't doing it! We just gave them salary increases, too. We gave them increases and that's how they're showing their appreciation. I say, if they don't shape up we fire their butts. That Kane's a pain. She says she wants more responsibility, we give it to her, and a raise, and then she comes in late every morning and drinks coffee all day long.

PARKS: Simmer down Randy. You'll have to admit we don't set much of an example. It seems like there is always a gang of supervisors in the coffee line at all times, and your secretary and her friends stand around the cigarette machine way after 8:00 A.M.

JACKSON: That's not relevant. You can't get cigarettes unless you stand in that line— cripes we can't go clear out to the lobby stand, can we? Oh, it's all right to grab a cup of coffee on occasion, but those two girls are always out together. They're abusing the privileges. They drive to work together every day, I've seen them, and then go into the cafeteria at 8:00 and have breakfast. It's got to end.

PARKS: Okay, okay. We'll have another chat with them. The offices and the whole back-of-the house are pretty lax in regard to timeliness. I agree we don't want reservations standing out as the worst offenders. Part of it is that they go out together, and that makes it conspicuous alright. I'm leaving town this afternoon, but I'll talk with them personally today and let you know before I take off.

JACKSON: Okay. Just make it good. We've got to stop abuses, or we'll just have to crackdown on everyone. It's always a few who make it hard on everyone.

On the way back to this own office, Mr. Parks detoured into reservations and found Ms. Jean Marshall, talking on the telephone. When she hung up, Mr. Parks related his conversation with Mr. Jackson. This was the second time in two months that Mr. Jackson had called the behavior of Kane and Palumbo to his attention. After a brief discussion, they decided that the proper thing to do was to call the two women into the departmental conference room and talk with them. When Mr. Parks, Ms. Marshall, Mrs. Kane, and Mrs. Palumbo had assembled, the following conversation took place.

PARKS: While I sure don't like to bring up a complaint a few hours before I go out of town, I've just come from Mr. Jackson's office. He has complained again about you two getting to work late and about you taking so much time away from your desks for coffee. He rather emphatically stated that he has seen you in the cafeteria after 8:00 several times and that you both seem to be there having coffee together every time he stops by. I believe Jean spoke with you about this several weeks ago. What do you think we ought to do about it?

KANE: Yes, Miss Marshall talked to us before about it. We've been trying to watch it since then. I believe we've been doing a lot better. You know how hard it is to get to work winter mornings, and we do go down once in awhile for a cup of coffee. The new cafeteria is so nice now. Everybody is using it more. Why shouldn't we?

PARKS: Yes, you're right, of course. More people are using the cafeteria more. You'll agree with me, I'm sure, that this property has a pretty relaxed attitude about getting to work on time occasionally and about getting out of the office for coffee or Coke or a smoke. But let's face it. Mr. Jackson is riled. If we abuse the privileges we have, it will be necessary for Jackson to create some rules that constrict us. We'll all suffer then. There must be some way you can work it out so you'll not be so conspicuous when you take a break once in a while? Isn't it possible for you two to get to work on time so when you take a break it won't be so objectionable?

KANE: All the other reservations women do it. All the office force does it. The smokers go out all the time. Most use the lavs, but it's always so crowded there we prefer to go down to the cafeteria.

PARKS: Part of the problem, of course, is that you two are always seen together. That makes you stand out. Why can't you split up, or go some other place? Mrs. Kane, you've indicated more than once that you want more responsibility in reservations. Let's face it, we can't get it for you if the GM thinks you're abusing the situation.

KANE: Of course that makes sense. What do you want us to do? Stop taking breaks altogether?

PARKS: Mrs. Palumbo, what do you think you should do?

PALUMBO: Gee, I don't know. We don't do anything that the others don't do. But we don't want to get into trouble. The Casino has been generous enough.

PARKS: The way things stand now, well you can see how things are. Both Mr. Jackson and Cooperider have commented on you. Jackson's the GM remember, he approves all job changes and all recommendations for raises. It's just not smart to have him on your case.

KANE: We want to do what's right, of course. I sure wouldn't want to do anything that would hinder my next promotion. I suppose we could go somewhere else and maybe not take so many breaks—at least not together. Suppose we lay low for a while until the top brass forgets about it?

PARK: And, get to work a little more promptly in the morning. Sure, all of us are a touch lax sometimes about getting in on time, but the finger is pointing at you, so how about doing a bit better than you've been doing of late?

KANE: Okay, but as you know, I've three kids to get off to school every day. What with car problems, the storms tying traffic up, it's awfully hard to get here on time.

PARKS: I'll leave it up to you. I know you're both good workers and I know you're both trying to get ahead here. You must realize that if old Jackson doesn't see an immediate turnaround, well, I'm not sure what he'll do. You've been talked to twice now. We wouldn't want our GM to do something that would hurt all of the staff now, would we? (Pause) Jean, what do you think is the best thing to do?

MARSHALL: You've outlined the situation very well, Mr. Parks. I think these women are attracting undue attention by going out together all the time. The whole staff has been lax about starting promptly. I'll certainly work with reservations to see that we put a drive on to get to work on time. I think they shouldn't take quite so many breaks, and not together. That way they won't cause so many negative comments.

PARKS: Well, it's up to these women. I'm about to leave for a conference—tonight, in fact. I'll be away so I won't hear anything. If Jackson gets in a twit, he'll no doubt call you down, Jean, and I know you'll do whatever he says. See if you two ladies can't stay out of trouble, please. I'll be back in five days. Good luck.

Roger Parks returned to this own office and telephoned Mr. Jackson. He told Jackson that he and Ms. Marshall had talked to Kane and Palumbo and that he believed that Jackson would see an immediate improvement. Parks asked Jackson to call Ms. Marshall if there are any further complaints. Jackson replied, "You're darn right I will."

ABOUT CASINO GRANDE

Casino Grande was an older, mid-sized casino hotel, employing approximately 2,000 people, on the boardwalk section of a mid-Atlantic city. Mr. Randolph Jackson was the general manager of Casino Grande and as such had the ultimate authority over all departments and functions at the property. He took an unusual interest in the human resource activities of the casino/hotel, establishing both personnel policies and office procedures personally. The ordinary interpretation of these policies and procedures, however, was handled by the department managers and section supervisors with consultation available from the Employee Relations Department.

Roger Parks was the manager of Casino Grande's reservations department. He had begun his employment with the casino in 1982 as a night programmer in the accounting department while he was finishing his B.S. in hotel administration from a prominent eastern university. After graduation, Roger continued to work in accounting for two years, then he requested a transfer to the newly established computer system group where he worked for another two years before he replaced a section head and, thus, acquired his first truly supervisory experience. In late 1987, Roger obtained an interview for a section manager's position in the front desk department, and for which he was hired. In 1990, Casino Grande significantly upgraded its computer facilities, including a sophisticated reservations system. Roger was transferred to the reservations unit to take charge of it. When he began to organize this function, he hired Ms. Marshall and two clerks. About a year later, when an opening occurred, Mrs. Kane was hired. In Mr. Park's opinion, Ms. Marshall was a "technical whiz" who got along fairly well with her people. She had a reputation within the reservations group of sometimes being impatient; she "kidded" her workers a lot and usually got a lot of high-quality work from them, but was considered somewhat lax in enforcing discipline.

Mrs. Kane, about 39 years old, had three children of ages 11, 8, and 6. Her husband was a sales trainer with a major manufacturing company and was away from home for extended periods. Mrs. Kane's mother lived with them, taking care of the children so that Mrs. Kane could work. She was made senior reservations clerk on January 1, 1992, receiving a substantial raise. At that time, Mrs. Kane was told she was doing excellent work, but had a quick temper that sometimes disturbed her fellow employees. She was also told that she often disrupted the office by talking too loudly and too often. The position of senior reservationist provided a wage differential over the others and required her coworkers to bring their questions about procedures and assignments to her. All other matters, such as salary and training questions as well as performance appraisals, were handled by Ms. Marshall. Mrs. Kane took her work seriously and expressed resentment toward the indifferent attitude of the younger reservation clerks. She was trying to get ahead financially. She did not like housekeeping or childcare and planned to continue working as long as her mother could look after her children.

Mrs. Palumbo was about 28 years old and a college graduate. Her husband was in the Army and had been in the Middle East for two tours after Operation Desert Storm. Mrs. Palumbo lived alone in a small apartment and planned on working only until her husband was posted in the United States. Mrs. Palumbo did a good job as a reservation clerk and got along well with everyone in the department. She also got a raise on January 1, 1992.

The office rules at Casino Grande did not permit smoking on the job, but allowed personnel to leave the office to do so, although there were no designated smoking spaces.

On Monday, August 15, 1992, the following notice had been posted on the bulletin board just inside the employees' entrance to the property.

TO: All Casino Grande Office Personnel

Some Employees have been taking advantage of our company's coffee break privilege. In order to be fair to those who are being reasonable about going to the cafeteria for coffee, we do not wish to rescind this privilege altogether. We do expect all office employees to start work at 8:00 in the morning—meaning come ready to work, already having had breakfast. There is no excuse for having coffee, therefore, after 8:00 A.M.

From now on the following rules will apply to coffee breaks:

1. No one should visit the cafeteria for coffee before 9:30 A.M.
2. Groups from the same department should not take breaks together, since this would disrupt the service provided.
3. No one should stay away from his/her workstation for longer than 15 minutes.
4. It is unnecessary to leave one's office for coffee or any other beverage more than once a day.

These simple rules should be clear to everyone. If, in the future, these rules are ignored, the coffee break privilege will be canceled altogether. Your wholehearted cooperation is expected.

R. L. Jackson
General Manager

CHEETAH RENT-A-CAR

Awakening to the telephone's ring, Christie glanced at the bedside table. It said 7:01 A.M. Picking up the telephone, Christie sleepily said, "Hello." Not unexpectedly it was Tony. "Did I wake you?" he asked. In reply to Christie's "Umm," Tony continued, "Sorry but could you come in early today?" After a pause, Christie said, "Ok," and hung up and lay back on the bed. After a few minutes she said, "I'm getting sick and tired of his early calls, his trivial questions, his inconsideration, and his damn self interest. Maybe I should just quit like everyone else." From underneath the bed covers, Christie's husband muttered, "Don't tell me; he's your boss. Maybe it's time you educated him again."

Cheetah Rent-A-Car was located on the northwest outskirts of Eugene, Oregon, about a half mile from the airport. The recently remodeled airport served several counties around the Eugene-Springfield areas, and the nearby towns of Corvallis and College Grove, as well as numerous farming and logging hamlets dotting the countryside. Both Eugene and Corvallis had universities, and Eugene, much larger, had two major malls as well as a well-developed downtown area.

The Eugene Cheetah Rent-A-Car also had a Ryder truck and trailer leasing franchise. The Cheetah station was an agency location, not a corporate one. Agencies were new to Cheetah; there were only five in the United States at the time, usually small, and all operating under the same policies as corporate locations. There were some conflicts between Corporate and owner-managed agencies. The Eugene Cheetah, for example, would have liked to have extra cars for walkup rentals (for customers who come to the counter without reservations). Corporate Cheetah, however, did not believe that walkups were a significant segment of the Eugene market and worth even forecasting for.

Tony Bartos was the owner-manager of Eugene's Cheetah. He was heavy set, 35 years old, married and the father of four. Before starting his Cheetah-Ryder business a year and a half ago, he sold cars for Eugene's largest automobile dealer. While very family oriented, Tony played golf whenever he could and never missed the University of Oregon's home football and basketball games. He expressed strong opinions on just about everything.

Until six months ago Tony's Cheetah location was staffed by two full-time rental agents and two full-time and one part-time service agents. The rental agent's job consisted mostly of checking cars in and out, handling phone reservations and questions, occasionally leasing trucks and trailers, and ensuring that the service agents were cleaning enough of the right type of vehicles. Rental agents used a computer a lot, both for reservations and recordkeeping as well as for the many reports that Corporate Cheetah required. Tony usually worked at the counter, serving customers.

The job of the service agents was entirely focused on cleaning and gassing the cars and trucks. Cheetah had very high standards for cleaning rental cars. An important part of the service agent job was keeping the ready line full of clean cars, that is, the six spaces closest to the office, based on the day's reservations. Service agents were continually moving cars up to the ready line from the back lot. The information on what cars or trucks to clean and get ready came from the rental agents.

Cheetah in Eugene was not all that busy, renting on average just 20 cars a day. At the next closest Cheetah location, at the Portland airport, about 250 cars a day were rented. While service agents stayed fairly busy, the rental agents usually had time to socialize and read between customers.

Christie, 23 and married, was a business major at the University of Oregon. She began to work for Tony part time six months ago. After just one week of work, Christie had decided she liked the job of rental agent. Everyday was different, interacting with a variety of customers and using the computer. Christie felt that she might have a career with Cheetah and decided she would try to learn as much about the business as she could. She also liked the fact that in slow periods she could get some of her homework finished.

One week before Christie began working at Cheetah, one of the full time rental agents gave her two week notice. The following day, however, she called in sick and subsequently never returned to work. Tony advertised for two part-time rental agents. Christie responded, was hired on the spot and immediately started work. Three weeks later the other full time rental agent gave her notice but, like the first agent, never showed up for work. This left Christie and Tony to run the counter. Christie began working over 40 hours a week in addition to going to school full time. She worked the long hours at Cheetah because she felt sorry for Tony. Christie's schedule quickly became exhausting, she got behind in two of her courses, and her husband began to comment that he barely ever saw her. Tony began to call Christie at seven in the morning when he arrived at work. His call always woke Christie. Tony would ask her a question about the previous day or if she would come to work early because he was tired or wanted to do something with his family or had been invited to play golf. The questions always seemed to Christie like they could have waited until she came to work. Tony would invariably ask, "Did I wake you?" and then apologize as Christie's answer was always "Yes." Being awakened a couple times didn't bother Christie, but when the calls continued over the next few weeks she became angry that Tony did not consider her needs although she never told him how she felt. After a while Christie began to refuse Tony's requests to come in an hour or two early and eventually just let the answering machine pick up.

Two and a half months after Christie began at Cheetah, Tony hired Phil as another part-time rental agent. Christie felt relieved; her hours were cut back to 20. Phil was 20 years old and an agricultural major at Oregon State. Phil enjoyed the work and the interaction with customers. He learned the rental agent's job quickly and always came to work on time. In his first month Phil received only one customer complaint, which was written to Cheetah Corporate. Christie and the service agents liked Phil a lot. Tony's early morning wake up calls and questions shifted from Christie to Phil.

After two months of Tony calling and requesting more hours from Phil, Phil told Christie one day that he'd "had it." The next day Phil gave his notice and left two weeks later. On Phil's last day, Christie approached Tony before her shift and asked to speak with him. She told him that even though the office was understaffed that she would not work additional hours because her grades were suffering. She asked Tony if she could give him some "constructive criticism." He smiled and nodded. Christie then went on to tell Tony that he needed to understand that when he hires students he had to accept that their studies come first, not work. She went on to say that he had to respect the hours they work and their privacy or he would continue to lose student employees as quickly as they are hired. Tony smiled, nodded, and thanked her for her "input."

When Christie came to work a week later, Tony introduced her to Andrea "our new rental agent." "She'll need your help learning the job, Christie," he said, then turned and walked away. Two months later, at 7:01 A.M., Christie's telephone awakened her. Tony was on the line.

THE CROISSANT PLACE

As Lisa walked out of the European style restaurant-coffee shop, she became aware that her heart was beating hard. It had taken her a whole week to work up to resigning, mostly because she felt she should apologize to Roshan personally. To her surprise he had said, "Lisa, don't tell me that. Think it over first. If you stay there'll be a raise for you. So be a good girl, we'll talk tomorrow." Lisa nodded, shouldered her purse and jacket and left.

The Croissant Place was located in a strip mall near the corner of El Camino Real and De Anza Boulevard, close to the town center of Mountainview, California. Mountainview was one of the series of adjoining towns north of San Jose collectively known as Silicone Valley. The high tech industrial base of the valley had been booming for some time. Mountainview, like its sister towns, had become more and more attractive to a diverse and growing population of younger professionals, singles and families alike, seeking a "California" life style. Businesses serving this fast-paced, materialistic, affluent area were often upscale and trendy. In the same strip mall as The Croissant Place, for example, were a day spa, a wine and cheese store, a woman's specialty jewelry shop, a realtor's office, an organic food store, a cellular telephone outlet, and an automotive detailing shop.

The Croissant Place was open Monday through Saturday, 7:00 A.M. until 4:00 P.M. and 7:00 A.M. to noon on Sunday. Upon entering the shop, a customer felt like an expected guest, greeted with the sight and scents of plates and bowls of delicious looking food, fresh coffee and especially a wide selection of fresh baked croissants and other pastries. In the mornings about 70 percent of the business was takeout. There was a counter with a dozen seats and 15 small tables and the place was bright and shining clean. Eighty percent of the customers were regulars, many greeted by name. The Croissant Place had recently received a certain amount of local fame in the San Jose Mercury-News' "Hit of the Week" food section as a "hands down winner" for its "scrumptious French-style croissants and poppy-seed scones topped with a thin orange glaze." A couple of weeks later the Mountainview Weekly, in an article called Best Bets, described The Croissant Place as a "haunt worth tracking down." The article went on to say:

> At The Croissant Place the tables are small and the parking sometimes tough. You may need a bloodhound to find the place. The service is uneven, the prices high and the daily specials are all too often gone before you decide.
>
> So why bother?
>
> For croissants to kill for, that's why. For fresh soups and salads that make most fast-food competition food taste like paste. For muffins that commuters buy more of than they need. And more.

The owner-managers of The Croissant Place were an elderly but energetic couple known to everyone by their first names, Flora and Roshan. Flora and Roshan had immigrated to California from central Europe about 10 years ago. In Europe, Roshan's family owned a prominent grocery wholesale business and were considered very well to do. While both Flora and Roshan understood English very well, both spoke with strong accents. They worked hard, one or the other at the restaurant about 90 percent of the time it was open. Typically, Flora was on site the first half of the restaurants' open hours and Roshan the second half. Roshan baked in the evenings sometimes quite late. During the day Flora and Roshan often worked along side their staff doing everything, no matter how menial. Roshan especially liked to chat with the customers.

Flora's middle-aged niece, Kara, and nephew, Don, worked in the restaurant about half-time. While friendly, they were quiet and serious and kept to themselves and never spoke about their personal lives. Kara and Don knew the restaurant's secret recipes, assisted in preparing the homemade dishes, sometimes purchased supplies and when Flora or Roshan were absent, supervised the staff (about 5 percent of the time). Otherwise they too performed any of the staff's tasks needing attention.

On the average, the number of staff members at The Croissant Place was nine, usually teenagers, but it varied a lot. All of the staff was expected to perform all activities except for baking, cooking, and managing. They made specialty coffees, sandwiches and salads, served everything, bussed tables, washed dishes, mopped the floor, and acted as host and cashier. All staff was paid the minimum wage even as they were trained. Roshan, Flora, or an experienced employee taught all new employees the appropriate method for completing all tasks on-the-job which usually took two or three weeks. Staff was allowed a 15-minute break and a half hour for lunch. They were allowed to make whatever they wanted for lunch up to a cost of five dollars, but this policy was never enforced. The staff ate whatever they wanted regardless of cost. Most of the staff took their breaks sitting at an inconspicuous table in the restaurant. A few went outside to smoke. When in the store Roshan or Flora would usually tell their employees when to take their breaks but would sometimes forget. Some employees would not speak up and thus not receive a break; others would request a break and usually got it. It was expected that if business became busy that the staff would cut their break short and help out. Most would. Over time many employees slowed in their work, didn't perform tasks carefully and fooled around when business was light.

When Flora noticed employees beginning to come to work late or talking on the telephone in the back room or sitting down at the counter and chatting with one another, she would call all the staff together and lecture them. She always said the same things: that some staff were better than others; that being late and "fooling around" was unacceptable; that she and her husband worked very hard; that she had to get up at 5:00 A.M. every morning to get to the restaurant and Roshan usually didn't get home until after midnight; that Roshan and she were not young anymore; and that Roshan shouldn't have to work so hard or he would have a heart attack. Upon hearing this every couple of weeks or so, the employees often talked among themselves about Roshan and Flora. They speculated that Roshan and Flora probably made a lot of money, and complained that still wages were too low and Flora and Roshan were too cheap to give raises to long-term and hard-working staff, having to work rush hours to make up for inexperienced employees, and that they were tired of constantly training new people. Over time many employees did work less hard and fooled around more. Eventually they were fired. Consequently, Flora and Roshan were constantly hiring and training new staff.

Job openings were never advertised since there were always a large stack of applications. Each month six to ten people would come into the restaurant seeking employment. Whoever was at the cash register would hand out an application, and when it was filled out, pass it on to Roshan. No prior restaurant experience was required as Roshan believed that the necessary skills could all be learned. Whenever he needed to fill a staff opening, Roshan would call the most recent applicants because he believed they would be the most available. If an applicant was still interested, Roshan would have the person come to the restaurant. He would then speak with the applicant for a few minutes and if he found them "presentable," he would immediately start the person's training by himself or Flora or most commonly by an experienced employee. After a couple of weeks, if the applicant's performance was satisfactory, Roshan would ask him or her if he or she would like the job permanently. Most applicants, eager for extra spending money and not yet fully aware of the negative feeling of most of the staff, usually accepted. Roshan would then help the new employee fill out the necessary employment papers.

LISA

Whenever she thought about her job at The Croissant Place, Lisa's feelings welled up. The high school senior felt unhappy about working there—her low earnings, the pressure of rush hours, Flora's lectures, the negativism of her colleagues, and continually having to train new employees. At the same time she felt so sorry for Roshan; he worked so hard and turnover was constant. Over and over recently Lisa had mentally quit but hadn't told anybody. Today had to be different. She'd resign. She would tell Roshan at the end of her shift.

And it had taken all of her courage. After the lunch rush Lisa helped clean up which took longer than usual because the Croissant Place was understaffed—as usual. Collecting her purse and jacket, Lisa found Roshan in the office. She apologized for interrupting and then quickly told Roshan she was giving her notice and that she could work only one more week. Roshan had sighed, asked her to think it over and offered her a raise if she would stay.

Leaving the Croissant Place Lisa felt pity for Roshan, who had become a grandfather figure to her, but knew she had to stick with her decision. But should she tell him why she and most others eventually quit? If so, what should she say?

THE DANBURY HOTEL

Reminiscing with Roger Johnson, his hotel manager, about all the changes they had implemented over the past few years, Nick DiCarlo, general manager of The Danbury Hotel, leaned back and sipped his iced tea. DiCarlo had been transferred to The Danbury three years ago, a year after Johnson had arrived. The two of them had worked together in Washington at another hotel run by the parent management company, Hotel Management International, prior to being reunited in Boston at The Danbury. After having learned he was going to The Danbury, DiCarlo called Johnson to discuss the hotel's weak financial performance. Although the year DiCarlo arrived the hotel had over $35 million in revenues, it was just breaking even.

"Well, I guess we have another project on our hands," DiCarlo said to Johnson.

"I got news for you," replied Johnson, "this is going to be easier than Washington. There are $20 bills on the carpet here. All you have to do is bend down and pick them up."

DiCarlo remembered wondering what Johnson had meant by $20 bills lying on the carpet. But when he got to The Danbury, it all made sense. Basically, ways to save money existed all over the place. Easy, simple, and obvious examples of over-spending were spread throughout the hotel like $20 bills. By making little changes over the past three years, DiCarlo had picked up a lot of $20 bills, totaling over $3 million in profits this past year. But it had not been easy. He had not anticipated the difficulties of making changes when the older, long-tenured employees appeared to fight him every step of the way. Most of the changes, DiCarlo believed, were relatively minor adjustments that saved thousands of dollars. However, making these changes had been more difficult than at any other property he had worked at before. How were he and Johnson supposed to make even more changes, perhaps even bigger changes, with these long-tenured employees who seemed to resist any kind of change?

HISTORY OF THE DANBURY HOTEL

She was the grand dame of hotels in Boston—a real one of a kind. The Danbury had a proud history of elegant hospitality with Old World charm. The lobby, located on the second floor, was accented with gold leaf, rich, brocade carpeting, and large, heavy murals. The stairs leading up to the lobby, over 20 feet wide and covered with a velvety red carpet, gave one the impression of walking into a palace. A large, crystal chandelier hung from the high ceiling, and directly underneath it sat an antique oval table with an urn filled with large, stunning fresh flowers. To the left, seven more red carpeted stairs led to the upper lobby, with a room size fountain for a centerpiece. The upper lobby had walls lined with mirrors and gold wall sconces, and was filled with many plush living room-like antique chairs. In the afternoons, tea was served to the mellifluous tones of a harp. The air was filled with luxury and a well-worn comfortable elegance. The Danbury had "white glove" refinement without being snobby.

The Pompeii Room, The Danbury's most prized banquet room, featured an Italian architecture style with a colonnade of columns covered in vines with tones of creams and gold, Tennessee marble floors, and crystal chandeliers. It was one of the most popular places for large weddings and banquets, seating up to 700 people.

The hotel was celebrating its 75th birthday, and the brochure "The Danbury Tradition: A Milestone in History . . .," outlined its proud history:

> The Danbury Hotel opened in 1920, and the March 1919 issue of "The Economist" reported that the structure would be "of unusual magnificence, nothing like it in appearance, arrangement or finishing having ever been attempted in this country . . ."
>
> Stylistically, The Danbury takes its balanced formal composition and restrained detail from the Italian palaces of High Renaissance Rome and Florence. Constructed of smooth limestone, the building is thirteen stories high. It rises from a rectangular base which changes at the third story to an H-shape. A distinctive feature of Italian Renaissance design found in The Danbury is the "piano nobile" which was the principal story, raised above the ground and contained the public rooms. This concept was especially appropriate for adaptation to a grand hotel. Canopies provide a sheltered entrance on both Hurstbourne Avenue and Linden Street. These are connected by an interior arcade which provides showcase space for various shops on the street level. In emulating sixteenth century Italian architecture, the designer wisely chose a historical precedent noted for the dignity and serenity of its design.
>
> The coat of arms, which appears on The Danbury's chinaware, linen, silver and other places, contains the phrase in Latin, "Aquila Non Capit Muscas," which simply means "an eagle does not catch flies." On the shield of this emblem is a wyvern (a winged dragon with a knotted and barbed tail) and directly above is an upraised arm holding a battle-axe. This crest was designed in Italy many centuries ago for The Danbury family (the original owners) and the true heraldic emblem was used by the family's warriors on their armor and personal possessions.
>
> The Danbury cost $10,000,000 to build, including land, building and furnishings. Its original seven hundred rooms were served by eight to nine hundred employees. Ever since its opening on New Year's Eve 1920, The Danbury has accumulated guest-book signatures of Queen Elizabeth and Prince Philip of

England, the Emperor of Japan, King Hussein of Jordan, Nehru of India, Winston Churchill, Eleanor Roosevelt, presidents Herbert Hoover, Dwight Eisenhower, Gerald Ford, Ronald Reagan, and many celebrities such as Charles Lindbergh, Walt Disney, and Charlton Heston.

In 1979, after being privately owned by various families, The Danbury was purchased by Devonshire Industries who, in turn, leased the property to the management company Hotel Management International. In May 1982, the hotel was proclaimed a historic place by the U.S. Department of the Interior and the State of Massachusetts. The Danbury completed a $30 million renovation in 1986 and was restored to its original splendor.

Although the hotel had 535 rooms and suites and 650 employees after the renovation, it still maintained an intimate, cozy atmosphere. Unlike some of the newer, more modern hotels, The Danbury gave the feeling of being in one's grandmother's parlor. The cushions on all the sitting pieces had been worn in comfortably, and the staff provided a warm and relaxed level of service. The hotel was busy year round and catered to both business and leisure travelers, but occupancy was busiest on the weekends due to tourists.

Despite the splendor of the hotel, the building was 75 years old and not without its problems. According to Lee David, the rooms division manager:

> The hotel is a nightmare to heat and cool. We have 35 room configurations (see Exhibit 1). I have all kinds of engineering problems. If I had a cookie cutter kind of hotel like the Holiday Inn where all the rooms are the same I wouldn't have all these problems. It would be simple. But I like the opulence; I want the hotel to be glamorous. It's a nightmare to keep clean and to keep up with because the traffic is so heavy. All these things need dusting and polishing. In a modern hotel you get a light that is flush with the wall that you don't have to dust. You don't have to dust the crystal things and that kind of thing. Yeah, you don't have any charm, but it's much easier to work with.

Yet despite the problems associated with an older, stately building, The Danbury had charm and character, and it went well beyond its physical assets. Many of the hotel's employees, after having worked at the hotel for 20 to 30 years, had become as much a part of the character of the hotel as its plush velvet red chairs and heavy crystal chandeliers.

MAKING CHANGES AT THE DANBURY

Nick DiCarlo was tall, easily six feet and a few inches, and had dark brown, almost black hair. With a full round face and a boyish haircut, DiCarlo looked more like an overgrown teenage boy than a "thirty something," experienced, aggressive manager. Not only was he general manager at The Danbury, he oversaw 11 other Hotel Management International properties as well, all outside of the United States.

Roger Johnson, on the other hand, was five feet eight inches, with a slight, well-kept build and a neat and tidy appearance. He wore finely tailored suits, which accented the elegance of his refined British accent. Although fully gray, in his mid-forties, and with an apparent refined appearance, Johnson also had a boyish quality to him, albeit different from DiCarlo's. DiCarlo had a booming voice and a "rough and tumble" appearance to him, while Johnson was more like a Cheshire cat.

Boston The Danbury Hotel
Operated by Hotel Management International

Room Type Definitions

The Danbury Hotel has a lot of different rooms varying in size and bed type. To ensure that the hotel maximizes its room revenue while maintaining a simple way of determining room types, the following room codes have been designed.

All room codes have two letters: the first letter stands for bed type while the second letter represents the size and features of the room.

First letter:
S = One oversized twin bed or single bed
K = One king bed
Q = One queen bed
T = Two twin beds
O = Two oversized twin beds

Second letter:
B = Standard room
C = Moderate room
D = Deluxe room—large room most with a seating area
E = Junior suite—used to be two rooms that were converted into one room
L = Room with a view of the harbor
S = Small suite with Murphy beds
V = Vista floor—top two floors with lounge privileges
F = Suite with harbor view with a large parlor
G = Suite with one bedroom
H = Suite with one bedroom and large parlor

EXHIBIT 1

Aside from The Danbury, Hotel Management International operated over 160 hotels in nearly 50 countries. In the United States, The Danbury was their top property, and DiCarlo had been pleased to make the move. Costs at The Danbury were out of control, and DiCarlo had been brought in to bring them back into line. Hotel Management International was not happy with The Danbury's performance. It was not in the hotel business just to break even. The competition was formidable—Hyatt, Sheraton, Westin, Ritz-Carlton, Four Seasons, and Marriott were all neighbors of The Danbury. Changes had to be made if The Danbury was to continue.

With the able assistance of Johnson, DiCarlo had been able to make changes and cut costs, but it had not been easy. Many of the employees at The Danbury had been there over 20 years, and some even longer. Having never attended a retirement party at a hotel before, Johnson attended his first at The Danbury—for an employee who worked at the hotel for 45 years. Lee David, the rooms division manager, was surprised to discover that another of the retiring Danbury employees had worked in the laundry for 35 years, and David was not even 35 years old! DiCarlo believed The Danbury was one of a kind in terms of having long-term employees:

I guess the difference in this hotel is that you do have a core of stable employees.
There are approximately 60 people in the kitchen and 55 of them are core employees

and there's like maybe three, maybe four positions that we turn over. And busboys . . . we've got more career busboys. We have busboys that have been here 25–30 years, and they absolutely love it and enjoy it. That's their career path and it stopped 20 years ago. You won't find that at other hotels. This hotel is one of a kind in Boston because a majority of the employees are very senior in time at the hotel.

Our core is much, much bigger than most hotels and I was just talking about this with the chef the other day. One of the hardest things in any hotel is getting your breakfast people to show up on time—your waiters and waitresses and the people in the kitchen. We had the opposite problem. We have some people that don't even have a home life. They take the midnight bus and get here at 1:00 A.M. and get dressed and sit on the bench in the locker room waiting for their shift to start at 4:00 A.M. I mean, it's crazy. You don't have to worry about it; our breakfast cooks show up on time. However, if you do change the schedule, they'll still show up at the same time and day. They've been doing it so long, they just show up.

According to DiCarlo and Johnson, although many hotel managers believe having long tenured employees would cure all their problems (see Exhibit 2), loyal employees do not come without their own problems. Said Johnson,

The most difficult thing is, if you ever want to introduce a new idea, like when Nick came, there were a hundred changes that needed to be made, and it's probably one of the hardest hotels I've ever worked in when actually changing anything. Even to change the quantity of soup that has been made here for 30 years was almost impossible to change. I mean, I wanted to change to make the quantity of soup equal to each day's sales. But try getting the cook to change. He knows what his start time is. He knows what time he needs to be here in order to get the soup made by opening time. You never have to worry about him showing up. He'll be here, no problem. He'll be late sometimes, but no matter what time he shows up, the soup will always be ready on time. He just switches to automatic pilot. And he does the same thing, every single day. So if you try to introduce this idea that, okay look, after 30 years, maybe there's a different way of doing this, you know, and by the way, the recipe will be slightly different because the volume is slightly different, you may get it changed if you stand over him for 3–4 days. Then leave him for 3 or 4 days and he may continue doing it. But after a week, he's back doing it the old way. You know, you just can't change it. It's very, very difficult. There are a lot of examples like that. It's a challenge.

DiCarlo had this to say about some of his experiences:

Oh, the orange juice! Orange juice was one of the biggest arguments. We used to make our own orange juice. And as you know, you have to use a blend of oranges, You can't just take Valencia oranges and squeeze them—they're too damn sweet. You've got to combine them with blood oranges which are more tart than others and sometimes they're not available. And because we had to blend our own oranges, we were throwing out cases of oranges because they were rotting because we were buying too many of some kinds of oranges, etc. Then we had to have someone on staff just to sit there and put the oranges through the machine. And then the staff would drink 90% of it. So then, I was thinking, this is a big city, and sure enough, there are

Human Resources Management in the Hotel Industry

Hotels are usually described as labor intensive. A 500-room hotel is likely to employ 300 to 600 employees depending on the level of service provided. When the hotel is fully occupied, anywhere from 600–1000 guests could be on the property. The total capital investment in such a hotel might be 100 to 200 million dollars. Compare this to a chemical plant costing about the same. It might be operated by a workforce of 25 employees, and might sell its products to only 2 or 3 large customers.

Hourly positions in hotels are typically low paying. Many jobs have to do with basic duties such a cleaning, carrying, and serving. Turnover in hotels is notoriously high, with turnover rates of 50 to 100 percent being common in some positions. Hotel managers tend to attribute the combination of low wages, high pressure from customer demands, and working nights and weekends (a hotel is open 24 hours a day, seven days a week) to the problem of turnover. A hotel with 500 employees and a 50 percent annual turnover rate must hire and train 250 new employees each year (one-half of its total staff). The human resources departments of many hotels are caught in a cycle of interviewing, hiring, training, and terminating. It has been estimated that the cost of turning over an hourly hotel employee is approximately $2,500 and $6,000 for a salaried employee. These costs include money spent or lost on separation (exit interviews, unemployment tax, administrative functions), replacement (advertising, interviewing, drug testing, uniforms, etc.), training, lost production (time for new hire to learn the job; loss from time employee decides to leave until actual separation occurs), and morale and public relations ("ripple" effect—one leaves and others follow; effect on customers from disgruntled employee or a new employee who doesn't recognize the customer or know his/her job very well). The monetary costs and customer service effects of turnover can be enormous, especially in light of trying to maintain consistent customer service standards with a constantly fluctuating staff.

Hotels have traditionally relied on young people (18–24 years old), women, minorities and immigrants for their labor. However, as the number of young people has diminished, some hotels are looking for alternative sources of labor. Hotel trade journals have suggested the use of older employees as a solution to the labor shortage and turnover problems, without indicating the problems associated with usage of such employees.

EXHIBIT 2

three produce guys that do this for a living. But the chef said it's not fresh squeezed. But I said, "Chef, they squeeze it at 2 A.M. and they deliver it here at 5 A.M. That's fresh squeezed in my mind." And he said "Ah, the first day it snows they won't show up." It's one excuse after another. What's the difference if we leave the blending headache to a professional? The guy supplies all our competitors: The Ritz-Carlton, The Four Seasons. He supplies everyone else, why are we special?

Oh yeah, and mayonnaise is another big one. We were making our own mayonnaise. If we were in the middle of a desert island, I'd say, yes, we should make our own mayonnaise for consistency and quality. Do we make our own salad dressings? You bet we do. But the base is mayonnaise and you can buy so many different types and styles. We tried them all, but the chef kept saying that they were no good and the guests were complaining about "this and that." So I said, "Chef, I'll find you someone that will make our exact mayonnaise at half the price." We used to have a mayonnaise lady in the morning—nothing but make mayonnaise. We actually found this company that makes the mayonnaise to our specifications and it costs half the price of making it ourselves.

Having gotten the chef to accept the orange juice and the mayonnaise, DiCarlo and Johnson had not anticipated their own wait staff would sabotage the changes. Said DiCarlo,

> Here I convince the chef to allow the produce guy to make our orange juice and then, after many taste testings, I even got the chef to stop making mayonnaise. But what I didn't expect was what the waiters were doing. Come to find out these guys were telling the customers not to order the orange juice because it wasn't fresh squeezed! Then I heard them telling customers that the sandwiches were terrible now because we weren't making our own mayonnaise anymore. Our own waiters were killing us. They were undermining everything we were trying to do. They were our biggest enemy.

Of course, having long term employees was not without benefits. Not only did such employees provide continuity and consistency, they built up a rapport with the guests. Said Johnson,

> The guests love to be recognized. It's vital. A guest may come only once a year, but the third year they're here and they're still recognized, then we've got them as a customer for life.

DiCarlo gave this example:

> One of the legacies of this hotel is its executive floor. You look at the executive floor concepts at other hotels, and ours is one of the few that I've worked at that works, one hundred percent. And people pay for it, full value. It's not like 90% of the other hotels you go to where very few customers are paying for it. At those hotels, they're upgrading their top corporate customers. Those people are not paying extra to be on the executive floor. Here, you got people who want to be there because Gladys, Maria, Estelle and Norma, the four people that work there, have been there forever. Gladys started here when she was 15 years old. She used to be one of the old elevator operators, so she knows everybody. These executive floor guests don't even call reservations to reserve a room anymore. Most of the people, and these are CEOs of companies, call Norma directly at home. "Oh, and Norma, by the way, can I have *my* room and I'll be coming in at . . ." and they know the room they want, exactly, and they come, and . . . it's amazing. Go up there and have a cocktail in that lounge and you'll see . . . Gladys, well, she knows everybody. It's like her parlor, like her living room. And she's been here 50 years, and you know, I was up there the other night and these two ladies walked in and their husbands joined them and they said, "Did you hear? Gladys had another grandchild!" Gladys is there showing the family pictures, and she says, "Oh look, here's my new grandchild" and geez, these are bloody guests! And then other guests come in and say "Gladys, you've had another grandchild," and I'm, sitting there with my wife thinking this is incredible. But it's the real deal—it's the real deal. These people come here because of that.
>
> And the downside? Is Gladys the best employee in the world? She's certainly the most friendly; she's certainly the happiest. But she's moving a little slower these days. She has her own pace. She's another tough one if you want to change something.

Johnson added:

If you want to get a housemaid to clean something under the bed, you feel sorry for them. Most of our room attendants are in their sixties. You know that at 65 years old, they can't get down on their hands and knees anymore. So what you know you need done, they are physically incapable of doing it. They can't do 14 rooms a day the way we need them to do it. So, it makes it unusual here. Then you get the ones that won't retire. They are 70 years old and falling asleep in places. It's very difficult. You can't retire people in this country.

THE ROAD AHEAD

DiCarlo, with the help of Johnson, had fought a long, hard battle with many of the employees over the past couple of years. Now he feared how difficult making additional changes would be. Plus he wondered what to do with all the older employees on staff. Did The Danbury need "new blood," he wondered, to keep the hotel at pace or ahead of the changing times? How would he keep labor costs in line if some of his employees appeared physically incapable of doing their jobs? DiCarlo poured himself another glass of iced tea as he pondered these questions.

EVERGREEN WILLOWS*

Evergreen Willows, a new convalescent home, had been in operation for several months. The large one-story building, which had been specially constructed for its purpose, was divided into two identical wings designated A and B. In the center of the building, separating the wings, was a large living room, a chapel, offices, and a middle wing, which included the kitchen, patients' dining room, and employees' dining room. A and B wings consisted of a nurse's station in the center with a corridor of patients' rooms to each side (see Exhibit 1).

Each nurse's station served the patients for its wing, and each was under the direction of a charge nurse. Other nurses and nurse's aides worked under the charge nurse. From the opening day, each wing had been staffed separately. The director of nurses had assigned the more experienced, older aides to A wing, where she planned to locate sicker patients. She assigned the less experienced aides to B wing, which was to have patients who were more ambulatory. Except on rare occasions, A-wing staff did not work on B wing nor B-wing staff on A wing.

The day shift on B wing consisted of one charge nurse and four nurse's aides. Normally the charge nurse was Jenny, a young registered nurse who had no previous experience as a charge nurse before working at the home. On her days off, she was replaced by Sue, a licensed practical nurse who worked part time. The nurse's aides had rotating days off each week so that, except when someone was sick and had to be replaced, the same aides were usually on duty at the same time. The B-wing aides were of similar age and experience, having been hired at the same time. All lived in the local community and tended to see one another socially after hours.

---

*Reprinted with permission from A. Cohen, S. Fink, H. Gadon, & R. Willits. *Effective Behavior in Organizations.* R. D. Irwin, Inc. 1995.

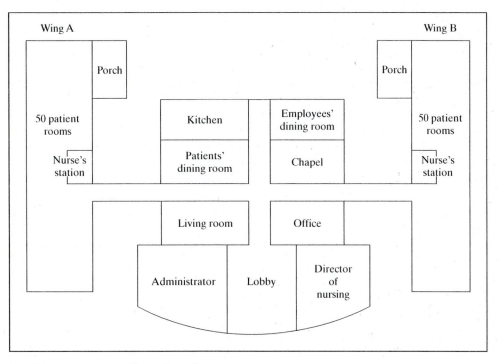

EXHIBIT 1   Evergreen Willows Floor Plan

Jenny's duties as charge nurse included dispensing medications, keeping charts and records up to date, and supervising the work of the aides. Actual patient care was the responsibility of the aides. Most of the B-wing patients were at least partially ambulatory. Caring for them involved assisting them in bathing, dressing, walking, and feeding, or what nurses call "activities of daily living." The aides also like to visit with the lonelier patients whenever time permitted. A number of the patients wandered around during the day, and it was often necessary for the aides to look for them, which consumed a great deal of time considering the size of the building. Jenny, in giving her medications, ranged all over the building in search of patients and was not always to be found on the wing.

From the opening of the home, Jenny had found that there was barely enough time in the day for the work she had to do. She did not give detailed instructions to the aides, and they developed their own routines in caring for the patients. One new aide even said that "it took me weeks before I felt I knew what I was supposed to be doing." Usually they would separate by corridor, each doing the work they saw needing to be done. All helped in passing out breakfast and dinner trays, feeding patients, and in answering lights when a patient called for assistance. All of the B-wing aides kept busy, although sometimes there were complaints by some who felt they were "getting stuck" with the more unpleasant jobs because no one else would do them.

Nonetheless, the atmosphere on the wing was friendly. The aides often spoke of how much they enjoyed the patients. While most of the aides had not sought a job working with older patients, even those who might have preferred a job in a hospital caring for younger patients soon discovered that the "old folks" were interesting people. Consequently, there was much friendly contact between patients and aides as well as among aides and among patients.

The patients enjoyed the atmosphere, although sometimes their families worried about the way the patients were allowed to wander about.

In contrast, A-wing patients were for the most part bedridden and required more actual nursing care. In fact, if a patient on B wing took sick, the home's policy was to transfer that patient to A wing where there was a larger staff/patient ratio. The staff consisted of a charge nurse, Elizabeth, and two or three R.N.s or L.P.N.s and six aides. The charge nurse took care of duties at the nurse's station and drug room, while the other nurses dispensed drugs and did treatments. The nurse's aides did patient care. Many of the patients were unable to walk or stand and helping them up to a chair involved heavy lifting. Fewer patients than on B wing were dressed, most wearing johnnies and bathrobes, and most remained in their rooms. Many of the patients who were confined to their rooms rang for the aides frequently throughout the day, often for only minor requests.

Elizabeth was an older, more experienced nurse than Jenny and supervised the aides working under her in a strict manner. Each morning the aides were paired in teams of two and assigned to 16 specified patients. The assignments were standardized, and the A-wing aides usually worked systematically and on a schedule to complete their work. There was little change from day to day, and patients were generally taken care of at the same time each day and were accustomed to this. Working in teams of two gave each aide someone to assist her when lifting was necessary. Assignments included patients located far apart on the floor, but aides usually cared only for the patients on their assignment sheets. When another patient asked for assistance, they would often answer "Wait until your nurse gets here." Elizabeth kept a close watch on her aides and was very critical of the work they did. Sometimes she could be heard over the intercom saying something like, "Girls, there are five lights on A wing." She insisted that the girls maintain a professional relationship with the patients. While the atmosphere on the wing was far from homey, the sick patient received good technical care and their families felt a good deal of confidence in the quality of care provided on A wing.

The administrator and director of nurses were cheerful and apparently well liked by the nursing staff. They appeared at meetings held approximately every other week for in-service educational training or to update employees on issues of importance. Their response to the work done by the nurses and the aides was favorable. However, they were rarely seen on the wings, and they delegated a great deal of responsibility to the charge nurses.

After several months the director of nurses announced at one of the in-service meetings that aides would now have assignments alternating them between the two wings. While she felt completely satisfied with the performance of both wings, she felt the aides should be more versatile and experienced with all types of patients.

When this new plan went into effect, a series of problems began to develop between the head nurses and aides of the two wings. B-wing aides on A wing found themselves answering lights not belonging to their own patients and falling behind in their own scheduled work. While working on one corridor, an aide would often forget those patients on the other corridor assigned to her, and those patients frequently had their lights on and unanswered for long periods of time. They complained to the head nurse when they had to wait. Thus the B-wing aides were under constant criticism from Elizabeth, but when they tried to talk to her they found she was not listening.

The help Elizabeth had from the other nurses allowed her more free time than Jenny had. She was often seen laughing and talking with the other nurses, but she did not socialize with the aides.

When on their own wing, the B-wing aides now found they had to do even more work than usual. Most of the aides from A wing were lost on B and needed much help in caring for the B-wing patients. Nothing was written down, and Jenny was too busy or not around to help them; so the responsibility of orienting them fell to the B-wing aides.

Stating that there was "nothing to do" on B wing, a few of the A-wing aides took frequent coffee breaks. The regular aides from B wing could not find them when they needed help or did not have the time to go to the employees' dining room to get them. One incident on B wing occurred when an aide was assisting a patient to bed, and the patient slipped to the floor. There was no one nearby, nor did anyone answer the emergency light when the aide called. The aide had to leave the patient to get help. When this situation was reported to Jenny, she reprimanded the A-wing aide who was not on the floor where she was supposed to be and recommended to the director of nurses that she be fired. It was the decision of the director that she "should be entitled to a second chance." The situation did not improve.

A great deal of resentment developed among the nursing staff. Several of the aides, including those considered to be the best workers, quit or began looking for other jobs. The attitude of the administrator and director of nurses was one of little concern. In the words of the director of nurses: "We have many applicants for each vacancy. Anyone can be replaced. Our turnover rate of employees here is better than in most nursing homes."

EXCLUSIVE RESORTS WORLDWIDE

Three months ago, at the end of the quarterly meeting of the Executive Committee, the CEO and president of the Exclusive Resorts Worldwide Corporation asked Anthony Hines, vice president of marketing, and William Spee, manager of the organization planning and development department, to get together and determine if better forecasts of tourist travel and reservations could be made available so that financial planning, recruitment, construction planning, and so forth could be improved. Kent Mathews and Steve Peale, who both worked for Spee, and David Helms, Henry Roberts, and Andre Foucard of marketing, were assigned by Spee and Hines, respectively, to a task force to work on forecasting issues. Peale and Helms, being older, more experienced, and regarded as more senior, quickly became the informal leaders of the task force. The work proceeded quickly and smoothly as the five men got along well together and quite easily divided up the technical aspects of the project. The task force members agreed at the outset that they should keep their respective superiors informed as they went along.

After the project had been underway for nearly seven weeks, David Helms told Steve Peale that he, Roberts, and Foucard seemed to be getting some "run around" by the divisional marketing managers. Helms also indicated to Peale that he felt reluctant to bypass the divisional marketing managers and speak to Mr. Hines, the vice president of marketing. Helms asked Peale to have his boss, Bill Spee, suggest to Hines that there should be a progress meeting to assess the work done to date. Peale spoke with Spee about Helms' idea and the reason for it. Spee then spoke with Hines who agreed to call a progress meeting as he believed a rapid resolution to the problem was desirable. Hines invited the five marketing division managers, William Spee, and the five-man task force to the meeting, and told Helms and Peale to set up a presentation.

As Helms and Peale began to plan for the meeting, they agreed that the three marketing members of the task force were in a tight spot. Helms, Roberts, and Foucard, not wanting to embarrass their superiors or themselves, asked Peale to make the presentation of the joint forecasting recommendation the task force had come up with.

At the appointed time, everyone invited to the meeting was present. Anthony Hines began the session by asking who would be reporting for the task force. Helms suggested that Peale was the best man to do this. Hines asked Spee if that was acceptable to him, and Spee agreed. Peale then spent about 40 minutes outlining the concept of their work. He emphasized that all task force members agreed on the adequacy of the data and its analysis, and that they all believed their recommendations were feasible and would be effective. Foucard and Roberts asked Peale to expand on certain points during his presentation. It appeared to Spee that they wanted clarification for their own managers who might not understand or agree.

After Peale's presentation, Hines asked his division managers to react to the task force's recommendations. Two gave the recommendations unenthusiastic support, the three other division managers then began a heated discussion among themselves—Helms, Roberts, and Foucard each tried to interject, but were ignored. Once when Foucard asked the western U.S. division manager a question, he was angrily told to "be quiet!"

As William Spee observed the meeting, he recalled that for a year or more these divisional marketing managers had rather consistently resisted all suggestions for changes in systems and operations—many stemming from the corporation's stepped-up strategic concerns. Spee believed that their opposition had begun to be detrimental to the company's development, and Spee knew the president expected him to step up the process of organizational change. While a staff officer, Spee also knew his relationship with the president was an influential one. He believed that Hines was open to change and was actually quite a sophisticated manager, but that he couldn't tolerate the opposition from his division managers much longer. Spee actually liked these older, experienced divisional marketing managers, and certainly didn't want to have their careers damaged if at all possible. Clearly, Hines had the formal authority to get things done in the marketing area.

As the two-hour mark passed in what appeared to have become a discussion going nowhere, Anthony Hines loudly cleared his throat and said, "Bill, you've listened to the meeting thus far, what do you think we should do next?"

AN EXPATRIATE MANAGER'S NOTEBOOK*

While the thoughts of most passengers onboard the American Eagle flight focused on the memorable vacations they were leaving behind, Tim Parker, a hospitality administration doctoral student entering his second year at Cornell University, had his thoughts elsewhere. Although he had spent the previous nine summers working for Sail Caribbean, a large charter sailing school, he had gone down this summer with an additional mission. His doctoral committee had allowed him to return to the British Virgin Islands conditional upon his keeping detailed notes regarding his interactions with expatriate and local managers and staff.

*"An Expatriate Manager's Notebook," Courtesy of Jeffrey P. Shay, Ph.D. Jeffrey Shay is Associate Professor and Chair, Department of Management and Marketing, The University of Montana.

The committee contended that this experience might provide the foundation for Tim's future research as well as afford the opportunity to become more aware of a culture's impact on leader–follower relations. Tim knew that his first meeting with his committee would center on what he had learned and realized that it was time to review his notes. Tim pulled his notebook out of his carry-on bag and began to read. Many of his notes seemed to reflect the nature of the local culture and the challenges that face expatriate managers.

NOTEBOOK EXCERPTS

June 6th

I arrived five days ago in Tortola,[1] British Virgin Islands (see Appendix A for details on the British Virgin Islands)—this is my tenth consecutive summer working here. I started working here as a skipper (i.e., responsible for one boat and nine students) and was promoted through the ranks for five years and wound up as one of the directors (i.e., responsible for 30 staff and 200+ students). The other director is my boss, Mike Liese. This summer is different because I have the dual responsibility of working as a director of Sail Carribbean's[2] programs as well as researching the influence of the Caribbean culture on the managerial environment for my studies at Cornell. Having taken a year's worth of classes in international management and cross-cultural management, I am anxious to find out how useful cultural models such as Hofstede's and Kluckholn and Strodbeck's (see Appendix B) are in helping me to better understand the underlying elements of culture here in Tortola and in the Leeward Islands (i.e., St. Maarten, St. Kitts, etc.) as well. My initial reaction is that the models have made me more sensitive to behaviors that in the past I may have overlooked. There's a long way to go this summer.

I have made some additional observations that are worth noting as well. To the best of my recollection, since my third summer down here, I have had very strong ties to local Tortolans—ties that appear to be free of racial prejudices or strains. I do notice, however, that a social distance seems to develop between my Tortolan friends and I when I am away from the island between September and April of each year. This, I think, is only natural. (I think the fact that I have returned year after year does make a difference, though I am not able to readily determine why.) The way that the locals break the ice though does have racial connotations. Due to my fair skin, I arrive each summer looking quite pale after enduring the long winters in the Northeastern United States. The locals are quick to inquire whether someone "bleached me down." What I find interesting in this case is that the locals acknowledge the difference in skin color but do not appear to use this difference as a means of ostracizing me from the group (i.e., the locals).

Although it has taken me a few days to regain my command of the local dialect of English, as in years past I am finding that my attempts to speak the language increases my acceptance by locals. I notice that, in reality, we meet somewhere in the middle between an East Coast U.S. dialect and an English Caribbean dialect. I have noticed both the locals and myself shifting gears into "pidgin" when we engage in conversation. As the summer progresses, I hope that my fluency in this local dialect increases even more.

---

[1] Tortola is the most highly populated of the British Virgin Islands. The capital city, Roadtown, is the largest city in the BVIs and also the home of the Moorings Charter company.

[2] Sail Caribbean is a for profit summer sailing school for teenage students from around the world. Mike Liese of Northport, New York, founded the school in 1979. The school has attracted more than 4,000 students who learned sailing, windsurfing, waterskiing, diving, marine biology, French, etc. while living aboard a 50-foot yacht.

It's great that our company, Sail Caribbean, is using the Moorings Charter Company again. It's so much easier to know all the people and be known by all the people in a company, regardless of whether it involves cross-cultural situations. The Moorings is the largest sailboat chartering company in the world, with chartering operations in 10 locations around the globe. Sail Caribbean charters its boats from the Tortola unit, an operation that opened in 1969. Today the Tortola unit has more than 175 boats.

Today I spoke with Zita, a 40-year-old Tortolan who has been with the Moorings for nearly two decades. She is one of the managers of the provisioning and supply department at the property. I inquired about the survey that I had sent through the Moorings management over the winter. I wanted to find out what she thought of it. Zita was quick to respond in a very surprised fashion, "So that was *really* a project that you were doing for school. I was afraid to answer your questions truthfully because I didn't think you'd ever get the surveys back. So, how did we do?" I found her remarks were surprising on two levels. First, I was surprised to find that she thought the survey was some sort of a test. Second, it surprised me that she was afraid to answer the survey with her real feelings. I think that the combination of a new general manager at the property, along with me not administering the survey in person, might have made the locals apprehensive. I wonder if the other respondents reacted in a similar way.

June 8th

Today I had a very insightful conversation with a long time friend of mine at the Moorings, Enrick. Enrick is from Tortola and has been moving through the ranks at the property—he's marked to be one of the senior local managers if he continues along his path. My inquiry focused on expatriate managers and what the locals *really* thought about them. Enrick explained that one of the major problems that locals have with expatriate managers was that, "these expatriates think that their job is to make us do things their way without taking into consideration the Tortolan culture. They don't respect what we have, why should we respect what they bring?"

He continued, "Managers don't realize that you have to ease into the culture, otherwise you create more problems. When a foreign (i.e., expatriate) manager establishes a negative relationship with his staff at the start, it takes more time for the manager to be accepted no matter what they do to correct the situation. They are starting with a very steep climb up the mountain if they do this." From this, I gather that the first impression that an expatriate manager makes is one that will be hard to overcome, especially if it is a negative first impression. By initiating changes prior to being accepted into the culture, you are demonstrating a general lack of respect for the host culture and therefore unnecessarily isolate yourself from the culture, a position which requires overcoming greater cultural barriers—those which are natural and those which you have helped build.

I wonder what these expatriate managers should do. They are hired by their companies to manage here, not to sit around and wait. There seems to be a difficult balance here between making things happen and showing respect. I wonder how the recruitment, selection, and training processes could be used to alleviate the potential for these problems (i.e., a negative first impression that severely hampers the ability of the expatriate to perform).

Enrick offered examples of two expatriate managers with different approaches. The first of Enrick's examples was Keith. Keith was hired as the food and beverage director for the hotel and restaurant facilities at the property. Enrick explained,

> At first we (i.e., the local staff) really didn't like him. He came in here from the
> States and tried to make too many changes too quickly. The Mariner Inn

Restaurant (the main food and beverage outlet) has always been known as one of the best places in Tortola. That's why so many weddings and social parties are held here at our restaurant. He comes in and acts like we didn't know how to do anything. I must admit he has finally figured out how to do his job . . . but it took a while. Unfortunately for him, a lot of the people here didn't like him for a long time because of what he did at first. Now we are almost to the point of liking him. But he will probably take another job soon anyway.

Enrick's second example was Paul, the new general manager of all operations at the property. Enrick thought that it was still too early to tell but that it seemed as though Paul had learned something from his predecessors. Paul has been here about six months and according to Enrick appears to be in the observation mode. Enrick indicated that the observation mode could have possible problems. Paul was observing operations from a distance and not interacting in depth with any of the local employees. "If Paul starts giving orders without speaking directly with us (i.e., locals), then he will face some challenges," Enrick argued. He continued, "How could he (Paul) know what to change if he hasn't been around us enough to know what changes are needed?"

Managing in this environment has always come relatively easy for me. But, in retrospect, my first three years down here I was sheltered from most cultural interactions. The directors have always been responsible for supplier, government, and other relations with locals. But even when you are a director, in our company, you direct a mostly American staff . . . so it's primarily just the external business contacts that involve any cross-cultural interactions.

June 10th

Tonight I had dinner in Roadtown, the capital of the British Virgin Islands, with two expatriate managers and a local national, Mike McLane, Mike Liese, and Deli Harrigan. The conversation is worth noting. Before proceeding with what I observed, I think it's appropriate to describe the individuals who provided some interesting insights into the culture. Mike McLane is a 36-year-old Canadian responsible for charter boat operations at the Moorings. McLane is a gregarious person and seems to have fit in very well with the locals during his six years here. Mike Liese is the 50-year-old owner-director of the company that I work for, Sail Caribbean. Mike has successfully run his sailing programs in the Caribbean for about two decades. Inquisitive is a word that would best describe how Mike approaches his interactions down here in the Caribbean. He is a person that truly seeks to understand the local culture through asking many questions and listening closely to the locals' responses. Deli Harrigan is a local national who is the most senior employee at the Moorings. In fact, Deli was one of the first employees hired by the Moorings. He started as one of the yacht cleaning crew and now is the chief mechanic of the Tortola base. During his tenure at the Moorings, he has seen many expatriate managers come and go. During the summer months Deli also works for Sail Caribbean as one of their skippers. I have known Deli for 10 years now.

Our dinner conversation revealed the many constituents that an expatriate manager must appease. McLane contends that the new manager of the Moorings Tortola operations, Paul (mentioned in an earlier notebook entry), is not meeting McLane's personal needs. McLane elaborated, "When they (the Moorings) bring in someone new as my boss down here I expect that I can learn something from him. This is just not the case with Paul." McLane argues that, "Paul seems very removed from the operations at this point and is not providing any of us managers with any guidance or direction." In essence, McLane seems to want someone who would really come in and "wow" him. McLane explained that Paul's predecessor, Dennis, was very helpful from the start, got things done, and commanded a great deal of respect. In McLane's opinion, the Moorings should have retained him because Dennis was able to implement changes, something that others had failed to do. "Dennis's biggest asset was that he really got his hands dirty down on the docks. Paul, on the other hand, has not yet mingled with the people and doesn't know the operations," McLane commented. As a result, to McLane it seems as though Paul's initiatives are not seen as reflective of what really needs to happen. McLane questions whether Paul's ideas are really going to improve things at the base.

Mike Liese, in his inquisitive fashion, asked for an example. McLane responded, "We've had an increase in thefts from the boats during the last few months. Paul's decision was to hire a guard and place him at the inboard end of the dock in an attempt to stop some of the stealing. This type of solution works for the first few days but does such an approach actually resolve the problem or address the issues at the core of the problem?" McLane remarked. After dinner I reviewed this part of the conversation, trying to determine the underlying reasons behind employees feeling comfortable stealing from their employer. Were there any cultural elements, either group or national culture, which might be influencing the locals' propensity to steal? The root cause of this problem needs to be explored.

Deli, the local having dinner with us, had an entirely different perspective on the situation. He feels that Dennis was not a good manager and that Paul is much better. "Dennis was always getting in our face. Paul is much more relaxed and is spending time getting to know how we do things down here," Deli remarked. Hence, I see the apparent contrast between what expatriate versus local national managers are looking for from their superiors. The local, Deli, prefers to have someone who will keep his distance while McLane, the expatriate, prefers to have someone who is visibly adding something to the company on a daily, hands-on basis.

McLane is also wondering whether the Moorings' management values his input. The company has sent him to several seminars and he has forwarded reports to upper management regarding how the company might do things differently without receiving any responses. To McLane, sometimes the management at the Moorings' main offices in Clearwater, Florida appears too removed from operations at any of the operating bases.

McLane made one additional remark at the end of the evening that will take further analysis at some time. "Tim, I noticed that you have been getting along very well with Small Craft lately," he remarked. "You must be doing well if you've got him." Small Craft is the name of a Moorings employee who works on the small dinghies. I interpret McClane's remarks to be reflective of the distance that Small Craft keeps from non-Tortolans. While Small Craft is quite animated when in the company of his local Tortolan friends, he is quite shy when interacting with most non-Tortolans. Perhaps the friendship I have established with Small Craft signifies his acceptance of me. There are other employees with whom establishing a friendship has been more difficult, however, I think that my presence in Tortola for so many years, in combination with the respect that I have shown toward the locals, is making the difference.

June 18th

My acceptance by the locals at the Moorings was demonstrated today when they invited me to attend their Fathers' Day party. Fathers attending the party pay $10 and the "mules," men without kids, pay $20. The Tortolans jokingly referred to me as an old mule because most of them have kids before they reach the age of 20. The party appears to have some cultural undertones as well. I think that Tortolans place a high value on perpetuation of their culture, perpetuation through fathering babies. This is consistent with the large families and that the culture does not frown on having more than one girlfriend. "You should have one wife that you love and live with, but it is OK to have girlfriends with whom it is also acceptable to have kids with," is what I have often been told by both male and female Tortolans. The difference here, relative to what frequently occurs in the United States, appears to be that the fathers do not shirk their responsibility to these kids and do contribute child support. Fathers who fail to support their children, whether the children were conceived in or out of wedlock, are ostracized by the locals.

There appears to be well-established roles for males and females in the BVIs. This is something that I have noticed on many occasions. The accepted norms for male behaviors, however, seem to be much more relaxed, as indicated by the multiple partners that males are allowed to have. A woman's role, on the other hand, appears to generally be in raising children. Most Tortolan women work, but few hold managerial or supervisory positions.

June 30th

Today, I had an interesting conversation with an expatriate whom I have known for about five years. Simon is a 28-year-old Englishmen who has been working as a dive master in the Caribbean for about six years now. We were discussing our impressions of a new manager from the States working at the Pusser's Restaurant (one unit of a chain in the Caribbean) on Marina Cay (a small island off the East end of Tortola). Simon heard from locals working at the restaurant that they thought Rob, the new manager, was "just another white guy passing through." Simon elaborated,

> Rob will be able to get some things accomplished because he is more of a people person but he has still taken some of the more common approaches that expatriates take when dealing with a new position in the Caribbean. For example, I find that most expatriates try to make vast changes in the beginning and often look down on the locals. Rob's actions indicate that he feels that he will be able to "whip these people into shape." The employees at the restaurant don't like this because they feel that they do things just fine. After all, many of them have been with the restaurant for several years.

In the back of their minds, Simon contends, the locals know that they will only have to "deal" with Rob for a year or two since Rob views the position as a temporary stepping-stone. "Moreover," Simon argued, "the locals are getting tired of having foreigners come in and take managerial positions. They want to know when it will be their turn to become a manager!"

July 3rd

Yesterday we brought one of Sail Caribbean's eight boat fleets back to the Moorings docks in Roadtown, Tortola. We only bring the boats back here about once every two weeks. It's part of the trip for the students and it is a great stop for the staff because we can get a new provisioning of food and get the boats worked on as well. The Moorings staff is always informed one week in advance which days we will be at the dock so they can be prepared. Most of the time, the Moorings and the provisioning companies that we use are well prepared and provide excellent service. Today was not the case. It is difficult to deal with because, although we know that there is some truth to the proverbial "island time," our schedule is very tight.

No matter how accepted I am by the locals, there is a fine line that always exists between locals and outsiders. Therefore, when things aren't done on time by the Moorings or the provisioning companies, I often have to be very demanding. At the same time, I often worry that I have overstepped my bounds and might ruin the relationships and trust that I have built with the locals. From my experience, however, I have learned that as long as you don't try to play hardball with the locals on a weekly basis, it is all right to be demanding if the situation warrants it. Another tactic seeming to work well is to make sure that if we (Sail Caribbean) are going to be demanding, then the messenger should be one of the senior staff with an established rapport with the locals. This may work because senior staff is perceived as being closer to an insider. Although I played hardball with the provisioners today because they were three hours late, the Moorings still has some time to complete the scheduled work before the fleet departs tomorrow afternoon.

July 4th—Attitude toward time!

About three hours before the scheduled departure of the fleet today, I went down to the docks to check on the progress of the repairs and maintenance. To my surprise, most of the work had not even begun. I made these arrangements two days ago with the Moorings staff to get three boats in our fleet fixed, specifying that this was only a pit stop for the fleet and we were on a tight schedule. We were looking at the possibility of having 80 people (staff and students aboard the 8 boats) being held up from the planned activities of the day. As a result, I had to be a bit more demanding, going above some of the mechanics and speaking with their supervisors. The supervisors spoke with some of the staff who provided some answers as to why things were moving so slowly. Apparently, several of the maintenance staff had left on a lunch break and were not planning on completing the jobs that they had started earlier, at least within the time frame that we had scheduled. They just didn't understand what our schedule was. When the maintenance staff came back after lunch they worked hard to meet our schedule, but in conversations with them it was clear that it wasn't just a matter of understanding what our schedule was—they couldn't understand how any group could be on such a tight schedule when they are in the BVIs. We departed the docks one and a half hours later than we planned.

July 7th

Today I ran into McLane, the man chiefly responsible for overseeing the maintenance department at the Moorings, and spoke to him about the recent delays that we experienced. He was apologetic about the whole situation and gave some insights regarding the difficulties he deals with every day.

> The guys in the maintenance department are great. They are all great at what they do but they have some limitations too. Their biggest limitation is that they have never been taught or rewarded for taking initiative. I heard about Sail Caribbean's problems the day after you left the docks. Apparently, some of the guys had completed the work to a point and then stopped because they thought they needed the OK from a supervisor to replace some parts. They should have realized that in their position that they had the authority. They know if the part needs to be replaced or not. So, because they didn't want to take the initiative, they were going to wait until we (the managers and supervisors) came down to them to tell them to replace the parts. It sounds ridiculous but in this place it's part of managing. You need to

go down and check how things are going periodically. It was unfortunate that I wasn't there that day.

July 28th

Today I finally decided to ask a question that had been plaguing me for quite some time. When locals are greeting each other they often say "respect" instead of a more traditional "hello." I asked Enrick at the Moorings what this meant. I became more interested because many of the locals with whom I have established friendships with were now using it to greet me. Enrick explained, "Don't worry, Tim, it is a good thing. When a person says to another 'respect' it means just that. It means I have respect for you and the type of person you are. It means we know you as a good person. The people who are saying this to you are making a compliment; not many foreigners have heard this from us before."

Enrick and I also got into a more philosophical discussion regarding another part of the greeting. I asked him to show me how he nodded hello to a person. His head tilted back and then returned to its natural position. I asked him what he would think if I nodded the other way, tilting my head down. He said, "That looks funny. It reminds me of what my mom said when I was a child. She said that white people often did that to show that they were looking down on us." We discussed it further and surmised that it may have come from the slave heritage of the Caribbean. Slave masters probably used this gesture in much the same way as his mother had described.

August 11th

Deli, the chief mechanic at the Moorings, and I have been friends for ten years now. He is one of the most genuine people I think I have ever met. He's also the most respected person, at least by the locals, at the Moorings. Today we were delivering a boat to the Leeward Islands (i.e., St. Maarten, St. Barts, etc.) and we talked about management, something we had never spoken about before. Deli began by telling me about how outsiders often don't realize how much power a single person can have in an organization. About fifteen years ago there had been a number of thefts at the Moorings. The rumor circulating at the Moorings was that because Deli was the informal leader of the locals, he had to know who had been stealing. The manager of the Tortola operations asked Deli to come to his office. When Deli arrived the manager gave him an ultimatum—tell the manager the name of the person who was stealing or Deli would lose his job. Deli refused to make any statement. I asked Deli why he didn't say anything. He explained,

> Tim, to this day I do not know who was stealing. If one of my workers was stealing from the Moorings, he was stealing from me. If I knew who was stealing, *I* would have taken care of it myself. Stealing is wrong no matter where you are. But this manager was claiming that I knew and that I was covering it up. That's just wrong. Down here you don't tell on other people. I didn't make a comment because I didn't have anything to say.

Deli continued,

> The next day the manager learned the power that we have. They may have all the money. But this is still our island. The next day, during the busy season, only five of the 160 workers showed up. The only five were the guys who aren't from here. That afternoon the manager called me up and begged me to come back to work.

We took one more day off and then we all went back to work. The funny part is that I didn't call for the strike. I just told people what had happened and how I was treated. We stick together down here.

It was surprising to me that I had never heard this story before. I decided that the time was right for asking Deli to tell me more about the Caribbean people and what a manager should know. Deli explained that Tortolans may be a little slower at getting things done but that they have a lot of pride in their work. They like to see a well-maintained boat making a charterer happy. He said that outsiders faced their biggest problems when they talked about or lied about their coworkers behind their backs. A manager who does this doesn't face just the person he was speaking about but the whole Moorings staff.

August 16th

Today, after being in the Leeward Islands for a few weeks, I heard one of the greatest compliments that an expatriate can hear. Many of the Moorings staff in Tortola said, "Welcome home, Tim." To me this meant that I was accepted by the culture and that Tortolans thought of this as not only their home but mine as well.

INTERPRETING HIS ENTRIES

A smile came to his face as Tim recalled writing the August 16th entry just a few days before. It had been a long summer made longer by staying up nights to expand his "shorthand" entries. However, after reading from his notebook he realized that he would have a lot to share with his committee.

He recognized that he needed to take his assignment a step further. He needed to use cultural models and management theories to interpret what he had observed. Were any of his observations reflective of Hofstede's dimensions of culture? Would Kluckhohn and Strodtbeck's dimensions be useful (see Appendix B)? What type of leadership style might work best given the cultural profile that he would develop? He took out a clean pad of paper and looked back through his notebook.

Tim's meeting with his committee was just three days away.

APPENDIX A: TOURISM BRITISH VIRGIN ISLANDS

"Discover nature's little secret." That simple phrase, used by the British Virgin Islands (BVI) Tourist Board to market the region, captures the essence of BVI tourism. Unlike neighboring islands, St. Thomas and St. Croix, that underwent massive development during the 1970s and 1980s, the BVI government carefully planned and restricted growth. The result is a carefully carved niche in the Caribbean market—positioning the chain in the exclusive/ecotourism market segment.

From 1950–1970 the BVIs hosted the traveling elite. However, with the introduction of bareboat chartering (cruising boats ranging from 28 to 50 feet that are rented to tourists qualified to take the boats out without the assistance of a licensed captain) to the region, the small island chain became affordable for the medium budget traveler as well. The calm waters and steady tradewinds the BVIs offered were soon filled with charterboats and the region became known as the premier chartering location in the world. Bareboat companies such as The

Moorings, West Indies Charters, and Caribbean Yacht Charters offered a unique vacation opportunity—one that connected tourists with the islands' rich natural beauty and intriguing history. Although some of the charter companies failed to survive a mid-1980 industry shake-out, a number of new operations quickly filled the void. By the early 1990s The Moorings, one of the few original companies to survive, dominated the BVI and world chartering markets with over 190 bareboats on the island of Tortola (BVI) alone.

As the charter industry grew throughout the 1970s, 1980s, and 1990s, so too did the number of hotels and resorts. However, the combination of strict government regulations constrained opportunities for new development projects and limited access through the small Beef Island Airport kept major developers out. As a result, the BVIs retained its natural beauty and avoided the threat of mass tourism. In essence, the islands remained "nature's little secret".

APPENDIX B

Hofstede's four cultural dimensions come from his book *Cultures and Organizations* (1991), McGraw-Hill Publishers:

> *Collectivism/Individualism*—Individualism is defined as the degree to which individuals focus on individual needs as opposed to those of the group. Collectivism refers to the degree to which individuals focus on the needs of the group and on establishing and maintaining membership in the group.
>
> *Power Distance* is defined as the degree to which members of a particular culture accept the unequal distribution of power in organizations and in the culture.
>
> *Masculinity/Femininity*—Masculine cultures view assertive, aggressive, and achievement focused behaviors favorably. Feminine cultures value supportive, nurturing behaviors and embrace gender role differentiation.
>
> *Uncertainty Avoidance* is defined as the degree to which members of a particular culture feel uncomfortable in unstructured, ambiguous, and uncertain situations and therefore embrace beliefs and institutions that seek to minimize exposure to such situations.

Kluckholn and Strodbeck's four cultural dimensions are:

Orientation toward Activity

A. *Doing*
  1. *Assumption:* Taking action is the most important activity
  2. *Finds meaning in:* Accomplishments, achievements
  3. *Meaning of work:* A "doer" *is* what he/she *does.* Work is pursued for a living (work = living). Relationships are secondary to the task. Work and play are separate activities, but "doers" often work hard *and* play hard.

B. *Being*
  1. *Assumption:* Self-expression is the most important activity
  2. *Finds meaning in:* Spontaneous expression, being oneself, affiliation
  3. *Meaning of work:* Work is not directly attached to the ego, nor is it strictly considered a separate activity from leisure. Social and work relationships may be closely intertwined. Relationship development at work is time well spent; it builds morale and group identity/feeling.

C. *Becoming*
   1. *Assumption:* Self-development is the most important activity
   2. *Finds meaning in:* Process, purpose, and intention of activity
   3. *Meaning of work:* There is a deep investment in the *type of work* and its process; both aspects add to one's personal development.

Orientation toward Time

D. *Past*
   1. *Assumption:* Today flows out of the legacy of the past
   2. *Finds meaning in:* Serenity, surrender, history as context and teacher
   3. *Meaning of work:* Work is a place to establish and nurture relationships and traditions. There is an awareness of, connection to, and obligation toward the legacy of such relationships and traditions.

E. *Present*
   1. *Assumption:* Today is the only reality
   2. *Finds meaning in:* Carpe Diem (seize the day)
   3. *Meaning of work:* Work, like life, is to be enjoyed. Present-oriented individuals often bring to work an energy and vitality not as frequently embodied by the other orientations.

F. *Future*
   1. *Assumption:* Today is a step toward tomorrow's goals
   2. *Finds meaning in:* Establishing and working toward goals, work ethic
   3. *Meaning of work:* Finds his/her identity through achievements in the workplace. Keeps one eye on deadlines and goals and evaluates the present in relation to its utility in moving toward the future. Is rarely satisfied with achievements, focusing in the next. Endorses ethic of "no pain, no gain."

Orientation toward Human Relationships

G. *Individual*
   1. *Assumption:* Each person is responsible for what happens in his or her life, and must watch out for his or her own rights and welfare.
   2. *Finds meaning in:* Personal accountability, competitive ethic
   3. *Meaning of work:* Work is a place to be recognized for one's own achievements. Upward mobility and other forms of recognition are expected from these individuals; group goals, rewards, and achievements aren't as satisfying.

H. *Ranked*
   1. *Assumption:* Each of us has his or her own place, and respect is due according to one's position
   2. *Finds meaning in:* Tradition, hierarchy, family, protocol
   3. *Meaning of work:* Work is a place to enhance or strengthen, but not necessarily advance, one's social position. Protocol is seen as maintaining the weave of the social fabric. There is a higher value placed on being respectful than on being frank.

I. *Mutual*
   1. *Assumption:* My purpose is to make a contribution to a larger whole
   2. *Finds meaning in:* Interdependence, group goals, affiliation
   3. *Meaning of work:* Work is a place to make a contribution to a group effort. The mutual individual needs to have a sense of belonging to projects and to see the connection to a

larger goal or effort. Public praise and competition among or comparison to others may cause embarrassment.

Orientation toward the Environment/Nature

J. *Controlling*
    1. *Assumption:* Human welfare is primary; nature serves to meet our needs
    2. *Finds meaning in:* Taking charge of challenges, mind over matter, effective use of resources
    3. *Meaning of work:* Work is a place to manage and control tasks, resources, employees. Problems are to be solved, knots in the system to be untied, hurdles to be jumped or dismantled.

K. *Yielding*
    1. *Assumption:* Nature is in charge of life on earth
    2. *Finds meaning in:* Nature rules mankind, we have little control
    3. *Meaning of work:* Work must be done. Within an organization such individuals may feel dominated by the organization and try to adapt to their roles and assignments rather than influence them.

L. *Harmony with Nature*
    1. *Assumption:* Our relationship with nature is symbiotic; care for the physical world will pay off with a balanced and peaceful existence
    2. *Finds meaning in:* Harmony, doing one's share
    3. *Meaning of work:* Work is part of a contract of balance wherein people contribute their share toward a symbiotic relationship with society, nature, and all aspects of life.

FOUR PEAKS BLUES

In 1969, Montana-born newscaster Chad Higgins had a dream of creating a ski resort where the world would come and experience Montana's scenic wonders without damaging the very elements they came to see. "All too often in the past, the men who have built resorts have ended up destroying what they came to seek," he said. "But at Four Peaks, we're establishing a new pattern: creating a resort without destroying the environment in the process."

In 1973, Higgins' dream became reality. Just before, Four Peaks Mountain had been partially logged and thus was ripe for development use which promised to return its scenic beauty. Four Peaks Mountain was just south of the Blue Pines Wilderness Area and 39 miles north of Eagle Feather Mountain. The city of Bozeman, with a jet airport, was a little less than a one-hour drive away. In the valley bottom there was the Golden River's blue ribbon trout fishing. Several major investors—all Fortune 500 companies—joined Higgins to purchase 10,600 acres alongside the mountain, making it one of the nation's few privately owned ski resorts (most others lease land from the U.S. Forest Service).

The years prior to Four Peaks' opening in 1974 held many problems. There was a four-year court fight resulting from protests against development in Golden Canyon and the resort's access road. The Forest Service wouldn't give approval to build a road up the mountain to haul concrete for the ski lifts. Elk moved onto the new grass of the golf course and soon overgrazed it. The Forest Service seemingly dragged its feet on a crucial land swap (allegedly at the bequest of President Nixon who was angry at remarks Higgins made about him). In spite of these and other obstacles, in four years the resort had four chair lifts, the 204-room Higgins Lodge, several condominiums, a golf course, a paved road to the base area, and most of the typical amenities of a major ski resort. Three days before the official opening of the resort in March 1974, Chad Higgins died. The oil embargo that spring took travel plans away from many Americans, and a national recession didn't help. With more than $40 million dollars spent, the major investors feared the worst.

In 1976, a Michigan resort company, Boytz USA, bought the resort for $7 million—barely the cost of the ski lifts alone. For the rest of the 70s and 80s Four Peaks limped along. The resort was vulnerable to power outages, animal damage, heavy snowstorms, and much else. Development proceeded, but very slowly. In the mid-80s Four Peaks was lucky to earn 100,000 skier days, the standard measure of ski area activity. The 1987–88 season was the turning point. An excellent snowfall and a new state-supported marketing program produced 163,000 skier days. In 1991–92 that figure had climbed to 216,000. Recently, the resort had opened a 20,000-square foot conference center with 94 adjacent condominium suites. New lifts had been built and another skiable mountain opened. There were now about 6,800 available beds in the area, a small shopping mall, grocery stores, a full-service bank, and numerous restaurants and bars. Summer business had quadrupled since the seventies. Besides the professional ski school at Four Peaks, there were now three fly fishing outfitters and three white water rafting guide services in the area. There were about 1,500 regular residents between the highway turnoff and the resort itself.

In 1992, the Peach Creek Lumber Mill in Skylerville, 40 miles north of Four Peaks, went on the auction block. With the 140,000 acres of timberland it controlled, 25,000 acres were adjacent to Four Peaks' ski area. The U.S. Forest Service, the Nature Conservancy, and private investors were all interested. Who would control this land and what they would do with it was one of the many concerns on the mind of Four Peaks' General Manager, Tom Collins.

To develop a more accurate and better communication system with the public, environmental groups and governmental agencies, Kurt Winner was hired in 1990 to fill the newly created position of Public Information Officer (PIO). The PIO reported to the marketing director of Four Peaks who was a direct report of Tom Collins. Kurt's job objectives were to inform the public of Four Peaks' policies and plans and to collect vital information from the nonclientele public for Four Peaks managers.

Tom Collins had been the general manager of the Four Peaks resort for one month prior to hiring Kurt Winner. Tom was 38 years old and had a B.S. degree in hotel administration from Michigan State University, and an M.B.A. from the University of Montana. He had extensive experience in the hospitality industry and had been a manager at three year-round resort properties in mountainous areas of the northwest, where he had gained a reputation for being concerned with people, developing the quality of service, and adapting to the needs of environmentalists and the public. Because of the public's interest in preserving the natural characteristics of Montana, a great deal of Tom's predecessor's time had been spent in relating to several state and federal agencies, as well as in public meetings. Most of these external relationships and meetings were used to inform the public and gather input with regard to Four Peaks' ongoing development (on and off the mountain), reforestation, aesthetic quality and sights, water and land quality, wildlife preservation, herbicide and pesticide use, road construction and maintenance, soil movement, and other issues.

A HAPPENCHANCE ENCOUNTER

On a late Thursday afternoon, Tom Collins, accompanied by a case researcher, was leaving the main offices of the Four Peaks Corporation at the mountain village. Seeing Debbie Marx at her desk, Tom casually asked her how things were going. Debbie responded by saying, "If you *really* want to know, I'm depressed. This job is not what I expected it to be, and I feel I'm going nowhere." Tom told Debbie he'd like to know more about her situation, but because he was late for an appointment that he'd get in touch with her as soon as possible.

The next morning, Friday, Tom called Debbie but discovered that she was away in Bozeman having a physical exam that day. Upon hearing this, Tom called Kurt Winner and the Human Resource Manager, Chris Keller, for appointments later in the day to learn more about Debbie's situation. These interviews are summarized below from the case writer's notes, who was shadowing Tom.

CHRIS KELLER'S VIEW OF DEBBIE'S SITUATION

"Debbie had been a clerk with the Westin Hotel in Seattle. The job involved filing, typing, and answering the telephone. Debbie found the job boring and had been frustrated by the lack of career opportunities. Debbie had an A.A. degree in Journalism from Seattle Community College and had received high performance ratings as a clerk.

"Debbie applied for and was selected for the new position of public information assistant at Four Peaks. This position offered increased pay, responsibility, and career advancement potential. Kurt later learned that Debbie decided to accept the position even though this meant breaking an engagement and leaving family and friends in Seattle.

"Kurt first got the idea of upgrading his clerical assistant to a public information assistant while attending a seminar on equal employment and upward mobility for lower-level employees. Kurt indicated on the position advertisement and job description for the new position that 50 percent of the job would involve writing news releases, speaking to service clubs and community organizations about Four Peaks, and assisting Kurt and Tom with presenting Four Peaks' development plans at public meetings. The job would also involve 50 percent clerical work, such as typing, filing, and answering the phone.

"After three months on the job, Debbie was doing clerical work 95 percent of the time. The other 5 percent was spent editing news releases written by Kurt and sitting in on management meetings as a recording secretary. Debbie had so much typing and routine clerical work to do that there seemed no time left to write news releases, speak to outside groups, or get involved in organizing public meetings. Debbie was unhappy in her new job, and the scuttlebutt around the office was that she was seriously thinking about resigning from Four Peaks Corporation and returning to Seattle.

"Kurt was not satisfied with Debbie's work performance and felt that she was sloughing off and looking for excuses not to get involved in higher level work. Kurt now feels that Debbie was a poor choice for this position, and has talked with me about how to get someone else into the position."

KURT WINNER'S VIEW OF DEBBIE'S SITUATION

"We created a position with the intent that it would be based as a stepping stone to a trainee PI officer—a professional one. We selected Debbie from a regional search that turned up many qualified individuals. All of the finalists had two years of college and had some appropriate experience.

"The job was to consist of some typing, answering the telephone for me and the marketing staff when they were out, but mostly answering inquiries of a general nature, preparing news releases under my supervision, and talking and assisting in presentations to various groups and organizations about Four Peaks subjects of public interest.

"Before Debbie arrived, there was some unrest since the selection had been someone off-resort, and several people here felt there were some highly qualified in-house people passed over. Again, our recruitment system had proved inadequate in arriving at a just selection.

"After a couple of months on the job, it looked like the grouches were right. The typing was sloppy, dealing with the public was curt and less than informative, and assignments for news releases were not timely and were often unacceptable.

"It was intended to start the job mix at almost 75 percent clerical and 25 percent public information with Debbie moving toward a 50–50 mix by the sixth month. The job mix by the third month had actually worked out to be 95 percent clerical and 5 percent public information. Debbie's predecessor, the clerical assistant, was able to accomplish the current clerical duties in about 60 percent of the total work time available. Debbie and I discussed the lack of progress, and I pointed out the following areas that seemed to hinder accomplishment of the clerical duties: three weeks of sick leave in the first three months on the job, reading editorials and classified ads when reviewing newspapers and magazines for items pertaining to Four Peaks, engaging in extraneous conversations with other employees, and arriving late and leaving early.

"At this point, it seems Debbie has the potential, but not the desire or stamina to advance to a more responsible and less supervised type of work."

DEBBIE'S VIEW OF THE SITUATION

The case researcher bumped into Debbie on Saturday in the mall, invited her for a cup of Seattle's Best coffee, and inquired about her views of living and working at Four Peaks. (The case writer's notes of that conversation reported below were shared with Tom.)

"I had worked for Westin Hotels for three years as a clerk-receptionist in downtown Seattle. Six months ago I applied for a job as public information assistant here. I was highly qualified for this position because of my three years of experience and my A.A. degree in Journalism. The decision to move was a difficult one since it meant leaving my family, my friends, and breaking my engagement. After being here for three months, I find the job is not meeting my expectations. The job description indicated half innovative work, such as writing news releases, speaking with public and civic organizations, and assisting the PI officer and other managers with presenting Four Peaks' policies and development plans at public meetings, and half clerical work, filing and answering the telephone. It turns out that I've been doing 95 percent typing, filing and answering phones, even more than at my previous job. This leaves me with so little time for the public information position of my job that I've become disillusioned and unhappy.

"I've tried to discuss my situation with my new supervisor, Kurt. But Kurt is very unresponsive and seems unwilling to give me added responsibility. I have several ideas I'd like to have a chance to try, but there's just no time. Also, the people in the office have been unfriendly and aloof. They don't go out of their way to help me feel comfortable or accepted in my job.

"Besides the job, the move itself has proved to be unsatisfactory. There are few opportunities for meeting people my age or with my interests. After three months, I still have no close friends. Also, I had hoped to find a nice apartment or small house to live in. Instead, I am living in an old, poorly insulated two-room trailer down near the highway, which is the best housing I could find or afford off the resort. It gets very cold at nights, I'm always shoveling snow, and I've had two terrible cases of the flu since I've been here.

"I am frustrated, physically run down, unhappy, and undecided about my future. Since this job has not turned out to be a career advancement at all, I'm considering returning to Seattle where at least my social life would be more satisfying. I guess I've got a bad case of the Four Peaks blues."

WHAT TO DO?

In front of his fireplace Sunday evening after reading the case writer's notes, Tom Collins ponders the situation. Tom is aware that any action will not only affect Debbie's future, but it may affect the morale and trust level of the Four Peaks organization. As the general manager, Tom would like to help the parties involved and encourage more emphasis on employee development in the resort. Tom believes that the PI function is important to the ongoing well-being of the resort and that disturbances in the PI unit can impact Four Peaks' relations with the public—always critical in Montana. The resort had turned the corner in the last couple of years and seemed poised to take off as a major destination ski and four seasons resort. Tom mused to himself, "This whole situation seems a lot like some of the cases we discussed in grad school. Then the profs always pushed lots of understanding before decisions or action. So, what do I now know, what do I need to know, and what do I do with it?"

THE GROUP REPORT

March 7, 2003

Todd:

I came by to see you about the Hospitality 210 case report due tonight. Unfortunately, our group had some problems that led to me being thrown out of the group. I will submit a personal letter about how our group worked as well as some of my own alternatives.

Thanks,
Maria

Professor Todd McGraw, the instructor for Hospitality 210 at the Arrington School, University of the Southwest, shook his head upon rereading Maria's note, then went on to read the notes he had collected from the group's members. What should he do in this situation? Of equal interest, he thought, what had caused this situation and what lessons could be learned from it?

In his Hospitality 210 course, it was McGraw's practice to assign a group case report about mid-term in the semester with a short time to work. This term, as in the past, he randomly assigned students into groups of five members. While the groupings had been announced in early February, work typically did not get underway until the report assignment was distributed (Exhibit 1 shows the report assignment).

The group that Maria had been assigned to was composed of two women—Maria and Jane—and three men—Art, Jerry, and Phil. When this group's report was handed in (on time), the report contained just three names—Jane, Art, and Phil. In McGraw's two sections of Hospitality 210 he had 28 groups. This group was the only one that had experienced what appeared to be serious issues.

Immediately after receiving Maria's note, McGraw had requested each group member to write his or her recollections of the group's experience. These individual accounts follow.

PHIL

Our group had a few problems but, all in all, I think things worked out. Jane, Maria and I met on the Thursday before the report was due. Maria could only stay a short while but Jane and I worked that night. Friday, Art was back and we worked through the weekend. On Monday, Jane and I put the report together and handed it in. We never saw that Jerry guy at all and only saw Maria for a half hour on Thursday, so we decided to include only the three names on the report.

I believe this assignment was an excellent way in which to conclude this section of Hospitality 210. Along with being forced to work with a deadline, it enabled each of us to see first-hand what it was like to work with others in a business-like situation.

I found both Jane and Art a pleasure to work with. Together, I believe that we have submitted an excellent report.

JANE

It all started Monday in class before the report was handed out. I suggested that we exchange phone numbers. I didn't get anybody's number but they all took mine. I said, "Let's meet at my place Tuesday night and we'll sort this thing out." I said that I would pick up the case Monday night so that we'd all have it Tuesday.

So Tuesday night rolled around and nobody showed up—nobody! So I started looking up phone numbers and phoning people. I got through to Maria and Phil and couldn't reach the other guys. I explained that I had an exam on Thursday and suggested we meet Thursday after my exam. Phil, Maria, and I met Thursday—I didn't know anything about Jerry or Art at that point.

At the meeting Thursday, Maria didn't like the way the talk had been going. She only had this one idea. I would kind of respond, "Well I don't know, what do you think of this and this and this?" Maria got really fed up I guess—stayed about fifteen minutes then she left. Phil and I went to the library that night and tried to sort this out. We didn't get anywhere.

Friday, Art came to class and said that he had had a family crisis—a grandparent dying—but he would do everything he could to get the report done for Monday; he said that he would spend all the time that he could. Phil, at that point, was like, well, you know, "checking in" everyday. He was saying, "How's the project going?" I'd say "It's still there" and he'd say, "Okay, I'll talk to you later." He phoned back everyday just so that he would get his name on the thing. I kept trying to get in touch with Maria. She kept saying, "I have an exam Saturday—don't bug me."

Art and I had been writing the report all day Friday and all day Saturday. Saturday night at 10:15 Maria phoned. She said that she was sorry she hadn't phoned earlier. She had had an exam that day and wasn't up to phoning until 10:15. I explained that we had kind of finished the project. She volunteered to type it. I said that my writing was too messy—I didn't think that anyone could decipher it, and the report had to be edited because it was too long. All of a sudden she blew up at me, screaming and yelling and freaking out on the phone, then she hung up. I said, "Forget her—I don't need this."

So Art and I did the whole thing with Phil checking in every day. I had an exam the Monday the report was due so I was up all night Sunday cramming for the test. Then Monday, after the exam, I had to type the report and get it in. That day Phil came over and totally screwed me up. I said for him to do the charts and he couldn't even do that. He'd ask what I thought of this and this, then he'd do them wrong. Everything was screwed up!

Well, we eventually got it in. I did not see Maria after and I never found out who Jerry was. It was really Art and I who did all the work. We had to put Phil's name on it because he had kept checking in. And that was it.

MARIA

We were put into groups and it was left up to us—to get together and to discuss how to approach the case and as a group to come to the decision. We were given the assignment Monday. Tuesday, Jane and I talked on the phone about getting together. She had a lot of work up till Thursday and mine started after Thursday. We agreed to meet on Thursday—which was probably a bad idea because I had just started to study for my Saturday exam. So we met on

Thursday. In the meantime Jane had consulted her brother, who was in the business school, about the case—how to approach the case, how to write a case and all that kind of thing. In the process, she had had more time to go over the case and had come to some decisions.

When we met on Thursday, there was Jane, Phil, and me, and the attitude that came out was one of "let's just do it, let's just get this thing done." The other thing that really got me was that I felt that the case was being approached from the wrong perspective—not as a human resources case. That was how things started to get off track. I guess I was a little tense already but I tried to be tactful. You know, it was our first meeting and I didn't want to be coming across as a big mouth. I tried to go around the problems but that didn't seem to work. I came up with some alternatives that had been going around in my mind and those didn't seem to go.

I gave up on that meeting. I thought that maybe it had been the time of day or whatever. The meeting had gone on twenty minutes or so and it had been twenty minutes of tension. It was two against one: he was siding with her—"let's get it done"—while I thought that it was interesting. So I said that I couldn't put any more time into the project until Saturday when my exam was over—they said fine. I said I would contact them when my exam was over and we would work on it then. I had thought that Saturday and Sunday would be when most of the putting together would have been going on. So I left the meeting and didn't talk to them 'til Saturday after my exam.

Saturday, I called and said that I was ready to work on the case. They said to hang on a minute—I heard a conference going on in the background. I asked if the problem was that I hadn't worked up 'til then. They said yes, they didn't think that I had put any time into it and that my name shouldn't go on the report. Okay, that was true, but we had made an agreement on Thursday.

That was how the whole thing blew up. I think that things definitely could have been avoided. I think that they were stubborn. There was absolutely no room for discussion. The fact that I didn't agree didn't seem to phase them.

ART

We got into our group on Monday. There was one person who none of the group members were familiar with. We had never seen him in class but we did try to get a hold of him. The first meeting I could not get to because of a family crisis. The group did meet but the meeting apparently lasted only fifteen minutes—the group members found it hard to get along and members had time commitments. Another meeting was set up but fell through completely. I was absent, Maria was absent for various reasons, Phil couldn't make the meeting and the other member could not be located.

The next step in the meeting process was between Jane and Phil. They met and discussed the case for a few hours on Thursday—nothing much came out of that meeting. I came back to San Angelo Thursday night and got in touch with Jane. Jane and I sat down Friday. We set up guidelines, a structure and a format we were going to use for the project. We did that until seven o'clock, then we got right into writing the report—Jane and I.

As far as the problems in the group, Jane thought that it was not in our interest to keep trying to call people to make it a group effort. So we went on with the case and worked at it through the weekend. We had the case finished by Saturday night. I met with Jane briefly on Sunday—I had other commitments—and left it up to her to submit the report by the due date.

As regards to our problems, one member never did show up—we never saw him. The two girls had a personality conflict, I feel, and Maria left the majority of the work up to the other members of the group. Phil was very interested in the case but he was not ready to listen to other people's ideas on how they thought it should have been done.

JERRY

The fifth member of the group never came to class. He made no effort to contract the group or the instructor.

Report Assignment

Date: February 28, 2003

To: Student Groups, Hospitality 210

From: Professor Todd McGraw

Subject: Instructions for Your Group Case Report

1. Your group is to submit a report on the Spirit Dude Ranch case. The guideline question is:

   As a group of consultants to the owner—managers of the Spirit Dude Ranch, do an analysis and diagnosis of their situation and make any recommendations you feel are appropriate.

2. Your report is due Monday, March 7. Deposit your report in my mail box in Room 412, Stevens Hall. Late reports will receive a grade of zero.

3. Reports should be typed double-spaced in a professional style.

4. Reports should have a covering, one-page (maximum), point-form executive summary. The summary should include: (a) the names of all group members, (b) a complete statement of the issues/problems, (c) a list of the major recommendations being proposed, (d) any other information that might be useful to a busy executive who has time to read only this one-page summary. The summary should not include any information not also included in the report.

5. Maximum report length is 1200 words of analysis, diagnosis and recommendations, and an executive summary (the exec. summary is not included in the 1200 words).

6. Submit one copy of your report. Every group member will receive the same grade.

EXHIBIT 1   Report Assignment

THE HARBOR VIEW

It was 2:00 on Wednesday, August 1, as Mrs. Caroline Craig, owner and manager of The Harbor View Restaurant, sat on her deck at home, pondering the events that had transpired over the weekend. It had been almost two days since Tom, the new head chef of The Harbor View, had informed her that he had tested HIV positive. For the last two days, she could think of nothing else. Caroline's thoughts were interrupted by a knock at the front door. As she got up to answer it, Caroline suddenly hesitated. She wasn't expecting anyone but then remembered Tom said he was going to stop by to discuss future plans with her. Although Caroline had been thinking of nothing else for two days, she still had no idea what she was going to say to him.

THE SETTING

The Harbor View Restaurant was located in a small fishing village in northeastern Maine called Round Pond. Legend had it that the town acquired its name in 1920 when some settlers from New York decided it would be an unprofitable place to develop because the harbor resembled a "round pond" rather than a real harbor. Thus, the original name, which no one seemed to remember, was changed, and the town was renamed Round Pond. Whether the story is true or not didn't matter. All that mattered was that the locals, as they liked to be called, believed it.

Round Pond was a relatively unspoiled area in comparison to the surrounding towns. Many of the residents were born, grew up and died there without ever leaving the state. This helped to preserve an enchanting "down home" feeling about Round Pond that few Maine villages possessed anymore. This also left the locals rather provincial and relatively uninformed about what was happening elsewhere in the world.

Since the late sixties, Round Pond had also become the year-round home for numerous young, well-educated, artists. These painters, sculptors, poets, and musicians had found serenity and inspiration in Round Pond. Although the natives and the artists initially clashed culturally and politically, they both came to accept and respect one another's viewpoints. The two groups assimilated in such a way that the artists came to be as important to the economy and the culture of Round Pond as the natives.

During the winter, the population of Round Pond was approximately 800 people. Most of the male residents, except the artists, made a living by fishing, carpentry, or by working at a boat building company about 20 minutes away. The women generally were homemakers except for the summer season when they worked in the tourist industry.

In the summer, the town's population more than tripled with summer vacationers who owned cottages in the town and area. This was also when the summer businesses, including The Harbor View, opened for a season that began in late May and lasted until mid October. Round Pond then became a Mecca for tourists who enjoyed it for its natural scenic beauty, lobsters, and simple life style.

The Harbor View had been an intricate aspect of Round Pond for over 40 years. Before Caroline bought it, it was not known for its culinary élan, but more because it had always been a popular watering hole for the locals.

CAROLINE CRAIG

The chance to buy The Harbor View was a dream come true for Caroline. She had grown up in New Harbor, a town about 10 minutes southeast from Round Pond. After graduating from Cornell University's Hotel School, she spent the next 15 years in California working in the food and beverage industry. Caroline had long desired to return to Maine. Although she had enjoyed her work, those years were also filled with heartache. She often ran into roadblocks because she was female, in her opinion, twice losing promotions to less qualified males. The long hours also meant she couldn't be at home very much, which she believed had contributed to the break-up of her first marriage. The most intolerable aspect of her work had been dealing with the prejudices her coworkers exhibited not only toward women but toward gays, lesbians, bisexuals, and transgendered people, people of color, and people from nonChristian religions. This had angered Caroline, and she vowed then to somehow, someday make a change. When she finally received the management position she desired in California, Caroline found her authority very limited and she doubted she would ever have the chance to make a real impact in the industry.

Although some of Caroline's past experiences had been negative, she consciously chose not to dwell on them. She instead decided to learn lessons from all her experiences, whether they were good or bad. In fact, in her resignation letter to the last company she worked for, she had directly addressed the lessons she had learned while working there. Caroline stated that she needed to fulfill her entrepreneurial desires and could never be truly satisfied until she had real autonomy. She also stated that if she were to someday operate her own business, she would never discriminate against another human being on the basis of race, gender, religion, etc. as she and many others had been discriminated against at that company. The resignation letter was very strongly worded and many of her friends believed that she was burning her bridges. Nevertheless, Caroline had decided that even if her own business failed, she would never again work at a company where anyone was discriminated against.

ACQUIRING THE HARBOR VIEW

When Caroline's father had called her, in the early fall of 1985, to tell her that The Harbor View was for sale, she was excited. However, that excitement soared when she found out that the selling price was in her range. Caroline immediately flew to Maine to take a look at the property. She was acquainted with the restaurant from her childhood days but hadn't been there in over 20 years. When she got there, she was pleasantly surprised with its condition. Although the dining room needed to be expanded and redecorated, the kitchen, electrical wiring, and plumbing were in great shape.

Caroline's mother, a market analyst, had put together a complete report for her concerning the feasibility of reopening The Harbor View. The projections looked good. The economy was strong and there weren't any signs of a recession. Maine's gross state product was growing rapidly. Unemployment was at one of its all time lows. Caroline also talked to some of the locals and received encouragement from them. The majority thought that if The Harbor View were successful, it would bring a lot of outside business to the other vendors in the local area. After talking with her new husband, her lawyer, and the bank, Caroline decided to go ahead. On November 18, 1985, she became the new owner of The Harbor View Restaurant.

Caroline and her husband moved back to Maine during the Christmas holidays. Her husband, an airline pilot, was able to transfer and fly out of the Portland airport. The couple rented an apartment in Round Pond initially but planned to buy a house if The Harbor View proved to be a success.

GETTING STARTED

Caroline began work at The Harbor View right after the New Year. She wanted the restaurant to open on Memorial Day weekend and that gave her little time to get a lot of work done. Her first order of business involved hiring an assistant manager and a head chef. The assistant manager would help her out with the dining room and the head chef would be responsible for the kitchen and menu planning. Finding the right people was not an easy task considering Round Pond and the surrounding towns did not have a very large labor pool of experienced food and beverage personnel. After numerous interviews, she finally found two people to fill the positions.

Beth Chapman, a local woman, was chosen to be the assistant manager. Although her restaurant experience was limited, Beth had a strong finance background, which Caroline lacked. Beth seemed incredibly well organized and Caroline thought that in time she could learn to deal with vendors. Beth was in her late twenties and had just recently gotten married and planned to settle down in Samoset, a town about 10 miles from Round Pond. Her enthusiasm for the job was refreshing and Beth appeared very eager to learn all aspects of the business.

Gordon Jacobs was hired as the head chef. He had worked his entire life in the restaurant industry from dishwasher to eventually owning his own seafood restaurant which he had sold a few years back to eliminate stress in his life. Initially Gordon didn't have any formal training, but in recent years he had gone back to culinary school to learn about current trends and techniques. His only drawback was his age. At 60, he informed Caroline he would be retiring within the next five years. But Gordon promised Caroline that he would then help her find a replacement for himself. Although this bothered Caroline, she realized his experience was invaluable and that The Harbor View had a greater chance of success with him in the kitchen.

Redecorating the dining room turned out to be a lot more work than Caroline imagined. The old dining room was light blue with light blue painted wooden banquettes instead of individual chairs. Caroline envisioned covering the walls with old barn clapboards, adorned with paintings and wall hangings from local artists. Realizing that this was too much work for her to complete alone, she hired a group of local carpenters to do the physical work. This included the building of a screened-in deck with an awning overhang, an addition which would double the seating capacity.

Often the locals would drop in to check out how the renovation was coming. Although they were generally pleased, they voiced some resentment that she chose to do away with the light blue banquettes. Caroline feared losing the local townspeople's patronage and asked for their input. After considerable discussions they came up with the idea of moving the banquettes to the bar area and painting them light gray. This way the locals would be happy because they could still sit at the banquettes and Caroline would be happy because the banquettes were out of her dining room and they weren't light blue anymore. This was the type of compromise Caroline knew she would have to make many times over to assure she stayed on the good side of the locals.

As the opening date neared, Caroline began hiring her staff. She advertised in the local newspaper but most of the applicants heard about the jobs via word of mouth. Caroline was surprised by the number of applicants. Many were college students, local and out-of-state, looking for full-time seasonal work. Caroline was especially interested in hiring college students because they had flexible schedules. She also believed they would have an easier time keeping up with the restaurant's fast pace than older women might. However, the college students would have to leave at the end of August and, since The Harbor View planned to remain open until mid-October, Caroline needed to hire people who could stay until the closing date. She decided to hire ten college students and eight older women as food servers. The college students would work full-time all summer, while the older women would work part-time until August, and then work full-time until October.

Gordon hired all of the kitchen crew. He organized the kitchen into specific stations: fry, salad, desserts, grill, broiler, prep, and dishwasher. Gordon then hired people for each station with the idea that they would work in that station for the whole summer. He acted as the expeditor and assisted as needed. Within one week of opening night, everything was up and running relatively well. The majority of the staff were trained, all the licenses were in order, and the renovations were nearly complete.

On opening night, things went well with one exception. The Harbor View got rave reviews about the food, and people thought the menu prices offered good value. Except for one party, all the meals were served on time. The atmosphere was a success because everyone loved the décor and the beautiful view of the harbor. The one problem was that Caroline had neglected to include Mount Gay rum as one of the liquors the bar offered. She had forgotten that Mount Gay was the locals' favorite liquor and if The Harbor View wasn't going to serve it, the locals weren't going to go there. Although this problem could be easily solved by running out to the liquor store to buy a few bottles until a liquor order could be placed, Caroline believed that she could not afford to upset the locals many more times. They were her bread and butter.

The rest of the summer went very well and Caroline was pleasantly surprised to find out that the income statement projected a rather nice end of the year profit. This especially pleased her because her only goal had been to break even her first season.

TIME GOES BY

The next few years progressed well. By 1990 business and profits at The Harbor View increased each year. Except for having to fire a few unmotivated dishwashers, the staff each year worked out well. Caroline would often brag about the fact that most of her employees, including the college students, would return each summer to work. A hard working server could make between $4,000 and $5,000 in the summer plus a nice end of the year bonus. The Harbor View gained the reputation of being the best restaurant to work for in the county and Caroline always had a large pool of applicants to choose from each spring.

Caroline was able to make many friends among the locals and found many of them much better informed than she had originally presumed. Several times after work she and some of the locals had engaged in rather in-depth conversations regarding politics. She was pleasantly surprised to find that the majority were very liberal, even the old timers who had lived in Round Pond their entire lives. Most of the town was very anti-George Bush (senior) which Caroline thought was amazing in a state in which 73 percent of the people voted in favor of him for president. This helped Caroline explain to herself why the artists and the natives were able to get along so nicely.

Caroline's private life had also been going well. She and her husband bought a nice house in Round Pond and a sailboat, which they kept in the harbor. Unable to have children of their own, Caroline and her husband adopted an African-American child in the winter of

1989. She had initial fears about the adoption because Round Pond was 99.3 percent white like her and her husband, and she wasn't sure how well the town would accept a white couple raising an African-American child. Caroline's fears were put to rest by George Poland Sr., one of the oldest and most well-known residents of Round Pond. One day at the bar, drinking his Mount Gay and 7-Up, George looked at Caroline and said: "Whether black, red, yellow or white, we are all the same when you turn out the light." It was all Caroline needed to hear.

The Craigs also found that the locals were beginning to think of them as part of the community. This was shown one night when a fierce storm hit Round Pond. Caroline and her husband got a call at about 10:00 P.M. that their sailboat had gotten loose from its mooring and was headed for the rocks. They ran down to the harbor to find a couple of dozen locals in boats risking their own safety to rescue the Craigs' boat. After about 45 minutes, their boat was back on its mooring and everyone was back on land, wet and tired, but unharmed. Caroline was overwhelmed by this hospitality. When she offered to pay them for their efforts, they just laughed and explained that it was all in a day's work.

1991 AND A NEW CHEF

As the 1991 New Year began, Gordon stopped by to discuss his retirement. He had just turned 65 and it was time for him to leave. This greatly saddened Caroline because Gordon had helped make The Harbor View the success it was. However, she was excited about bringing in a new chef, because it would be an opportunity to make several changes to the menu to accommodate the 90's trends.

After interviewing numerous candidates, Caroline and Gordon found someone they believed to be the perfect replacement for Gordon. His name was Thomas Barrelstone, a 1985 graduate from the Culinary Institute of America. Since graduation Tom had been the head chef at a seafood restaurant in Rhode Island. He came to Maine because he was hired to teach culinary arts courses at the University of Southern Maine. Due to state cutbacks, his job had been limited to the spring semester; he needed to find a job for the summer and fall, which The Harbor View was able to offer him.

From the start, Caroline was impressed by Tom. His management ideas were quite modern as shown by giving the kitchen employees more autonomy over their own jobs. He also believed in rotating jobs so every employee could learn each job if he or she so desired. Even though he wanted to make a lot of changes, Tom was careful not to change everything Gordon had built up for that would upset some of the senior employees. Tom also had some exciting new ideas for the menu. Realizing the need for a healthier, low fat menu, he added one pasta dish and one fish dinner that was steamed in parchment paper and served French style. He also suggested having live music in the bar and considered doing some outside catering.

Because Tom was new and had such an important role at The Harbor View, before the 1991 summer season began Caroline decided to hold a "Get to know you" party at her house to give all the previous and new employees the chance to meet each other and Tom. The party was a huge success and everyone seemed to like Tom as much as Caroline did.

Caroline viewed the 1991 season as one of her most important years. The state was in a recession which could possibly have detrimental effects on the tourist industry. However, she was still very positive because Round Pond's summer population had increased greatly over the last few years. The Harbor View had also gained statewide recognition and recently had received a three and a half star rating from the *New England Restaurant Journal*. Caroline also hoped that a new chef with innovative ideas would help to attract new customers.

On August 1st, Caroline was pleased to announce to the staff that the cover counts and sales were up 10 percent from the previous year. The state might have been in a recession but The Harbor View wasn't. In celebration of the great news, Caroline decided to throw a party for the employees after work that night. All the employees attended, except for Tom who very quietly declined the invitation and went right home after the work shift was over for the night. This bothered Caroline because Tom was a very social guy and it was unlike him to miss a party. The party was not only going to celebrate the successful summer, but also the fact that Tom had just signed a seven year contract with The Harbor View. In fact after signing the contract, he immediately went out and had his physical (covered by the restaurant's group insurance plan) so that he could be put on the Harbor View's insurance program right away.

The morning after the party, Caroline got a call from Tom saying he needed to take a few days off because of a personal problem. Realizing he wouldn't ask unless there was something seriously wrong, and knowing the kitchen staff could cover for him, Caroline granted his request and he quickly hung up. The call troubled Caroline because she knew there was something definitely not right with Tom. He was always so friendly and yet in the last few days he was on the verge of being rude with her. Caroline had not wanted to pry, but she was dying to know what type of personal problem Tom had. Caroline knew him well in the business sense, however she knew next to nothing about his personal life. She did know that Tom lived alone and that he liked it that way. Caroline also knew that Tom was very close to his family, but rarely saw them because they lived in Seattle. She had never asked him about his past or present personal relationships, nor had he ever volunteered information about them to her. Some of the waitresses had gone out with Tom on a social basis, but they all said it was strictly platonic, which was not by their choice. They all said Tom was fun to party with, but he would usually only drink a beer or two and absolutely abhorred smoking. Caroline also knew that Tom had developed friendships with many of the local artists and would come to dine with them at The Harbor View on the days he wasn't working. Tom also hung-out with the local lobstermen as well. He loved the ocean and would often go out in the morning with some of his lobstermen friends to help them haul their traps. By Tom's own admission, he was a health nut. He had developed a strong physique by biking about 20 miles a day. He often encouraged the rest of the staff to exercise saying it would increase their energy and add years to their lives. While it bothered Caroline that this was all she knew about Tom, she was sure in time she would develop a deeper understanding of him.

TOM'S NEWS

When Tom returned to work, after the four personal days he had taken off, he seemed just as chipper as ever; Caroline assumed everything must have turned out all right and so after greeting him she went back to her office to do some paper work without questioning him. Ten minutes later, Tom came into her office and asked if he could speak with her. It was then that she learned that her initial assumption that everything was fine was in fact gravely wrong. Tom informed Caroline that his insurance physical had shown that he was HIV positive. Her reaction was shock and disbelief. She was aware of HIV and AIDS, yet she had never known someone personally who was afflicted with the disease. After a few moments of silence, Tom proceeded to explain the events, which had transpired over the last week.

On Monday, the day of the party, Tom had been called to his doctor's office. The doctor informed him that he had tested HIV positive for the AIDS virus. The doctor explained to

Tom that although he was HIV positive, it didn't mean he had the AIDS virus. In fact it could be anywhere from one month to ten or twelve years before he ever felt the effect from AIDS.

Tom then took the next few days off from work to collect himself and to make plans for the future. He had consulted Dr. Dewey Franklin, an AIDS specialist in Portland, who immediately placed Tom on AZT, a drug that would help his immune system fight off the AIDS virus. Due to the great physical condition Tom was in, Dr. Franklin felt that he had a good chance of fighting the AIDS virus for many years. The doctor informed Tom that it was important to exercise, eat well, and continue a normal lifestyle. Dr. Franklin went on to emphasize that being positive, physically and mentally, were important in combating the disease.

At this point, Tom handed Caroline a letter that was written by Dr. Franklin (see Appendix). The letter basically stated that there wasn't any reason why Tom could not continue working at his position at The Harbor View. The virus was blood-to-blood transferred and could not survive outside the body. Thus, it was impossible for the AIDS virus to be transferred to another human being through food service work.

After reading the letter, Caroline placed it on her desk, clasped her hands and put her head down. Tom sensed her unrest and assured her he would be all right. During his time off, he said that he had experienced numerous emotions. He had experienced a great deal of anger and often asked God "why me?" Tom had become depressed and had contemplated ending his life. Tom reported that he finally came to the decision that he was going to fight it. It would be years probably before he ever felt the effect of AIDS and maybe by then, there would be a cure. Caroline was impressed by his courage and determination.

Tom went on to say that he felt it was important that the rest of the staff know about his condition. He had decided he would start wearing latex gloves around the kitchen, just as a safety precaution, and surely the staff would wonder why. Tom also believed that God had given him this disease for a reason, and the reason was to educate others about AIDS. By keeping it a secret, he would only be projecting AIDS as the shameful disease that many people believed it to be. Realizing Caroline needed some time to let it all sink in, Tom quietly said goodbye and told her he would stop by her house in a few days to discuss the future.

CAROLINE REFLECTS

As Caroline continued to sit on her deck, she realized it was time to make some decisions that would effect the future of The Harbor View. Tom believed it was important that the staff was informed that he tested HIV positive. But, how would she tell them? Or, better yet, would they understand? Caroline thought highly of her employees, yet many of them probably lacked the information to deal with an issue such as AIDS. Most of them thought it was simply a homosexual disease and a certain death sentence. Although they liked Tom a lot, out of fear for their own lives, she thought many of them would probably quit. It would take massive education on Caroline's and Tom's part to teach their colleagues that they were not at risk.

Even if she was able to educate her employees, would the customers understand? Although there were no known cases of customers being infected with the AIDS virus through food, there was always the chance it could happen. An AIDS paranoia was running rampant throughout the nation and Caroline feared this paranoia might just drive away her clientele. She shuddered at the thought that this could mean the loss of her business.

Caroline also wondered about the reaction from the town. The locals were very conservative on some issues and very liberal on others. Would they be able to accept this issue or would Caroline be asking too much from them? She thought of Ryan White, the young AIDS victim recently in the news who was driven out of his home town because he had AIDS, but was then welcomed with open arms by the bordering town. Would Round Pond open its arms or would they drive Tom away?

And what about herself? While she had always seen herself as being socially responsible, could she come to grips with this issue? She had worked so hard to achieve success in her own business and she was now faced with a situation that could destroy it all. Caroline had no desire to fire Tom because he had done nothing wrong and was an important asset to The Harbor View. Even if Caroline had wanted to, her lawyer had informed her it was against the law to discriminate against people with AIDS or those who are HIV positive. It made her sick to think that she was even thinking about firing Tom. For him to recover Tom needed to have a positive mental attitude; firing him would surely destroy his resolution and make him sicker.

What if Tom's illness were kept a secret? Although he wanted everyone to know, secrecy would surely eliminate future problems. Caroline hated to think in these terms, yet considering what was at stake, she could not help herself.

Would it be fair to the staff and to the customers to keep Tom's condition a secret? By law, HIV or AIDS victims do not have to inform anyone about their illness. Yet Caroline had always believed in being completely open and honest with all her employees and guests and this would go against that. If knowledge of Tom's disease were to leak out, the effects of lying about it could also be detrimental to her business.

Was it fair to ask Tom to keep it a secret? Tom had already told Caroline how important it was to him to educate people about the disease. By asking him to remain quiet, she was knowingly going against Tom's own wish. Could Caroline live with her conscience if she asked Tom to keep his illness quiet? She had always blamed the president for his lack of initiative in the AIDS education field.

APPENDIX: LETTER FROM DR. FRANKLIN TO CAROLINE CRAIG

Memorial Hospital and Healthcare Center
AIDS Research Department
Lakeside, Maine 03432
(207) 563-5555

August 5, 1991

Dear Caroline Craig:

By now, you are aware that Thomas Barrelstone has tested HIV positive for the AIDS virus. As Tom's doctor and at his request, I am writing you to help explain the aspects of Tom's disease.

Tom has tested HIV positive, however he does not have AIDS. When an individual tests HIV positive, that individual has a 96.6% chance of coming down with AIDS in the future. After testing HIV positive, the onset of AIDS could be anywhere between 1 month to 12 years. There are several patients whom I treat personally that have been HIV positive for years and have yet to have contracted AIDS.

AIDS is a virus, which repeatedly attacks the central immune system. As it weakens the immune system, the body is unable to defend itself from other viruses and bacteria. AIDS does not cause death. An AIDS patient dies from illnesses such as pneumonia, forms of cancer or even the common cold which their body is unable to recover from.

I have placed Tom on AZT, which is a drug that helps the immune system fight off other illnesses. It was developed in 1987 and although it does not cure AIDS, it helps to prevent the onset of AIDS. There are limited side effects to AZT, and for the most part, patients take to it very well.

I and most doctors feel there are 3 methods in which an HIV patient can fight off the AIDS virus. First of all they must take AZT or a similar drug. Second of all, they must maintain a healthy diet and exercise program. And last of all, they must have a positive mind set and continue to live life as they did before.

Tom is a risk to no one. HIV and AIDS need a blood to blood transfer to successfully transfer from one person to the other and the virus dies immediately if exposed to oxygen.

I do hope this letter gives you a better understanding of the disease. If you have any questions, please don't hesitate to call.

Sincerely,

Dr. Dewey Franklin

HARRISON HOTELS INC.

Harrison Hotels is a chain of wholly owned and operated large hotels. All are located in the down-town areas in 12 major North American cities. The corporate headquarters of the company is in Chicago, Illinois. All Harrison Hotels are now over 15 years old. The company has, over many years, developed standardized ways of organizing and managing its hotels and almost all hotel managers have many years of seniority in their current positions. The corporate officers spend much of their time traveling throughout the chain, monitoring hotel business and guest services practices.

Recently the vice president of operations stayed at one of Harrison's hotels for 10 days while on business. While he was in residence, as was his practice, he talked with many members of the hotel staff. Disturbed by some of the things he heard, he contacted you—an old acquaintance and well-known hospitality management consultant. After agreeing to meet with him you asked him to send you, by way of your getting prepared, a list of some of the things he heard at the hotel (he called them "problems") and a copy of the hotel's organization chart. He has done this (see Exhibits 1 and 2).

"Problems" at the Harrison Hotel

1. Too much is being spent on manager/supervisor salaries.
2. Supervisors are extremely dissatisfied. They complain that it takes too long to get decisions made when things have to be referred upstairs—which is too often. Front desk workers complain that the reservations department overbooks and that rooms are not clean enough. Everyone complains that the purchasing department takes care of them last. Shift supervisors complain their counterparts leave work undone. The housekeeping supervisors for floors 1–5 complain they have more rooms to care for than their counterparts.
3. The HR director complains that the line managers don't seem to pay much attention to him and constantly fight the suggestions he makes or the programs he wants to get done. He says his supervisors get resistance from the other supervisors and that in disputes—which are many—the GM always sides with his managers against him.
4. The supervisors in purchasing, banquets, the spa, and engineering complain they are supervised too closely. Many managers say the same thing—that they are constantly being checked up on by the directors and assistant directors.
5. Supervisors complain that they are not allowed to make enough decisions and that they have to refer too many to their bosses for answers. They also say they don't receive enough information from "upstairs" and that they don't have much of an idea of what is going on in other parts of the hotel. Yet the managers say that the supervisors are not capable of making decisions because they do not have enough of the "big picture."
6. Supervisors complain it takes too much time to get an engineering person when something goes wrong. Supervisors call the engineering department by phone but usually the engineering staff is all busy so they have to get their manager to put some pressure on. Supervisors say that with everyone competing for engineering, especially for maintenance, the guys who are friends with the maintenance supervisor get helped first.

EXHIBIT 1   "Problems" at the Harrison Hotel

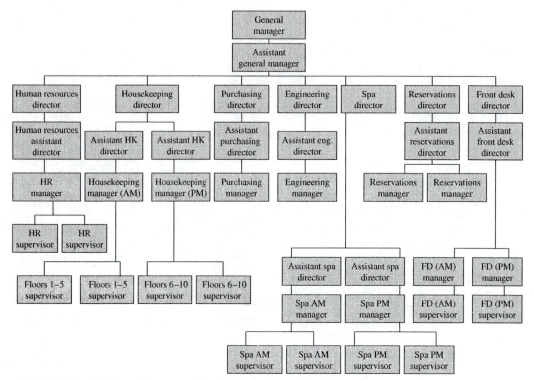

EXHIBIT 2   Harrison Hotels Organizational Chart

Soon you will meet with the vice president of operations. As preparation you study the materials he has sent to you. What about the way the company and/or the hotel is organized seems to contribute to the "problems" listed? What changes in the organization structure might you recommend and why?

JUAN PEREZ

In the spring of 1998, Juan Perez was employed as a machine operator on the night shift in the laundry department at the Miami Towers Hotel. He was assigned to laundry work with a promise from the human resources department that he would be transferred to another job in the maintenance/engineering area when an opportunity arose. Before working at the Miami Towers Hotel, Perez had been employed as a machinist at a utility company. The engineering group's primary activities at the hotel centered on maintenance of the building, its heating and air conditioning systems, the elevators, the equipment of three kitchens, and the electro-mechanical systems of the other operating departments. Perez was neither experienced nor qualified for these activities, although he was a good mechanic.

Perez was a slender, short Mexican-American about 40 years old. He was married to his childhood sweetheart, and had a 14-year-old daughter, who, as he often stated, were the "apples of my eye." Juan had attended high school in Los Angeles and frequently noted that Robert Redford went to the same school. His hobby was raising miniature orchids, and he dreamed that someday he would have the money and time to own a commercial orchid greenhouse. He did have a small greenhouse attached to his garage, which netted him nearly $6,000 a year, a sum which was enough to maintain his small home and provide his family with an annual vacation.

In the laundry department where Perez worked, all of the bedding, linens, and uniforms used in the hotel were sorted, laundered, pressed, folded, and bundled or racked according to where they went. The principal tasks in the department were laundering and pressing. Machine operators loaded and unloaded large washing machines, added measured amounts of detergent, and cleaned machines between loads. During the wash and dry cycles, they sorted clothes and bedding for the next loads. Pressers used steam presses and mangles to iron linens and uniforms smoothly, counted them, and placed them in bins or racks to be sent to the appropriate department.

Working conditions in the laundry department appeared both difficult and undesirable, especially for the machine operators. They wore rubber aprons, boots, and gloves, and were required by law to keep their hair contained in caps or nets. The heat and steam from the machines and their nonporous rubber attire caused them to sweat continuously. The laundry was known throughout the hotel as "the pits" and the people who worked there were generally referred to as the "arm-pit gang." The machine operators, however, enjoyed working together. By speeding up the loading and sorting tasks, and doing this at the same time, they could have a few minutes to talk and rest. The laundry supervisor didn't object to their practice of chatting with one another as long as they got their work accomplished.

There were approximately 15 workers on both the day and night shifts. It was hotel practice to hire younger people for the department and most were between 20 and 25 years of age with a few slightly older women pressers. The work of the department did not require previous experience, and all jobs could be learned on the job in about a month. Wages in the laundry were about average for similar jobs in the Miami area. Ralph Blake was the department supervisor.

The night shift of the laundry department was very congenial and shift satisfaction with the department was high. A number of the department members attended trade schools or the community college during the day. Blake himself was attending the local university. The night shift employees planned many social functions together. During the summer, when the students were not in school, the group sometimes lunched at the beach, and swam and played volleyball before going to work. Occasionally during the winter, they attended the university intramural basketball games and cheered for Blake who played on one of the teams. Once in a while they had a picnic at a nearby park to which they took their spouses or boy or girl friends.

Perez was terrified of water and thus did not participate in the beach activities. He was active in all of the other departmental social activities; he enjoyed helping to plan parties and he and his wife always volunteered to buy the hamburgers and hot dogs. One night Mrs. Perez sent an ice cream cake to work with her husband which was shared by the department at their mid-shift break. This ice cream or cake eating at the mid-shift break became a custom thereafter with everyone taking turns providing the "goodies."

In addition to loading and unloading his machines, Perez was the department's machine troubleshooter, fixing minor breakdowns and inspecting all of the laundry department machines for required maintenance. These were tasks of considerable responsibility. He also oriented and got any new employees started on their jobs, something he enjoyed very much. He went out of his way to be helpful to anyone with a problem; he was well-liked as well as respected by everyone. There were, however, no opportunities for promotion within the laundry department.

After two years an opportunity for a transfer to another job became available to Perez. Blake remembered that Perez had been promised a transfer and arranged it since he thought highly of Perez and wanted to help him get promoted. The opening was in the hotel maintenance unit of the engineering department, and Perez was assigned there to do regular inspections of the lighting in the public areas and guest rooms. There were several men in the electrical group, all of whom did separate, specialized activities. This group had excellent wages, often worked in the nicer areas of the hotel, and had more possibilities for advancement than the workers in the laundry. The employees in the electrical group were busy on their own throughout the hotel, and so had little opportunity to talk with each other. The electrical supervisor seldom spoke with his men, but would often appear where they were working and stand staring at them with his thumbs in his belt.

Perez did satisfactory work from the beginning. His weekly earnings would have increased as soon as he had passed the one-month probationary period, but before that had gone by he requested a transfer back to the laundry department, which was granted.

When Ralph Blake earned his degree in the late spring of 2000, he joined the hotel's human resources department. About a year later, he was routinely visiting each department on all shifts and one night happened to meet with Juan Perez.

BLAKE: Hello, Juan.

PEREZ: It's been a long time since I've seen you. How's it going?

BLAKE: Good, I'd say very nicely. How about you?

PEREZ: Okay.

BLAKE: How about your orchids? Are you making any money?

PEREZ: Hey, better than before. I've got several new varieties that are pretty popular. There's a lot more social events now around here, those Cubans do like to show off, you know. I'm doing just fine. I've bred a special one, which Ruth is going to wear to her prom. She's my daughter, you'll remember.

BLAKE: How is Ruth?

PEREZ: Lovely and smart, too. She's a senior now, popular and with the boys starting to hang around. My wife and I just received a letter from the principal telling us that Ruth made the Honor Roll again. She wants to go to college, but that's pretty expensive, isn't it?

BLAKE: Well, it really depends on where she wants to go.

PEREZ: I'm not sure. All I know is that I've got to start putting more money away for it. The recession is starting to hurt the hotel business. Actually, it isn't so great right now!

BLAKE: What are you saying?

PEREZ: Well, I don't mean we haven't got lots of work to do. Some in our department say we've too darn much work. I guess the hotel's going to be doing fine for a while. What bugs me is all the changes being made around here.

BLAKE: I can see there've been some changes.

PEREZ: You bet your life! A guy like me just doesn't know where he stands any more. I used to be the troubleshooter and inspector. Now, maintenance gets the calls. Since we've changed over to more automatic washers and added a couple more, the only thing I do now is load and unload. It isn't much fun around here any more. No picnics, no parties, no talking with the other operators— just work all night long. I hardly get to know the others in the laundry. There's nearly 22 now, mostly new kids.

BLAKE: Do you still help them get broken in?

PEREZ: Nope. Our new supervisor has changed everything. We've all become "specialists," just do one little job. I don't think the super likes me. When I try to help a new person with their job, the super says, "Mind your own business, Perez; you do too much gabbing for your own good." All I ever try to do is help the new folks get straightened out with their equipment. It's not so easy when you're new. I think they appreciate a helping hand. But our super, maybe he's jealous or afraid I'll show him up in front of the others, I don't know. He's not as smart as he thinks he is. See that new conveyor belt over there? It breaks down all the time and the super hollers for maintenance. I offered once to change a safety device that was shorting out but he told me to get back to my washer. I don't think he knows what a short is.

BLAKE: Did maintenance repair it?

PEREZ: Sure, they changed the safety switch so it wouldn't short out! It works fine now. You ought to see us turn out laundry now—with the new machines and the conveyor and everything, we really pour the work through here. We're pretty much specialists now, each of us just does one thing, over and over. It's sort of a production line arrangement. It's ok. Our laundry puts through nearly twice as much as when you were here.

BLAKE: That's impressive.

PEREZ: It sure is. Sometimes we work extra days too, and that helps with the pay check. We get time-and-a-half for anything over 40 hours a week. Those organizers last fall helped us too.

BLAKE: In what way?

PEREZ: Well, the management crumbled and gave us all a raise to keep the union out. We got seniority rights too.

BLAKE: I don't follow.

PEREZ: Any reduction in force, they mean cutbacks, within a department, is done by seniority. We older folks go last; it's a pretty good deal when you've been around here as long as I have.

JULIE'S CALL

Glancing at her watch, Marcie saw that it was nearly 8:00 P.M. Conscious that Julie was going to call her in about a half hour, Marcie pushed aside her homework and reached for the file of her field notes (see Appendix) on Julie's store. Julie was going to want her ideas on empowerment and she'd best get her thoughts sorted out.

Marcie Garner was a last-semester senior majoring in hospitality management at Old Ivy University. Earlier that year, anticipating a job offer from the Triple Hot Mexican Restaurant Corporation—a chain of fast food restaurants—Marcie had approached one of her professors to talk about Triple Hot's newly initiated employee empowerment program—one of the reasons she had interviewed with the company. The professor wasn't very helpful to Marcie, but did raise several questions about the program. While he and Marcie agreed that the idea of employee empowerment sounded good in general, they also wondered how easy it was to implement and if it was actually working as designed. Marcie was encouraged to find out first-hand by visiting several Triple Hot stores and interviewing a sample of employees.

While she was quite busy finishing her program at Old Ivy, Marcie did telephone several Triple Hot managers in two nearby cities to try to arrange some visits. One of the managers contacted was Julie, the operations manager of the north Syracuse Triple Hot who seemed at first reluctant to have Marcie visit, but finally agreed to a mutually convenient day in mid-semester. On the appointed morning, Marcie drove to north Syracuse, met and then interviewed Julie twice, as well as four of her employees, each once, and was able to observe store activities for several hours. Near the end of the afternoon, just as Marcie was leaving, Julie approached her and said, "Your visit has made me think about whether I'm doing the right things about our empowerment program. I'd like your thoughts. May I call you in a couple of weeks when you've had time to digest what you've learned here today?" Marcie agreed, gave Julie her telephone number, and they set a date and time for the call.

At 8:30, Marcie's telephone rang, interrupting her note reading. Answering with "Hello, this is Marcie speaking," she heard Julie's greeting followed by, "I hope this is a good time to talk, Marcie. It's been quite a long day for me. Both Doug and Dan, you remember them, well, they gave me notice they're leaving next month, and now that spring has finally come, business is picking up. I've been jumping all day. I know you've been busy too, but have you had any thoughts about training and empowerment and such at my store?"

APPENDIX FIELD NOTES: NORTH SYRACUSE TRIPLE HOT MEXICAN RESTAURANT

BACKGROUND

The Triple Hot Mexican Restaurant is located in North Syracuse in between two strip malls. It is a free-standing, brick-and-mortar style Triple Hot. There are a few other fast-food restaurants in the immediate area, including a Kentucky Fried Chicken. About two blocks away is a medium-sized mall whose anchor store is T.J.Maxx. Most of the other stores in the mall are

Reprinted (with modifications) with permission from Teri Tompkins (Ed.), *Cases in Management Organization*, Prentice Hall Publishers, 2000.

also discount shops. The area looks a little rundown. My guess is that the building of the new and very large Carousel Mall, less than five minutes away, did not help this section of town.

The store opened last August and everyone I spoke with was hired at that time. The empowerment program was discussed prior to opening the store (Julie heard about it at a training session during the summer). Employees have slowly been eased into taking on more and more responsibility.

There are four crew members and a manager or shift leader during slow times (one on the cash register, one on drive-thru, and two on the line). During peak hours there are four crew members on the line (two doing regular orders and two doing special requests).

PEOPLE INTERVIEWED

All of the employees are male and most are in high school. However, the operations manager and assistant manager are both female. Julie is in her late twenties to early thirties. She was not wearing a uniform. Instead, she had on black pants and a short-sleeved blouse. She has been with Triple Hot for $3^1/_2$ years. Julie had previous supervisory experience as an assistant manager with McDonald's and with a franchised Kentucky Fried Chicken. However, when she came to Triple Hot she had to start as a crew member (line employee) because there were no management positions available. As soon as she started working she was in training to be a shift manager. Julie works directly under Rob Robertson who is a multi-unit or "TMU" (team-managed unit) manager. Rob spends about one day a week in Julie's store. In addition to Rob and Julie, there is an assistant manager and a shift manager.

Darryl is presently training to be a shift manager. He is in his mid-twenties and has varied work experience. Besides working at Triple Hot, Darryl is a cook at a fine dining establishment.

All of the crew members who were interviewed have been with Triple Hot since the store opened in August. Doug is a high school senior. Previously he worked for Burger King. He often makes the schedules and is an "empowered" employee, so he can open the store without a manager being present. Dan is also a senior at the same school Doug attends. Before coming to Triple Hot he was working for a family-owned fish and ice cream restaurant and had some experience in telemarketing. His sales experience has led to him being put on a team that does OPS (off premise sales) calls. The third high school-aged worker is Floyd, who is a junior. This is his first job and he has not been given any additional duties, but expects to be empowered this summer.

JULIE ON TRIPLE HOT AND EMPOWERMENT

"I first heard about empowerment at a training class I attended this past summer (at that time the concept was being called teaming). I've never worked for a company that talked about letting line employees get involved in traditionally managerial functions."

"At the other fast food restaurants I worked for, managers were instructed to be in control at all times. At Triple Hot, crew members are in charge of all kinds of things including preparing deposits, going to the bank, completing the closing paperwork, and opening the store in the morning."

"The employees of Triple Hot have much more freedom to think for themselves. They are encouraged to try to come up with something new instead of just being told how it has always been done. There is not one person who is in charge of making all of the decisions; everyone gets to contribute. The employees make more of the decisions. If they take action and make a decision, ultimately they will make the correct one and do the right thing. If they make a mistake, we'll help them fix it. What could they possibly do that we couldn't fix? Also, you don't have to ask permission for everything. Managers just say, go for it, and you don't stop."

"You have to be careful, though. It's not one day you're not empowered and then, voila, you are. It's a constant thing. There is always something to be learned at every level. Since there is always stuff to learn I don't think a store can ever be totally empowered. There is constant training going on and new people coming on."

"I think overall the restaurant is better off because of empowerment. It lets the employees have ownership in the store. They will point to something and say, 'Hey, that needs to be cleaned,' or, 'It's slow, someone should go home.' That never would have happened at McDonald's. [My employees] have much more of an awareness of what's going on around them."

"It really seems like the crew members are interested in learning more. Some of them are surprised when we tell them about stuff that we used to not be allowed to talk about to employees. In other places, they never were allowed to know the sales, food cost, or labor cost. It is nice because they ask about it and they can get familiar with it. I think the reaction overall has been positive. Of course there are some people who don't want any responsibility—they don't like empowerment. They just want to come into work, punch a cash register, and go home. Those people don't stay. If there is ever such a thing as total empowerment, those people won't be part of the team any more. They will be put out by other team members."

"Since we started really getting into this empowerment stuff, I think customer service has improved. Food cost is down and labor cost is beginning to come down too."

"If you are going to work at Triple Hot, you should know that people are capable of doing more than pushing buttons and sweeping floors. The biggest blockade to empowerment is management who think employees can't do anything but push buttons. There still are some old-style managers who think this way. Really, [employees] can do whatever you show them to do."

"Corporate is trying to teach these managers about empowerment. They gave all of us this packet on how empowerment is supposed to work. According to the packet, there are four levels of empowerment: (1) know what you are doing, (2) scheduling and stuff like that, (3) opening and closing the store, (4) doing everything without a manager. I think we are doing a little bit at each level, but not all of any. People need to go at their own pace. I knew most of the information in the packet already but everything I read helps."

PERCEPTIONS OF EMPOWERMENT

Out of the 12 crew members at this Triple Hot, two are empowered. This means that those two employees have been trained to open and close the store without a manager being present. When asked what "empowerment" meant, the following answers were given:

JULIE: All the employees being self-sufficient in their jobs and having all aspects of the restaurant run as a team instead of the way it is traditionally.

DARRYL: Empowered employees can open or close the store.

DOUG: Letting employees open by themselves. Giving regular employees the power to run a shift. I opened the store without any managers and that's empowerment. Other places they wouldn't let you manage.

DAN: Had never heard the term "empowered."

FLOYD: Being able to work by yourself without having a manager here with you. You're in charge that way.

EMPLOYEES SPEAK ABOUT EMPOWERMENT

DARRYL: You get a little more money for being "empowered" but not for doing scheduling or something like that. That is just for variety. Money does matter at some point.

DOUG: At Triple Hot you get a lot more responsibilities and privileges. At Burger King I only did one thing—I made the food but never worked the cash register. Here I've done everything. There is more variety. I like it better here. Sometimes I like to see the financial statements too. You want it to do good, but you don't want it to get too busy. That isn't too much fun. I would like to have some say in hiring. I think we'll get that soon.

DAN: It used to be only the manager who made the schedule. When we started doing it we saw how difficult it was. I understand the manager's job better now. I appreciate how difficult their job is. It's a little harder—I don't think I'd be able to do a lot of the stuff they do. I couldn't work the computer. They have to make the final decisions like on inventory. Basically there is a lot of stuff I don't even know about with the computer. I'll stay away from the computer. I figure I'll probably never be manager (I'm not 18 yet). I'll just stay where I am. When you do that extra stuff you don't get paid any more. It is just something to learn. That's fine with me. The more I know the longer I can stay here and the more hours I can get.

FLOYD: I look forward to coming to work. It's fun. We don't fool around but it's fun working with your friends and sometimes the managers will go out in the dining room to do something and it's like you're in charge doing everything.

I always thought that only a manager could do opening. That is why some of the crew members want to do it—so they could be like managers in a sense. This summer I am going to be empowered. This is something only Triple Hot does. It is something to work towards and look forward to. They show us the computer or something like that on a Sunday when it gets slow. They'll take us back there. It's nothing that big but it's something else you can do. It's a little higher.

I think it is better if employees do the schedule. It is easier to talk to them if you can't work a certain time. We all go to school together so you can just see them in the halls and let them know.

Sometimes the managers go sit in the back. They don't want to stoop down to being an employee that way—sweep or do the dishes or something like that. Everybody should be considered on the same level. It makes everything easier. Some people quit because they think the managers are better than them.

This store could be run without managers with the people who are here. Sometimes you do. The managers will be in the office and someone will just take over. Maybe we couldn't do the computer work. But since they're showing us how to do it we probably could if they just told us.

COMMENTS ABOUT MANAGERIAL STYLE

When asked about what her role as manager would be if employees continued to take on managerial duties, Julie seemed a little taken aback. Finally she replied,

JULIE: "I don't know. I never thought about it. That's a good question. Things change so quickly you don't have time to think about what your role is going to be. You just figure you'll free yourself up to do other things than working the line and saying, 'You do this and you do this.' We'll do community relations and get new accounts. I'd like to have more time where I could get out from behind the line. Now I spend about 90% of my time on the line."
Later in the day, after she had thought about the question a little longer, Julie stated, "My job is to teach them my job."

DARRYL: "I won't ask anyone to do something I wouldn't do myself. So how could they complain? I am very fair. Also, I don't yell a lot. People like working on the shifts I lead because I'm easy on them. Also, if I have a good idea I'll do things my way and show others that way. That makes it easy on everyone. I don't care how Corporate says we should do it."

DOUG: "Over at the other place I worked the managers didn't know what was going on. They would stay in the office. They weren't in touch with the employees. These managers do everything with us. They make food and help us out. These managers keep things in order, keep things moving along. Also, they keep us in line. Still, the managers are nicer here. They let us do more stuff and don't get mad at every little thing."

DAN: "This isn't very different from my previous job except that being a corporation they're not as mean to you. At the other place they used to yell a little more if things weren't done on time. Here, people only get yelled at when they are not doing their job. They'll say 'Do this' once, then 'Please do this' and then they'll raise their voice. Overall, this job is more fun. I mean any job I got at least I get paid but I like the people and the managers are nice. I got my friend to work here. I said 'It's a good place to work. People are nice, and I can probably get you good hours.'"

FLOYD: "The managers are nice and everybody who works here is friends. You can tell if someone's gonna leave real quick. Like if they didn't want to do the dishes they aren't going to last. They have attitudes and get fired for talking back."

CUSTOMER SATISFACTION

Employees are expected to do whatever they think is necessary to satisfy the customer. The crew has power to correct any problem a customer may have. For example, they can comp food. However, sometimes customers want to see a manager. They feel that only a manager could solve their problem.

Dan described an incident when he had to go outside corporate regulations to satisfy a customer. "One time a woman came in and ordered a taco. She was from San Francisco or somewhere in California and said that there they come with olives for free. Here we charge for them. She was getting really mad so I asked a manager. She said 'If that's how it is then just give them to her' because, you know, Total Customer Satisfaction. Make the customer happy at all costs. If they say you gave them the wrong change you just give it to them and you just tell the manager you might be over or under. You ask the manager first, I do, I don't know if you're supposed to but I check everything with the manager so I don't get yelled at. If I hadn't asked it probably would have been okay because the lady was getting upset and starting to raise her voice and demanding to see a manager."

TRAINING

When a new crew member is hired they spend their first few days on the job shadowing another employee or working on the line between two experienced employees. Julie would like to change the way training is allotted financially so that new employees could complete a more comprehensive training program before they were expected to perform. Presently, Corporate's totally automated computer operations system's Fast Labor program calculates how much time should be allotted to training based on the volume of the store. For Julie's store it comes out to 45 minutes a day. Julie explained, "Well, a person is not going to work a 45-minute shift. Everyone moves at their own pace. You can't have a program that says that on day one you should know this, this, and this. We don't have enough time for conventional one-on-one training. It's like 'We have time, let's do it now.' It'd be nice to be able to go step by step."

Due to the lack of training, turnover has been high. Recently, the training program was reevaluated and some of the problems have been resolved. Julie explained how these changes came about: "The employees let the managers know that training was a problem through round-tables with the training manager and the market manager. They had three of these discussions in one month and then never had one again—that was overkill. They had roundtables with two employees from each store and at all three roundtables the employees said that the training was not what they wanted it to be. So we looked at that and said 'They're right' instead of getting upset and saying 'Who are they to say this?' We started to use the existing program more consistently. Trainers have to be certified to show they are qualified to train others. This program of certification came from Corporate. It was fine at first, but now I don't want to have a lot of different titles because we're supposed to be a team and all on the same level. Having titles would defeat the purpose. So now if you're certified, you should know it well enough to show someone else."

Crew members have been very eager to learn new skills and take on new responsibilities. They report approaching a manager and asking to be taught how to complete a particular task. Every once in a while a crew member will ask to take on something that management doesn't think they are ready for. For example, if a crew member often calls in sick, they are not ready to be in charge of opening the store. When this situation arises, Julie said, "I tell them honestly why I am not going to train them now and that gives them incentive to improve. At other restaurants the managers would just lie to the employee and say, 'I'll show you next week' and just keep pushing them off even with no intention of ever training them. It's great to be able to be honest with them, they are surprised, and appreciate it. Then they'll try to improve so they can prove you wrong and show you that they are ready to learn new responsibilities. In this way, training acts as an incentive."

Presently Julie is in the process of training the crew members to conduct employment interviews. For the first time, she has come up against a lot of resistance. "It is really scary for them. You can show them how to do a food order and they say, 'Okay, no problem, this is fun' or how to do the schedule and they say 'Okay, no problem, this is fun.' But put them face to face and they're like, 'Don't leave me alone,' " she explained. To alleviate this fear she is letting them sit in on interviews she conducts. However, Julie cannot always coordinate her schedule and the interviewee's schedule with when the crew member is working and presently the need to hire people is overriding the need to train crew members.

MISCELLANEOUS COMMENTS

When [Darryl] becomes a manager he says he'll have to cut his long hair. This came from the corporate policies. He thinks this is "ridiculous" because they hired him with long hair and he can keep it as long as he's not a manager. Also, he says they make a distinction between men and women.

> JULIE: "We have more of a feeling of people working together than at other fast food restaurants. Even from store to store. There are less rumors going around and people talk less."
>
> "You get more knowledge of the overall picture. Everybody gets to look at the overall picture not just the RGM (regional general manager). You get to know where we are at with everything. It's not just well this is where we are at with everything. It's not just well this is where we are at and what we're going to do about it. You look at where you are at and decide what you are going to do about it."
>
> "Whoever opens the store in the morning is the only one allowed in the safe until the shift changes. This means at times the manager has to ask permission of the employees."

THE KEVIN STEWART CASE

It was late in the afternoon on a Friday in mid-June. Professor Steve Davis sat at his desk outlining the activities he intended to do the following week. As he was jotting in his calendar book, he looked up at the knock on his open door. There stood one of his former students, Kevin Stewart.

> DAVIS: Hi Kevin, what a nice surprise. I thought you were off selling yourself in the marts of men?
>
> STEWART: Well, not exactly. I was in the building, ah, applying to the graduate program and thought I'd stop by and see how you were doing!
>
> DAVIS: You know me Kevin, busy, busy. This last semester has been a brute for me. I was just sitting here getting my head straight about some writing. Remember that research project we talked about last winter? Well I think I'm about ready to write up the closing for it.
>
> STEWART: Yeah, I'd like to see that. If there's anything I can do to help let me know. I'll be around sort of floating until summer term gets underway. I'm working evenings so I've plenty of time.

DAVIS: So you aspire to our Master's program? We'll no doubt be seeing more of each other. But didn't you just go off to Colorado or someplace and start a job?

STEWART: Yes, that's so. It's kind of a funny story. I feel sort of strange about it. It would probably make a good case.

DAVIS: Well why don't you tell me about it and we'll see if it has the makings of a case or not. Let's see, you graduated just last month didn't you?

Kevin Stewart then related his experiences since graduation. Professor Davis listened, occasionally interjecting a question. When Kevin had finished Professor Davis encouraged him to record his experiences, both because it might be the basis for a teaching case, and, organizing his thoughts to record might serve Kevin to learn from his experience. A week later Kevin left a cassette with the following account in Professor Davis' mailbox.

* * *

Well here we go Prof. I think this is going to be a little more difficult than I thought it would be as I have tried several times already to start this without much success. I am going to try and relate to you my experiences in campus recruiting and job hunting, say in the past eight months. Before I do this I will fill you in on my educational background, my previous work experience, and some of my attitudes.

I graduated in 1996 from the Episcopal Academy, a private boy's school in Philadelphia. I was in the top half of my class and a C+ student on a very easy grading scale. I participated in almost every sport there and lettered in swimming my senior year. My SAT scores totaled 1,100, with a 570 in English and a 530 in Math. I applied to three universities, Penn State, University of North Carolina at Chapel Hill, and here. I was accepted at all three and came to Texas for a number of reasons, among those being the fact that it was far away from Pennsylvania, near a large city but not downtown, co-ed, down south, and warm weather. I thought I'd like the place.

As you know, I graduated last May 20 from here with a degree in Business Administration. My grade point for the four years was a 3.0 which qualified me for Honors Day Convocation—3.0 to 3.5. I had a 3.15 cumulative grade point in the Business School, as well as a 3.4 grade point for my junior and senior years. I participated in several extracurricular activities. My freshman year I was a squad leader in Cheeros, a freshman cheerleading organization. Throughout my college career I was a member of Beta Beta Phi, the pledge trainer there in the fall of 2000, and I was a goalie on the now defunct water polo team in the fall of my junior year. In addition to these activities, I was also a teaching assistant for several business school courses, including, as you know, in the Introduction to Organizational Behavior and the Management course. My course of study in the Business School was pretty much of a general course. I had nine hours of Management, nine of Accounting, six of Finance, six in Business Law, and approximately twenty-seven in various operations courses including the one-time case writing course with Dr. Clutts. In addition to the university required courses I also took approximately 21 hours in political science; the reason for this being that I felt at one time that I was going to go to Law School and eventually become a lawyer.

My previous work experience consists mostly of summer time jobs. I have been a forklift operator, gravel shoveler, a tire changer, a car washer, salesman in a men's clothing department, short-order cook, lifeguard, janitor, waiter, and even a painter. These jobs ranged from $4 an hour to $8.25 an hour in pay and I have worked anywhere from 25 hours a week to 70. I have worked every summer since I was 14 and I have used the money I made during these times to buy cars, clothes, and pay for my books and social expenses while in school. I am 22 years old, 5' 10'' tall, and 165 lbs. I have medium length light brown hair, brown eyes and am clean shaven.

Before getting into describing my experiences with campus recruiting I would first like to briefly tell what my previous postgraduate plans were. For my first three years of college I secretly intended to go to law school after graduation. My father is an attorney, a partner in his own firm and is quite successful. I always viewed law as a profession which seemed quite interesting to me, as well as being very rewarding. It wasn't until the summer after my junior year after talking with my father for an extended length of time that I decided that law school was not what I wanted to do. I could not justify three more years of school as well as the additional cost of the education when it seemed like the law field was not as good as it used to be. With Legal Defense Societies, no-fault insurance and with thousands of lawyers coming out of college each year, and only a few openings, it did not seem this was quite the field I thought it was. After deciding not to go to law school I felt that graduate school in business was my next alternative. I felt that I would like to go to some place like the University of Washington, maybe Stanford if I could get in, Dartmouth, Cornell or SMU. About the middle of the fall 2000, I decided that I would not go to graduate school but would concentrate my efforts towards finding a permanent job someplace after graduation, even in hospitality.

My next step in obtaining a job was to sign up for some campus interviews. I had two before Christmas, one with Southwestern Bell and the other with Southwestern Life. Although I was to find out later that the recruiters were only interested at that time in December graduates, I felt that signing up for these two interviews ahead of time would not only indicate to them that I was interested in finding work but it also gave me some valuable experience in interviewing. I think that for the first two interviews I was pretty nervous. I really didn't know what to expect from the interviewer and didn't quite know what kind of questions he was going to ask. For these reasons I think I was pretty poorly prepared and probably didn't do that well in the interviews themselves. Most all of the interviews that I had that semester all seemed to ask pretty much the same type of questions: age, high school background, extracurricular activities in high school, your summer work experiences, types of courses taken in college, the ones you liked and disliked, grade points, and extracurricular activities in college like fraternities, sports, and assorted other types of things. They also asked you questions as to where you would like to live, if you minded relocating, but more important they asked what you were expecting or looking forward to as far as a job and the type of company you wanted to work with. These last two questions for me were the most difficult to answer and as would be indicated by my changing of plans from law school to graduate business to just finding work. I don't think that I was totally sure just what I wanted to do and with this in mind I was quite unable to formulate a specific answer to that question. As a stop gap measure I told most of the people who asked that I was interested in some sort of management or administrative program which would lead me on to upper management and eventually some sort of executive position. As far as the company I was looking for, I felt that a company that had a good background, promoted from within on the basis of performance rather than on seniority and one that generally afforded me the opportunity to progress in responsibility, position, as well as financially, was the type of company that I was looking for. I did not view relocating as being a critical factor as I didn't think I had any ties and moving around would not be a big thing for me.

My next step, I felt, in finding a job was to sign up for as many interviews as I possibly could. I felt that by signing up for a greater number of interviews that this would increase my chances of finding a good job at the end of the school year. I will try to list the companies I interviewed with, though I am sure I will leave some out, in hopes you will have some idea of the types of companies I was interviewing with. I had two interviews with Southwestern Bell, one as I said before Christmas and another in February. I had one interview with Southwestern Life and was asked to sign up for another but as I said before I was not interested in an insurance company and signed up for that one only for the interview experience. I also had interviews with quite a number of retail department stores in Houston and Dallas, Sanger-Harris, Titche's, Nieman-Marcus, Sears & Roebuck. I had interviews with Mobil Oil, Penzoil, Missouri-Pacific Railroad, National Chemsearch, Proctor & Gamble, Anderson-Clayton, a food processor and wholesaler, and some others which I cannot remember at this time. As I said before most of the interviewers seemed to ask pretty much the same questions, and they all would talk for a little while about their specific programs at the end of which the interviewee was supposed to ask some questions which I found to be quite difficult. Not knowing too much about the background of each company I found that most of the questions I thought of to ask were already pretty much answered by the interviewer in describing their particular program.

I did not have too much success with these interviews. I eliminated some of the companies, Procter & Gamble for one, Mobil Oil, Missouri-Pacific Railroad. I eliminated these myself because I didn't think I would want to work for them. Other companies eliminated me on the basis I guess they didn't think they wanted me to work for them and most of these were the retail companies. Penzoil was looking for a land development man in petroleum and I had no experience in that so I was eliminated there. All the letters I got back from them were very encouraging letters. They seemed to think that I was a nice young man, intelligent, and had done well in school, but that my particular educational background in college was not as strong as they would like in their particular areas.

I had two basic offers through these interviews, one being a very definite one from Sears & Roebuck and a tentative offer from Anderson-Clayton. After my campus interview with Sears I received a letter from them requesting that I come to their territorial offices in Dallas and take their executive battery of psychological tests as well as talk with several of the people there. The tests that I took were relatively simple and I think were designed to test a person's motivation, his attitude, as well as his chances for success. I found these tests relatively easy to take. I have had a certain amount of experience in these types of tests and I knew what they were looking for so answering the questions on them was relatively easy. When I completed the tests I went in and talked to several people about the program. They answered the questions that I had as to pay, where the training program would take place, although they never did say much about the actual program itself. I think that if I had a little more experience or had a little better idea of what I was doing, I could have cleared up that issue before going to Denver.

My second feeler was with Anderson-Clayton. They said they were interested in me and invited me down to talk to a number of their executives as well as take some of their tests and have lunch with them. Of the two I think I was more impressed with Anderson-Clayton than I was with Sears although I never really did get a firm offer from them.

All of these events took place before spring vacation and the week before spring break I got a definite offer of employment from Sears & Roebuck. They said that they felt that I had excellent potential to succeed in their retail management program and were happy to offer me a job. The starting pay would be approximately $2500 a month at a rate of around $630 a week. I had a choice of four training locations: Denver, Colorado; Houston, Texas; Midland-Odessa, Texas; and Lincoln-Omaha, Nebraska. In my original campus interview with them, the recruiter stated that I would have my choice of the four so I didn't think that would be much of a problem.

Also before spring vacation I was supposed to have heard from Anderson-Clayton. My interview with them was I recall a week and a half to two weeks before spring break was supposed to start and they indicated to me that they would have a decision for me one way or another before I left for spring vacation. Unfortunately such notification did not arrive and when I returned from spring break I had expected to have heard from them either by phone or by mail. This presented an interesting problem for me because I felt that if I did get an offer from Anderson-Clayton that I would work for them but on the other hand only having one offer with no more interviews signed up, I could not really afford to spend too much time in waiting to notify Sears. For this reason I inquired of several faculty, Professor Stone and you, as to the correctness or properness of calling Anderson-Clayton and inquiring as to the status of my application for employment. I found out that this was an accepted thing and wouldn't be looked down upon so on Tuesday after Easter I called Anderson-Clayton to ask them if they had made a decision on my application. They said that at that time they had been involved in other things and had not decided on how many people they were going to hire this spring but would let me know by the end of the week. About this time a little over two weeks had passed since I had received my offer from Sears and I was getting a little anxious because I felt that if I took too much time the offer might get retracted. On the following Wednesday, the day after I had called Anderson-Clayton, I received another letter from Sears saying that my application and file were still being held open and that they would like a decision one way or another on my part as soon as possible. On Friday I called Anderson-Clayton late in the afternoon and was informed by them that they were not going to hire anybody this spring but that sometime in the next six to eight weeks they were planning a major expansion and there would be job opportunities open after that time which they felt I was qualified for. They said they were very sorry that they would not be able to hire me at this time but that they were very interested in me and would keep in touch.

That Friday afternoon I called Sears and made a verbal acceptance of their offer and on Monday I sent them a written letter accepting their offer and requesting Houston as my training site and Denver as a second choice. I would say at that time I felt pretty good about this whole situation in that I had what appeared to be a good offer of employment and acceptance with a national company which many people told me was quite good as far as employee benefits and other things went. I personally was happy that I had a job when others around me didn't seem to be able to figure out what they wanted to do and take any action towards it. A lot of my friends signed up for interviews and did not get any offers or did not interview much at all. About three weeks from the end of school I received several letters from Sears, one from the territorial office in Dallas stating that I had been assigned to the Denver-Cherry Creek store for my training program and another from my coordinator up in Denver, welcoming me to Denver and giving me some basic instructions of what I was to do when I got to Denver. From that point until the 22nd of May I pretty much goofed off, did a couple of final exams, and coasted into graduation although I did not attend the ceremonies.

On the 22nd, in the morning I packed my car and drove to Denver. I took the trip in one day and to tell you the truth it was probably the worst trip I have ever taken anyplace. Outside of Childress, Texas I got a speeding ticket for going 80 in a 70 mile an hour zone, which I didn't know I was doing because my speedometer doesn't work, but I had to drive back to Childress, wait 45 minutes for a Justice of the Peace, and fork out $42.50 for the speeding ticket. I continued my trip on to Denver and just as I got into Colorado one of the fender skirts of my car fell off, took a big gouge out of the car, tore off the hub cap and flew out into the road. I pulled my car over to pick up these items but before I had a chance to, a tractor-trailer ran over them and flattened both the hubcap and the fender skirt. I walked out into the highway, picked them up and threw them off the road. By the time I got to Denver I had a sore throat, a fever, a cough, and generally felt pretty lousy. It was pretty late at night and I watched TV for a little while before going to bed.

Wednesday morning I called my coordinator, Mr. Ken Davis at Sears, and arranged to go in and talk with him for a little while about the program, to introduce myself to him and ask him to help find a place for me to live. That afternoon I went in and talked to Mr. Davis. He outlined my training program, which was to last until the end of January or the beginning of February on a week-by-week basis. It was basically comprised of a job rotation beginning with four weeks in sales, and then moving on to shipping, receiving, personnel, credit, customer services, back to sales as an assistant group manager trainee and then back to several of the other departments, moving back finally into being an assistant group manager in sales which would wrap up my training period. I was not too impressed with this program. I had previous experience in a retail store in a sales capacity and did not find it very enjoyable or very rewarding. I had hoped to avoid this aspect of Sears when I accepted the job but as I look back on it now, a store basically deals in sales, so their training program is probably going to have a large amount of sales in it. After my training program was completed Mr. Davis said that I would more than likely, and in fact he almost assured me, that I would be transferred someplace else other than Denver where I would start out as assistant group manager and work into a group manager position in one of their branch stores. He cited several places as examples, such as Wichita, Kansas; Omaha, Nebraska; and some other places like that and said that my chances of going to Dallas or Houston or some of the larger cities would be rather slim. I was not too impressed with this for the simple fact that I had been raised and spent most of my life near or in a large city and had come accustomed to the advantages a large city offers as opposed to a smaller city. We talked for a little while about our own backgrounds as a way of getting to know each other. I asked him about how much would be taken out of my paycheck of approximately $630 a week and he said my take-home pay would be anywhere from $450 to $510. The deductions were for Federal tax, Colorado tax, Denver city tax, and Sears' benefits such as health and insurance. I was rather disappointed in this from the standpoint that I had hoped to make a little more than that and honestly couldn't justify working such a low grade of pay when I could change tires or shovel gravel for more. I asked Mr. Davis, since I was going to stay in Denver, if he knew where I could find an apartment in a reasonably good neighborhood, you know a nice clean apartment, but one that would not cost too much. He said that he had only been in Denver for four weeks himself and he really wasn't familiar with the town but he showed me on a Denver city map a good spot in town where I should be able to find an apartment and he gave me some street names and things like that. I asked him if he knew if there was anybody in town that I could possibly room with, like another trainee. He said there was one but he had no way of getting in touch with him because they didn't know where he was.

I left Sears that afternoon and drove out to the area that he had indicated to me on the map and attempted to find an apartment. I spent the next hour and a half driving around in my car and saw only one apartment building and the manager wasn't there. He lived someplace else. By this time I was thoroughly confused and getting a bit on the pissed-off side so I stopped in a gas station and called up the parents of one of my fraternity brothers and explained to them my situation and asked them if they knew of any place I could find an apartment in a good neighborhood and would fill the other qualifications I was looking for. They said that they did not know of a place but suggested that I come over to dinner and possibly spend the night and that we would look for something in the morning. I drove to their house and sat down with the gentleman, Mr. Victor Organenzo, a retired jeweler in Denver, the author of several books on diamonds and a very respected man in his field of jewelry. By the time I got to his house I was so depressed about the whole thing about Denver and Sears, frustrated at not being able to find an apartment and from spending the afternoon driving around in my car. I felt like just getting back in my car and driving back to Texas. Mr. Organenzo was able to talk me out of doing this and succeeded to a large extent in calming me down. We spent the rest of the evening talking about my various alternatives if I was to leave Denver, among these we felt that I could go back to Houston and attempt to find employment there or that I could go to graduate school or see if Sears would be able to transfer my training program to Houston which would be more along the lines of what I was looking for as opposed to Denver. That evening I went to bed pretty early and spent most of the night awake trying to figure out what I was going to do. I suppose I had a pretty troubled night's sleep. It wasn't the best. I had several nightmares about selling on the floor in Sears and when I woke up in the morning I felt that I had reached some sort of decision of what I was going to do.

The next morning I called Mr. Davis over at Sears and told him that I would like to come in and talk to him again, which he agreed to do. At eleven o'clock I went in and talked to Mr. Davis and I told him I would like to have my training program switched from Denver to Houston, that I felt I would be a lot happier in Houston than I would in Denver. I saw all my efforts in Denver saving money, and things like that, would only go towards getting out of Denver and going someplace else, preferably Dallas. I had hoped that I would have ample opportunity to visit Dallas on the weekends to see my girlfriend and other friends. At Sears in Denver I would not be able to do this. The stores there are open seven days a week and most holidays except for Christmas day, New Years day, probably Memorial Day, and Thanksgiving. Although I would be working a five-day week for them he said very rarely would I be able to get two days off back to back and would end up working a lot of Saturdays and Sundays, which I did not view as something I wanted to. I talked to Mr. Davis and asked him to talk to the proper people about having my training program switched to Houston and he said that he would do it and that he would give me a call in about three hours. At approximately 3 o'clock, Thursday, May 24, Mr. Davis called me at the Organenzos' house and said that he had talked to the territorial placement office in Dallas and they had talked to the people in Houston and there was no room in the Houston training program and that they really wanted me to stay in Denver. He said that they felt I had tremendous potential and very much wanted me to stay with the company and take my training program in Denver. I told Mr. Davis that I thanked him very much, that I thought he was a pretty nice guy, that he had treated me very fairly but that I was going to go back to Houston or Dallas and either go to graduate school or find a job there in town.

I felt pretty happy about making this decision. I felt that, at that time, and I still do, I had made the correct decision. Mr. Organenzo said that if I was not going to be happy with Sears or Denver that I had made a good decision and that the means that I had used to make the decision were good. Instead of making the decision when I was in a bad mood and which would have more of spur of the moment decision and which I may have regretted, I weighed my alternatives, my possible moves to graduate school, my ability to find work in Texas, and generally I think my alternatives were better coming back to Texas than they were if I had stayed in Denver.

After talking to Mr. Davis I called home to tell my parents what I had done. I felt that they would be tremendously disappointed and maybe even mad at me; after all they had spent a lot of money providing an education for me and I felt that they would be pretty unhappy that I had quit my first job even before I started. As it turned out, their reaction to my quitting Sears was the exact opposite reaction to what I thought it would be. They said that if I was not satisfied with the program at Sears that I was best getting out of it before I started my career off on the wrong foot. They said that if I needed any help while I was in Dallas that I should feel free to call them and that their feelings and desires should not be a part of my criteria for making a decision as I was out on my own and the decisions I would have to make would be the ones I would have to live with. I found this to be very comforting and it only further reinforced my belief that I had made the right decision in quitting Sears.

The next day I drove back to Dallas. I got back here OK and the day after Memorial Day began looking for work. Most of my efforts in finding employment were centered in looking through the newspaper in the want ads section as well as trying to work through three personnel agencies in Dallas. I did not have much success in either one of these. I had decided while I was in Denver that I would like a career in banking, based on numerous reasons. After relocating in Denver I found that I really didn't want to relocate, that I had more ties here than I thought I had, and that Dallas was really the place I would like to stay, at least for the next several years, if not the rest of my life. As for banking, I felt that it was a very secure job, no travel, no relocating, as well as being interesting and secure work, so my preliminary efforts at finding employment in Dallas were directed towards securing some sort of position in a bank, whether in management training or as a loan officer trainee, or something like that.

As I said, my efforts were directed basically through three personnel agencies, with an emphasis on one. I would not recommend anyone attempting to find a job through these personnel agencies as I feel they really do not work in your best interests and are only out to find you a job so that they can collect their commission. At one agency the fellow that I was working with said that he had contacted all of the banks in Dallas and the greater Dallas area, all the Savings and Loan banks and things like that and there were not any openings available at this time. He said though, that there was one bank, Federal Savings Bank, that seemed interested in me and he would attempt to arrange an interview for me. In the meantime we had agreed that he would try to find some sort of management training job with a corporation here in Dallas. He had very little success in this area but succeeded in arranging an interview with Greyhound for me two Thursdays ago. I went in for the interview and talked to their personnel director about the job which was to be a supervisor over thirty women in their accounting department. I asked him what the potentials were for this job as far as promotion and advancement and there were none, although among the fringe benefits for working for Greyhound is that you get a free bus pass. I went back to the personnel agency and told them that I did not want to work for Greyhound or anybody like that and that he had better do a little better than he was doing because he had yet to find anything that was even remotely interesting to me or better than the Sears job. He arranged for a second interview for me as an underwriter trainee for an insurance company in Dallas. I went in for that interview and though they were very friendly and nice people I did not want to work for them either.

I was getting pretty frustrated with this whole thing and quite discouraged which I was told would happen so I began doing some of my own soliciting. I looked in the newspapers to find ads for trainees, executive trainers, managers and things like that and began calling these people on my own. I arranged several interviews, one with Dallas County Bank, another with Prudential Life Insurance and neither of these interviews produced anything. After the Dallas County Bank interview I decided that there was not much future in working through personnel agencies and that the type of job I was looking for was really not available at this time so I decided that I would submit my application to graduate school and go on to get a Master's in Finance and Banking which would eventually lead me to a job at a bank in Dallas.

Looking back on this whole thing I believe that I made several mistakes. My first mistake was in not determining what I wanted to do. The problem there was that I wasn't sure. I really didn't know and had no idea of really what I wanted to do and felt that if I went with some company and training program eventually the whole idea would dawn on me and that everything would work out fine. I don't think that you can find a job through campus recruiting if you don't have a good idea of the type of career that you want. The second mistake that I made was not really knowing what I was looking for in a company. I should have questioned the type of training program that they had a lot closer than I did, the benefits, the pay, promotion aspects, relocation and things like that that I didn't think would be all that important when I was in the interview but when I actually got out I found that they were more important than I had thought. The third mistake I think that I made was in the relocation aspect. As I previously stated, I didn't think that relocation would be an important factor for me as I didn't think I had any ties, didn't have any responsibilities, and that travel and moving around from city to city wouldn't bother me that much. As I look back on it now, when I actually had to do it I found that I had more ties and did not want to relocate so that this became more of a factor than I thought it would have.

My fourth and probably even my biggest mistake was in accepting the Sears offer. I felt that I was totally correct in doing that from the standpoint that it was my only offer and it was that or not having a job at all. I should have looked a little more carefully into the type of program that Sears had, what it would require of me, what I should expect from them, the relocation aspects, financial aspects, the program itself, what I would be doing during the training program, what I'd be doing when I got out, and importantly, where I was going to be doing it. All these things I didn't look into. From the standpoint that it was my only job, I accepted it and there were no other alternatives that I saw at that time.

Now that I've been through all of this I think that I have learned quite a bit about myself, about the things that I want to do for the rest of my life, and how I am going to get them. I believe that I didn't quite know or understand prior to now exactly what I wanted to do and where I wanted to do it. On the basis of this whole experience I think I maybe can offer some advice for someone else who might be or will be going through a similar experience. First of all you have to decide what you want to do before you go job hunting. That's probably easier said than done and in order to do that I think you have to have some basic information about the various kinds of jobs that are available, the programs and the kind of future you will have with them, and the lifestyle that a particular job will imply. As I said before, I didn't have much knowledge on this and kind of walked into the Sears job pretty blindly so I would recommend to a person looking for a job, whether it is after completing undergraduate work or graduate work, to find out these things before they accept a job. If you can be sure about these things, you can make a correct decision as to the job and the kind of lifestyle it implies, then you can probably avoid some of the mistakes that I have made.

Another thing that I think is important is picking your company carefully. Although several people had told me that Sears was a great company to work for, that their employee benefits and profit sharing were second to none, I found that Sears were not the people that I wanted to work for. I honestly did not want to work on Sundays or Saturdays or holidays, I did not want to relocate, I did not want to travel, and even more so, I did not want to sell. So I took a trip up to Denver to find all of these things out, which I could have found out in school in the several interviews that I had or just by calling about them before I left for Denver. I think in a first job you have to get off on the right foot; that if you make a wrong step and possibly trip, you might carry the scars or the bad feelings about it possibly for the rest of your career.

In conclusion, I would like to say that success in interviewing probably depends upon knowing what you want to do and understanding the kind of lifestyle a particular career will imply. I think that for me I arrived at this decision too late and as a result made several mistakes. But I feel that I have learned from them so that right now my application is in for graduate school. Several people have told me that I shouldn't have any trouble getting in, and I hope I don't. I am working as a busboy in a local restaurant now and will move up to waiter in several weeks and should be able to finance this whole thing myself and, hopefully, a year from August I will be able to work for a bank in Dallas, fully understanding that kind of lifestyle it implies and the work involved. I think it is what I am looking for.

Prof., I think this may not be as full of information as you would like. When you get it transcribed, we can see what else we can add. Thank you.

MAMA LINGUINI'S

Mama Linguini's Inc. was a chain of family-style restaurants in the middle Atlantic and southeastern regions of the United States. Beginning with one restaurant in Richmond, Virginia, in the late 1960s, the chain had grown each year until by 1988 there were 85 restaurants in eight states. Each restaurant operated almost independently, doing all of its own purchasing, hiring, promotion, maintenance, etc. Employment of each restaurant manager, however, was done personally by the President, Mr. Sam Latona, primarily on the basis of kitchen experience and good work habits. The financing of each restaurant, after the first 12 that were started, required the new manager to contribute 15 percent of the costs of opening the restaurant, for which the manager obtained 15 percent of the annual profits in addition to a modest salary. Sam Latona took pride in the fact that each Mama Linguini restaurant developed a "feel unique to the community it served, yet was recognizable as a Mama's anywhere."

The headquarters of Mama Linguini's was in Little Silver, New Jersey, Mr. Latona's home town. Twice a year, all restaurant managers gathered in Little Silver for a two- or three-day meeting just before which they were required to submit their financial statements. It was at the early December 1987 meeting that Sam Latona began to confirm what he had been suspecting for the past year from his unannounced visits to Mama Linguini's restaurants, namely, that employee turnover for all positions was escalating. Each of the assembled managers had his or her own explanation of this turnover. No general pattern of factors explaining turnover, however, was discernible.

Over the Christmas holidays, Sam Latona and his wife Linda were entertained one evening at the home of Dr. and Mrs. Richard Dayton. The Daytons' daughter Heidi, a sophomore at Cornell's School of Hotel Administration, was home for the holidays and joined in the after dinner conversation between her dad and Sam. During the conversation, Sam mentioned his puzzlement and concern about turnover at Mama's restaurants. Heidi questioned Sam about the costs of turnover. As Sam spoke freely about customer satisfaction, recruitment and training costs, and lowered morale, Heidi went on to question him about the managerial functions typical at Mama restaurants. Sam seemed to enjoy this interchange and Dr. Dayton beamed more and more with pride in his daughter's obvious growing knowledge of business and management. Driving home through the quiet, tree lined roads of Little Silver, Sam Latona dwelled on one of the things Heidi had said to him, "Your selection of managers and your financially focused semi-annual meetings . . . sounds like no one is really paying attention to personnel matters." Sam suspected she was on to something; he certainly did pay most of his attention to the financial side of his business.

Sam's concerns about turnover and Heidi's comments began to occupy more and more of his thoughts after the new year. Sam continued his long-standing practice of dropping in unannounced at Mama Linguini's restaurants. He personally saw how employee turnover was increasing everywhere, and he also noted that recruitment, orientation, training, and appraisal were given relatively little attention by his managers.

It was late March when Sam Latona met Captain William Klein, a tall and very erect retired U.S. Navy officer, at a cocktail party in Little Silver. Sam immediately liked "The Captain" as everyone called him. The Captain, after retiring from the Navy three years ago, had become a partner in a successful executive recruitment firm in New York City, but had recently sold his interest in it. While he freely admitted he had only his military experience in personnel matters, he stated to Sam that restaurants probably should be managed so as to become more "ship shape." "After all," he said, "a tight ship is a worthy ship." The Captain's personableness and obvious self-confidence impressed Sam and he offered The Captain the newly created position of assistant to the president for personnel. The Captain immediately accepted Sam's offer and set about studying the records of Mama Linguini's Inc. in anticipation of the forthcoming managers' meeting in June of 1988.

At the June meeting in Little Silver, Sam Latona introduced "My friend and new associate, Bill Klein," to the assembled managers with the comment, "Now we have someone to help us with our turnover problems." The June meeting, however, was conducted as usual, focusing almost exclusively on fiscal control and revenue matters. The Captain mostly listened at the meetings although he did get a chance to meet many of the managers during coffee breaks, cocktails, and meals.

In the week after the June managers' meeting The Captain met with Sam Latona and outlined his plan for improving the personnel function of Mama Linguini's. As first steps he proposed to construct a manual for restaurant managers which would contain chain-wide personnel policies for recruitment, selection, compensation, personnel appraisal, and the like, as well as step-by-step procedures to follow for these activities. He stated that he intended to get advice and suggestions for policies and procedures from the managers. As The Captain explained it to Sam, "That way, the best ideas for managing personnel matters would be shared throughout the chain and each restaurant manager would become a more conscientious as well as a more skilled personnel manager." Sam Latona quickly approved The Captain's plan.

The next day Captain Klein dictated the following letter to his secretary and asked that it be sent immediately to all Mama Linguini's restaurant managers:

Dear Mr./Ms. _____:

Our president has recently approved of a plan to standardize personnel practices in all of our company's restaurants. To help me get started, please send me, in writing, your success experiences in attracting, managing, and retaining your employees. I'm sure you'll agree that company-wide personnel practices will go a long way toward alleviating your employee relations problems and will serve the interests of the Mama Linguini's Corporation.

Sincerely,

Captain William Klein,
USN Retired
Corporate Personnel

During the next few weeks, faxed replies came into The Captain's Little Silver office from about 25 restaurant managers. A typical faxed reply was:

Mr. William Klein
Assistant to the President
Mama Linguini's Inc.
440 Rumson Road
Little Silver, NJ 09554

Dear Mr. Klein:

We have received your letter about standardizing company personnel practices. Your suggestion seems to be long overdue. We wish you well and look forward to seeing you at the managers' meeting in the fall.

Yours truly,
XXXXXXXXXXX

Sipping a cool drink together after a hard fought tennis match at the Little Silver Country Club in early July, Sam Latona mentioned to The Captain that the restaurants he'd visited in the prior two weeks, "were doing business as usual." In fact, it looks like we'll have an excellent summer season. Most Mama's are starting to add summer help, but many still seemed shorthanded," Latona said.

THE MONTVILLE HOSPITAL DIETARY DEPARTMENT

Rene Marcotte briskly walked home from her part-time job with the Montville Hospital Dietary Department. "Mom," she said as she entered the house, "they may have to close down the hospital! The Montville Department of Health has just found the Dietary Department's sanitary conditions to be substandard. Mrs. DeMambro, our chief supervisor, said that we are really going to have to get to work and clean the place or the hospital is in trouble!"

THE HOSPITAL

As Rene continued to tell her mother about this latest event, she thought about her part-time job at the hospital which she had had now for almost a year. Montville Hospital was a 400-bed community general hospital located in suburban Montville outside of New York City. Montville itself was a racially mixed community of low- and middle-income working families.

Reprinted with permission from A. Cohen, S. Fink, H. Gaddon, & R. Willits. *Effective Behavior in Organizations.* R. D. Irwin, Inc. 1995.

However, Montville, along with most hospitals, was operating under severe financial pressure and needed to constantly find ways to reduce costs. It offered a range of medical services, but due to the nature of the Montville population, it had an appreciable number of elderly terminal patients. The hospital was well thought of by the community both as a place of treatment and as a source of employment. Through the years it had received strong financial support from the community and had grown as the community had grown. It currently was building a new wing to keep up with expanding demand, and this added to its tight financial situation.

THE DIETARY DEPARTMENT

The Dietary Department, where Rene worked, was located in the wing that had been added during the previous expansion project a little more than 10 years ago. This department employed approximately 100 employees (mostly female) and was under the direction of Mr. Thomas Ellis, food service director. The department employed cooks, dietitians, and "kitchen workers" (of whom Rene was one). The department had two major responsibilities— namely, the planning, preparation, and serving of three meals a day to every patient, and the operation of an employees' cafeteria. Since most of the patients required special diets, such as salt-free diets, the food for each was quite different, although cooked in a common kitchen.

Rene well remembered her initial contact with the department. When applying for a job, she was first "screened" by the hospital personnel office, then sent to be interviewed by Mrs. Kelley, the chief dietary supervisor (CDS), and after a second interview by Mrs. Kelley, given a "tour" through the kitchen facilities by one of the supervisors. She never saw Mr. Ellis or Mrs. Johnston, the chief dietitian. As she later learned, Mrs. Kelley did all of the hiring and firing while salary and raises were determined by the payroll department. Rene felt as if Mr. Ellis were some kind of "god," when she eventually heard of his existence two weeks after starting work.

Upon being hired, Rene was put right to work with no formal instructions in standards or procedures. She, as every other new employee, was expected to learn by watching others and asking her peers. Rene, who undertook the job with a deep sense of responsibility, well remembers one of the older kids saying to her, "Hurry up, you're taking too long; don't bother to clean up those spots of spilled soup."

Along with Rene, the majority of the employees were kitchen workers (diet aides, dishwashers, and porters). Ninety-five percent were female. Twenty-five were full-timers working 40 hours per week and 50–60 were part-timers, as was Rene.

Ten years ago the Dietary Department was smaller and under the direction of one of the current dietitians. There were no food service director and CDS positions. While the kitchen was centralized at that time, tray preparation was not. This was done in a kitchenette located on each floor of the hospital. The workers moved from floor to floor serving food from bulk containers onto individual trays on each floor. The dishroom also was separated physically. When the new wing was built, everything was centralized into one location from which carts of setup trays are sent out to each floor. Now, only the diet aides went to the floors and only for the purpose of distributing and collecting trays from the patients.

THE FULL-TIME EMPLOYEES

The full-time employees were mostly older women (40–65 years of age) who had been working in the department for a long time, some for 15–20 years. All lived in Montville; most had a high school education; many were married, and most helping to augment the family income so that their children could be the first in their family to go to college. With few exceptions, they worked a morning shift from either 6:30 A.M. to 3:00 P.M. or 8:00 A.M. to 4:30 P.M.

Most of the women had worked in this organization back in the old days before the hospital expanded and the kitchen was rebuilt. They had many stories to tell about how it used to be and how much easier and less chaotic their jobs had been before the change. One woman, who had recently been reemployed, had worked in the same Dietary Department 20 years ago as a teenager. She was amazed at how different everything was and said how she felt she was in another world from the job she used to know and love 20 years ago. The women, however, took great pride in their work (many had been doing the same job for years). Each woman had her own assigned task which she did every day and there was little shifting around of positions. The dessert- or salad-makers never learned much about the work routine of the tray-coverers, silverware-sorters or juice-setter-uppers. Every woman was set in a specific routine during a day's work. This routine was heavily controlled by the tight time schedule everyone had to follow. There was no fooling around even though the working atmosphere was very congenial and everyone was on a first-name basis, including the supervisors. There was considerable conversation among the women while they worked, but it did not distract them from doing their jobs—perhaps because management required the workers to completely finish their assigned tasks before leaving for home, even if it meant working overtime, without extra pay.

There was a striking cross section of cultural backgrounds among these full-time employees. There were about equal numbers of whites, blacks, and [Asians], and many were immigrants. Many spoke Spanish and very little English. Although a language barrier existed between many of the employees, feelings of mutual respect and friendliness were maintained. Malicious gossip due to racial or ethnic differences was uncommon, and the women helped each other when necessary to finish their jobs on time.

The women often expressed their concern about not getting their jobs done on time, especially when they were manning the assembly line. This assembly line consisted of sending a tray down a belt, along which, at certain intervals, each worker put a specific item on the tray as designated by the menu for each patient. After each tray was completed, it was put in an electric cart with each cart containing trays for different floors of the hospital. The carts were then pulled (by men porters) into elevators and transferred to the designated floors. At this time, pairs of diet aides (not working on the line) were sent to the floors to deliver the trays to the patients. Speed and efficiency in delivering trays were very important. If the trays were sent up and then left standing for a long time before delivery to each patient, the food got cold and the Dietary Department received complaints directed at the dietitians. The complaints were relayed to the supervisor, who in turn reprimanded the diet aide(s) responsible for the cold food. This temporarily disrupted the very informal and friendly working relationship between the diet aides and their supervisor, whom they liked and respected, causing uncomfortable guilt feelings for the diet aides. As a result, reprimands were seldom necessary among the full-timers.

At the same time, the diet aides were expected to meet certain established standards governing such matters as size of portion, cleanliness of kitchen facilities, and cleanliness in food handling and preparation. At times, in fact rather often, the standards were overlooked under the pressure of time. For instance, if the line was to be started at exactly 11 A.M. and if by that time the desserts were not wrapped or covered, as required by sanitary regulations, the line might begin anyway, and the desserts went to the patients unwrapped.

The full-time employees received pay raises designated by a set scale based on continuing length of employment. Starting salary was about average for this type of work. They were allowed a certain number of sick days per year as well as paid vacations (the length of which were based on the numbers of years of employment). The uniforms they were required to wear were provided (three per person) by the hospital and could be laundered free of charge at the hospital laundry service. Also the workers paid very little money, if anything at all, for meals eaten at work. Technically they were supposed to pay in full for meals, but seldom did, because of lack of consistent control.

Work performance was evaluated on the basis of group effort. Individual effort usually was not singled out and rewarded in any tangible way. However, supervisors would often compliment an individual on how nice a salad plate looked or how quickly and efficiently a worker delivered the patients' trays. For instance, the woman who prepared fancy salad plates and sandwiches could take pride in the way they looked. Furthermore, the aides recognized that their work could affect a patient's well-being and therefore could be important, and sometimes a patient was a former hospital staff member or neighbor known by the aides. When delivering a tray, a diet aide might chat with a patient and discover particular likes or dislikes which, when reported to the dietitian, sometimes led to a revision in the patient's diet.

Extra care was often taken in arranging food on the tray in an attractive manner to please the patient. Sometimes this dedication produced minor problems such as when a diet aide violated certain rules in order to do something extra for a patient or to promote her own version of efficiency in doing a task. This type of individual initiative (and creativity) was not encouraged. Management set down rigid guidelines for performing all tasks as the only correct way, since they worked out for so many years. Any recommendations for changes in these techniques were approached with caution by management. The equipment also had changed little in the past decade.

THE PART-TIME EMPLOYEES

There were 50–60 part-time employees in the Dietary Department whose level of pay was appreciably less than that of the full-timers. They were divided into two teams (team A and team B); each team worked on alternate days of the week and on alternate weekends, a device adopted on the advice of some efficiency experts as a way of avoiding having to pay overtime to anyone. There was no specific supervisor for each team; instead each might have one of two supervisors depending on the day and/or week. Two different shifts exist for the part-timers: 3:30–6:30 and 4:00–8:00 (the kitchen closed at 8 P.M.), but on the average all part-timers including Rene worked a 16-hour week. Their duties were the same as the full-timers, except that part-timers served and cleaned up after dinner instead of after breakfast and lunch. The majority of these workers were young, mostly high school age (16–18 years), working for extra money and because friends were working. Most had not worked in the hospital very long as there was a constant turnover as individuals left to go to college, etc., but other kids were readily available to take their places. There were also several older women working on a part-time basis, who had been with the organization for many years.

The part-timers' situation exhibited a striking contrast to that of full-timers. There were no permanent tasks assignments; each night a part-timer did something different, and the kids often asked to do this or that different task. As a group, the night shift was not as unified in spirit or congeniality as the day shift (full-timers). The younger workers tended to form cliques apart from the older women and gossip and poke fun at non-English-speaking workers.

Most of the teenagers also took their work much less seriously than did the older women (the full-timers), doing only what was required at the most minimal level. As was the case with the full-timers, they worked on a tight schedule and their working behavior was heavily controlled by it. However, they seemed more anxious to get their work done as soon as possible. Once they had finished, they were free to leave no matter what time it was at no loss of pay; that is, if everyone was finished at, say 7:45 P.M., all could leave yet still be paid until 8:00 P.M. It was not uncommon for work areas to become messy, for hands to be left unwashed, and for food to be handled and touched even though it shouldn't be. They also tended to devise their own ways for doing the job, partially to promote efficiency and decrease the time needed for completion. It was not uncommon to hear a more experienced teenage part-timer tell a newcomer, "Oh, come on, we don't have to do it that way. Don't be so eager; relax and enjoy yourself." The supervisor seemed to have little control over the teenagers. They ignored her comments or talked back to her and continued doing things their own way. The working atmosphere was informal and friendly with everyone on a first-name basis except for the supervisor. At times there was a high pitch of excitement among the kids as everyone kidded one another, sang songs, and generally socialized together. At times this led to mistakes being made, which infuriated the supervisor but didn't bother the kids, as they had little respect for her.

Conflict existed between the supervisor and the teenagers about wearing the required hairnets (especially the boys) and aprons and such procedures as not eating during work. They seldom took reprimands seriously, saying that they "hated their job" but needed the money. In general, however, these young diet aides did complete their required tasks in the time allotted, although the quality was often substandard. There was not a total lack of concern for quality because if so, they would have lost their jobs, and they knew this; but quality was maintained most strongly only when "it didn't take too long."

There did exist some conflict between the older and younger workers during the night shift. The older women did not approve of the young people's attitudes even though those older women who worked at night did not exhibit as much pride in their work as did their daytime counterparts. They resented the teenagers' new and different ways of doing jobs, as was especially evident when an older woman was assigned to work with a teenager for the evening.

THE MANAGEMENT

With regard to the management staff of the Dietary Department, there were several people involved. Mr. Ellis was the man to whom everyone else was ultimately responsible as the food service director. He was an older man, hired by the hospital about five years previously. A flashy dresser, he wore no uniform and spent most of the day in his office. He rarely talked to anyone in the department except the chief dietitian and the CDS. He communicated to the rest of the employees by way of memos posted on a bulletin board in the kitchen. His memos usually contained instructions, telling the workers to change or improve some facet of their jobs. He also relayed messages down the ranks via the supervisors to the workers. About once a day he would walk through the kitchen in a very formal manner apparently observing what was going on. The diet aides (and supervisors) became very conscious of their actions as he walked by, hoping they were doing everything right. When questioned about this man, the workers expressed feelings of curiosity mixed with an element of fear. The only time a diet aide came into direct contact with him was on payday, when she entered his office to receive her check after he signed it. One recently hired employee said that she thought that his main job was signing paychecks. There was obviously much confusion by workers concerning who this man really was. He was the mystery man of management to them.

A second management person was the chief dietitian, Mrs. Johnston, a woman in her late 30s. Her job was mainly administrative in nature, acting as a consultant to the dietitians and assisting them when the workload was heavy or someone was out sick. She also helped out in the kitchen once in a while if the kitchen staff was especially shorthanded. In general, however, she tended to remain relatively formal and distant from the workers, although, when she had suggestions to make, she often went directly to the workers instead of using memos. Her relationship with the four dietitians was informal and friendly, and she was highly respected by them for her technical excellence as a dietitian.

The CDS, Mrs. Kelly (about age 44), was in charge of hiring and firing. She was also responsible for making up employee schedules week by week, especially those involving the scheduling of the part-time workers. Workers went to her with gripes and requests for favors and special days off. She was generally sympathetic to employee problems, having been one of them about six year ago before she became the chief supervisor. In general, she was relatively informal with the workers although not on a first-name basis. The employees respected her and her authority was rarely questioned or challenged by any of the workers. She seemed to be regarded as the real boss, rather than the two people who ranked above her.

These three people constituted the main power structure in the Dietary Department. They tended to keep to themselves socially as well as physically. They never ate with the workers and seldom communicated with them except about their work. If any changes, plans, or decisions were to be made, they were made by these three people, the final say being had by the food service director. The supervisors were then told of any new policy and expected to inform the workers and implement the change. The CDS seemed to act as a middleman between the director and the workers. When she (or the director) felt that the workers were "sloughing off," a staff meeting would be called and she would exhort everyone to shape up. For instance, a meeting was called after an unusually large number of complaints were received about patients receiving cold food. The CDS said, "We are here to help these patients get well as best we can—they are sick and deserve the best possible care. They won't eat cold food, and that slows down their recovery. Keeping the food warm is more important than whether or not you want to hurry to get the day's work done."

Other members of the management staff included the supervisors, whose main responsibilities involved the diet aides and other kitchen workers. The supervisors, who in all cases were former diet aides, worked in the kitchen. They assigned jobs, made sure they got done, maintained discipline and order (hopefully), and helped out when needed. In general, they saw that everything ran smoothly. Altogether, there were three supervisors, one of whom was part-time. They took turns covering the weekends, and thus had contact with all employees, although they worked with one group most of the time.

The cooks and the dietitians were the other members of the department. The cooks' job was to prepare the food according to standard recipes and to put it on the serving line at meal times. They did their jobs efficiently and effectively. They kept to themselves, eating together and not mingling with the diet aides. The dietitians also kept to themselves both physically and socially. They had their own office and ate together. Little was seen of them by the workers; however, when approached, they seemed quite friendly.

THE CURRENT PROBLEM

The State Board of Health makes periodic, unannounced visits to the Dietary Department to determine whether it meets certain sanitary standards. Although the hospital believes that the Board of Health interprets the regulations too strictly, there is little it can do except make efforts to satisfy any criticisms made by the inspectors.

In the past, the director of the Dietary Department managed to find out when the inspectors were coming and prepared for the visit by a frantic two- to three-day major clean-up campaign. Historically, this has resulted in Montville passing the inspection. However, over the past two to three months, the inspectors have become more successful in making their visits a complete surprise. Frantic efforts to clean up took place the last time during the brief period of time it took the inspectors to get from their car to the kitchen. As a result, the department recently failed the inspection and was given a limited amount of time to correct the situation or else face being shut down. The department did pass a reinspection, but only because of a lot of extra pressure put on workers to do extra cleaning during and after working hours (for overtime pay) for several days. If the organization should fail inspection repeatedly, it will be required to shut down indefinitely. The impact of this would be catastrophic for the hospital as a whole, since it must provide food for both patients and employees! Rene wondered what the hospital would do about the situation and how it might affect her job situation.

ON THE WAY TO THE PINNACLE

"So there you have it. That's exactly what I heard," said Linda to Susan. She continued, "So can you see why I'm concerned? I mean, I had no idea Carmen felt that way. You would never know by looking at her that she's considering leaving. I wasn't sure I should tell you because I don't know if it's really our concern, but I thought you should know."

Linda Stewart, the Human Resources Assistant, a young, bright, bubbly woman, started out in the sales department when she first joined the Pinnacle Hotel. Now as a part of her job in the Human Resources Department, Linda was responsible for taking the newly hired employees on a tour of the property during their orientation program. The Pinnacle conducted employee orientation every Monday. Because she was one of the first people new employees got to meet, and because she got to speak with them on a more informal basis when giving the property tour, Linda was rather friendly with most of the employees. With a total of 600 employees, sometimes rising to 650 employees during busy times, the Pinnacle kept Linda very busy.

Susan's hair was sticking to the back of her neck. "Oh why on earth didn't I put my hair up today," she sighed as she pulled her hair back into a pony tail and held it for a moment before letting it fall back down to her shoulders. "Here's what I think," said Susan as she straightened herself in her chair.

Susan Pollack, Director of Corporate Training for the Royal Hotel Company (RHC), the management company for the Pinnacle, had recently been given the additional title of Director of Human Resources at the Pinnacle property. The Pinnacle was one of 40 properties managed by RHC. As Director of Corporate Training for RHC, Susan was responsible for overseeing training programs at all the properties. Because of the additional Pinnacle human resources duties bestowed upon her as of last year, Susan was constantly juggling her schedule to be at the Pinnacle as much as possible and still travel to the other properties.

Susan continued, "I really thought we had fine tuned our orientation and training programs. I'm not certain about exact turnover figures, I mean, I know they're higher in housekeeping than I would like, but with the physical demands of that job it's not unexpected. That's why I'm concerned about Sarafina, that housekeeper we just hired, staying with us. But in the other departments, turnover doesn't seem to be a big problem. We're probably average with the other hotels in the city, maybe even a littler lower. So I guess I just assumed everything was okay."

"That's what I've been thinking," said Linda. "I mean, I get to talk to all the new hires informally when we're on the tour, so I guess I feel like I know them. And Carmen appeared by all accounts to be a confident, polished, professional young woman. She's exactly the kind of person we love to have in reservations. But then I hear her talking to Sarafina about how she doesn't have any friends here and how comfortable she felt at her old job, even though it seems like she really didn't like it there, and I wonder what is really bothering her. Is it really all this stuff about not having anyone to go to lunch with? Is that really it? Or is it something else? And what am I supposed to do about it, or I mean, is human resources responsible for making sure every single employee is happy, or at least has someone to go to lunch with? Is that our job Susan?"

Susan leaned back in her chair, and turned to gaze out the window. After a long pause, she turned and looked at Linda thoughtfully. "You know Linda, that's a really good question. And I'm afraid I don't know the answer."

Susan wondered if the heat was getting to her. This summer of 1995 had brought a terrible heat wave, and everyone appeared to be a little on edge, distracted and irritable. Wishing she had put her hair up today, Susan brushed a lock out of her eye. "So Linda, tell me once again how you know all this," asked Susan. "If I remember correctly, you overhead Carmen talking to Sarafina, is that right?"

COMPANY BACKGROUND

RHC was founded by Isaac Robinson. While in architecture school as a young man, he dreamed of one day owning his own hotel. His dream eventually led him to developing smaller hotels (approximately 250–350 rooms) that would some day become luxury first-class properties. But to be a first-class property, to be the best, the property had to be distinct. Robinson decided RHC would offer service second to none, and to do so, rules for ensuring quality service were necessary. What he did was to take corporate standards and fit them to the management style at each Royal property. To produce service second to none, the hotel would have to offer the best service possible on a consistent basis. Service that is good on Monday and lousy on Tuesday is not first-class service. Consistency is the key. Robinson believed other hotel companies lose out in not being consistent. This consistency at Royal properties has led to 45 percent repeat customers.

RHC was an international company. In 1992, RHC took over management of the Lee Hotel Company based in Tokyo. As a result of the takeover, RHC now had properties in Australia, the South Pacific, and the Far East, as well as North America. RHC has maintained the Lee name on the newly acquired properties because of the strong reputation for quality the Lee name has developed over the years. Recently, the Lee hotel in Tokyo was voted the number one hotel in the world.

Management of the Pinnacle property, built 20 years ago by another company, was taken over by RHC approximately two years ago. The Pinnacle, one of RHC's oldest properties, was also one of its biggest properties, with 430 rooms. The Pinnacle prided itself on the personal service it offered to its guests: the business center; valet services, such as one-hour dry cleaning, mending, and laundry; and spa services via the Pinnacle Club fitness center. The Pinnacle was voted the number one hotel in the United States by *Conde' Nast Traveler*, a favorite magazine of international business travelers.

The executive committee of the Pinnacle was headed up by Nickolaus Lamb, the general manager and regional vice president. Mr. Lamb also oversaw other RHC properties in Chicago, Philadelphia, and Toronto, Canada. Richard Conners was the resident manager and did all final employment interviews, whether the position being filled was for a housekeeper, a cocktail server, or the director of marketing. As such, every employee at the hotel had met him. Richard and his wife had an apartment at the hotel, and ate at the hotel's restaurants often.

OVERHEARD IN THE FOX'S DEN

Linda proceeded to relate the incident to Susan. She overheard Carmen talking to Sarafina in the cafeteria. The Pinnacle's employee cafeteria, called the Fox's Den, was located on the 12th floor of the hotel and provided a spectacular, panoramic view of the city. The word around town among hotel employees was that the Pinnacle had the nicest employee cafeteria of all the hotels, and the hotel was quite proud of this honor. Everyone enjoyed the cafeteria, and even the general manager was known to occasionally stop in when at the property. Employees were given one free meal per shift, and could eat as much as they wanted. A well-stocked salad bar with the typical salad fixings as well as specialty vegetarian and low fat salads, a variety of hot and cold entrees, and many beverages to select from, all made the cafeteria a popular place to eat. Linda ate there just about every day, as did many of the employees. On this day, Thursday, July 20, sitting at a window table overlooking the city, Linda imagined how hot it would be by the time she got off work. The previous day, at 6 P.M., the temperature was still a sweltering 96 degrees. On days like this, she didn't mind working. The commute into the city, however, was agony—already 85 degrees at 7 A.M. She felt sorry for the other employees who lacked air-conditioned homes. How could they sleep? Everyone was suffering from the heat. Across the city, over 400 people had died, and the city's health department was predicting still more heat-related deaths. Linda was daydreaming about the heat when she found herself inadvertently picking up on a conversation nearby. She quickly recognized the voices of the two women talking—Carmen Morales, a new reservations agent, and Sarafina Williams, a new housekeeper.

"I hope I can make it. Oh I just hope I can make it!," Sarafina was lamenting to Carmen. "My friends keep telling me 'We know you can. Just hang in there Sarafina,' but sometimes I'm just so tired." All of her friends at the Pinnacle had made it. Sure, they too were tired in the beginning. But after a couple of months, they all adjusted to the work. Sarafina continued. "I just want to succeed. I know that working hard is the only way to make it. And I do want to make it here in the United States. But I'm worried I won't be able to keep up with the job."

As a new housekeeper at the Pinnacle, Sarafina Williams was trying her best to keep up with the demands of her first job in the United States. She had come to the United States to marry and live with her fiancé. In June, she was encouraged to apply to the Pinnacle by a few of her neighbors who were employed there. Sarafina found housekeeping in the United States very different than back in England. According to her, the job at the Pinnacle consisted of "so many details, so many things to clean in the room." The housekeeping training packet she was given during orientation was 39 pages long, detailing even the smallest task to be completed. Each housekeeper was responsible for cleaning the equivalent of 13 rooms, with each room taking approximately 30 minutes to clean. As such, housekeepers had to work at a swift pace in order to clean their rooms in the 7.5-hour work day.

"Well, I've never been in housekeeping, but I know you can do it. You can't give up now," Carmen urged Sarafina. "You've put too much into this place already. And besides, everyone has doubts when they start a new job. Even I have doubts about the Pinnacle."

"Really?" Sarafina said in disbelief. "You seem so confident, so at ease."

"Oh, it's not that I don't know how to do my job in reservations, it's just that I don't know if that's what I really want to do. I don't know if I'm all that much happier than at my last job" explained Carmen.

Sarafina looked incredulous. "How could you not like it here? The Pinnacle is such a beautiful place. It's such an opportunity to work here. I don't understand how you could feel that way," said Sarafina.

"It's not that I don't like it here. I mean, they treat me well and everything. It's just that because the phone lines always need to be covered, we have to take turns going to lunch. So I have to go to lunch alone. And aside from a few people in reservations, you're one of the only people I've gotten to know since I started working here," Carmen admitted.

Sarafina looked puzzled, "Now I'm even more confused. Maybe you should start at the beginning."

CARMEN JOINS THE PINNACLE

After working at Hotel Atlantis for two years, Carmen Morales was still in an hourly position. She had thought by this time in her career she would be a supervisor, but the Atlantis offered no advancement opportunities. Leaving her job appeared to be the only means for advancing her career and putting her hospitality-tourism bachelor's degree to use. It was early March, and she decided to keep one eye on her job at Hotel Atlantis and one eye on the job market as well.

She responded to an ad placed by the Pinnacle Hotel for a front desk agent. Although it was an hourly position, Carmen explained in her cover letter she was looking for a supervisory position. It was worth a shot. If the Pinnacle was interested in her for a supervisory role, they would call; otherwise, she didn't expect a response. When she received a letter with the Pinnacle address on it, she knew it was a rejection. She was, however, impressed the hotel had responded at all. The stationery was elegant and sophisticated. In the letter, the Assistant Human Resources Director explained no supervisory positions were currently available at the front desk. She suspected she would never hear from the Pinnacle again.

Three months later the Pinnacle called. A position in reservations had become available. It was not a supervisory position and Carmen wondered if she should go in for an interview. During the past three months, her job at Hotel Atlantis had gotten worse. "What the hell" she thought. Though currently responsible for accounts receivable, she had worked in reservations for a year prior to that position. She knew what a reservationist's job would entail. At worst, taking a job at the Pinnacle would be making a lateral move. Besides, she thought, it couldn't be any worse than her job at Hotel Atlantis, and the Pinnacle was a larger, upscale five-star hotel, probably with more advancement opportunities. In fact, her hourly pay as a Pinnacle reservations agent would be more than what she was making having full responsibility for accounts receivables at Hotel Atlantis.

Her first interview was with Zack Shoemaker, Assistant Director of Human Resources at the Pinnacle Hotel. As he explained a bit about the job and the benefits, Carmen wondered if she should tell him she didn't want to be a reservationist her whole life. Would Zack find her too ambitious and worry she wouldn't be able to stick it out in reservations for any length of time? Before she could finish this thought, visions of her current job flashed before her and she decided she had nothing to lose. Her career was going nowhere. She couldn't risk the same thing happening at the Pinnacle. If no prospect for promotion existed, then in the most important way, the Pinnacle would be no different than where she worked now. She confided in Zack and told him of her desire to move up in the company.

By the time the interviewing process was over, Carmen had interviewed with four different people. Zack from human resources had been first. Next was Nancy Shaffer, the reservations manager who would be Carmen's direct supervisor. Since she didn't have an office, Nancy met with Carmen in the human resources training room. Mark Mink, the rooms division manager, was the third interviewer. A tall, silvery-gray haired man, he warmly welcomed Carmen into his office next to the front desk. Richard Conners, the resident manager, was her final interviewer. His office was located next to Mark Mink's, and Mark had walked her next door and introduced her to Mr. Conners. Carmen couldn't help noticing that Mr. Conners and Mr. Lamb were the only people addressed formally at the hotel.

It was during her interview with Mr. Conners that Carmen suspected she had the job. "Well I guess the only thing left for us to do is get you a schedule," said Mr. Conners. Carmen was delighted. As she left Mr. Conner's office, she noticed Nancy, the reservations manager whom she had already interviewed with, waiting for her. "Well thank you for coming in Carmen. We'll be in touch in a few days." Carmen thought it curious that Nancy didn't know Mr. Conners had already, in essence, offered her the job. Perhaps it was just Nancy's standard statement to all interviewees, Carmen thought. She rushed back for her shift at the Hotel Atlantis.

Carmen had been at work less than an hour when her mother called. Zack from the Pinnacle had phoned and wanted Carmen to call him back. She couldn't help smiling as she said good-bye to her mother. Why else would Zack be calling? She knew she had the job.

ORIENTATION AT THE PINNACLE

Carmen had worked almost two weeks at the Pinnacle before she went through the orientation program. The Fourth of July holiday had eliminated the weekly orientation, and so Carmen was scheduled to go through the formal property-wide orientation on Monday, July 10.

She was the first one in the training room. Located around the corner from the human resources office in the basement of the hotel, the training room was rectangular in shape with one door, no windows, and only overhead lighting. It was 8:15 A.M. and orientation was to begin at 8:30 A.M. A small table had been set up near the door and was loaded with coffee, decaf, tea and Danish, muffins, and croissants. Small butter triangles, orange marmalade, and strawberry jam were available, as well as cream, lemons, sugar, brown sugar, and sugar substitutes for the coffee and tea. The coffee was being kept hot by the sterno underneath the beautiful silver coffee urn. The china, consisting of cups, saucers, and small plates, was white with a royal blue and gold rim. The tablecloth on the table was swaggered, like the bottom of a southern woman's ballroom dress. As Sheryl, another new employee, would later explain, some employees in the hotel were hired just to do that—swagger. Sheryl had worked but one day at the Pinnacle Hotel, but she was already quite proud of her new position as a swaggerer.

At the far end of the training room, a marker board lined the length of the wall. An easel with pad was set up in the far left corner of the room, displaying directions for completing the employee identification card forms. Pictures of the hotel's Planning Committee members hung in a frame facing the doorway. The Planning Committee consisted of the GM/Regional VP, the Hotel Resident Manager, Rooms Division Manager, F&B Director, Human Resources Director, Chief of Engineering, Director of Marketing, Director of Security, and the Controller. On the wall to the right of the door hung pictures of the other properties owned by RHC. The conference table filling the middle of the room had nine chairs around it with an orientation packet and employees' name tags placed at every chair. Outside on the bulletin board next to the door to the training room were listed the names of the new employees going through the orientation program that day. All employees had to pass that bulletin board after dropping off their IDs with security before heading to the locker rooms. The lockers, training room, uniform office, and human resources office were all on one of the basement floors. The security office and the hotel kennel were on the same floor as well.

Other new Pinnacle employees gradually joined Carmen: Jason, a young graduate from a hotel management program, was an assistant manager in banquets; Becky had been hired to work in the Open Air Café doing cocktailing; Carlos had already worked about a week as a greeter; Daniel had started as a houseman. Daniel had never worked in a hotel before. Sarafina, who had been working in housekeeping for five days already, came in and sat down next to Carmen. They had met two days earlier in the Fox's Den and had struck an immediate friendship. Sheryl arrived just as Jason was introducing himself to the rest of the group as instructed by Zack Shoemaker. Zack was to conduct the first part of the orientation, and later in the afternoon, new employees would go to their respective departments for further training. Nancy Shaffer, Carmen's supervisor, had already arranged her schedule to train Carmen in the afternoon. And Sarafina's supervisor, Edgar, has asked Sarafina to come back to the training room in the afternoon to begin her department training.

Zack started the program by explaining he had been with RHC, the management company for the Pinnacle, for five years and described how the hotel was broken up into the rooms and the food and beverage departments. After reviewing the history of the hotel and the importance of consistent quality service, Zack explained RHC's concern with safety. "If ever there was to be a fire here, we have to make sure you know how to protect yourself. You can't help a guest if you're not safe and in control yourself." Zack put in the fire safety video and asked Carlos if he would come and get him in the human resources office when the video was over.

The next video, described by Zack as being very dated, but having a message as relevant today as it was years ago when the video was made, was entitled *Royal-ty Everyday.* It depicted the visual story (no words are spoken, just background music) of a housekeeper and other employees during their work day at a Royal Hotel property. A housekeeper drops off her daughter at a dance class and then heads to the Royal. She spends the rest of her day performing various duties, interacting with other employees and guests, smiling, and laughing. The video captures a Royal doorman helping a family (husband, wife, and young daughter) hail a cab. In the commotion of getting into the cab, the little girl inadvertently drops her teddy bear. The cab pulls way with the bear lying in the gutter. The Royal doorman picks it up, quickly flags down a cab, and indicates "Follow that cab!" When his cab finally catches up with the family's cab at the next traffic light, the doorman jumps out and presents the bear to the grateful parents and delighted little girl. Wrapping up the end of the video are employees of various nationalities saying in their native language, "So nice to be special."

At this point in the orientation program, Linda Stewart took the new employee group on a tour of the hotel. She led them out of the training room and down the hall to one of the two service elevators. Linda explained that one of the elevators was used by room service in the morning for ensuring prompt delivery of breakfasts and thus was unavailable for use by other employees. At other times, some groups using meeting space needed to use the other service elevator to get materials to their meeting rooms. Patience was needed with the elevators, said Linda, especially for the housekeeping staff trying to get up to the guest rooms. After approximately four minutes, an elevator appeared and the group headed to the kitchen areas. Employees were busy working to the low hum of the ventilation system. The kitchen was spacious, clean, and air-conditioned. The

Pinnacle's award-winning restaurant, The Dining Room, was next on the tour. The room was paneled with rich wood and spacious seating. A three-foot tall chocolate sculpture, created by one of the chefs, was situated near the door of the restaurant. Linda told of rumors that one of the bottles on the wine list was selling for $2,500. She went on to boast that the chef of the restaurant, a young woman, a native of the area, had recently won numerous culinary awards. Other highlights of the tour included viewing some of the meeting rooms, The Bar, The Greenhouse, and the steward area. A guest room was not available for viewing (occupancy that day was 99 percent) and eight other rooms were having new carpeting installed. Attempts to meet with Mr. Lamb, the general manager, or Mr. Conners, the resident manager, were unsuccessful. Linda was embarrassed by her inability to show a guest room or to arrange a meeting with a manager, and apologized profusely.

DEPARTMENTAL TRAINING WITH EDGAR LUNA

Housekeepers and housemen at the Pinnacle had traditionally been trained via the "buddy system." More senior housekeepers would be given an increased hourly wage for training a new housekeeper. However, over time, different training housekeepers had their own way of training and doing things. The new housekeepers were picking up the bad habits or shortcuts being taken by the particular trainer and consistency, the principle most important to the founder of RHC, had gone by the wayside. So last year, the position of housekeeping training manager was created in order to ensure consistency in housekeeping training. Edgar Luna held this position.

Edgar shared a space with the executive housekeeper and the assistant executive housekeeper. Although three desks were situated in the office, none had the appearance of really being used—no personal name plates or pictures of loved ones. There was just a general mess to the place, although the floor was clean. Every available nook and cranny had guest room amenities and cleaning supplies in it—candle holders, potpourri, vases, body lotion, coffee filters, light bulbs, decorations, etc. One of the desks was centered at a window with sliding glass panels to another housekeeping room with desks for other supervisors and coordinators.

Edgar had started out with the Pinnacle as a houseman. After 17 years, he was now the housekeeping training manager. Not bad for a Hispanic man in the United States, he thought. But that was also his gift to the housekeeping department. Most of the housekeeping staff spoke Spanish and Edgar's ability to communicate was a plus. Since he had taken over, turnover has been reduced dramatically. However, even with this reduction, the housekeeping department still had trouble keeping people. He believed that arranging for child care took its toll, as did the physically demanding nature of the job. Many of the new housekeepers were not fully aware of how tiring their job would be.

Edgar was proud of the work he had done in the housekeeping department, but he knew he still wanted to do more. He had worked with human resources to develop a training program in Spanish, but it had been back-burnered while the new Human Resources Director, Susan Pollack, got into place.

Before the morning company-wide orientation, Edgar had instructed Sarafina and the new houseman, Daniel, to meet him back in the training room in the afternoon for departmental training. In addition, he asked Sean, who had left after seven years employment to pursue an opportunity with a new hotel and was subsequently rehired by the Pinnacle as an assistant executive housekeeper, to attend as well.

Edgar handed out training packets (see Figure 1) to all of them and asked Sean to read the packet to the rest of the group. Occasionally, Edgar would interject with additional

---

Job Breakdown
HOUSEKEEPING ROOM ATTENDANT

Job	How To Do It
Cleaning the bathroom	Spray the toilet, bathtub, and soap dishes with all-purpose cleaner (APC). This will allow the APC to work in while you are cleaning the counter.
Marble Countertop	• Clean all ashtrays and soap dishes with glass cleaner. Wipe dry with a glass rag (pink-striped cloth, or pink-dyed rag). Bring mini bar tray back to mini bar.
	• Move everything to one side of the counter and spray counter with water. Use the yellow sponge to clean the surface as well as the ledges. Rinse well with cold water. Wipe dry with a rag and repeat the process for the other side of counter top.
	• Spray the mirror with glass cleaner and clean the mirror with a glass rag. *Do not* use any APC on the mirror as this will cause it to have streaks.
	• Clean the sink basin with APC and wipe dry. Be sure to check the sink stopper. The sink stopper should be placed in the up position when done. Hair dryer should be wrapped/brand name facing up.
Bathtub	• Clean the bathtub, tiles, and soap dishes with APC and the yellow sponge. Rinse well with hot water and wipe dry with a rag. Polish all chrome free of water spots. Shower head should face inside wall and tub stopper should be placed on the inside corner. Soap dish should be free of soap scum. The shower liner should be placed on the inside of the tub opposite the chrome.
Additional Information	• Marble is delicate; use mainly water and soft sponge to clean.
	• In an occupied room, the countertop still needs to be cleaned, but you should not move the guest amenities around. All guest amenities that lay flat should be put on a washcloth with labels facing upwards. All amenities that stand should be put on the ledge with labels facing forward. Any electrical cords from blow dryers or curling irons should be wrapped neatly. The hand soap should be cleaned and the used soap should be flipped over to allow the wet side to dry.
	• If water continues to drip after closing the faucets, notify housekeeping.
	• In an occupied room, the soap dish must also be cleaned, and the used soap should be flipped over to allow the wet side to dry. The soap does not need to be replaced unless necessary (clean all soap dish edges).
	• If the guest left the amenities in the tub area, arrange them neatly on the marble ledge of the bathtub with labels facing forward.
	• Shower curtains should be checked on a regular basis and changed as needed.
	• The bathtub tiles should be free of mildew. If the mildew cannot be removed with your brush, then notify your supervisor.

FIGURE 1 Housekeeping Training.

comments and ask for questions. Sarafina found it a little boring having someone read to her about how to clean a bathroom and vacuum a rug. She learned better by doing, and she had already gone over some of this during the five days she had worked prior to this training. The session finally ended at 4:30 P.M. She went home and Daniel went back to his department to work until 7:00 P.M.

RESERVATIONS DEPARTMENTAL TRAINING

Nancy Shaffer suggested to Carmen that they head to the Fox's Den for the training session. Nancy's desk was in the room with the other reservationists, so they would have had to whisper. The employee cafeteria was crowded, but they managed to find an empty table.

Nancy wore a "uniform" similar to the front desk agents: a royal blue tailored suit, with a slim fitting skirt an inch above the knee and a beautiful, double-breasted jacket. A white blouse and blue pumps completed her outfit. Carmen thought Nancy and the front desk agents looked great—professional, stylish, and classy. Her reservations uniform, unlike Nancy's, consisted of a royal blue skirt, flared at the bottom and ending midway down her calf. The shirt was patterned, long sleeved, and tied into a loose bow at the neck. Carmen felt ugly and dowdy in it, and she wished she could wear a uniform like Nancy's.

Nancy opened up a folder containing training materials. "Let's open up with the Pinnacle's First Day Orientation Checklist (see Figure 2). I have a copy here for you. As we go through it, just initial it as we go down the list in order, and if you have any questions, just let me know," she said.

Nancy proceeded to read each item on the checklist, elaborating where needed. Everything from hours of operation, policies for name tags, meals, breaks, parking, sick leave, and schedule requests, to employee problems, transfers, warnings, payroll sign in/out procedures, evaluations, etc., were covered. In addition, the company's philosophy, benefits, orientation, guest comment cards, outlets and services, hotel history, lost and found procedures, and OSHA hazardous chemicals procedures were explained. After each item, Nancy would ask, "Are there any questions?"

Carmen was trying so hard to remember everything, she couldn't even think about asking questions.

Nancy continued, "No questions? Great! Okay, then you want to initial over where it asks for the trainee's initials." This procedure continued until all 27 items on the checklist were explained and initialed by Carmen. After two hours, Nancy showed no signs of weariness, but Carmen's head was swimming with information. She was tired and looking forward to going home.

"I HAD NO IDEA!"

Carmen had worked for the Pinnacle for three weeks now and the timing of her commute to work was still unpredictable. On this day, the traffic was horrible and it was nearly 86 degrees at 7:45 A.M. Carmen thought about the Hotel Atlantis and the friends she had left behind. Hotel Atlantis had been close to her house in the suburbs—it never took more than 20 minutes to get there. As a Pinnacle employee, however, she had to drive into the city and pay $5.50/day for parking. Everything about her job seemed new. She had to make new friends, try not to get lost making her way to the cafeteria, and determine what management expected of her. As she sat in traffic with her car air-conditioning on high, Carmen spotted a U-turn

First Day Orientation Checklist			
Job	**Trainer Initials**	**Trainee Initials**	**Date Shown**
The Pinnacle Philosophy • Customer is always #1, if it is possible, we will do it. • Attitude must be cheerful, pleasant, willing, and caring in both dealing with guests and fellow employees. • Professionalism, cream of the crop employees, we expect it from our employees to act in a very professional manner at all times. • Promote from within.	————	————	————
Department's Hours of Operation	————	————	————
Uniform: Specification • Shoes (women) • Shoes (men) • No colored nylons (women) socks (men) • Makeup • Hair • Nails • Earrings • No jewelry in excess • Housekeeping procedures?1 for 1 for uniform exchange • What to do when uniforms become dirty during shift • Policy on wearing uniforms on/off property	————	————	————
Name Tags • Must be worn at all times • How to replace when lost or broken	————	————	————
Employee Meals • One meal and one snack per eight-hour shift • Cafeteria hours	————	————	————
Lost and Found Procedure • Call Security office in order to record information	————	————	————

FIGURE 2   Reservations Training.

ahead. She knew the Hotel Atlantis would take her back. All the friends she had made at the hotel still worked there. And although she had had disagreements with some of the other employees and supervisors, she at least knew what the arguments would be about. Her days were predictable. The U-turn was getting closer. All she had to do was get in the left lane and she could easily turn around and head back to the Hotel Atlantis.

Sarafina gasped. "I'm so surprised! I had no idea you felt this way. You seem so happy. I can't believe you would really consider leaving here!"

· Carmen was shaking her head. "It's not that I'm so *un*happy, it's just that I'm not that much happier than I was at the Atlantis," Carmen went on. "This is the first time I've changed jobs. The Atlantis was my first job out of school. I was comfortable there. Here, everything is so new, so different. You have to be so friendly and look so enthusiastic and energetic. Learning a new job is tiring, and having to make new friends and get to the point where you feel comfortable with them is even more tiring. At least at the Hotel Atlantis, I knew everyone. I didn't have to worry about having someone to go to lunch with. In reservations here, we never get to go to lunch together because we have to cover the phones. Well, I don't know anybody else, so I end up eating alone most of the time. Unless, of course, I run into you, Sarafina."

"WHAT IF YOU HADN'T OVERHEARD?"

"I really thought Carmen was happy here," Linda mused. "She always seemed so happy, so friendly. When I asked how she liked it here at the Pinnacle, she said she really liked it and everyone was so nice. I just don't get it. I mean, I understand why Sarafina might be doubting herself, and I am worried about her as well, but I don't understand what's going on with Carmen. I guess the reason I'm telling you all of this, Susan, is because I'm afraid she might quit."

Susan Pollack was looking at Linda so intently she didn't say a word after Linda finished talking. As if in a trance, Susan gave her head a quick shake, waking up her thoughts. "I'm sorry, I was just thinking. The whole time you were talking, I kept thinking, 'What are we doing wrong here? What are we missing?' Just when I think our orientation and training program has really come together, I feel suddenly like we're missing a big piece of something. And what if you hadn't overheard Carmen's and Sarafina's conversation?"

THE PROSPECTOR HOTEL

This month, July 2001, John reflected, was the 14-month anniversary of his becoming the general manager of the Prospector Hotel. While business was improving, John Austin was not yet satisfied with the way the hotel was operating, especially the front desk. In fact, two of the front desk clerks, Reese and Estelle, had recently come to him and requested that he hold a meeting with the front desk personnel. John knew that some of his recent decisions as well as those of his direct reports had met with staff resistance. A meeting, the first of its kind, had been scheduled with the front desk staff for five days hence. John had to prepare himself for this meeting very, very carefully.

THE FRANKLIN YEARS

For over 25 years, Charles "Chuck" Franklin had managed the Prospector as general manager. He had also served as the president of the hotel for the last 15 years. Chuck had been very successful as a general manager. He learned his trade through apprenticeships and on the job experiences, as opposed to formal schooling. He was very autonomous, rarely solicited input from department managers, and he alone made almost all decisions, ranging from selection of vendors of toilet paper to staff hiring on his own. Between 1995 and 1997 he successfully executed a 110-room expansion of the hotel, bringing the total number of rooms from 106 to 216, more than doubling its room supply. Franklin turned 60 years old in 2000. The rumor was that his family had demanded that he slow down. After considerable thought, Chuck finally decided to leave the general manager's post but to remain as the Prospector's president.

Franklin chose John Austin, the sales and marketing manager, as his successor. John had started his career with the Prospector hotel in 1988 as a front desk clerk. He was then about to complete his B.A. degree in English from the local university. John was very shy and didn't seem to fit into the culture as did the other young people who worked with him at the front desk. A story circulated that long-standing family trouble had put its mark on the young man. John was serious minded and very different from his more outgoing coworkers. Chuck, however, seemed to like John and, in 1990, John was promoted to front-office manager. The Prospector's two main divisions were food and beverage, and rooms. As front-office manager, John was effectively in charge of the Prospector's rooms division. The food and beverage manager, however, had more experience than John and was also the Prospector's assistant general manager. In 1992, Chuck Franklin saw an opportunity for expansion of the hotel. To concentrate his efforts on this expansion, Chuck leased out the hotel food and beverage operation to a partnership formed by the managers in the existing department. This lease secured a fixed income for the hotel from its food and beverage operations, a department that had historically drained cash flows. Now, the only real operating unit of the hotel was the rooms division. John's title changed from front-office manager to assistant general manager, although his duties didn't initially change at all. Eventually, John took on sales and marketing assignments from Chuck, but John realized as the years went by that he wouldn't get promoted further at the Prospector as long as Franklin remained as the general manager and president. John's frustration with the job only increased when Franklin never solicited John's input on the design of the new addition of the hotel. In spite of the exciting times that seemed to be ahead at the Prospector, with the opening of the new wing in the summer of 1996, John didn't feel he had reached his full potential. That fall, John was approached by a local developer, who had a 100-room Holiday Inn hotel under construction. John accepted an offer to become the Holiday Inn's general manager and left the Prospector in January 1997. The hotel gave a minor farewell party for John but only the front desk staff showed up to wish John well in his future endeavor.

The Holiday Inn opened in July 1997, two months after its scheduled opening. John felt both relieved and relaxed at the Holiday Inn. He seemed to thoroughly enjoy his job. The Holiday Inn had a hard time establishing itself in the market, however, in part because it opened two months later than originally scheduled because of construction delays. This was troublesome to the owner as the hotel was heavily leveraged, but didn't seem to affect John at all. John had attracted some staff with him from the Prospector, possibly due to the excitement that comes with opening a new hotel. John also managed to attract many of the

Prospector's regular customers to the Holiday Inn. His enthusiasm for his position at the Holiday Inn was evident. He even worked with the construction crew and several hotel workers during the last weeks before the opening, carrying mattresses into the rooms, fitting light fixtures, and moving furniture around. Despite John's efforts in marketing the hotel, the Holiday Inn never quite generated enough revenues to cover its debt service. Six months after the hotel opened, the owner had to file for bankruptcy and the mortgage bank took over the property. Due to John's lack of financial background, he was reassigned as the Holiday Inn's operations manager while a young and locally prominent businessman was brought in as general manager.

In the meantime, Franklin had trouble finding a replacement for John at the Prospector. He hired Bob Stockmen, who had a background in public relations and in the travel business, as assistant general manager to focus on sales and marketing. Franklin had not considered an in-house candidate for the position. Bob began hiring his friends into sales to handle room reservations, although these positions historically had been filled with people from the front desk. The front desk staff developed an adversarial relationship with Bob. Bob had never worked in a hotel before, and his staff in the sales office produced erroneous reservation forecasts that seriously affected the front office. Harriet, the front desk clerk with the longest tenure, and others actually began talking about the good old days when John was in charge, because "then you could at least rely on the room reservation count." Whether it was due to serious frictions with the front desk or due to his inability as a manager, Franklin eventually terminated Bob in late 1998.

The economy was hit by a recession in late 1998. To replace Bob, Franklin wanted an assistant general manager with a finance background. He hired Steve Stoller, an MBA from the University of Rochester, who, while locally well known, did not have any hotel experience. The economic recession affected local restaurants and food service establishments very hard, and the partnership that had leased the Prospector's food and beverage operation had to file for bankruptcy in early 1999. Franklin terminated the lease immediately and the hotel took back the food and beverage operation. Although most employees in the food and beverage department retained their jobs, Chuck Franklin had to fill its managerial positions since the partners who previously managed had left.

JOHN RETURNS

With Steve Stoller installed as financial manager, Chuck Franklin needed someone to manage sales and marketing at the Prospector. He contacted John Austin at the Holiday Inn and quickly made him an offer that was accepted. There were mixed feelings at the front desk about John's return. Some people welcomed him back, as they were tired of the confusion that had existed ever since his departure. As sales and marketing manager, however, John didn't get involved in front desk operations. He did supervise the reservations department, which was in very close contact with the front desk. John got his old office back next to Chuck's office, while Steve moved to another office down the hallway. John was soon quite successful in managing the marketing and sales function of the hotel. Since its expansion in 1996, the hotel hadn't been able to secure its fair market share, but 1999 seemed to be the first year the hotel would regain it. The front desk staff seemed somewhat more satisfied with the way things were going—at least reservations were more accurate now than they had been in the recent past.

In March 2000, a year after John's return, Chuck Franklin prepared to retire as the general manager of the hotel. He approached Steve to offer him the position. Steve declined the offer and resigned from the Prospector a month later. Franklin then hired Brian Brown who had been a financial manager at a small computer firm but had no hotel experience. Franklin was interested in having the hotel's internal control system revised and considered Brian a good choice as financial manager. Brian in turn, with Franklin's permission, hired Tom Piper to be in charge of the hotel's internal control function (accounting). Tom was a graduate of Florida International University's hotel program and had actually worked at the front desk under John's supervision 10 years earlier.

One Saturday morning in early July, Emily, the telephone operator on duty, was reading the newspaper. To her surprise, there was news in it about a new general manager at the Prospector Hotel. The article said that John Austin was to replace Charles Franklin as the hotel's general manager with Franklin remaining president. The news spread swiftly around the hotel, that John would replace Franklin as general manager as of next Friday. At noon, when John arrived at the hotel, people congratulated him on the news. Reese, president of the staff club, congratulated John on the news, but also expressed concern that the staff wasn't notified before the press on the change. John felt a little embarrassed.

Despite the shift in top management, nothing in the hotel seemed to change. Franklin was still the president of the hotel and continued to occupy his office. There was no party or any formal ceremony for the new general manager. No one replaced John as the sales and marketing manager of the hotel.

Within two weeks, John decided to move his office to the space occupied by the reservation department next to the front desk. The reservation department in turn moved into a section of the sales office. John's stated rationale for the change was that he wanted to maintain closer contact with the guests. The gossip among the front desk staff was that John switched offices so that he could observe them more carefully. Not only could John now observe everything that went on the front desk through the glass doors to his office, but he could also overhear the back room of the front desk where front desk clerks typically took breaks to chat over a cup of coffee.

THE FRONT DESK

Because John's hotel background was in front-office operations he believed that the front desk was the nerve center of the hotel, and he was very concerned with having it run smoothly. Karen Thompson, Franklin's daughter-in-law, had been the rooms division manager for four years. Two shift managers reported to Karen and supervised the front desk clerks. Karen's regular day-to-day duty was to perform the morning audit and balance the accounts receivable from the previous night as well as to hire and schedule the front desk employees. While the front desk clerks liked Karen, they never approached her when there were problems but instead went to the shift managers with their concerns.

The front desk was predominantly staffed with women. Their average age was below 30. Although the turnover was quite high compared to their competitors, most employees had worked there sometime before. The clerks seemed to like their jobs as they frequently returned after being away a year either at school or at some other job. The front desk job was busy and thus interesting. All clerks had to work both day and night shifts. The younger clerks liked the night shift because then there were no hotel managers around. During the wintertime, especially during midweek when business was slow, the clerks frequently had time to watch TV, read books, or just chat and get to know each other. Consequently, the clerks got to know each other extremely well and many of them developed strong friendships. The few older front desk clerks were typically women in their midthirties. There were so few because most of them did not like the assigned night shifts for all clerks. When John became general manager, there were just two older clerks, Grace and Harriet. Grace had worked at the front desk for two years, whereas Harriet had worked there for almost six years. Harriet was single and didn't mind working night shifts; she was also the most familiar with the computer system, which frequently broke down, especially during the night. She was frequently consulted when the system crashed.

The hotel provided the front desk clerks with uniforms. They were supposed to wear a white blouse that was provided by the hotel with the uniform as well as a bow tie. The clerks, however, frequently wore their own blouses. Karen, Franklin, and John never reprimanded the clerks for doing this. Karen wore her black uniform any way she wanted. The front desk clerks, as well as Karen, also had the habit of arriving 10 minutes late at work almost everyday. The front desk staff, however, consistently received outstanding ratings from the guests of the hotel, better than any other department.

As the front desk was located adjacent to the hotel entrance, it could become quite cold in the wintertime, especially during the night. For quite a while, the front desk clerks had asked to have the skirts replaced with pants since the skirts were too cold to wear in the wintertime. Franklin, and John, had always been against it, as they thought it was more appropriate for female employees to wear skirts rather than pants. Christine, the personnel manager and an avowed feminist, had recently persuaded Franklin to change the uniform.

Although Franklin was no longer the general manager, he still seemed to be in charge of most things at the hotel. While he didn't often interfere with things in the rooms division, Franklin was quite involved with the food and beverage department. For example, he decided to run an upcoming state banquet in honor of Tony Blair, Prime Minister of England— something the Prospector had never done before. Yet John felt Franklin's presence. One day John asked one of his staff to buy new telephones as a safety stock for the hotel rooms in case of breakage. Franklin however, liked neither the color or the design of the phones chosen. "This is what happens when people start to think," he said to an acquaintance.

John soon started his old habit of going behind the front desk to observe the clerks working. One thing got especially on their nerves. John frequently positioned himself behind a desk clerk when that clerk was registering a guest. This would make the clerk nervous as well as the guest uncomfortable. If the clerk made an error, John would intervene and start ordering the clerks around or even reprimand them in front of the guest. One day he caught a front desk clerk directing customers to the banquet room in a manner he didn't agree with. John shouted at her in front of the guest, and just before slamming the door to his office was overheard to say, "I am glad she is leaving, that stupid girl."

In the fall of 2000, several front desk clerks quit. The younger clerks were frequently recent high school graduates who had dropped out of college and believed their job was a temporary one. Frequently, they returned to college after a year or two at the Prospector. The turnover of the front desk clerks was always higher in the fall. This fall, however, both shift managers quit to resume their studies at the local university. Luckily, at the same time, Jackie Ross, who had worked with John at the front desk seven years earlier, approached him for a job. John, who always had liked Jackie, hired her immediately as a shift manager. Harriet had informed Karen, who was one of Harriet's best friends, that she could barely stand the night shifts anymore. The night shifts were tiring and Harriet, who was overweight, found them difficult.

Harriet's extensive work experience at the front desk, in Karen's mind, made her an ideal candidate for the other position. Reluctantly, John agreed to Karen's proposal to promote Harriet, although he had some doubt about this decision.

In early 2001, Amy Eastman, a recent graduate of California State Polytechnic University's hotel program, also approached John for a job. Amy had worked as a front desk clerk and supervisor at the Los Angeles Sheraton. John thought Amy would be an excellent candidate for a shift manager, but there weren't any openings. While John never expressed any concerns regarding Harriet's performance as a shift manager, he now had Amy as a candidate so he hired her as a shift manager at the front desk without conferring with Karen (see the Appendix for the hotel's organizational chart). Harriet resumed her duties as a front desk clerk. Amy's supervisory style was different from what the front desk clerks were used to. She became unpopular with the other clerks as well as with Karen. Instead of arriving 10 minutes late to work, she arrived 10 minutes early. She frequently reprimanded the clerks for spending too much time in the back room as opposed to staying at the desk itself. She also asked clerks frequently to type letters and reports for her as if they were her secretaries. Her behavior toward guests was very different from theirs. In the past, shift managers had always been hired from the ranks of front desk clerks, with only one exception when five years earlier John had hired an outside person as front-office manager. That woman was made uncomfortable by Harriet and Karen, who then were shift managers. Amy never approached Karen with any problems. She went to John.

A NEW SYSTEM

One of John's first major decisions as general manager was to select a new property management system for the Prospector. The current system frequently broke down and maintenance costs were alarmingly high. John wanted to install the new system by March. John showed Karen demonstration packages of three systems. Karen in turn consulted Harriet on which system to select. John ended up choosing the system that Karen and Harriet liked the least. The system John chose had never been installed in a hotel as large as the Prospector. John especially liked a feature that allowed the sales department to book function rooms directly on the computer. The rumor was that Franklin liked this system as well, because it had "nice color screens." Neither Karen nor anyone at the front desk knew of John's decision until he approached them on a Tuesday and told them that the new system would be installed during the upcoming weekend. He installed a personal computer in Karen's office and asked her to translate the menus in the system because it came from a foreign vendor. Karen managed to translate the menus with minor difficulty. The system was installed over the weekend. The front desk clerks didn't receive any training on it, because they could "pick it up on their own" as John put it. There were major problems with the new system—more serious than the problems experienced by the front desk with the old system—the first three months after it was installed. Karen, Harriet, and other front desk clerks were quite upset, in part because they hadn't been consulted on the selection of the new system. Furthermore, they learned from the sales department that they weren't using the function room feature of the system enough that John liked so much. However, Jackie and Amy, the new shift managers, seemed to accept the new system. Amy quickly developed more competency in the system than everyone else.

The summer of 2001 looked quite prosperous in terms of room reservations. Several veteran desk clerks returned to work during the summer, which was historically an extremely busy season. Reese and Estelle, who had been attending college during the winter, returned. Since they had worked the prior summer, they were already familiar with the hotel but not familiar with the new computer system. Sally, who was about to finish her law degree, and had worked at the Prospector two years earlier, also was hired on to work at the front desk over the summer. Sally had worked with the old computer system and had been quite familiar with it. She had worked on the same shift as Harriet and they had gotten to know each other pretty well. Sally and Harriet were almost best friends. She was also a good friend of Karen. Sally quickly developed a dislike of the new computer system, condemned it frequently, sometimes with reference to John's incompetence as a manager.

Karen, the rooms division manager, went on an extended vacation in June. In the past, the shift managers had filled in for her. Karen's absence never seemed to slow things down at the front desk in the past. This time, however, John replaced her with Clarice Grubman. Clarice had worked at the front desk three years ago. The past two summers, however, Clarice had worked in the accounting office. Last summer, she had actually become close to Brian, the financial manager. Brian, who was divorced, and Clarice had started dating that fall. While Clarice was well liked by the front desk clerks, the rumor spread that Clarice got her summer job because "she slept with that guy in the accounting office." Clarice was a very quiet and reserved person. Her experience at the accounting office made the morning audit easy. The rest of her days she spent doing some minor accounting work, while she replaced the clerks and the shift managers on break. Clarice, however, seemed unaware of the tensions that existed within the front desk staff and between the front desk staff and John. At this time, Brian became increasingly aware of a problem related to the front desk's cash drawer; no two counts of the cash balances in the drawer ever seemed completely balanced. Rather, they fluctuated in an overall downward trend. As financial manager, Brian believed he had to do something about it. He also believed Karen was an incompetent manager and resistant to change. Brian decided to make changes while Karen was away. The problems with the cash drawer at the front desk had existed at the hotel for over five years. Neither Karen nor John had ever taken the time to try to solve the problem. One Monday morning Brian took the book where clerks registered their counts. He saw that the cash balances over the weekend had fluctuated dramatically between counts. Both Harriet and Sally had been on duty over the weekend. In red ink, Brian wrote comments all over Sally's counts. Later that afternoon, he designed a new form to be used to log counts, and posted the following memo in the room behind the front desk:

TO ALL FRONT DESK CLERKS

This form should be filled out each time you count the drawer and should be included with your audit to the cashier.

Brian

The clerks were furious over Brian's initiative. He hadn't ever consulted anyone at the front desk before making the changes. Sally condemned Brian's approach in doing this, as well as Clarice's lack of supporting the clerks, only referring to her as "the chick that sleeps with him." Jackie and Amy, however, seemed to support Brian's decision and they were pleased that someone finally had taken the initiative of getting a problem solved. John was not aware of what had happened. The tensions started affecting the already strained relationship between the clerks and Amy. Reese, who had worked under different shift managers last summer, complained to Jackie about Amy.

After their shift one day, Reese and Estelle approached John asking him to initiate a meeting with the entire front desk staff. Reese was well liked by the front desk clerks and by John. John said he was happy to have the opportunity to meet with the front desk clerks and told Reese and Estelle he would schedule a meeting for next week. The meeting would just be general in nature. It became widely known among the front-office personnel that Reese and Estelle wanted to discuss Amy's supervisory style, Sally wanted to discuss Brian's behavior, and everyone wanted to discuss the computer system.

John scheduled a separate meeting with Jackie to prepare for the general meeting. Jackie told John about the friction between Amy and the clerks. John was surprised that this problem had existed so long, for nearly seven months. It seemed strange to him that a hotel that did such a great business would have problems of this nature.

APPENDIX: PROSPECTOR HOTEL ORGANIZATIONAL CHART—2001

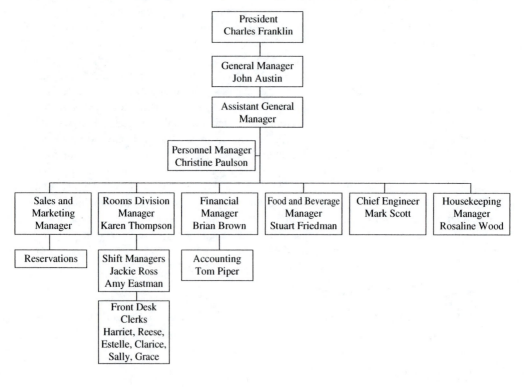

SIMON SAYS

Simon poured himself a cup of coffee and sat down at the staff table at the back of the kitchen. Glancing out of the window he saw it was still raining and night had fallen. February seemed colder than usual. As he sipped his coffee, Simon reflected on the telephone conversation that he had just had with Mr. Nissenbaum, the general manager. The GM had asked Simon to meet with him the next morning to review the poor scores that the front desk department had received on the mystery shopper's report. Mr. Nissenbaum had said that he expected Simon to come up with some new ideas on how to improve the level of service. Simon suspected that his meeting with the GM could affect his future with Hotel 3000. He knew that he had to come up with ideas to turn the front desk service around. The problem was that he had no idea why service wasn't better. That very morning he'd lectured his staff about customer service just as he'd frequently done since becoming the front-office manager six months ago. As the rain began to pound harder on the windows, Simon wondered who was to blame.

HOTEL 3000

Hotel 3000, opened in January 1999, was the first luxury hotel built in Tel Aviv in 20 years. It was located on the beach 10 minutes from downtown. This five-star, 560-room hotel catered to an international clientele, business and leisure travelers from around the world but especially from Europe and the Americas. During the week most of the hotel's guests were business travelers, while weekends were filled with leisure guests. In addition the hotel hosted Israeli conventions, and on Jewish holidays many European families. It was not unusual to have diplomats, heads of state, celebrities, and other VIPs as guests. Since its opening, the hotel had had an occupancy of 80 percent and a strong average daily rate (ADR) of $145.00. In addition to its strong room revenues, Hotel 3000 had a large banquet facility and three restaurants. The hotel was modern throughout. The lobby, for example, was stunning, a combination of white and green marble and warm earth color furnishings. On one side of the lobby was the front desk, concierge, and bell stand. On the other side were the elevators. The western wall of the lobby was a dramatic 10-story high glass window giving a view of the swimming pool area and the Mediterranean Sea. Behind the elevators was a large lounge designed as an atrium, the center of which was a round sushi bar. Around the lounge were two theme restaurants and an Internet café.

While Hotel 3000 was the newest and most luxurious hotel in Tel Aviv, top management believed that the way to successfully compete with the other five-star hotels was to provide only the best service. From its inception therefore, all new employees were required to attend an extensive orientation and training, both of which stressed service issues. The three-day orientation was conducted in one of the hotel's meeting rooms by Dan, the training manager. Dan gave presentations on many topics, from what constituted service excellence to service recovery, from appropriate body language to interdepartmental communications. In addition Dan informed employees about the hotel's rules and regulations regarding fire safety, sexual harassment, stealing, uniforms, personal hygiene and grooming, outgoing phone calls, and much else. All new employees had to sign a list indicating that they acknowledged all rules and regulations. During orientation, all department heads spoke about their departments and how they worked. At the end of the third day Dan gave a tour of the hotel's public spaces, a few guest rooms, and the presidential suite, which he said sold for $2,000 a night.

After orientation, all employees were given cross-training in other departments than that in which they would be working. All new front-office employees, for example, were cross trained in room service, housekeeping, reservations, telephone service, and concierge. After this, front-office training was a day of instruction on the Property Management System (PMS), and then trainees were scheduled to work the front desk shadowing an experienced employee. As an average day would include 200 check-ins and 200 checkouts, the front desk staff was very busy, often too busy to properly instruct newcomers. Trainees often had a difficult time answering guests' questions or providing routine guest services. In fact guests often complained about the abundance of trainees at the front desk, "who don't know what they are doing." Sometimes trainees were so frustrated that they resigned before the two-week training period was over.

THE FRONT-OFFICE DEPARTMENT

The front-office department was managed by Simon Dell. Reporting to Simon were three assistant managers, Michelle, Bruno, and Sharon, and a night manager, Ronny. Reporting to the assistant and night managers were six shift leaders and nine receptionists. Also reporting to Simon was the head concierge, William, with three concierges and ten bellmen, and the telephone operation manager, Maggie, with eight operators. William's and Maggie's units were quite independent from the rest of the front office and Simon and the assistant managers rarely dealt with them.

Simon was born and raised in England, and educated at the Swiss School of Hotel Administration. After graduating, he worked as a front-office manager at a 75-room luxury boutique hotel in Geneva. When Hotel 3000 opened, Simon was hired as the guest-relations manager. He was promoted to front-office manager six months ago when his predecessor was fired. Simon worked long days, usually from 8 o'clock in the morning until nine or ten at night. Daily, Simon met with the resident manager, and the sales and reservations managers. He also met frequently with the GM. He personally took care of various human resource matters, too. Simon thought of himself as ambitious and believed he could grow with Hotel 3000. He made no secret that his real interest was to become a GM someday. The hotel's GM, Mr. Nissenbaum, was quite fond of Simon, telling him more than once that he had "the right attitude" for accommodating the hotel's international clientele.

Michelle and Bruno both had a great deal of hotel experience but no formal education in hotel management. Michelle actually ran the front desk operations with Bruno's help. Michelle was the assistant manager who the front-office staff came to with their questions and concerns. At times, however, Simon overrode her decision, usually on the floor in front of the staff. Sharon's job as an assistant manager included front-office training and monitoring overtime pay. She kept track of trainee progress and did one-on-one training sessions. Sharon's days, usually just two a week because of her university studies and extensive traveling with her family, were spent writing reports on various training initiatives, working with Dan, and doing other front-office daily tasks. Her training of new employees was often interrupted, always on days when she was manager-on-duty. While well liked by most front-office staff because she was usually in good spirits and was the front-office cheerleader, Sharon was not respected for her absences and lack of hands-on knowledge of the work. A common joke was, "Sharon is always in a good mood because she is not at the desk very much."

Shift leaders at the front desk, beyond doing reservations, supervised the reservationists, printed reports at the beginning and end of each shift, preblocked rooms, coordinated with housekeeping, and took care of guest requests that the receptionists didn't have time or skills to resolve.

THE FRONT DESK

The front desk's line employees were a diverse group, some born and raised in other parts of the world. One receptionist was from Japan, for example, and another from Canada. The majority, however, were Israelis from the Tel Aviv area. Since both the hotel's staff and clientele were international, the prevailing language was English. The front office was quite informal. Everyone referred to each other by their first name, including the managers. Since the hotel was always busy there was very little time for socializing on the job, and people were generally occupied with their work. However, at slow times, typically on Saturday morning, there was more time to talk and joke around.

Most of the staff started working at Hotel 3000 at the time Simon became the front-office manager. The front office in general, and especially the front desk, had a very high turnover rate. Between the time the hotel opened in January 1999 and February 2000 all of the reception staff had changed. The turnover in shift leaders was not that high, but some of them were promoted to other jobs in the hotel. Most of the front desk staff saw their jobs as temporary ones. All of the Israeli employees had completed their military service and some were preparing to go to university. Most of the older employees considered their future career to be in the hospitality industry. Wages in the front office were hourly, based on the minimum wage in Tel Aviv. Only managers received salaries. Since front-office wages were low compared to the rest of the labor market it was hard to attract and retain employees. Because this situation was true of the whole industry, the Israeli government had initiated an incentive plan a year ago to encourage young people who just got out of the army to work in tourism-related jobs. This program included a one-time government grant to any person working in a hotel for seven months or more. Thus many of the front-office employees stayed for only seven months and left after receiving their grant.

The front desk staff typically had good relationships with their supervisors and assistant managers. They all worked very closely together and would frequently help each other out. The assistant managers would often have lunch at the employees' cafeteria with the receptionists and the shift leaders. Simon never did. Most of the front desk staff thought he was a snob. They resented the fact that he never helped at the desk and that when he did go out to the desk he would start helping a guest and then let the receptionist finish the "dirty work." Simon would also use his cell phone when standing behind the desk, something strictly forbidden by all employees.

All hourly front desk employees worked eight-and-a-half hour shifts, which included a 30-minute unpaid lunch break. The daily tasks of the front desk included checking guests in and out of the hotel, exchanging currency, performing any billing-related activities, accommodating guests' requests and questions, answering phone calls, checking in groups, and making reservations when the reservations office was closed. In a typical shift there would be three or four receptionists and a shift leader. The shift leader was the person in charge and the receptionists would go to him or her with any questions. In case a shift leader ran into any difficulties, an assistant manager could usually be found. Because much of the shift leaders' work was related to reports and other back-of-the-house duties, they were often in the back office. Receptionists had to walk to the back office whenever they needed assistance. Many of the receptionists' tasks required a shift leader's authorization, such as rebating charges from guests' accounts, upgrading guests, and so on. The receptionists thought this was silly and just caused a lot of extra paperwork. Shifts were often very busy, often so busy that the front desk employees would not have time to go down to the employees' cafeteria for lunch. People would be working a full eight-and-a-half hours without a break, but would still be paid for eight hours.

It was also common that the shifts would not end on time. Because shifts were so busy, the front desk staff found it very hard to finish their end-of-the-shift tasks while they were out at the desk. They would often end up staying anywhere from one to three hours after a shift just to finish up. On average, every employee would work five to six hours of overtime per week. In order to get paid for overtime, employees had to fill in a form and leave it in Sharon's folder. Sharon was to go over these forms daily and authorize any overtime. Front desk employees did not like staying after their shifts and only did so when they had to, therefore Sharon would usually authorize all overtime. Employees had complained to Simon that overtime made their day very unpredictable and that they could never plan anything after work because they never knew when they would finish. Because Sharon was often absent from work, she would go through the overtime forms just once a month. Months might go by with employees not being paid for their overtime. One front desk employee had to talk to Sharon, to Simon, and to three people in the accounting department before she was paid overtime. Simon would never reprimand Sharon for not keeping track of the overtime. One shift leader once said: "He could never fire her anyway, she's too connected in the industry." Also some employees would be scheduled to work a six-day workweek instead of a five-day week, but were never asked whether they were willing to work the additional day and would only find out about it once the schedule for the following week had already been published.

THE GUEST SATISFACTION SURVEYS

Hotel management emphasized a high level of guest service. All employees were expected to be polite and courteous when in contact with guests and to do their best to make the guests' stay enjoyable. Once in a while Simon, Sharon, or Michelle would talk to the front desk staff about smiling, greeting, answering the phone promptly, and following up on guest requests. Receptionists were encouraged to have all guests fill in guest satisfaction surveys. These surveys were supposed to assist managers in determining what needed improvement. The front desk staff, however, often used those surveys as a device to get "annoying guests" off their back. Simon would announce at the end of every month at a daily briefing the previous month's results and goals for the upcoming months. Most of the front desk staff saw these figures as detached from reality. While they were generally committed to providing good service, they were having a hard time completing their daily tasks, let alone providing exceptional service.

Between October and January the surveys did not show any improvement. At the daily briefing of the front desk staff, Simon would often scold the staff saying that they were not doing their jobs. He would also say that he expected them to go out of their way for guests, adding that he would make sure they did. Following these meetings, Simon would keep a close eye on the receptionists' interaction with guests. During busy hours he would stand in the lobby and observe how receptionists were handling their guests, although he would rarely help in the check-in process.

THE MYSTERY SHOPPER

During the month of January there was a rumor throughout the hotel that management was expecting a mystery shopper. Hotel 3000 has a worldwide practice of having each hotel reviewed at least twice a year by a mystery shopper. The mystery shopper would check into the hotel under an alias and examine all of its services, amenities, and facilities. The mystery shopper would then write a detailed report about the hotel and how well it met Hotel 3000 standards. The general manager of the hotel, the regional manager, and the CEO of Hotel 3000 would all receive copies of this report. Following the rumor, Simon warned all of the receptionists to treat every guest as if he or she were the mystery shopper.

On February 18th Simon summoned all the front-office staff to a special meeting. Immediately everyone realized that this was not about good news; good news would have been mentioned during daily briefings. Simon opened the meeting by announcing that indeed a mystery shopper had stayed in the hotel. He said that while he had not read the full report, he had read the initial findings concerning the front-office department. He said the findings "were all substandard." Simon then went on to list the standards that had not been met. For some of the employees this was the first time they had ever heard of some standards, for example Hotel 3000's standard of trying to up-sell a guest to a more expensive room upon check-in. Simon continued saying that although none of the units in the front office had met all the standards, his main disappointment was with the front desk. He stated that, "I feel like all my efforts have been in vain," and that "everything I've been teaching you has fallen on deaf ears." He expressed his disappointment in each and every receptionist. Silence followed. Simon frowned, turned, and went to his office.

SMOKESTACK VILLAGE, INC.

Thomas J. Bronston, chairman of the board of trustees and general manager of Smokestack Village, was worried about the developing problem between his employees and Karl Olson, the man he wished to have replace him as general manager.

Smokestack Village was a tourist attraction located near the Continental Divide in central Colorado. It offered visitors a large railroad museum and daily excursion rides on old railroad lines. The museum had over 40 steam locomotives on display and many other exhibits relating to the days of steam railroading. The excursion rides were operated during the summer and fall months over 26 miles of track winding through a valley high in the Rockies. It had been founded by Miles E. Smith, a semiretired railroad buff, with Mr. Bronston's assistance in arranging financing.

Mr. Smith served as general manager during the early years of slow growth. When he was unexpectedly killed in an automobile accident, Mr. Bronston tried to find someone to take care of the day-to-day operating responsibility. This included short-range planning, ordering supplies, handling the finances, and coping with "nosey federal inspectors." When unsuccessful in

Reprinted with permission from A. Cohen, S. Fink, H. Gaddon, & R. Willits. *Effective Behavior in Organizations*. R. D. Irwin, Inc. 1995.

finding someone he considered satisfactory, he reluctantly took on the task himself. This meant closing up his own business as an investment counselor and moving from Denver to Grenoble, which was closer but still 45 miles from Smokestack Village.

He had been general manager for the past five years. During that time, the museum had started running the excursion trains, and the many engines that had been sitting around the turntable rusting had been stored under cover during the winter and restored on a regular basis. Attendance had tripled over the five-year period. He now felt that it was time for "new blood" in management, and he was informally looking for a replacement. The long commute was also getting to him.

Assistant manager Jim Harris, 28, was in charge of restoration, painting, lawnmowing, and ticket sales. Working for him were three girls who sold tickets and staffed the exhibit cars. Also under his direction were five high school boys who worked around the locomotive displays, painting, restoring the engines to their original looks, lawnmowing, weeding, sweeping walks, and doing trackwork. Jim spent most of his day making sure the boys were working and not goofing off from what they considered to be "just a summer job in which you put in your 40 hours."

Contact between Harris's crew and a crew that operated the excursion trains was limited because of the physical layout of Smokestack Village (see Exhibit 1) and the jobs they did. The train crew spent the day either in the station or up the line, while the museum crew was working around the display engines a distance away.

Sven Olson was in charge of the train crew and was also the engineer on the train. Sven was a veteran of 50 years' service as an engineer for the Great Western Railroad, and he knew his business. The other employees used to joke that he knew more about railroads than they

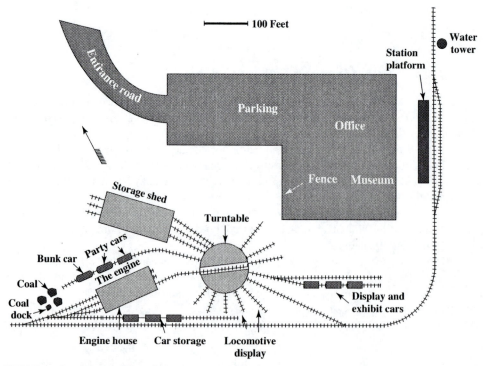

EXHIBIT 1   Smokestack Village layout

would ever have time to forget. At 75, he was still capable of working longer and harder than most of the other employees 55 years younger than he.

Ned Bronston, 17, the son of Mr. Bronston, was the fireman. He lived with Sven in the bunk car parked near the enginehouse. It was the first summer working at Smokestack Village for both of them, although Ned had spent many days at Smokestack with his father over the years.

Working with them were three other employees who had worked at Smokestack Village in the past. Bob Johnson, 30, had worked for the village for four years as conductor for the passenger train in the summer and in the office in the winter.

The brakemen were Al Stanhope, 18, and Peter Townshend, also 18. They had worked at Smokestack for the past two summers on the museum crew, and it was their first summer on the train.

The five of them became fast friends. They worked well together and enjoyed each other's company both during and after work. It was not unusual for them all to go out to dinner at the end of the day or sit around the bunk car half the night talking about railroads. Al and Peter kept sleeping bags at the bunk car and frequently stayed overnight.

Al, Peter, and Ned, with Sven's consent, traded jobs occasionally; Ned worked as brakeman while Al or Peter fired the engine. Frequently Sven would allow the fireman to run the engine while he fired. Most railroads allowed this, and Mr. Bronston knew that with Sven in the cab, nothing could go wrong. The practice allowed for the training of future engineers. Mr. Bronston only asked that the train leave and arrive in the village on time. How this was to be done was left up to the five of them. They found it best to work as a team; each of them knew the other's job well enough from the practice of switching jobs to know what to expect from the others. Arguments were few and far between.

The day started for Sven and Ned at 8:30 A.M. Being a fireman, Ned had many duties to tend to before the engine could be run that day. The fire had to be rebuilt from the day before, lubricators filled, water worked out of the cylinders, and the engine coaled. The coal dock was 75 yards from the enginehouse, and this gave Ned an opportunity to run the engine a bit. If he had time and the engine warranted it, he would polish the engine, wiping oil and cinders from the boiler and wheels.

While Ned was working on the engine, Sven would be preparing a sumptuous breakfast for the two of them. He would also boil a large pot of coffee for Bob, Al, and Peter, who would arrive at 10. Breakfast started at 9:30, and the train crew would join them at 10 for a half hour of railroad talk. The talk usually turned to girls, sports, and movies; the breakfast hour was enjoyed by all.

At 10:30 it was time to take the engine and passenger cars down to the station in preparation for the first run, leaving at 11. Mr. Bronston would be waiting on the platform for the train's arrival. He would climb into the cab to talk with Sven about the engine. He would inquire as to whether the engine was running well, the coal supply was lasting, and any other details related to the operating department. Satisfied that all was going well, he would head back to his office.

Mr. Bronston felt that he had a responsible crew working on the train. There was an unstated understanding between him and the train crew that as long as things went smoothly, he would not interfere in their routine. Sven worked hard with the train crew, drilling them on railroad procedures and safety measures. Running a railroad is serious business, and they all knew it. Fooling around could not be tolerated when 800 people were on the train. There were instances where local kids had tried to derail the train by placing ties and spikes on the track. Al and Ned had managed to catch the culprits, and they were turned over to the state police.

The arrival of the train back in Smokestack Village after the first trip marked the beginning of lunch for both the museum and train crews. Ned would buy lunch for Sven and himself and return to the engine. One of them stayed on the engine at all times. After eating, Sven would climb down off the engine and wander around talking with visitors, while other visitors would climb into the cab for a look around and maybe a chance to blow the whistle.

Two more trips would be made before the end of the day at 6 P.M. It took Ned about an hour to shut down the engine for the night. If the train crew was going out to dinner together, they would all pitch in to get the work done, otherwise Sven would start dinner for Ned and himself while Bob, Al, and, Peter would head home for dinner.

There were times when the engine needed major repair due to some malfunction. When this happened, the museum crew would join the train crew in repairing the locomotive. Sometimes the work would take all night—nobody complained. It had to be done if the train was to run the next day. Sven and Ned would work with the crews until midnight and then retire. If they were to function the next day, they needed their sleep. The two of them put in the hardest day of all the employees.

Each morning at 3 A.M. Ned would wake up and go out to the engine to check the water level, steam pressure, and the fire, which was left burning from the day before. The engine had a habit of building up steam pressure when left unattended, and this led to difficulties the next morning, the worst being a boiler explosion.

In doing this, Ned violated federal law, which requires that railroad employees not work more than 16 hours followed by a 10-hour rest period. Ned was well aware of this law but chose to ignore it. Smokestack Village would have had to hire a night hostler to watch the engine, and this was costly. So he did it himself.

Employees turned in their time cards each Wednesday. They were to write down the hours they had worked and what they had done. Average pay for the museum and train crews was $1.60 an hour. Bob earned a higher wage since legally the responsibility of the train and the hundreds of passengers was his, and his higher pay was justified. The train crew only put in for a 44-hour week, although 50 and 60 hours of actual work was not unusual. They never asked for pay for the nights they worked repairing the engine. Working on steam engines was considered a privilege. Al, Peter, and Ned spent many evenings working on one engine in the exhibit area that was their favorite. They had painted the engine and spent many hours hunting through the storage shed and spare parts boxcars looking for gauges, valves, and other parts to replace ones missing from the locomotive. They didn't ask to be paid for this.

The museum crew, for the most part, did the same thing with their time cards. They only asked for overtime when the work was not with the engines. They had a few pet projects that they also worked on after hours; for example, they had been painting the railroad name on the sides of the passenger cars, doing one side of one car an evening.

During the times when the two crews were working in the evenings, Jim Harris and Sven were never around. The evening projects were the idea of the employees involved, and they wished to do it on their own. Mr. Bronston, on his daily inspection tours of the grounds, would only offer suggestions as to what might look better or more realistic. The final decisions were left up to the crews. The two groups stayed to themselves most of the time. The only time the two crews worked together was when the engine that Al, Peter, and Ned were working on had to be lettered. The museum crew stenciled the engine for the three of them to paint. The museum crew had offered to do the job, and the offer was gladly accepted. Once the job was done, the two crews went back to the original format of working by themselves.

The museum crew's attitude of it being "just a summer job" changed during the month of June. Once the lawnmowing and trackwork and other tasks were done, they were permitted to work on the engines, which was much more interesting and enjoyable to the point that they stayed late on their own time.

Sven had one son, Karl, 50, who lived in Wyoming. Karl was a successful mechanical engineer with a long list of patents to his credit. He had been involved in the production of a sound movie projector for a large camera producer, and his expertise had helped send a man to the moon. He had started many engineering consulting firms with clients like NASA, the armed services, the automobile industry suppliers, and railroads. He had sold his businesses over the past few years and was now in semiretirement, taking on consulting work out of his home when he wanted.

During the month of June he made several trips with his wife Henrietta to Smokestack Village and the area to visit his father. He would ride in the cab of the engine, and Ned would sometimes let him sit in the fireman's seat. Karl considered this a privilege and was grateful to Ned. Sven and Karl got along quite well. Karl never interfered with Sven's work, realizing that he was in the presence of one of the best and most well-known engineers in the country.

It was not long before Karl was seen in the office with Mr. Bronston discussing Smokestack Village. Karl had many ideas on how to increase patronage at the museum. He knew some people in the TV advertising business, and he arranged for low-cost TV commercials to be aired in major cities of the area.

Karl started spending more and more time at the museum. Mr. Bronston, realizing that Karl had plenty of spare time that might be put to constructive use at Smokestack Village, asked him if he would be interested in becoming a trustee. Karl accepted the offer, and he and his wife moved into a local motel for an indefinite stay.

Prior to Karl's becoming a trustee, Mr. Bronston had asked Ned what he thought of Karl. Ned couldn't think of anything negative at the time and told his father that he would get the other employees' reactions. The museum crew didn't have much contact with Karl; only Jim knew who he was, and he thought Karl was OK. The train crew had only known Karl for a month at that point and didn't register any complaints about him either. They knew that Mr. Bronston was looking for a replacement, but since Mr. Bronston had left the operating department to them and didn't interfere, they didn't care who was the boss. In the next two weeks they would all have reason to care after all.

Karl, now a trustee, began to make his appearance in the bunk car every morning at 9 to start issuing orders. The train crew started to grumble that they didn't need this intrusion in their morning routine. Karl no longer allowed the morning coffee break. The work that Al, Peter, and Ned did in the evenings was now to be done in the morning starting at 9. Ned, having to work on the engine, couldn't participate. Ned's work in the morning was under constant fire from Karl. As a result, the "extra bit" Ned did polishing the engine was neglected. Karl also ordered that the engine and train be ready in the station at 10:15 each morning. Sven and Ned were incensed at this. It meant getting up earlier and rushing breakfast on what they considered to be their own time. Sven was also told by Karl that when the engine was moved even a foot, he had better be at the throttle or Karl would find a new engineer. Ned was no longer allowed to run the engine to the coal dock, and the firemen were not allowed to run the engine on the mainline. At lunch time Ned could no longer leave the engine to get lunch for Sven and himself from the cafeteria in the station. They were both to stay on the engine at all times during the day. The conductor and brakemen were not subjected to the same restriction, and this caused hard feelings between the engine and train crews. When Sven had asked Karl how he was to get lunch, Karl told him to bring a sandwich with him in the morning. Sven told the four men he worked with to ignore Karl. Mr. Bronston had given Sven his orders and those were the ones to follow. Karl seemed careful not to give orders when Mr. Bronston was around.

The employees began to look around to see if Karl was watching and, if he was, to do it his way. Nobody dared cross him. But the trips allowed the train crew a chance to get away from Karl and do things their own way. Once the train left the station, they would stop looking over their shoulders to see if Karl was watching. Bob got in the habit of signaling Sven to start when Karl was nowhere in sight, while Al and Peter would walk the length of the train to see if Karl had gotten on while they weren't watching and, if so, tell the engine crew through a prearranged hand signal. If Karl was on the train, the trip would be slower and the whistle wasn't blown as much, which upset Sven because he felt that the people had paid for a train ride and he was going to give them a ride they would never forget.

Mr. Bronston had told the employees that Karl had been made a trustee but had not made any mention of any authority that Karl might have when dealing with employees. The Smokestack Village board had 15 trustees on it. They were all known by the employees, and many of them came to Smokestack on weekends to look around. They frequently asked the employees how projects were coming but never ordered anyone around. For the most part they were fund-raisers for the organization and policy makers. On one trustee's visit, he asked one of the museum crew workers to wear cleaner clothes because the employees were in the limelight. It was the only incident where a trustee other than Karl confronted an employee all summer.

Karl had made it understood that anyone who didn't do as he said would be fired. The way he gave orders, the message was clear: "Do it my way, or you're out."

Morale hit bottom. Employees came to work at 9 and left at 5. Before, when the engine needed repair, Jim had asked who would like to stay late to help fix the engine and the museum crew would head for the phone to call home to cancel dinner or their girlfriends to cancel dates. This was no longer true. Sven and Jim had to plead with the museum crew to stay, and they would agree only if it were understood that they were free to leave if Karl showed up. Ned and Al and Peter would stay, even if he did show, because they needed the engine. The time cards started to show exactly how many hours each employee worked. Fifty and 60 hours was not unusual, and the payroll was doubled with the overtime.

About two weeks after Karl's appointment as a trustee, Mr. Bronston was made aware of the payroll increase by his secretary, Jean, who handled the payroll accounts. Jean, the employees' "second mother," offered no explanation, although she did know what has happening. Mr. Bronston decided to accept Sven's standing invitation for dinner in the bunk car with Ned and himself. The conversation that night finally turned to Karl. Sven related some of the incidents that made him angry with his son Karl. Ned, at Sven's insistence, let it be known that Karl was ruining a good working environment. Employees were rebelling by "misplacing" valuable locomotive tools and parts, painting and restoration work was slowing down, and little jobs such as picking up trash were not being done. If Mr. Bronston wanted the stenciling and lettering of the passenger cars finished, he would have to order it finished on Smokestack Village's time. Ned also stated that he and most of the other workers felt it difficult to follow two bosses. They were all at a loss as to whose orders to follow: Karl's, as he was always around the grounds, or Mr. Bronston's, who was the boss even when he was working in the office.

Mr. Bronston thanked the two of them for dinner and got in his car for the 45-minute trip home. As he drove, he reflected upon the situation. Karl looked like a man capable of taking his place. He had plenty of spare time, which he was willing to devote to the village, and was a successful businessman with many connections in the railroad industry. Karl would make the village his life, something that Mr. Bronston didn't want to do. Living in Grenoble, a poor mill town, wouldn't bother Karl as he didn't have any children and didn't much care what his wife thought. Ned had overheard Karl tell Sven that his wife had cancer, "so she'll be gone soon."

The present circumstances cast a doubt in Mr. Bronston's mind as to whether he could entrust Karl with the museum. The next trustees' meeting would be in October. He knew he would have to stay on as general manager until then, when Karl might take the job. Now if he could figure out a way to keep peace until then . . .

SUMMER SUN CASINOS, INC.

David Lloyd, vice president of human resources for Summer Sun Casinos, Inc., watched Anne Furlong leave his office. He sat back and reflected on the meeting they'd just had. It wouldn't be many months before they would have to staff the new $160 million Midnight Sun Hotel and Casino property nearing completion with an estimated 1,800 to 2,000 employees. David and Ann had agreed that staffing for a hard opening[1] was always difficult and always crucial to the initial success of a property. David had participated in the opening of several new hotels and casino hotels in his career. As he had opinioned to Ann as she was leaving "We've just got to do it better. Maybe it's worth doing it differently than we've ever done it before."

THE COMPANY AND SETTING

Summer Sun Casinos, Inc., began in 1976 as The Casino, a 5,000 square foot gaming property in Las Vegas, Nevada. During the 1980s, The Casino was transformed and enlarged to become the Blue Sun Hotel and Casino. It now had approximately 25 times the space of the original property. In 1993 the company went public with what became the most successful gaming offering in the history of Wall Street. Since that year, Summer Sun Casinos had opened a new property every year. At present Summer Sun Casinos had five properties in Las Vegas, including the Blue Sun, and two casinos in Missouri. Soon to be opened in the summer of 1997 was the newest Summer Sun property, the Midnight Sun Hotel and Casino.

Las Vegas had been the center of legalized gambling in the United States for many decades. Casino hotels clustered downtown and for several miles along "The Strip." In recent years there had been a surge of new openings, several every year. Las Vegas had been the fastest growing city in the United States for the past four years. While growth in the gaming industry accounted for much of Las Vegas's recent growth, it also had been attracting high technology firms and other light industry as well as retirees and others who wished to escape the pollution and congestion of large cities such as Los Angeles and Chicago. More and more, new casino hotels strived to be family-oriented, having some distinctive entertainment theme, regular exhibits or activities, for example, the erupting volcano in front of The Mirage, the

---

[1] A "hard opening" was when a property opened its door with all services at full or nearly full capacity.

pirate ship battle in front of Treasure Island, or the jousting matches in the Excalibur, to differentiate themselves from their competition.

RECRUITMENT IN LAS VEGAS

Recruitment for new casino hotels was a straightforward process. Companies typically ran advertisements in local newspapers announcing staff hiring with a series of days noted for interested people to show up. Applicants came to the appointed place, got in line and waited until their turn, when they were given an application form to fill out. When the form was completed, it was handed in to one of several recruiters who then scanned it. If an applicant possessed minimum qualifications, they were either given an appointment for an interview or interviewed right then. On the first day of this process, as many as 3,000 people might show up to fill out an application. Some might have to stand in line for half a day or more. As Ann Furlong, the human resource director for the new hotel and casino noted,

> When you open the first day, your objective is to attract people. Then, when 2,000 people show up, your objective becomes how do we get these people out of here. And this is totally opposite from what you are trying to do. Your mission changes from what you are trying to do. Your mission changes from one of evaluation to processing, and you can't staff a property properly by just processing.

Furlong added, that to help ease the pressure of the situation, she and her staff sometimes even stood in line with applicants, telling them jokes, serving coffee in cold weather, anything to keep them from feeling frustrated.

David Lloyd believed there were real weaknesses in the conventional recruitment process. For Summer Sun Casinos, finding and keeping the best employees was believed to be an important way to keep a step ahead of the competition. The Summer Sun Casino philosophy was simple in concept: hire the best employees using the best selection process available. Summer Sun's goal was to have applicants enjoy the selection process so much that, even if not hired, they would return as customers. Yet there were many barriers. According to Lloyd:

> Managers have some real problems today. Their pressure is to fill a job while focusing on the operations part of the business. Their number one priority is "get someone in here," their number two priority is "get someone in here who can do the job," and their number three priority is "get someone in here who can do the job and is the best candidate available." It's very hard for them to step outside the operation and give recruiting the attention it deserves.

MIDNIGHT SUN HOTEL AND CASINO

The newest property of Summer Sun Casinos, Inc., was to be the Midnight Sun. Located on 160 acres of concentrated, commercially developed land, the property under construction would include a 527-room hotel tower and 80,000 square feet of casino space. There would be six full-service restaurants. Other features of the property were to include a microbrewery, a 13-screen movie theater, and much more. Like other casino hotels, Midnight Sun would operate seven days a week with most services available around the clock.

WHAT TO DO

The more David Lloyd thought about the staffing of the Midnight Sun ahead of him and Ann, the more he was sure that it was time to reexamine the entire selection process. Taking out a pad of paper he began to sketch his ideas. Two objectives immediately came to mind: to increase the applicant flow and to decrease the number of candidates selected to complete the full interview process. Jotting these objectives down, David paused, turning these into numbers, even rough numbers was the next step. And, he didn't want to just focus on the Midnight Sun for this was an opportunity to reconceive recruitment for the whole corporation.

David knew that the corporate annual applicant flow was about 38,000 and in the past that the company had selected about 4 percent. Since his general objectives seemed reasonable, and he thought that his staff probably could spend time with about 20,000 selected applicants, it meant that to be more selective would mean hiring 2.5 percent of these 20,000, who, according to his experience, would come from an applicant pool of 80,000. Jotting these figures down on his pad, David leaned back and grinned to himself. It seemed like a pipe dream. Human resources would have to have its own building and additional staff. To upgrade the quality of hires and fill jobs in a more timely manner while increasing the applicant flow more than 50 percent seemed impossible. Turning his desk chair to look out the window David Lloyd mused to himself, "I'm sure there is some sort of high-tech, high-touch solution. I'll start looking around to see what's available."

In the ensuing weeks David Lloyd began to research available options. He realized that whatever was chosen would be put to the test in the staffing of the soon to be completed Midnight Sun. After several conversations with the Midnight Sun's HR director, Ann Furlong, Lloyd concluded that what was needed was a technology assisted telephone-screening device to take the routine, time-consuming work of getting applications and initial screening out of the hands of his HR staff and operations managers giving them more time to focus on the better candidates.

Lloyd discovered that a firm in Laramie, Wyoming called Birch Tree Software (BTS), Inc., had developed computer-assisted products to improve several human resource activities such as managing customized internal databases and exit interviews. What intrigued him about BTS was both its ongoing validation research on its products and the high level of customer service offered. Contacting BTS, Lloyd quickly learned that it had recently developed a new screening system and wanted a site in which to test it. The BTS Computer-Assisted Phone Screening (CAPS) system, however, was designed for situations where approximately 1,500 to 2,000 employee prospects were expected to be processed.

With the CAPS system, Summer Sun Casinos would run advertisements in local and regional newspapers informing readers that they were about to staff a new hotel and casino. Interested people were instructed to call a telephone number provided and answer a series of short questions over the phone. If the caller met the minimum qualifications for the job in question, programmed into the software, he or she was transferred to a HR assistant and scheduled for an appointment at his/her convenience at the Midnight Sun hiring center. On arrival at the hiring center, the person would complete an application, participate in a group interview, and then talk with an employment manager one-on-one, a process lasting no longer than two hours per applicant.

Lloyd and Furlong met to talk about how well this new system might work from both the company's point of view as well as from the applicant's point of view. Was the CAPS system worth trying?

THE TWO ANGELS INN

Sally Lapson sat stunned in her car parked in the flower-lined circular driveway only dimly aware of the fountain's spray and the shadows of the palm trees. What had happened to Hap and Holly's dream, kept repeating in her head.

Sally, the first morning home from college for her spring break, had driven over to visit her former employers Hap and Holly Sanders at the château-styled inn, The Two Angels. Sally had looked forward to seeing the Sanders, who she considered as her friends, as well as once again experiencing the inn she had grown to love. As she parked, she immediately saw the new sign, "La Quinta Lake Resort." Upon entering the formerly serene, crystal chandeliered foyer, there was of all things a desk like any other hotel might have. Glancing to her left into the dining room she saw a portable coffee jug and plastic cups on the end of the table.

As Sally's eyes adjusted to the shadowed interior, a young man stood up behind the desk and said, "Hi, I'm Mack, do you have a reservation?" Upon inquiring after the Sanders, she learned that they were no longer the managers. When Sally explained that she had formerly worked there, Mack sat back down. Sally then asked about Dawn and Maria. She was told to check with "the help upstairs" with the warning that "those old women don't speak English." So Sally excused herself and went back to sit in her car. What had happened to Hap and Holly?

THE VALLEY

Paralleling Interstate 10, between the Little San Bernardino Mountains to the east and the Santa Rosa Mountains close on the west, were a string of well-known resort towns—Palm Springs, Cathedral City, Rancho Mirage, Indian Wells, Palm Desert, La Quinta, and Coachella—collectively called "The Valley." The area is what southern Californians call the High Desert, very dry and sunny. Winters are considered the best season with daytime high temperatures averaging 70 degrees. Summers, however, can be quite unpleasant, the mercury consistently well over 100 degrees (with 120 degree days on occasion). A canal from the Colorado River and deep wells kept the many golf courses, man-made lakes, and home lawns, shrubs, and flowers luxuriant.

People came to the Valley from all around the world, drawn to its winter climate, many resorts, and events such as the Bob Hope Classic and the PGA West. It has been home to many celebrities, for example, Frank Sinatra, Cher, and Gerald Ford, as well as where many well-off retirees, for example, "snowbirds," spend their winter months, and where many people from greater Los Angeles have weekend second homes or condos. In general, the visitors to the Valley desired the high-quality lodging, restaurants, and shopping that have long typified the "Springs" (i.e., Palm Springs).

La Quinta was one of the relatively newer and smaller towns in the Valley. The town fathers knew that their town could not compete with the number of large major lodging properties up the Valley such as the Four Seasons and Marriott. They believed in and actively encouraged smaller, unique, high-quality businesses in La Quinta.

HAP AND HOLLY'S DREAM COME TRUE

Harold (Hap) and Hollister (Holly) Sanders had been married for nearly 40 years. They lived in Cleveland, Ohio, where Hap, since graduating from Yale, had worked as an executive in his family-owned and managed chain of midwest department stores. Childless, Hap and Holly traveled extensively worldwide but over the years returned more and more to provincial France and Palm Springs. In 1997, the 100-year-old family company was sold; Hap who had earlier inherited a great deal of money from his father's estate now acquired nearly $2 million more. Nearing 60 years of age, Hap and Holly decided to leave Cleveland and "semiretire" to a warmer climate. They bought a large home in the Valley just north of La Quinta.

Upon returning from a visit to the south of France in 1999, they dreamed of opening a French château in the Valley because châteaus to them had always embodied wealth, comfort, and a retreat from the stresses of everyday life. A prime piece of vacant land bordering a small lake near La Quinta's best shopping became available. Hap and Holly immediately purchased it. Although the Sanders had no prior experience with a hospitality business, they decided to build their dream château because they enjoyed catering to people and making them feel welcome, and, in Cleveland, had achieved a local reputation for throwing wonderful social gatherings. They decided on the name of their enterprise before even scouting for a contractor—The Two Angels Inn. Their inn was to be basically their home into which guests were invited and given individual attention for a reasonable fee.

Hap and Holly quickly located a renowned architect and worked closely with him on the Inn's design. Their overriding criterion was to create a serene retreat that catered to its guests. Construction went quickly. Hap and Holly actively consulted with the interior designers to make their inn feel, as Holly often stated, "like an exquisite mansion." A boathouse with two spacious suites was also built on the lakefront. The layout of the completed inn was unique. The front doors were very tall and wide. They opened to a generous open space with a beautiful crystal chandelier above and a wide sweeping staircase to the second floor resembling an entry to a home. Through a wide arch beyond the entryway was a large living room. Photo albums, menus of local upscale restaurants, local pictorial history books, and large vases of fresh flowers topped several coffee tables. Multiple French doors opened on to a broad terrace overlooking Lake La Quinta. Extra large, plush couches and chairs were arranged in several conversational groupings. A fireplace burned every evening. To the left of the entry through another wide arch was a large dining room with antique sideboards and a long oval, glass-topped table with seats for 20 people. To the right of the entry was a library-den with a wet bar and several leather couches where guests could help themselves at all hours just as if they were at home. In the arch to the den was a carved table for morning coffee, tea, and juice amenities. All the fine china had a gold band and a Two Angels crest. The 12 guestrooms on the second floor each had a large bathroom and dressing room as well as French doors opening to a balcony overlooking the inn's gardens or the lake where warm breezes wafted. Each room had its own unique theme, furnished mostly with furniture and decorated accents the Sanders had collected during their travels. Safari, Indian, Bali, and Geneva were some of the themes. The comforters, linens, personal bathrobes, and bath amenities were of the finest quality.

Every morning Hap made breakfast which he began serving at 8:00 A.M. The menu varied daily with a minimum of three main entrées and five side dishes but special requests were welcomed. Holly made a special blended drink each morning—a different combination of fruits, juices, and other flavorings, which she would name—and invite the guests to guess its ingredients. The Sanders would make restaurant suggestions and reservations for their guests, sometimes even when room reservations were called in. Each evening at 5:00 P.M. Hap and Holly invited their guests to a wine hour with homemade hors d'oeuvres. Most guests attended and socialized with one another and the Sanders. During the day if a guest needed to speak with Hap or Holly they almost always could be found in the Inn's kitchen or garden.

THE STAFF

Dawn and Maria were the only employees. Maria Hernandez was the housekeeper. She came to work each morning to clean and prepare all of the guestrooms. Every other day, she also did all of the laundry. Maria was very efficient. She seldom spoke with anyone except in response. Married, Maria's own household had two of her five children as well as a variable number of relatives. Maria had begun her employment at The Two Angels when it first opened over two years ago. Currently Maria had some health problems necessitating time off. Recently, too, she had requested time off for one son's birthday party, to go to a funeral in Mexico, and to nurse an ill relative.

Dawn Johnson, a retired single woman, lived alone just a few minutes from the Inn. Dawn would come to work early and help serve breakfast, do the clean up, and then return home. In the evening she would return for turndown. Turndown required entering guests' rooms while they were away for dinner or other evening events, pulling back the comforter, ruffling the sheets in a designated way, and placing a signature book and two angel shaped candies on the bed. She also replaced any used towels and amenities and pulled down the curtains. She worked quickly and seldom made errors. When finished with all occupied guestrooms Dawn would go home. When Maria was away from work, Dawn would willingly take over her work. Any time the Sanders needed to go out of town, Dawn filled in for them too, for example, making reservations and breakfast, hosting the wine hour, etc. Often she was heard to say, "The Inn is my second home." When Dawn couldn't do her tasks, Holly would do them.

THE HIGH SEASON AND SALLY

The inn was not busy all the time. While the year round occupancy was 68 percent, summers were generally low and winters high. As the 2001–02 high season approached, both Maria and Dawn missed more and more days at work, a couple of times on the same day. Holly, even with Hap's help, had trouble completing all of the inn's work. Neither of the Sanders had the energy they had when they were younger. While the 12 guestrooms were not now at full occupancy, they soon would be. Hap and Holly decided they needed some part-time help.

Not having had to find employees since they had opened their inn, the Sanders were unsure of how to go about it. They placed advertisements in the local newspaper and the local radio station and spread the word around merchants in town. As the high season was nearing, the larger resorts were also recruiting. After a month, the Sanders had had only four inquiries about their opening—none with any lodging-related experience. Holly then had a new idea; she called the hospitality department of the local community college. Her call was transferred to Mr. Meyers who taught the Introduction to the Hospitality Industry course and supervised the department's job shadow program. Mr. Meyers invited Hap and Holly to be guest speakers in the course, to talk about managing a small, high-quality lodging property and to invite part-time job applicants. Within a week the Sanders spoke to Mr. Meyer's class utilizing many color slides of The Two Angels Inn and its grounds. After class only one student came up to the Sanders to talk about their inn. Sally Lapson had been impressed by the elegance of the inn, how guests were pampered, and the evident enthusiasm displayed by the Sanders. She made an appointment to visit the Sanders for the next day.

After touring the inn, Sally was even more impressed with it and how nice Hap and Holly treated her. She believed that she would learn a lot and enjoy her time there. The Sanders liked Sally and her appreciation of all that they had accomplished with The Two Angels. When they discovered she was willing to work any day or shift needed they hired her immediately. Sally began work the next weekend. She learned quickly, and was diligent and guest-attentive in their opinion. Soon the inn was running smoothly.

In the weeks before the Christmas holidays, Sally worked more and more at The Two Angels. She filled in for both Maria and Dawn who missed several days at work. The inn was now full each evening. Hap and Holly also had Sally assist them in elaborately decorating the inn for the holidays as well as assist almost daily with the wine hours. They often praised her work and called her "a natural."

SALLY'S DECISION

In early January, Sally began to think about what spring semester courses she wanted to register for. She was pretty sure now that she wanted a hospitality career—her parents, Mr. Meyers and the Sanders were all encouraging, and she loved the ambiance and the variety of people and tasks at the inn. The more Sally thought about it, the more sure she became.

On the second weekend after New Year's and before registration for classes, Sally and several friends spontaneously decided to drive to Las Vegas for a few day's excitement. While there she visited the University of Nevada, Las Vegas campus, discovered the major hospitality program there, inquired about transferring, and acquired application and financial aid materials. Within two weeks Sally was provisionally accepted for the upcoming semester which was to begin immediately.

Hap and Holly were stunned by Sally's decision to leave. On her last evening at The Two Angels, they used the wine hour as a going away party for Sally. As she left the Inn, Hap, Holly, and Sally tearfully hugged and promised to stay in touch. Sally promised to visit in two months when she came home on her spring break.

A VISIT TO FAST FOOD HEAVEN

Bob and his wife Joan were driving down to the Maritimes for their summer vacation. It was late in the morning, and the young couple were on the Nova Scotia throughway, headed up toward Cape Breton Island. The scenery was new and exciting, and their home seemed a long way away.

At noon they decided to eat a fast lunch in the next town they come to. Accordingly, a few miles later they exited the throughway, wondering where should they go. But the question was answered for them almost as soon as it had arisen, for at the bottom of the exit ramp was a familiar sign: a blue cloud with a halo on it. "Fast Food Heaven—Straight Ahead One Mile," it read.

Fast Food Heaven! Hamburgers! French fries! "Why not eat at Fast Food Heaven," Bob suggested. "After all, we don't know where else to go, or what their food's like."

"Sure," Joan agreed. "I could use a good cheeseburger, maybe even a double Heaven cheeseburger."

About a mile further on was a large shopping mall, and at the far end of its parking lot the blue clouds of Fast Food Heaven were plainly visible.

Bob and Joan entered the restaurant, walked down the center aisle between uniform rows of spotlessly clean tables, and examined the menu that was posted behind and above the service counter. Exactly the same menu as the one back home! They made their selections quickly and approached the counter.

"What can I get you?" inquired the counter girl, smiling at them.

"Two double Heaven cheeseburgers, two small fries, and two large root beers to go please."

The girl punched the order into her cash register and looked up. "Will there be anything else sir?" she asked.

Bob looked at his wife, who shook her head. "Er, no. Thanks anyway."

Not at all put out, the girl hit a key on her register to total up the sale and stated the amount in a clear voice. Bob gave her a 10-dollar bill.

"Ten dollars," she said, counting out the correct change and giving it to Bob before putting the bill in her cash drawer. Change delivered, she turned to assemble the order.

Joan, meanwhile, had been watching the other members of the staff at their various tasks—one taking a new batch of French fries from the cooking oil, another loading burgers into their special boxes, a third bustling from table to table, cleaning as he went.

"They certainly are efficient," she remarked.

"They're trained to be," Bob smiled. "I worked for Fast Food Heaven one summer when I was in college. You know, they actually managed to make an efficient cook out of me! Of course I didn't start as a cook. You have to work up to that."

Joan shook her head in disbelief. "But you're hopeless in the kitchen."

"Yeah, but the trick was, here everything was done for you. The patties were premade, all the same size so you didn't have to guess. And there was even a timer you set, so that the burgers were cooked for exactly the right length of time. Anyone could do it." In his mind's eye, Bob saw again the kitchen in which he cooked, his fellow workers waiting for the burgers to come off the grill so they could be dressed with just the right amount and mix of condiments, put in buns, and delivered to the counter people. "A hundred and seventy to a hundred and eighty sandwiches per gallon," he muttered to himself.

"What?"

Bob smiled. "I said, 'a hundred and seventy to a hundred and eighty sandwiches per gallon.' That's how many servings of Heaven sauce the manual says you should get from a jar of the stuff. Let me see . . . twenty-four to twenty-eight sandwiches per pound of lettuce. One hundred and eleven to one hundred and thirty-five slices per pound of pickles. Mustard, now that was a hard one to control—you were allowed anywhere from forty-two hundred to seventy-four hundred servings per gallon! I learned all the regulations 'cause I thought I might want to be a manager one day. There's a whole book of regulations for Fast Food Heaven you know. It tells you absolutely everything you need to know to run an outlet. I mean everything! Why, the manual even gives you a special chore for each day of the year. July 25, clean the potato peelers, November 2, check up on the snow removal contract, April 7, have parking lot repainted. I don't remember the exact dates of course, but that was the general idea."

By now the server was getting their drinks. "Watch," said Bob. "She'll fill the cups with ice up to the bottom of the clouds on their sides."

And that was exactly what the server did.

"How did you know?" asked Joan.

"Easy. It's in the manual. Everything is. I know how that girl was trained, for example. First she was given a guided tour of the store. Then she watched videotapes, showing how typical Fast Food Heaven jobs are done. Then she worked with a trainer for about ten hours. Right now she might be on probation for this workstation—the counter, that is. At the end of two months, if she gets a good evaluation she can advance to another station."

Joan laughed. "You make it sound really well thought out."

"You're right! Each position has a very definite set of jobs, and you have to learn them all before you can go on to the next station. Of course, you're evaluated at each station in terms of efficiency, as well as for your manner, grooming, and so on. Eventually, when you've learned all the stations, you're promoted to crew trainer. From there, you work up to crew chief, then part-time manager, manager trainee, and so on."

"OK then," asked Joan, "what's that station over there?" She pointed to where a neat-looking teenager, probably a high school student, was working busily.

"That's the bun station. The person at that station loads buns into the toaster, which incidentally has an automatic setting to make sure the buns are cooked just so. When a batch is cooked, he'll take them over to the dressing station."

"I'm impressed," admitted Joan. "It must be hard, making sure all these stations put out just the right number of buns or hamburgers or whatever at just the right time."

Now their order was being placed into the bag that the counter person had placed ready for this moment. In went the double Heaven cheeseburgers, each in its distinctive package. On top of them, two bags of French fries, each filled to precisely the same level. Finally the drinks went in, and the bag was folded with a double fold. "Thank you," said the counter girl, handing the bag to Bob and giving the couple a wide, sincere smile. "Come again."

"Does the manual say she has to fold the bag twice?" asked Joan as they left the restaurant.

"It sure does," replied Bob. "You've got the picture."

Joan glanced at her watch as they got into their car. The whole experience had taken just a couple of minutes. During those minutes, she had totally forgotten that she was a thousand miles from home, so familiar was the restaurant they had visited.

Soon they were back on the throughway and the smell of hot food filled the car. Bob bit into his double Heaven cheeseburger. "Perfect every time!" he said with satisfaction.

WHAT TO SAY?

As I waited outside the hotel manager's office, I sat back and thought about what I was going to say. The way I answered the questions that were coming in the next 30 minutes or so might seriously impact my entire hospitality career. When the general manager of the hotel, Tom Rayside, had asked for this meeting, he had said he had two reasons to talk with me. One reason for this meeting was to talk about my internship program which I had just gone through. Since it was the first college internship that this company had ever sponsored, Tom had said he was very interested in what I had to say. My guess is that he would probably use my comments to justify whether or not to host interns in the future. The other reason he'd indicated for this meeting was to go over my thoughts about the hotel, its systems and staff, and especially the management members that I'd worked with.

I had met a lot of really nice people during my four and a half months with the Cascade Hotel, and I had also learned quite a bit. These people were the main reason why I had learned so much. I had also discovered a few faults that I thought the general manager should be aware of. The problem was that, by bringing up these faults, it could result in people losing their jobs. Another problem was that many of these managers had numerous contacts in the hotel industry and they said they would use these contact to help me get a job upon graduation from college next year. If I were to say anything negative about them, they would probably not help me in my pursuit of future employment. As I thought back over my time at Cascade, a number of memories came back.

I remember being home for break last Christmas and getting the call from Tom. He and my father had been friends for over 20 years, and our two families had skied together for about five years. We had become pretty good friends. When he found out that I was looking for an internship for the summer between my junior and senior years, he said, "Look no further." His hotel was in a city one thousand miles away from my home in New York, but I thought it was a great opportunity so I immediately accepted.

A few days later, I started receiving letters from Tom and a few other executive committee members about the structure my training would take. They informed me that it was the first time that the hotel had done a program like this so there were no standard activities for internships; they would be making it up as they went along. The overriding message that everyone continued to stress was that they had never done it before, but they were all very excited about it. Tom sent a letter to me saying he was going to give me the title of manager intern. His plan, he said, was to put me in the awkward situation of being between the line staff and management. I would be pulling normal front desk duty and some housekeeping shifts, but at the same time training with the frontline managers and the department heads who make up the executive committee, basically learning what they do from day to day (see Appendix).

I recalled that my first day at the hotel was no disappointment. Everybody was very friendly and encouraging. They gave me a tour of the property, introduced me to lots of people, and showed me where I would be staying. The next day, my first day of work, was also very exciting. The Director of the Rooms Division, Mr. Brooks, personally trained me in all aspects of the front desk and reservations. My coworkers were also very nice and they all tried very hard to make me feel at home. I spent half my day working at the front desk and the second half of the day working with Mr. Brooks. Everything seemed to be going very well.

MEMORIES

The problems started about a week and a half after I began work. I spent more and more of my days just doing the front desk shift, and less and less time with the rooms manager. In fact, I soon hardly saw Mr. Brooks out of his office. When I asked my fellow front-office workers about it, they said that's what he usually does. They said, "He comes to work, sits in his office all day and then goes home early." This lack of supervision seemed obvious by the lack of procedures at the front desk. Everyone had their own way of doing things, but as long as their bank balanced at the end of the day, no one asked questions. I tried to approach Mr. Brooks with questions about operations at the desk, but he always referred me to my coworkers. I continued working my shifts at the desk and found myself feeling more and more frustrated. Mr. Brooks did meet with me once a week, and we got along very well socially, but whenever I changed the subject to work or my frustrations at work, he just told me that either, "This is how things are," or, "I'll look into that."

After all the things I learned at my college about front desk operations, the way things were run at the hotel did not live up to my expectations. It did not seem to me that there were any major problems at the front desk; instead everyone did what they wanted. So I just finished up my time at the desk and prepared for my tour with housekeeping.

After housekeeping, I entered the services department. I was first introduced to the director of services and then to his two assistant managers. I was assigned to Charles, one of the assistants. He was going to teach me to open and close the weekly accounts and to do scheduling and payroll. I was very excited about this job; I quickly felt I was contributing a lot and learning a lot more. I soon became very good friends with Don, the director of services. I started to go to Don's house for dinner fairly often and we would sometimes go out for a few beers after work. After a while we began talking about the job, the department, and what he thought of the rooms manager. He did not have many kind words. He said that he thought that Brooks was lazy, a poor manager, and that he felt like he was constantly covering up for all the mistakes that Brooks made. Don said he wanted to go to the general manager with his complaints, but he did not have anything concrete.

One week before I was supposed to leave the hotel, Tom called a meeting of all the managers which I got to attend. He then proceeded to yell at everyone about the low guest satisfaction scores and that the owner had told him if things did not improve, he was going to make some changes. All of the managers were directed to go to their respective departments and make some plans and take actions to solve the guest satisfaction problem. After the meeting Tom took me aside and said he wanted to meet with me in the morning and hear any of my suggestions. He said that since he had been out of town for much of the last month and hadn't talked with me, he wanted to hear about the last month of operation through my eyes. He also wanted to go over the program I had gone through as well as get my thoughts about the people who ran it.

That night all the directors and managers took me out drinking as a sort of good-bye party. That night brought back memories of the first night that I arrived, when everyone was in a good mood and saying all these nice positive things. Both Mr. Brooks and Don said they really enjoyed working with me, thought I was competent, and that they liked me a lot. Brooks took me aside and gave me a couple of business cards of vice presidents of some major hotel companies and told me to keep in touch with him and he would help me get a good job when I graduated.

BACK TO THE PRESENT

So here I am sitting outside Tom's office waiting to go in. Do I tell about all the problems I saw and get Mr. Brooks in trouble? Should I go into specifics or stick to generalities? Do I really know what I am talking about, or is this the way things usually are in hotels? Should I risk a possible future job? Tom did give me this great opportunity this summer. What will spilling the beans mean for our friendship? For other interns from my college? For how Tom and my Dad get along? What should I say to him?

APPENDIX: THE NARRATOR'S PARTIAL ORGANIZATION CHART

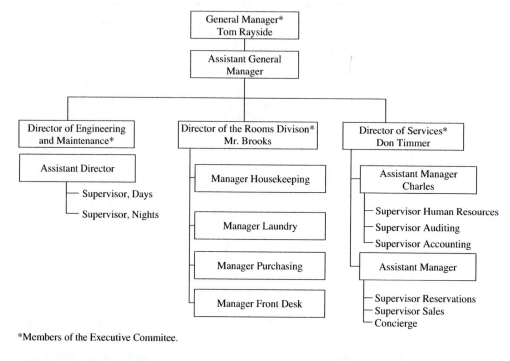

*Members of the Executive Commitee.

THE WHITERIVER GOLF AND COUNTRY CLUB

Near Quechee, Vermont, located just a few miles west of the river dividing Vermont and New Hampshire that gave it its name, was the Whiteriver Golf and Country Club. Quechee was about 15 minutes west of Hanover, New Hampshire, the home of Dartmouth College and a regional medical center. The Quechee area was settled long ago and still had many small villages and farms. In recent decades, however, the area had acquired many retirement and professional families as well as weekend and recreational homes.

Referred to as The Club, the Whiteriver Golf and Country Club had two excellent and very scenic golf courses, half a dozen outdoor tennis courts and a large swimming pool, all centered about a spacious clubhouse. The clubhouse had a well-appointed members lounge and locker rooms and a large dining room with a comfortable bar that could be opened up to a large flagstone terrace. The clubhouse was surrounded by carefully attended lawns and pocket gardens. The club's membership was composed of families with children, many senior citizens, and professionals from the Quechee, White River Junction, and Hanover areas. During the summer season and early fall, golf was the main attraction. At all seasons, the club's dining facilities and bar, open to the public, were consistently well utilized.

Mr. Nathan "Nat" Collins, the Whiteriver Club's general manager, believed that the increasing revenue of the food and beverage (F&B) department was essential for the club's success. Dining on a typical mid-week summer evening would have about a hundred covers.

The club also hosted a growing number of special events such as anniversaries, birthdays, luncheons for professional groups, as well as theme-related sources. Nat Collins attributed much of the F&B department's success to the club's chef, Juan Moreno. Chef Moreno, originally from Puerto Rico, had joined the club's staff five years ago. He was very well liked by the members of the club as well as its staff. Chef Moreno reported to the general manager as did the clubhouse director, the F&B director, and the directors of the Tennis, Golf, and Grounds departments. Chef Moreno oversaw twenty employees—two sous chefs, line cooks, and dishwashers—usually seven per shift except for special events when his staff increased.

THE FOURTH OF JULY

The largest event each year occurred on July 4th. A large tent was rented, set up next to the Terrace, and about 450 members attended. A lavish barbeque was served beginning at 5:30. A seven-piece band from Boston played on the Terrace to entertain dinner guests. At dusk there was a fireworks display on the grounds near the tent. As soon as the fireworks were finished, well after dark, the members began to leave. The annual Fourth of July barbeque and fireworks was the largest and most exciting event of the year for both members and club employees.

This year, the newest sous chef had bought $150.00 worth of fireworks and sparklers in his New Hampshire hometown to celebrate his birthday. While it was illegal to set off fireworks in Vermont without training, the sous chef and most of the kitchen staff went to the field behind the clubhouse and proceeded to set off these additional fireworks, soon after the main display. Everyone got involved and the sky was again lit up and the air reverberated with explosions. The kitchen staff then decorated Chef Moreno's car with glow sticks before heading home for some well-earned rest.

THE NEXT MORNING

At 7 A.M., July 5th, Mr. Jacob Karl, a former president of the Whiteriver Club and current board member, appeared in the genaral manager's office above the kitchen. Mr. Karl was furious. He shouted that "the chefs had set off fireworks in the field behind my house." He went on to say, "I can't believe you'd let these kids run out of control and act so unprofessionally." Mr. Karl emphasized that since the employees were on duty the club was liable. He went on to threaten the general manager of seeking a lawsuit and forcing the club into bankruptcy. With that accusation, Mr. Karl loudly demanded that Nat "take action or else!"

As some of the kitchen staff had assembled at 7:00 to begin preparing for the day, they had observed Mr. Karl storm through the kitchen and someone had even overheard his comments to the GM. Quickly conferring together, the kitchen staff all agreed to deny their involvement in or knowledge of the incident. Soon the GM called Chef Moreno into his office to find out what had happened the night before. Chef Moreno said that he'd heard something about some local kids setting off fireworks. He said that he didn't believe that any of the club's employees were involved. The GM next asked the sous chef who had bought the fireworks and about what had happened. This sous chef responded just as Chef Moreno had. The GM then called the other sous chef into his office. This sous chef had just come to work and hadn't been part of the earlier agreement to "play dumb." He told Nat how the kitchen staff had set off their own fireworks display.

Nat Collins then proceeded to go around the clubhouse asking everyone, from wait staff to dishwashers, who had worked the previous evening if they had participated in the fireworks. When asked directly, most denied their involvement.

As his questioning of the staff went on for the next hour or so, the general manager grew increasingly distressed. He began to wonder if he could ever resolve the situation.

THE WOODWARD HOTEL

After walking the 16 blocks across town from the Woodward Hotel to the Port Authority bus station, Doug Devoto always looked forward to the half hour's bus ride to Montclair, New Jersey. The ride home was a time to unwind and reflect upon his day. As his bus entered the Lincoln tunnel, Doug's mind returned to Louisa's comment to him on leaving work, "I wonder what Dan will do after all of us GSMs talk to him about Shoshana?"

THE WOODWARD

The Woodward was a 115-room, European boutique style hotel located in Manhattan (New York City) on West 55th Street between the Avenue of the Americas (6th) and 7th Avenues. The Woodward was centrally located—quite close to the theater district, Radio City Music Hall, Central Park, and much of New York's fine shopping and restaurants. There were three types of rooms. Most were bed-sitting rooms with marble baths. Standard amenities included a color TV, refrigerator, microwave, dinnerware, hairdryer, and a safe. Suites had in addition a separate dressing room and a comfortably furnished living room. On the top two floors of the hotel were spacious, multiroom penthouses each with a Jacuzzi, fax machine, and two or three TVs in addition to the hotel's usual amenities. A continental breakfast room, a small business center, and a few conference rooms shared the hotel's second floor with the hotel management offices. On the street floor a small lounge flanked the lobby on one side, with the front desk, concierge, bell stand, and luggage room on the other side with reservations, PBX, and auditing behind the front desk.

The Woodward was owned by Mr. and Mrs. Charles Sabo. Mr. Sabo had also acted as the hotel's general manager until 10 years ago when he hired Dan Kerwin as the GM. The Sabos lived in one of the penthouses. Both were 79 years old and increasingly infirm. Mr. Sabo had a hunched back and walked very slowly with the aid of a cane. Mrs. Sabo always walked with her arm linked through her husband's. Mr. Sabo continued to take an active interest in the hotel. He reviewed occupancy and reservations data sheets daily, met with Kerwin daily, and often walked around and chatted with hotel staff. Mr. Sabo repeatedly stated in conversations with guests, staff, and friends that staff "conviviality" was the most important thing about his hotel. He stressed the importance of friendly relationships between guests and employees but especially between employees. One of Mr. Sabo's standard comments to new employees was, "You have a lot of very nice people here to learn from and enjoy yourself with. Everybody gets along with everybody else. You never have to worry about anyone being nasty here."

DOUG JOINS THE WOODWARD

Doug remembered exactly how his employment had happened. It was on June 20, a Wednesday, when he had decided to seek a summer job in the hospitality industry. While he had had opportunities to return to prior summer jobs, life guarding and pizza delivery, since he was going out of state to enter a college hospitality program it just made sense to work in the industry. Sharing this decision with his parents at dinner, Doug's mother had said, "I have a connection with a hotel in the city. Should I give him a call?" That very evening Mrs. Devoto had called Mr. Sabo and asked if Doug could work at the Woodward that summer. In a minute Mr. Sabo had said yes, and that Doug was to call him in two days. That Friday Doug had called Mr. Sabo and thanked him for the opportunity to work at the Woodward at which point the Woodward's president told him, "You are very welcome. Just come to the Woodward on July 4th in proper attire—dark blue slacks, a white dress shirt, and brown dress shoes. You will be given the hotel's tie on arrival. Ask for Mr. Kerwin, my general manager."

At seven o'clock in the morning on July 4, Doug entered the two heavy bronze-edged front doors, crossed to the front desk, gave his name, and asked to see the manager. One minute after being informed of Doug's arrival by telephone, Mr. Kerwin showed up at the front desk. "Welcome to the Woodward," he said to Doug, "I'm glad to have you with us." To Doug's surprise he was neither interviewed nor asked to fill out a job application. Instead Mr. Kerwin took Doug on a 30-minute tour of the hotel, mostly of the guest rooms, where he explained that Doug should be familiar with the room types and their amenities in order to accurately describe them to guests over the phone. Next, Mr. Kerwin introduced Doug to most of the office employees and all of the front desk staff on duty. Doug noticed that Mr. Kerwin knew everyone's name.

After touring the hotel and meeting employees, Doug was eager to start working. His first job was to be in reservations after which he would go to the front desk. Betty Cruz, the head reservationist, was to train him until he was ready for the front desk, where he would have direct contact with guests and have many tasks to accomplish in a short period of time. Before starting his training that morning, Betty had Doug complete a few administrative tasks that included filling out an application and requesting a copy of his birth certificate and passport. Doug's starting wage was $10 per hour, the most he had ever been paid.

To get acquainted with Doug, Betty conversed with him for 20 minutes. She insisted that he call her Betty. Doug learned that this Dominican woman with a Spanish accent had two children and a husband. Betty also revealed that she was trying to lose weight and had starting eating a healthier diet.

During the three days that he trained with Betty, Doug learned the reservation computer system in order to understand how to make, modify, and cancel the various types of reservations. He also learned the proper protocol for answering the telephone and communicating with guests making reservations. There was an order to asking for certain pieces of information from a caller that allowed for a more timely and efficient method of typing the reservation into the computer. The reservationist asked the caller what dates he or she was interested in and then how he or she had heard about the hotel. This allowed the reservationist to first check the computerized date book to see if rooms were available and then to fill in a survey question dealing with referral sources. After these two steps were completed, the main reservation screen on the computer showed up automatically and the remainder of the reservation information could be typed in. Lastly, he was taught the functions of the internal phone system, which included transfers, holds, and wakeup calls.

THE FRONT DESK

For each of the next two mornings Betty would send Doug up for a free breakfast in the continental breakfast room when he arrived. In the afternoon, she asked repeatedly if he was hungry, and made jokes about his voracious appetite. At the end of the three-day training session, Doug had felt pretty competent as a reservationist. He really liked Betty and was reluctant to leave her department.

On his fourth day at work, Betty took Doug to the front desk manager's office to begin his training as a "GSM," or Guest Service Manager, a title that, as Doug would soon learn, meant he had to do many things beyond the usual front desk clerk. Doug's new manager was Louisa Legaspi, a five-foot tall Thai woman in her thirties. From the beginning Louisa always made sure Doug had a good grasp on what he was learning. When it took him longer than she expected to learn a task, she would say, "Come on, you should know this by now." She frequently talked about her husband and reminisced about past group social events of the hotel employees. She also joked a lot, for example, about how Doug stepped on her shoes and crushed her toes, which he did more than once by accident.

Even though Mr. Kerwin had stated that Doug was Louisa's trainee, the other GSMs helped him almost as much as she did. Anthony Guerro, Larami Lapitan, and David Hurt were the other GSMs on the day shift who helped Doug learn the GSM position.

At the front desk, Doug learned a variety of operations. He learned how to check guests in and out; handle complaints; take calls from rooms; sign temporary visitors in and out; and coordinate with maintenance, housekeeping, and the bell stand. He also learned the surrounding area well because many calls required directions and questions about location. One common phrase he was taught was, "We are very centrally located five minutes from the theater district, Radio City Music Hall, and Central Park." At the end of each shift, GSMs also checked housekeeping reports and balanced out credit card charges.

During Doug's second day at the front desk, he met the concierge, Shoshana, who had been with the hotel for over 10 years. Her desk was at the end of the front desk. She was an Israeli woman of about 45 years of age, overweight, and who breathed heavily while she spoke. Most guests liked her because she got requested tour and theater tickets and restaurant reservations on time and better than average seats for most events. Many guests even asked for her by name over the telephone. She received numerous gift baskets from guests as tokens of appreciation for meeting and exceeding their requests. Doug overheard guests describe Shoshana as a "life saver" or a "miracle worker."

One morning, during his second week at the front desk, Mr. Sabo took Doug to the continental breakfast room. Over a long breakfast Mr. Sabo showed Doug the data sheets he reviewed daily and explained what he was looking for, "because you'll be doing this someday after you graduate." As they parted, Mr. Sabo gave Doug his staff conviviality speech, ending with, "If ever anyone isn't helpful, just tell me."

THINGS ARE NOT QUITE WHAT THEY SEEM

During his first three weeks at the Woodward, Doug knew that he had learned a lot! Betty and Louisa had set a fast pace to be sure but also gave him a lot of attention. The GSMs Doug worked with had been extremely helpful too, and he noticed, always helped each other and were always friendly too. Doug told his parents one evening that Mr. Sabo's climate of conviviality was "the real thing."

Two days later Doug was left alone at the front desk. Only the bell captain and the concierge were in the lobby. A guest approached Doug and requested him to change a hundred dollar bill. As he had yet to earn a key to the bank drawer, Doug explained to the guest that he needed a moment to find someone with a key. Doug walked over to Shoshana and asked her if she would make change for him. Shoshana looked at Doug, sighed loudly, and said nothing. Doug repeated his request. Shoshana shouted, "I can't help you. I don't do bank stuff for GSMs." Doug was taken aback. Overhearing Shoshana, Samra, a reservationist who had just come out to the front desk to look for something, quickly said to Shoshana, "He is new here and you must help him. Don't just tell him you won't do anything for him!" The guest stared with her mouth open. Samra, who had a key to a bank drawer in the back room, then assisted the guest. As Samra left the public area, Shoshana said, loud enough for Doug to overhear, "That little skirt. I can't stand her. I've hated her since day one."

In the days following, Doug listened more carefully to how his front desk colleagues talked about the concierge. Mostly they complained to one another about how Shoshana would take a smoke break outside the hotel every 45 or 50 minutes, during which her phone lines sometimes backed up with four or five callers either on hold at the same time or forced to leave messages. Doug heard other things, too. Tony Guerro often spoke negatively about Shoshana, for example, once saying, "That greedy bitch." David Hurt said to Doug one day, "She can be a very nasty lady so I just do my best to stay clear of her." Even Louisa told of the day that Shoshana had made her cry.

As the concierge, Shoshana was entitled to a commission on the tickets she sold. On her days off the GSM who substituted for her received the commission for any tickets sold. On one of her days off, she gave Anthony Guerro a list of bus tour prices to use to sell tickets. He misplaced it and had to search Shoshana's desk for another price list, which he found. The same day around three o'clock in the afternoon, he also found the original list that she had given him. He noticed that the prices on the list found in her desk were much higher. He examined this list and, with the help of other GSMs, determined that it had been altered by computer from the original list sent out by the bus tour company. The altered list overstated prices by about 25 percent. All of the GSMs on duty at the time unanimously concluded that Shoshana was ripping off customers in order to gain a higher commission.

Over the next couple of days, most of the conversations among the day shift GSMs were about Shoshana, her fraudulent tour list and mostly their negative feelings about her. While Doug did not actually hear who first suggested it, the GSMs had finally talked about informing Mr. Kerwin as a group.

WHAT TO DO

The more Doug thought about the Shoshana situation and what the GSMs seemed to be planning, the more his stomach tightened. What if the GSMs expected him to join them? What could happen? What might it mean for him? As his bus came into Montclair, Doug was only sure of one thing—he'd have to decide what to do very carefully.

INDEX